THE CORSAIRS
OF SAINT-MALO

THE MIDDLE RANGE

THE MIDDLE RANGE

Edited by Peter S. Bearman and Shamus R. Khan

The Middle Range, coined and represented by Columbia sociologist Robert Merton, is a style of work that treats theory and observation as a single endeavor. This approach has yielded the most significant advances in the social sciences over the last half century; it is a defining feature of Columbia's department. This book series seeks to capitalize on the impact of approaches of the middle range and to solidify the association between Columbia University and its Press.

The Conversational Firm: Rethinking Bureaucracy in the Age of Social Media,
Catherine J. Turco

Working for Respect: Community and Conflict at Walmart,
Adam Reich and Peter Bearman

Judge Thy Neighbor: Denunciations in the Spanish Inquisition,
Romanov Russia, and Nazi Germany, Patrick Bergemann

Concepts and Categories: Foundations for Sociological and Cultural Analysis,
Michael T. Hannan, Gaël Le Mens, Greta Hsu, Balázs Kovács, Giacomo
Negro, László Pólos, Elizabeth Pontikes, and Amanda J. Sharkey

THE CORSAIRS
OF SAINT-MALO

Network Organization

of a Merchant Elite

Under the Ancien Régime

HENNING HILLMANN

Columbia University Press

New York

Columbia University Press
Publishers Since 1893
New York   Chichester, West Sussex
cup.columbia.edu

Library of Congress Cataloging-in-Publication Data
Names: Hillmann, Henning, author.
Title: The corsairs of Saint-Malo : network organization of a merchant elite under the
Ancien Régime / Henning Hillmann.
Description: New York : Columbia University Press, [2021] | Includes bibliographical
references and index.
Identifiers: LCCN 2020028804 (print) | LCCN 2020028805 (ebook) |
ISBN 9780231180382 (hardback) | ISBN 9780231180399 (trade paperback) |
ISBN 9780231542661 (ebook)
Subjects: LCSH: Merchants—France—Saint-Malo. | Privateering—France—Saint-Malo.
| Harbors—France—Saint-Malo. | Saint-Malo (France)—Commerce. | France—Foreign
economic relations. | France—Economic conditions—17th century. | France—Economic
conditions—18th century.
Classification: LCC HF3560.S3 H55 2021 (print) | LCC HF3560.S3 (ebook) |
DDC 381/.1094415—dc23
LC record available at https://lccn.loc.gov/2020028804
LC ebook record available at https://lccn.loc.gov/2020028805

Cover design: Lisa Hamm
Cover image: Ambroise Louis Garneray, *Capture of the prize ship* Triton *by the French corsair*
Le Hasard. Archives départementales d'Ille-et-Vilaine, 4Fg63.
Wikimedia Commons/Public domain.

Enfermés le soir sous la même clef dans leur cité, les
Malouins ne composaient qu'une famille.
—François-René de Chateaubriand, *Mémoires d'Outre-Tombe*
(vol. I, book 1, chap. 4)

CONTENTS

ACKNOWLEDGMENTS

I t seems only fitting that this book on organizational networks has spawned its own network of colleagues and friends to whom I am deeply indebted for their support throughout this long book project. It all began a long time ago while I was working on an article on the overseas investments of English merchants in the seventeenth century. A group of investors in the data I had set aside, perhaps for some follow-up study, were engaged in privateering enterprise. One day, my wife, Christina, rather innocently inquired who these privateers were. My routine response to this question was: "they were somewhat like pirates." Any mentioning of pirates usually piques the interest of people—well, until I would add the much duller detail that privateers were different because they were sanctioned by a state, and that there was an entire legal apparatus in place that regulated their actions. Christina is of course a very smart economist and has a fine instinct for interesting research questions. So, we ended up writing an article together on English privateering enterprise as an economic opportunity. My ambitions grew once I stumbled upon some rather detailed historical data on the corsairs of Saint-Malo in France. The initial plan was to write a comparative economic history of privateering enterprise in France and Britain. Yet, once I had immersed myself in the archival holdings in Brittany, I realized that these sources were so rich that the corsairs and the networks they had created deserved a full book of their own. The rest is indeed history.

The project first took shape while I was a freshly minted assistant professor at Stanford. In our joint workshop on political mobilization, my senior colleagues Susan Olzak, Doug McAdam, and Andrew Walder were among those who offered encouragement and suggestions for my very first ideas. The Scancor seminar series, then chaired by Woody Powell, and the Social Science History workshop, directed by Gavin Wright and Avner Greif, both offered helpful venues to receive comments as the initial empirical findings were forthcoming. At this early stage, Guillaume Daudin shared his intimate knowledge of French colonial trade and steered me to a number of valuable sources. More than anybody at Stanford, I am deeply grateful to Becky Sandefur, Monica McDermott, and Dan McFarland for their friendship and for listening to my half-baked ideas about privateering networks. Few research projects are accomplished without the dutiful help of student research assistants, and the work behind this book is no exception. Hence, this finally is my opportunity to thank Jackelyn Hwang, Laure Négiar, Andrew Parker, Diana Peng, James Greenberg, Warner Henson, and Denis Trapido, all of whom have long moved on to academic and professional careers of their own, for all their extraordinary contributions. This is also the place to express my gratefulness for the financial support of this research project by the National Science Foundation (grant number SES-0550848) and the Stanford Office of Technology Licensing Research Incentive Fund.

As I moved on to a new position at the University of Mannheim in Germany, the project did, of course, travel with me. It was in Mannheim that something resembling a book manuscript began to emerge. Here again, I could always rely on first-class student research assistants: Kristina Zapp, Nina Vallen, Pascale Müller, Jonas Richter, Björn Seitz, Jan Grau, Michel Maier-Bode, and Benjamin Rohr all went way beyond the proverbial call of duty. Three graduate students, in particular, were pivotal for the often-complex data analysis that went into the chapters that follow: Timo Böhm kept all taxation and partnership data in tight order and patiently translated many of my abstract technical ideas into tangible R-code. Pavel Dimitrov's programming skills proved to be invaluable throughout. Katharina Burgdorf did much of the same for the sequence analysis that underpins the study of merchant careers in chapter 7. Little of this book would have been accomplished without them. I also wish to thank the Mannheim Center for European Social Research for its administrative and financial support.

Among the numerous conferences, workshops, and department seminar series, during which I had the opportunity to present early and later findings from this book project, three stand out. The first was the 2007 Cliometric Society Annual Conference in Tucson, Arizona. I still remember it vividly as the very best conference I have ever attended. It was also the first occasion I had to get in touch with Phil Hoffman, who continued his support for my privateering project while he was editor of the *Journal of Economic History* and as a most helpful reviewer for the book prospectus. The second was a small yet immensely fruitful workshop on political elite networks, organized by Tod Van Gunten at the Juan March Institute, University Carlos III, Madrid. In retrospect, the comments and suggestions offered by John Levi Martin and my old graduate school friend Paolo Parigi were crucial in setting my analytical narrative on the right path. The third was an invitation to present at the Centre de Sociologie des Organisations at Sciences Po, Paris in 2015, which turned out to be just as influential. I would like to thank in particular Claire Lemercier, Pierre Gervais, Emmanuel Lazega, and André Lespagnol for their enormously generous and insightful input that steered me away from pitfalls and in the right direction.

As with every long-term research project, there are those friends and colleagues whose influence and input are so important that they have become invaluable. First and foremost, there is Peter Bearman. Since 1998, when I first met him as a graduate student, Peter has been dissertation advisor, coauthor (almost), colleague, friend, and my toughest, yet most appreciated, critic. Words can do little justice to all the help and guidance he has provided throughout the years. My guess is that his intellectual influence can be felt on every single page of this book. After all, he taught me what relational thinking is all about. Thank you, Peter.

In their very own personal ways, Richard Lachmann and John Levi Martin have likewise followed and read my work with sincere interest, and I continue to benefit immensely from their sense of seeing what is sociologically meaningful in historical analysis. Emily Erikson has been a colleague and friend since our days in graduate school at Columbia, and to this day, I enjoy reading her work in historical sociology as much as I am grateful for her critical eye when it comes to my manuscripts. I especially appreciate her unrivalled feel for tone and an appropriate choice of words in academic writing. Richard, John, and Emily all have read and commented on several, sometimes even all, draft chapters of this book. Some of my deepest gratitude is to André Lespagnol. Anyone familiar with French maritime history will recognize his intellectual impact on the field over the past forty-five years. I cannot imagine anybody more knowledgeable about the history of Saint-Malo than André. At the same time, he has always been the most gentle and generous senior colleague I have had the pleasure to meet. Noting that retirement does not necessarily mean more spare time, he nevertheless read the entire final manuscript of this book in no time, and then sent me several single-space (font size eleven at best) pages of unbelievably detailed comments, deep probing questions, and corrections of historical errors I had slipped into the text. I will be forever grateful to him for sharing his thoughts.

At Columbia University Press, I very much wish to thank Eric Schwartz and Lowell Frye. One cannot possibly wish for a better editor than Eric, who has always been patiently supportive, from gentle reminders on delivery dates to questions of cover design as much as substantive guidance on how to best respond to the manuscript reviewers. Lowell has been just as patient in leading me through all the necessary paperwork that awaits authors beyond the manuscript itself.

Finally, our family had to endure many a vacation where my laptop computer joined us an uninvited guest who overstayed his welcome. Over the years, they had to listen to endless excuses by this perfectionist author as to why "the book" was still not ready. Now, that it is indeed done, the least I can offer is to dedicate this book to Christina, the love of my life; her brother Uli; and Kathrin and Christian. This one is for all of you.

THE CORSAIRS
OF SAINT-MALO

CHAPTER 1

INTRODUCTION

On March 22, 1759, the *Villegénie*, a seemingly modest ninety-ton vessel of the snow type, left the port city of Saint-Malo on the northern coast of Brittany to sail across the Atlantic toward the French West Indies. The command on board was held by Pierre Anne de Chateaubriand, sieur de Plessis. With fifty-seven able seamen and armed with fourteen cannons, Captain de Plessis and his crew had a clear mission: to intercept and seize merchant ships of the enemy and their valuable cargo as prizes, and to bring them into the nearest French port. The British were the enemy in question, for this was at the height of the Seven Years' War (also known as the French and Indian War, where it concerned Anglo-French hostilities in North America). Chateaubriand de Plessis was a *corsaire* (or privateer in English): his commerce-raiding campaign may have looked like piracy, but it was legally sanctioned and in fact encouraged by the French royal government during times of war. As such, he carried with him a royal commission of *guerre et marchandise*, literally a permission to engage in both war and trade.

De Plessis and his crew accomplished their mission quite successfully. Cruising the Atlantic, they captured two prize ships and took another two for ransom. Unfortunately, one of their captures was retaken by a British vessel of greater firepower. De Plessis and his crew managed to bring the other ship, and a sloop seized along the way, into the port of Bayonne, where both prizes were sold at auction. The *Villegénie*'s journey continued. After a stint in the Caribbean at the French colony of Saint-Domingue, weathering hurricanes and taking a few more ransoms, de Plessis eventually returned to Saint-Malo on December 28, 1759. Considering all sales of prizes and all ransoms, the entire campaign fetched a net return of more than 730,000 *livres tournois* (*lt.*).

Needless to say, fitting out a corsair ship for such a campaign incurred costs: whoever owned the ship had to buy it; the crew received a salary and often an advance payment; victuals, equipment, and weaponry had to be paid for; and several administrative fees were applied. This was not only a risky undertaking but also costly. The owner of the *Villegénie* and the main promoter, or *armateur*, of the campaign was a certain René-Auguste de Chateaubriand, the captain's older brother and father of François-René de Chateaubriand, who would become an influential diplomat and one of France's most eminent writers. For René-Auguste, this was the brilliant beginning of his career as an *armateur* of maritime ventures.[1] To launch these ventures, he sought business partners who would share the costs and risks yet also benefit from the returns that such undertakings generated. Apparently, the first voyage of the *Villegénie* was so lucrative that René-Auguste had no trouble finding partners (*consorts* or *intéressés*) to finance another raiding cruise against the enemy (or *faire la course sur les ennemies de l'état*, which was the routine expression used in the archival sources). The fitting costs of 28,291 *lt.* were shared by René-Auguste de Chateaubriand; his two brothers Pierre and Joseph; the chevalier du Boisteilleul (his cousin); the sieurs de la Villesboinet (who also invested in the first voyage); Mousset de Villeneuve; du Rouvre (likewise a previous partner); the Marquise de Saint-Pern; Madame du Plessis-Grénédan; and Madame Bonin de la Villebouquais. All of the partners were private investors in an enterprise that effectively contributed to the French war effort. This observation explains why the French *guerre de course* often is translated into English as privateering enterprise, and the French term *corsaires* is rendered as privateers in English.[2]

On March 1, 1760, the *Villegénie* set sail with eleven officers, Pierre de Chateaubriand as her captain, and sixty-nine seamen on board. The campaign at the mouth of the English Channel yielded at least a dozen prizes, which were brought safely into Saint-Malo and Morlaix, and about as many ransoms taken, sometimes with the help of a few gunshots. On April 5, however, the *Villegénie* made a fateful encounter with the British *Antilope*, a warship armed with sixty cannons. Hunter became hunted, and as the *Villegénie* was no match, she was captured. The crewmembers were treated as prisoners of war, but the brothers Pierre and Joseph de Chateaubriand eventually were able to return home to Saint-Malo. Still, the prizes and ransoms they had taken earlier rendered once again a large enough profit for Chateaubriand to buy a new, and even larger, ship, the 150-ton frigate *L'Amaranthe*. As before, he set up a partnership (*société*) to mobilize the capital necessary for another privateering campaign. Among the shareholders were his brothers and trusted partners from his previous ventures, including the sieurs de la Villesboinet (father and son), Mousset de Villeneuve, and the sieur du Rouvre. They were joined by fresh recruits who nevertheless were not entirely unfamiliar faces to the *armateur*: Bertherand de la Closerie from Nantes was brought into the partnership by the Villesboinets; Chateaubriand, de Saint-Etienne, was René-Auguste's cousin. Magon, sieur de la Villehuchet; Jean-Baptiste Hippolyte Lebonhomme, sieur de Lafontaine; Le Gentil; and Nicolas Jean Brignon, sieur de Léhen were all four from distinguished families of Saint-Malo. As partners in the *société*, they all received substantial returns on their investments: the *Amaranthe*'s campaign in 1760–1761 resulted in at least a dozen prizes and five ransoms, amounting to 357,216 *lt*.[3]

René-Auguste de Chateaubriand was merely the latest in a time-honored lineage of *armateurs* engaged in the *course*. Each of his several undertakings was but one case among hundreds of other venture partnerships that were established in Saint-Malo during the same historical period. Yet, even if we consider just a few selected cases, a pattern emerges. Sharing the costs and risks with their business partners enabled *armateurs* in Saint-Malo and other centers of maritime commerce to spread their capital and invest in multiple enterprises at once, and not just in the *course*. For Chateaubriand, the expeditions of the *Villegénie* and the *Amaranthe* were stepping-stones for much greater ambitions. As we will learn in later chapters, using the funds from his privateering endeavors, he expanded his business interests to include the slave trade from Guinea, fish harvesting around Newfoundland, and long-distance trade with the West and East Indies.[4] As illustrated by the groups of investors for the *Villegénie* and the *Amaranthe*, for each of their undertakings, *armateurs* like Chateaubriand repeatedly relied on trusted partners and also forged new partnership ties with other members of the trader elite. As they continued to maintain and build new relationships while dissolving others, they collectively gave rise to a finely laced network. As I will show, this network provided social cohesion for the merchant community as well as a reservoir for the future collaborative partnerships that were so vital for commercial success.

The *course*, or privateering enterprise, is at the heart of this book. My interest, however, is not in its military history—neither its strategic role in state rivalries nor its tactical aspects in naval operations. Instead, my focus is on the local organization of the *course* in the exemplary setting of Saint-Malo under the Ancien Régime. How exactly, beyond just a few anecdotal cases, did the partnerships for these *course* ventures form? How did they entwine with parallel partnerships the same *armateurs* formed to promote their ventures in overseas trade? How did these various partnership networks combine to yield social cohesion within the merchant community? And, finally, how and why did this social fabric wax and wane over the course of more than a hundred years, from 1681 through 1792, from the reign of Louis XIV, the Sun King, to the French Revolution? As the chapters in this book unfold, we will see that the *course* played a pivotal role in upholding social cohesion among the local merchant elite in Saint-Malo. When opportunities for the *course* were absent, however, fragmentation rather than cohesion prevailed.

Beyond these concerns with organizational networks, the privateering enterprise also offers insight for understanding endogenous institutional change.[5] Change in this regard is endogenous: it emerges bottom-up, from within the merchant trader community. Certainly, the *course* in Ancien Régime France was channeled by national legislation of the royal government. Its tangible organization was done locally, however, by merchant entrepreneurs and their shareholding partners, and hence, we may think of the *course* as a local economic institution as well. To the extent that it was these very same merchant entrepreneurs who formed, adjusted, and shifted their partnership ties, any change in the resulting pattern of venture networks, including the *course* as a local economic institution, would also be endogenous.

COMMERCIAL EXPANSION AND MERCHANT NETWORKS

The local community of Saint-Malo's trader elite, from the late-seventeenth to the late-eighteenth century, was embedded within a much broader development. It found itself at the tail end of what we now call the age of European overseas expansion (c. 1500–1750), an era in which colonies were settled, empires were forged, and ever more distant markets and trade routes were explored that eventually encompassed the known world in a global exchange network.[6] Just like other port cities along the French Atlantic seaboard—Bayonne, Bordeaux, La Rochelle, Nantes, Lorient, Le Havre, Dieppe, and Dunkirk[7]—Saint-Malo made its contributions to this worldwide commercial expansion. The Malouins, as the residents of the city were called, provided Western Europe with a staple food from their traditional stronghold in the Newfoundland cod fisheries. When they were not employed in fishing, their vessels served as cargo carriers throughout the Mediterranean. Saint-Malo emerged as an important center for the import of Spanish and Portuguese colonial goods. Malouin ships would bring fine Breton linen cloth and lacework, which were much coveted in the American colonies, to the Iberian ports in exchange for Andalusian wine, fruits and oils, all kinds of colonial wares, and, most important, silver bullion from the mines of Mexico and Peru. Silver had become the principal currency in the trade with Asian markets, and the Saint-Malo merchants put it to good use when they fitted out expeditions for China and established trading posts on the Malabar and Coromandel coasts of India, all to make spices, silks, and other valuable textiles available to European consumers. At the same time, they had begun to link with the Arabian markets for coffee. To satisfy the ever-growing craving for sugar, plantation economies were set up in the French West Indies and on the islands that today are known as Mauritius and La Réunion. Plantations were run on forced labor and thus led to the flourishing trade in slaves from Guinea and Mozambique, an opportunity that few *armateurs* from Saint-Malo did not seize. Indeed, a truly global network of commerce changed the outlook of the members of the local merchant elite, the *Messieurs de Saint-Malo*, as historian André Lespagnol has called them. They remained local residents, yet fashioned themselves into "citizens of the world," to borrow David Hancock's fitting description.[8]

All of these early modern trades, whether pursued by the French, Dutch, English, Danes, Portuguese, or Spanish, had to traverse the Atlantic Ocean and thus gave rise to what has been called the Atlantic System, or an Atlantic Economy.[9] I have alluded to partnership networks that linked merchant *armateurs* and investors in their joint ventures. To say that the Atlantic Economy and the world of commerce beyond it were anchored in merchant networks certainly is not a novel claim.[10] It helps us, however, to situate the findings of this study in the wider economic history of European trade expansion. One recurring theme in the scholarship on merchant networks points to the problem of uncertainty, stemming from information asymmetries as well as insufficient public-order institutions for contract enforcement. Confronted with such challenges, merchant entrepreneurs forged trust-filled ties to enable the exchange of reliable information about new business opportunities. At the same time, cohesive ties among these merchant groups offered benefits of social control to the extent that they limited opportunistic behavior and thus encouraged the more efficient employment of agents in long-distance trade.[11] In other instances, the relationships that merchants formed in business spilled over into other spheres of life: in some settings, they brought about political alignments; in others, they eased marriage arrangements that cut across class divisions, thus facilitating the consolidation of emerging elites.[12]

These observations do not mean, of course, that network organizations in trade were immune to failure. Under unfavorable circumstances, they could and sometimes did lead to undesirable outcomes. Information sharing and monitoring therefore did not always succeed.[13] One reason certainly was that building and maintaining trust networks proved to be easier within well-bounded communities in which personal bonds mapped onto a shared sense of ethnic, religious, or regional belonging. This became a much taller order once merchant ties were expected to encourage cooperation across cultural, ethnic, and national boundaries. If we are to believe recent scholarship, the emerging Atlantic System largely succeeded in creating an integrated network of exchange, insurance, and credit relationships over long distances.[14] As Hancock has shown for Madeira wine, commodities often were produced in one particular place (in this case, a tiny Portuguese island), then transported across the ocean, and eventually sold to consumers in foreign marketplaces.[15] Some failures notwithstanding, the idea that merchant networks "constituted the most common institutional form for international trade during this period" is now commonplace within the literature.[16]

Accordingly, my point is not merely to reiterate that networks mattered in early modern trade. Instead, my focus is on the local organizational foundations of those far-reaching trading connections. As the chapters that follow show, promoting new ventures in Saint-Malo, fitting out ships, recruiting crews, and mobilizing capital to finance them remained firmly within the hands of local mercantile elites, even though shareholding partners from outside were increasingly brought into the fold. Documenting these local organizational networks, however, is only a first step. As noted earlier, a competitive advantage in trade was gained on the basis of cooperation. Even within such a tightly knit merchant community as Saint-Malo, not all relationships displayed cooperation. The port city boasted several trading houses, led by elite families that more often than not competed with each other. They pursued their own agenda, which did not necessarily align with the interests of their peers. How, then, was cooperation in local networks possible in the face of these competing interest groups? Answering this question requires moving beyond merely showing that cohesive networks of cooperation existed toward identifying the social mechanisms responsible for their emergence, reproduction, and change. To do so, it is helpful to draw on the empirical insights and theoretical tools of organizational sociology.

ORGANIZATIONAL LINCHPINS AND CAREERS

If cohesive networks within merchant communities were conducive to cooperation and information sharing, then the general question is where such social cohesion originated. Put differently, and in light of the previous discussion, the present study considers a classic sociological question: what bonds hold a community together if it consists of different interest groups, each with individual ambitions, preferences, and traditions? In modern-day settings, the answer points to formal organizations as platforms for integrating varied, and often rival, interest groups into collective action.[17] In the field of politics, for instance, we may conceive of parties as organizational structures that bundle diverse factions and splinter groups into a coherent political agenda and partisanship, hence, the notion of a party line. In the economy, firms may be regarded as serving a similar function: economic transactions are most efficiently pursued through contractual agreements. We also know that contracts are limited, leaving room for loopholes and opportunistic behavior. Instruments put in place to reduce opportunism in turn increase transaction costs. When transaction costs become exorbitant, integrating the two contracting sides within a single firm may prove to be a more efficient arrangement. The reasons for integrating previously separate factions in politics or contracting sides in markets may be worlds apart, but the means to do so—formal organization—is remarkably similar.

What distinguishes eighteenth-century Saint-Malo and comparable historical cases from modern-day contexts, however, is the lack of adequate formal organizational platforms that can serve as vehicles for social cohesion. Certainly, we may think of the chartered joint-stock companies as such formal organizations. Few would deny the leading role these companies played in the development of early modern trade expansion.[18] Still, at least in Saint-Malo, overseas trade and privateering enterprise alike were almost exclusively managed as private-share partnerships, the size of which was on a much more modest scale than a large joint-stock company. Granted, at one point, the headquarters of the French East India Company indeed were in the Breton port city. But the *Compagnie des Indes Orientales de Saint-Malo*, as it was called, was a short-lived enterprise (1707–1719) and a company in name only because it was run as another private partnership by an exclusive set of a dozen shareholders, all of whom save one were high-profile members of the Saint-Malo trader elite.[19] If narrowed down to a single question, then, this book's central concern is how social cohesion and a cooperative community can be achieved when firms, parties, or similar formal organizations that reach across rival interests are absent or in their infancy.

A useful way to think of social cohesion is in structural terms, in which a community is cohesive to the extent that its members are embedded in a social network that connects them through multiple independent pathways.[20] Imagine a near-ideal typical medieval or preindustrial village, where little escapes the watchful eyes of one's neighbors, while helping hands can be expected from all corners of the community.[21] The image and underlying concept imply that any two randomly chosen members within such a cohesive community are able to reach each other through multiple pathways. These pathways, of course, depend on the members who maintain them. Consequently, the presence of multiple independent pathways ensures that connectivity and reachability remain robust even if some members leave the networked community. If we further understand cohesion as a continuum, then we find segregation into multiple subgroups at the opposite end. In the extreme, the subgroups may be internally cohesive, but very small and without any links between them, such that structural holes separate them and fragmentation results.

In the absence of formal organizations that reach across the structural holes between subgroups, we may first think of brokers as an informal alternative at the level of interpersonal relations. In its most basic form, brokerage refers to the mediation between two unconnected actors by a third party, the broker. Visually speaking, brokerage thus implies an open triad of relationships, in which the missing leg represents the structural hole between the two unconnected parties.[22] Once we move up our analytical lens, from intermediaries between individual people toward macrolevel mediation between groups, then brokers act as boundary-spanners who build bridges to at least one member of the group on the other side of a structural hole.[23] Bridging ties, however, provide a rather fragile foundation for macrolevel cohesion in a segregated landscape.[24] For one, building and maintaining a bridging tie depends on two actors who are not close to each other in social space precisely because they are representatives of two different groups. Consequently, their willingness to maintain a bridge may be modest. Furthermore, to the extent that social closeness translates into stronger bonds between actors, any two members of the same group are likely to share a strong relationship. An equally strong tie that either of them maintains with a third person implies that the latter is likely to be a member of the same group. By the social mechanism of transitivity ("a friend of a friend is a friend"), a closed triad will be observed. By the same token, a tie that either one maintains with a third person who is a member of a different group is likely to be a weak relationship because social distance is greater between than it is within groups.[25] If it were strong, then, again by the tendency toward transitivity, the third leg in the triad should be strong as well, resulting in a closed triad, which in turn would draw all three actors into the same group. In sum, bridging ties are likely to be relatively weak relationships and thus are at risk to decay and break.

I propose an alternative foundation for social cohesion that does not rest upon individual brokers and bridges. Within a community that is segregated into subgroups or stratified into layers, as was the case in the historical setting of Saint-Malo, its macrostructure may be visualized as consisting of distinct social circles. We just discussed the notion that bridges between social circles are a weak basis for macrolevel connectivity. Instead, sequential overlap among social circles, similar to the crosscutting sections in a Venn diagram, offers a more robust basis for community cohesion. Even better suited for this purpose are the middle sections where most social circles crosscut and overlap with each other.[26] Translated into our historical context, where trade and seafaring were at the heart of people's identity, an activity that attracts members from all strata of the local merchant elite would have created dense overlaps. I call these opportunities for cohesion organizational linchpins (see figure 1.1). Organizational linchpins are informal platforms that provide a focus and a foundation for integrating diverse sets of actors and their relationships.[27] Just as linchpins ensure that different moving parts of a technical mechanism are being held together, organizational linchpins operate as social fasteners that hold different groups or strata within a community together. Another analogy is a keystone that secures the vaulted ceiling of a medieval church. Removing the keystone will erode the structure of the ceiling, just as the absence of organizational linchpins in social networks will undermine cohesion.

To the best of my knowledge, Noah Friedkin's concept of ridge structures comes closest to organizational linchpins in network theory.[28] The main idea is to think of social structure as similar to a contour map of a mountain range.

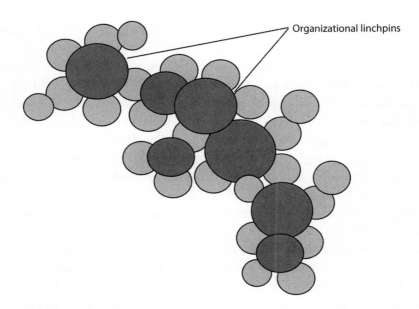

Organizational linchpins

FIGURE 1.1 Organizational linchpins holding up a cohesive macrostructure among distinct social circles.

Source: Adapted from Friedkin (1998, 134–35).

We may trace the contours by drawing a line from one peak to the next, but doing so would not reveal the full structure of the mountain range. Instead, if we draw the tracing line at a lower elevation, we would recognize ridges in between the peaks. Where ridges dip deeply and rise steeply on the other side, they appear as valleys. Where ridges rise high, no such valleys separate peaks from each other. Now, if social closeness in social space is represented by elevation, then we see subgroups emerging that correspond to peaks. Structural holes separating them correspond to deep valleys. Sufficiently high ridges then would correspond to "chains of sequentially overlapping, densely occupied, regions of social space" that, much like sections in a Venn diagram, create interfaces between different sub-groups.[29] Those subgroup interfaces are the linchpins in organizational networks. In keeping with this analogy, most hikers would probably prefer a well-trodden pathway along a ridge to a brittle bridge suspended between two peaks.

The linchpins within organizational networks that I have in mind still rest on people (merchant traders in my setting) and the social relationships in which they are embedded (mostly partnership and kinship ties in my setting). What, then, is the micromechanism that gives rise to a cohesive macrostructure that is held together by organizational linchpins? Building on models of network macrostructures that derive from balance theory, Friedkin has shown that the tendency toward transitivity in social relationships is consistent with the concept of ridge structures.[30] In a similar vein, I suggest that a variant of transitivity that operates sequentially over time serves as a micromechanism for a cohesive mac-rostructure. To get a sense of this mechanism, consider the development of mer-chant traders' careers in the historical context at hand. As I have illustrated, using the example of Chateaubriand's various undertakings, *armateurs* in Saint-Malo mobilized business partners to join them in collaborative partnerships to launch their overseas ventures. Following the successful conclusion of an initial ven-ture, they routinely reinvested the returns and moved on to their next venture. Seeking partners for the new venture, they relied on trusted peers from earlier enterprises as much as they recruited new investors to contribute to their joint venture. Hence, repeated ties connected an *armateur*'s successive partnerships over the course of a trader's career in the field of overseas commerce. At the same time, an *armateur*'s erstwhile partners may well have collaborated in still other private enterprises, whether or not our *armateur*, say Chateaubriand, partici-pated in them as a partner. In other words, as the careers of Chateaubriand and those of other *armateurs* like him unfolded over time, they yielded sequences of connected ventures as well as sequentially linked ties among former, present, and future partners. Cohesion among the merchant elite emerged from this enchain-ment mechanism of sequential ventures.

WHY SAINT-MALO?

In his influential book *La Noblesse commerçante* (*The Commercial Nobility*), published in 1756, the Enlightenment man of letters Gabriel François Coyer referred to Saint-Malo as a "stronghold of commerce," "a nursery of merchant entrepreneurs," and "a seminary of heroes."[31] Put in a more sober tone, what the abbé Coyer sought to emphasize was the central place that Saint-Malo held in the larger scheme of France's ambitions on the seas. The importance of this port city, perched on a small rock on the coast of northern Brittany (figure 1.2), rested on two pillars: the substantial contribution of its residents to entrepreneurship in various strands of maritime commerce and their equally strong dedication to the *guerre de course*, or privateering enterprise (the heroic part in Coyer's statement). Indeed, next to Dunkirk, Saint-Malo was one of France's hotbeds of privateering. In Coyer's view, these multiple maritime activities offered an ideal schooling for seamen and therefore also benefited the French Royal Navy in the long run.[32] The Malouins were of course not alone in their role, as other French port cities pulled

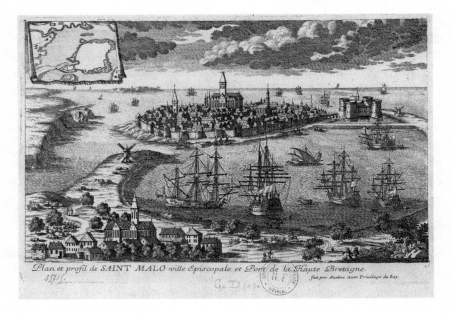

FIGURE 1.2 View of Saint-Malo, by Pierre Aveline, c. late seventeenth century.

Source: Bibliothèque Nationale de France.

their weight and held similar strategic importance. If anything, then, Saint-Malo was an exemplary metropolitan port in the development of the French Atlantic Economy (see chapter 2).

Precisely because Saint-Malo was not alone, its merchant elite faced stiff competition from other ports in the realm, especially when it came to securing trading privileges from the royal government. Not every single place could enjoy trade monopolies or the benefits of being a free trade port; otherwise, these would cease to be exclusive rights. Given such a competitive environment, not the solitary efforts of a few traders but rather cohesion among local merchants was supportive of sustained collective lobbying campaigns.

In times of war, competition from within was too often met with tangible threats of destruction from outside. During the five armed conflicts that occurred between the late seventeenth century and the French Revolution, English (British by 1707) and Dutch forces mounted repeated attacks on Saint-Malo. The city's location, exposed as it was to the open sea, proved to be a strategic advantage in commerce, yet also made it vulnerable to such strikes. Again, local cohesion was helpful in mobilizing citizens to collectively defend their city. In contrast, inner feuds surely would have been a recipe for undermining such defensive measures.

Turning from violent conflict to commerce, the very nature of long-distance journeys and the exploration of new trade routes entailed uncertainty. Consequently, gathering reliable information about fresh opportunities and the most efficient ways to seize them was essential to translate uncertainty into calculable risk. Dependable information to minimize risk would have to come from trustworthy sources, and arguably few would have been trusted more than one's neighbors, kin, and business partners in a well-connected community. Of course, some amount of risk—of losing one's ship, valuable cargo, crewmembers, and hence wealth—always remained, and in most cases, it was too much for any single *armateur* to bear alone. So, once again, a cohesive community of fellow traders provided an ideal pool for cooperative relationships, both to float seaborne ventures in the first place and to spread risk across several shoulders.

Early modern Saint-Malo thus makes for a compelling empirical case to explore this issue of cohesion in local network organization. As this book is a historical case study, alert readers may wonder how much of a selection on a particularly successful case it entails. In the chapters that follow, I trace the multilayered networks among Saint-Malo's merchant elite over a 110-year period (1681–1792), from the height of Louis XIV's absolutist reign to the French Revolution. We will see that, during this long time span, Saint-Malo's economic development followed a trajectory that was far from linear and progressive. The city's golden age lasted from the 1680s to about 1715, when the Malouin merchants benefited greatly from lucrative wartime opportunities in privateering and interloping trade with the Spanish American colonies, coupled with privileged access to markets in the East Indies and Arabia. After 1715, economic growth turned into a remarkable decline: a relatively long period of peace until the 1740s removed the kinds of high-risk, high-return ventures that had enriched the Malouin *armateurs* during the previous conflicts. Monopoly rights, especially for the trades with India and the South Sea, were revoked or not renewed. Even the *course* lay dormant until the War of the Austrian Succession. New opportunities, such as the growing sugar plantation economies in the French West Indies, came to be controlled by merchants from Bordeaux and Marseille, and not Saint-Malo. A slight recovery set in only with the Seven Years' War (1756–1763), when a new generation of Malouin trader elites dedicated their business interests once again to privateering enterprise, the East Indies, and the slave trade. Economic growth returned to Saint-Malo, although the city never again reached the levels of wealth it had enjoyed until the beginning of the eighteenth century. In other words, what makes the economic and social development of Saint-Malo in this period so intriguing is not a straightforward winner story (that lacks at least the possibility of failure for comparison), but rather its notable within-case variation.

Few would doubt that exogenous changes, beyond the reach of our merchant traders on the ground, had their hand in the ups and downs of Saint-Malo's trajectory. The leading historical interpretation, however, finds primarily endogenous social dynamics within the merchant elite at work.[33] A more detailed discussion of that interpretation will follow later in this book (see chapters 2 and 3). For the moment, a summary will suffice. According to its main argument, the merchant elites of Saint-Malo profited to such an extent from their ventures in commerce and the *course* that they came to think of themselves as a quasi-nobility: they increasingly turned away from seaborne enterprises and invested in landed property, sought marriage affiliations with the Breton nobility, adopted the lifestyle of the landed gentry, and ensured that their offspring would pursue careers in the royal administration rather than in commerce and seafaring. As compelling as this narrative of upward mobility and status aspiration may be in its explanation of Saint-Malo's decline in the early eighteenth century, it leaves a number of substantive concerns unresolved. It is these concerns, one might even say empirical puzzles, that motivate the case-specific questions of this study. For one, the narrative entails an implicit assumption that the local merchant elite was a unified bloc of likeminded members whose shared interests led them to turn their backs on the very foundations of their wealth at about the same time—and that they would do so at the very moment of their greatest success. In contrast, the evidence

I propose in chapter 3 reveals that although Saint-Malo's merchant elites shared a number of characteristics, they also differed clearly along a crucial dimension: their wealth. Of course, we know from a wide range of comparable historical settings that elites rarely display uniformity and routinely split into competing interest groups, even opposing factions.[34] In Saint-Malo, and undoubtedly in other French port cities as well, variation in wealth was crucial because what financial resources merchant traders had at their disposal determined the number and kinds of investments in ocean-bound ventures they were able to make. Given that forming partnerships for ventures was indeed at the very heart of their identity, the question is how these merchants were able to bridge what set them apart to come together as partners. Put differently, what was the organizational platform that facilitated their collective action? Throughout this volume, I argue and show that the *course*, or privateering enterprise, served as the kind of linchpin organization I introduced earlier (see the section "Organizational Linchpins and Careers"). It was the one enterprise that attracted interested parties from all corners of the local merchant elite. Hence, at the macrostructure of organizational networks in this time and place, it was the *course* that prompted cohesion, whereas its absence led to fragmentation.

The second case-specific question follows from the same historical narrative: if the reigning elites did indeed withdraw themselves so completely from seaborne commerce and privateering that even their sons and nephews began to opt instead for careers in the royal administration, then where did the generation of *new men* come from that emerged in the 1750s and 1760s? Within a short time span, they had assumed a social standing and wealth that made them look remarkably similar to the first generation of great Malouin *armateurs* at the turn of the eighteenth century. I have outlined how the unfolding of individual careers through the enchainment of sequential ventures can work as a micromechanism that yields a cohesive macrostructure. In chapter 7, I demonstrate how the new generation of merchant *armateurs* used their engagements in privateering, in particular, as launching pads for their later careers in maritime commerce. Not only did they build their personal careers in this manner but also, in doing so, they helped along the rise and maintenance of a cohesive macrostructure among their various enterprises and, hence, among their partners and peers.

Finally, few of these novel insights would have been gained had it not been for the unusually rich archival holdings on the trading and privateering endeavors that the merchant elites of Saint-Malo undertook. It is these well-preserved historical sources that permit us to reconstruct the partnership networks in all their complexity over a more than a hundred-year time span (1681–1792).

DEFINING A TRADER ELITE

Who exactly were the main protagonists when it came to the organization of maritime trade in Saint-Malo and Ancien Régime France at large? The first intuitive step to identify the Saint-Malo trader elites is to inspect the sources that document their core activity: the contractual agreements of the share partnerships (*actes de société*) they formed in the pursuit of maritime trade and privateering enterprise. The contract for the 150-ton frigate *La Concorde*, drawn up on February 1, 1697, may serve as a case in point.[35] The document names Nicolas Magon, sieur de la Chipaudière, le Jeune, as one of the owners of the vessel ("prop.^{re} en partye et armateur du navire") who fitted it out for a privateering raid against the enemies of the state ("le voyage quelle est prest de faire en course contre Les Ennemies de L'etat"). A list follows of Magon's associates who held interests in the share partnership of the *Concorde*, all of them residents of Saint-Malo ("ont Comparu Les cy apres nommés marchands et bourgeois négociants dem.^{r} en Cette ville de St. Malo"). In some cases, more than just one owner of a ship was listed, but otherwise the entry for the *Concorde* is fairly standard and representative of the 3,250 share partnerships registered at Saint-Malo that have survived to this day.[36] Browsing these sources, one encounters three distinctive terms that contemporaries used to denote those who partnered in trading and privateering ventures: *marchand*, *négociant*, and, already familiar to us, *armateur*.

Consider the first term that designates the role of Nicolas Magon: *armateur*. Its meaning was precise and referred to the functional role of "ships' husbands," as J. S. Bromley has reminded us. The *armateur* was the person in charge of organizing the entire venture, including all economic decisions and orders. In our previous case, Magon was also one of the owners of the ship, although management and ownership could be separate. In his role as *armateur*, he was the one who selected the ship and captain; oversaw the recruitment of the crew with the help of the captain; managed all necessary preparations for the voyage, including obtaining victuals, equipment, and weaponry; prepared all necessary paperwork and submitted it to the Admiralty; and raised contributions from shareholders. Finally, in the event of a successful privateering cruise, the *armateur* also took care of the safe storage of prize goods and, once the court decision and auction sales were concluded, distributed the gains among the shareholders.[37]

Whereas *armateur* refers to a mostly technical role, the terms *marchand* and *négociant* denoted occupational positions and socioeconomic status. According to most historians' accounts, *marchand* is the older category, which traditionally referred to retail merchants who dealt primarily on local markets, confined to their town and surrounding countryside. Crucially, within the corporate order of Ancien Régime society, these merchants were guild members and therefore required to complete an apprenticeship in their trade before they could open a shop. As such, they also had access to an exclusive judicial mechanism, the merchant courts, to resolve disputes between merchants over merchandise.[38]

The new figure of the *négociant* as a wholesale (*en gros*) trader emerged in the mid-seventeenth century as commerce expanded from regional to national and finally to global markets. Institutional developments, such as new financial instruments that facilitated the extension of credit and economic transactions over long distances, helped the trader's rise, along with the *société en commandite* partnership form that opened investment in trade to a range of social strata whose members previously were barred. These strata included the nobility whose members were now encouraged by the royal government to participate in commerce, a move that had been unimaginable among noblemen for fear of losing one's status. Under these favorable circumstances, the emergent role of the *négociant* elite was first defined by its scope: what Pierre Jeannin has called "polyactivité" and a cosmopolitan outlook in commerce that went well beyond the traditional limits of the guild-regulated and retail-focused local *marchand*. What distinguished great *négociants* like the members of Saint-Malo's Magon dynasty from mere national or regional traders, and placed them at the top of the world of commerce, was the wide range of choices available to them. These choices included the ability to trade wherever opportunities arose and to pursue their interests in multiple fields of commerce at once—from regional to national to worldwide markets—and to do so in diverse roles, as shareholders, bankers, providers of assurances, and first and foremost as *armateurs* of ambitious seafaring enterprises. Second, as a distinct mercantile elite, the ideal *négociants* represented not only extraordinary wealth but also, and perhaps even more important, the embracement of quasi-aristocratic virtues in commerce. As Savary exclaimed in his *Parfait Négociant*, because the realm of the *négociant* is "more honorable" and "noble," it "rises above" that of the retail *marchand* but is "also more dangerous" with "more risks to take." Hence, the willingness of *négociants* to brave the dangers and risks of their enterprises on the international stage came to be regarded as every bit as honorable as the military exploits that noblemen pursued in the name of king and country.[39]

For all the ideals attached to this new role, in practice, the terms *marchands* and *négociants* were still used concomitantly and often interchangeably, as the partnership contract for the *Concorde* illustrates ("marchands et bourgeois négotiants").[40] In terms of sheer numbers, in most eighteenth-century towns in Brittany, with the exception of the main port cities of Nantes, Lorient, and Saint-Malo, few traders went by the professional title of *négociants*. No such titles are found in the tax registrations of the Breton capital, Rennes, in 1706 or in 1721. In 1786, only fifteen residents of Rennes declared themselves to be *négociants* for purposes of taxation. Even in Lorient, the earlier tax registers of 1739 identified merely four *négociants* compared with thirty-six *marchands*. In the smaller port of Morlaix, thirty-two were listed and another five were noted in Saint-Brieuc. The evidence suggests that the term *négociant* was not fully established and recognized in Brittany before the end of the eighteenth century.[41]

BOOK OVERVIEW

The argument I make in this study unfolds over the course of the next six chapters and the conclusion. Chapter 2 sets the scene by portraying the origins and gradual establishment of Saint-Malo as a center of the French Atlantic Economy. It is largely a descriptive chapter that introduces readers to the historical setting, and in particular, to the kinds of enterprises the local merchant community engaged in. I draw on the experience of leading figures in that community to illustrate what it meant to be an *armateur* in the business of overseas trade and privateering. The chapter also begins a narrative arc that traces the development of Saint-Malo and the social structure of its merchant elite over time, from the 1680s through the onset of the French Revolution in the early 1790s. Thus, chapter 2 ends with the observation of Saint-Malo's reversal of fortunes at the beginning of the eighteenth century.

In chapter 3, we enter the empirical analysis. I draw on poll tax data for the city of Saint-Malo to show the extent of stratification within the merchant trader community. These findings are combined with an assessment of the costs involved in the fitting out of voyages in various trades as well as in the *course*. Chapter 3 concludes that the *course* emerges as the prime candidate for an organizational linchpin in the network of merchant partnerships.

Next, knowing what role it played in the organizational networks, we may wonder what the *guerre de course*, or privateering enterprise, is all about. Chapter 4 therefore presents a detailed history of its origins and the legal regulations that embedded the private war at sea within a strict institutional framework that sharply distinguished it from outright piracy. I further describe all the preparations that were necessary for a typical privateering campaign, from the purchase of a suitable ship and the recruitment of an experienced captain and able crew to the purchase of weaponry, equipment, and victuals, and, crucially, the mobilization of capital from shareholding partners. An essential part of the discussion considers what meaning these merchants attached to the partnership ties they formed. Drawing on a sample of journals that the captains of privateers were required to keep by law, we also witness some of the events that took place during the campaigns, from fateful encounters with storms and enemy battleships to successful captures of valuable prize ships.

Chapter 5 examines the outcomes of privateering enterprise, and in particular, its financial returns. I consider the administrative and judicial procedures that were necessary for the *armateurs* to comply with once their corsair ship returned from a successful raiding campaign. At the heart of the chapter is a systematic quantitative analysis of the costs and benefits of *course* ventures that allows us to assess the profitability of the whole enterprise.

Chapter 6 carries most of the weight of the network analysis of partnership ties over the 110-year period from 1681–1792. This chapter demonstrates how much cohesion within the macrostructure of organizational networks depended on the presence of partnerships in privateering. Aided by several robustness tests, I show that the linchpin role of *course* ventures holds no matter which subperiod within those 110 years one considers. I assess to what extent the selection of shareholding associates on the basis of kinship affiliation and geographical closeness influenced these observed patterns in the partnership networks.

Chapter 7 then picks up the narrative arc from chapter 2 and moves it forward to the second half of the eighteenth century, when Saint-Malo experienced a resurgence of its economic growth. The members of a new generation of *armateurs*, whom I call the *new men*, are at the center of this analysis. In parallel fashion to chapter 2, I draw on the exploits of selected protagonists to illustrate how their initial engagement in the *course* served as their entry ticket into the world of commerce. In line with the argument I made previously, as their careers as *armateurs* unfolded and they kept drawing other merchants into their evolving personal network of partnerships, they contributed their share to the cohesion of the merchant network at large. Anecdotal evidence from individual cases is often useful to breathe life into abstract concepts and ideas, but this chapter's conclusions are also supported by a systematic quantitative analysis of the enchainment mechanism described earlier.

The conclusion revisits the book's central findings and connects the various threads of the argument. It does so by recalling the career paths and undertakings of exemplary *armateurs-négociants*, both from Saint-Malo's earlier golden age and from the generation of *new men* who rose to prominence in the second half of the eighteenth century. I also draw parallels with *new men* who stepped to the fore in other historical settings, and in particular their tendency to play a key role in political change. This emphasis on politics leads us to consider the growing rift within Saint-Malo's elite that eventually placed the old patriciate and the *new men* on opposite sides at the beginning of the French Revolution. These political conflicts thus clarify the limits of the integrative power of partnerships formed in *course* ventures.

CHAPTER 2

SAINT-MALO IN THE FRENCH ATLANTIC ECONOMY

Approaching the city of Saint-Malo from the seaside, the visitor may have the impression that this granite city is just as much at home in the waters that surround it as it is connected to Brittany's coastline—only the *Sillon*, not much more than a narrow isthmus of sand dunes, had prevented it from being an island altogether (see the map in figure 2.1). Henri Sée, one of the pioneering economic historians of Saint-Malo, once portrayed this port as rising "proudly from its rocky islet, surrounded by ancient walls, like a vessel about to put out to sea."[1] The vivid image of a ship being readied for its ocean-bound voyage emphasizes how much the ever-present lure of the sea shaped the city's history. What, then, are its historical origins?

The earliest traces of human presence along the mouth of the river Rance and the Clos-Poulet, the large peninsula that forms Saint-Malo's rural hinterland, date back to prehistoric times. By about 80 BC, a Celtic settlement by the name of Aleth had been established in what is now the suburb of Saint-Servan.[2] After the Roman conquest of Gaul, Aleth kept its Celtic name but became a Roman port in 56 BC. The Romans erected fortifications and connected Aleth to their extensive network of roads that spanned all of the major towns in the provinces of Gaul. Excavated coins that display the portraits of various emperors suggest a Roman presence in the area until about 400 AD. Further evidence exists that Aleth served as a garrison for soldiers of the Martenses legion as well as the seat of a Roman prefect and his administrative staff in the fourth century. Still, beginning in the fourth century, settlements along the Armorican coast suffered from recurrent raids at the hands of invading Saxon tribes. As in other border regions of the Empire, Roman military superiority waned, and by 420 AD, the Romans had left the Cité d'Aleth behind.

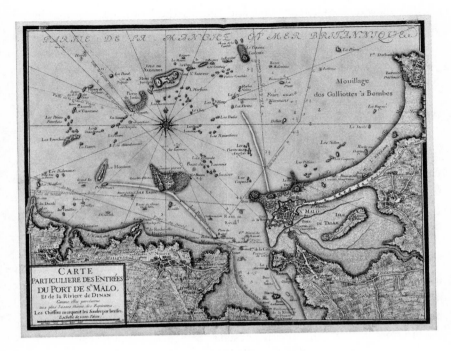

FIGURE 2.1 Map of the entrance to the harbor of Saint-Malo.

Source: Bibliothèque Nationale de France.

Merovingians followed the Romans, and Carolingians followed the Merovingians as the new rulers of the lands. Much of the history during these times is shrouded in mystery because direct evidence is severely lacking. But just like other prominent places that wish to invoke a rich historical legacy, Saint-Malo has its own foundation myth. And it does not come as a surprise that the foundation is thought to be seaborne. Legend has it that in 507, a hermit named Saint Aaron took refuge on that rocky islet facing Aleth. Having landed at Brittany's shore, a Welsh émigré monk and missionary by the name of Maclow (also known as Maclou or Maclovius in Latin) was among Aaron's followers. Following the death of Saint Aaron, Maclow became bishop of Aleth in 541. As Saint Malo, he is still recognized as one of the founding saints of Brittany. Maclow followed the hermit's example and settled on the *rocher d'Aaron*. He ordered the construction of a first chapel and probably founded a monastery on the islet. Eventually, the patron saint's name graced the rock as well as the settlement that gradually emerged upon it. Aleth, meanwhile, suffered from repeated pillages, first by the

Carolingians under Charlemagne, and later by the Normans. Prepared by the foundation of a Benedictine monastery in 1108, Bishop Jean de Châtillon finally transferred the Episcopal See from Aleth to Saint-Malo in 1146. Local ecclesiastical influence and political power had shifted from the ancient site of Aleth to Saint-Malo.

By the late Middle Ages, a growing community of entrepreneurial merchant traders and seafarers turned Saint-Malo into a prospering port, the commercial center and most important town within the Clos-Poulet region. Its growing wealth and strategic coastal location, however, made it a prized possession, coveted by the rival political powers within the region and beyond. During the dynastic War of the Breton Succession (1341–1365) and the Hundred Years' War (1337–1453), Saint-Malo changed hands numerous times between the independent duchy of Brittany, the French crown, and the English crown until it was integrated into the *domaine royale* of France in 1493.

The entanglement in these conflicts and the repeated threats of destruction instilled a strong sense of local identity among Saint-Malo's citizens. Several communal revolts over the course of the fourteenth century attest to their attachment to what they apparently felt was very much "their own city."[3] In a similar vein, in 1590, the Malouins openly refused to recognize the royal authority of the Protestant King Henry IV. As staunch defenders of the Catholic faith, they considered his claim to the throne illegitimate. Most likely, however, the Malouins' opposition was an attempt to stay clear of the confessional troubles of the time and to protect their own interests. The episode of the city's quasi-autonomy was short-lived and lasted barely four years.[4] In 1594, allegiance to the crown was restored as soon as the king had converted to the Roman Catholic faith and reinstated all of the city's erstwhile privileges.

Setting aside foundation myths and romantic images of a valiant port city whose burghers defended hard-won liberties, we may be tempted to regard the events as rather typical for early modern European state-building: on one hand, we witness centralizing rulers, whether Breton dukes or French kings, who aim to tighten their political authority over their territory; on the other, we find fierce resistance to the state's encroachment of local communities like Saint-Malo, often born out of vested economic interests.[5] Such an interpretation emphasizes confrontation over cooperation between royal power and local interests under the Ancien Régime. This view misses that the relationship between "crown" and "country" often entailed the granting of privileges to towns and provinces that enabled rather than constrained their economic development.[6] In the case of Saint-Malo, one of the more significant privileges dates to 1395. In this year, King Charles VI issued letters patent that granted the citizens of Saint-Malo a generalized exemption from paying various kinds of impositions and taxes within the realm. Perhaps even more important, the royal order explicitly stated that these liberties also extended to all foreign merchants who sought to pursue their trades at Saint-Malo. Likewise included were transactions whereby traders brought merchandise into the port, only to be reexported again. The royal warranty thus provided the legal foundations for an entrepôt and effectively turned Saint-Malo into a free port. As the privilege provided clear economic incentives for foreign traders to do their business here and not elsewhere, the merchant elite of Saint-Malo was keen to defend and preserve it. Indeed, the exemption was recognized and renewed by every reigning duke of Brittany and king of France up until Louis XIV.[7]

Such favorable institutional conditions coupled with Saint-Malo's gradual commercial expansion into the Atlantic and beyond. As exploration combined with commercial expansion, one of Saint-Malo's most illustrious sons, Jacques Cartier, played a pioneering role. During his voyages between 1534 and 1542 in search of the fabled northwestern passage to Cathay, the "Christopher Columbus of France" claimed the Canadian shores for the king of France.[8] Considering the broader economic impact of his explorations, Cartier also paved the way for the dominance of Brittany, and Saint-Malo in particular, as the exploitation of the Newfoundland cod fisheries grew rapidly in the sixteenth and seventeenth centuries. Further explorations across the Atlantic and the tentative establishment of trade routes into the eastern hemisphere followed. French seafarers had crossed into the Indian Ocean as early as 1508, and in 1601, a company of merchants from Saint-Malo, Laval and Vitré sent two vessels, the *Corbin* and the *Croissant*, for the Moluccas in the East Indies. These and further exploits inscribed Saint-Malo firmly on the map of leading ports within the emerging French Atlantic Economy.[9]

Taking a closer look at the map, we quickly recognize that Saint-Malo was only one among a series of cities along the French seaboard that thrived on the returns to transatlantic trade, including Dunkirk, Dieppe, Rouen, Le Havre, Honfleur, Nantes, La Rochelle, Bordeaux, Bayonne, and Marseille (see figure 2.2). Indeed, a long-standing tradition in French historical geography has suggested a division, one might even say a bifurcation, of early modern France into two distinct economic and social structures: one consisting of a chain of port cities lined up along the Atlantic coastline, oriented toward commerce, with an open, wealth-generating bourgeois culture, and enjoying some degree of municipal political autonomy, and the other, a continental zone reaching inland to the east, dominated by subsistence agricultural production, but lacking sufficient circulation of specie, burdened by tax extraction and administrative

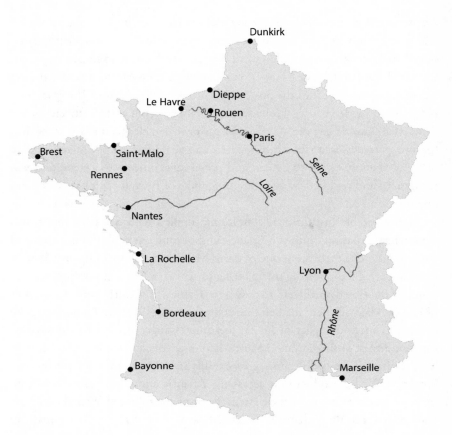

FIGURE 2.2 Map of leading French port cities, using present-day boundaries.

constraints, and suffering as sites of military confrontations. Where exactly the boundary line should be drawn is a matter of debate. Some argue for a meridian running north-south through Paris and down to the Mediterranean, which inconveniently puts Marseille and Lyon on the less-favorable eastern side. Others have suggested a horizontal line, in this case, running from Nantes to Lyon (or, a slightly tilted line, from Saint-Malo all the way down to Geneva). This alternative boundary would have separated an industrious and urbanized north that relied on open-field agricultural production and grew rich from trading across the Channel, from an economically stagnating south. The broader lesson is twofold. First, whatever division existed, it probably was much more malleable and shifted over the course of history. Second, France did not participate in the early modern commercial expansion *en bloc*, as a single and uniform entity. Still, no matter how the line is drawn, the interpretation is always the same: the relatively narrow band of Atlantic France represents prosperity and progress, and the larger central bloc of continental France denotes economic and political backwardness.[10]

Whether we consider a north-south or an east-west divide, Saint-Malo invariably fits neatly into the more favorable economic and political climate of the "other France," that is, the Atlantic France. This placement among such an exclusive company of wealthy ports as Le Havre, Nantes, La Rochelle, Bordeaux, or Marseille probably would have come as a surprise to contemporaries who never tired of emphasizing that Saint-Malo was not as gifted by nature as her rivals. One further glance at the city's geographic position reveals that it was exposed to attacking enemies and the elements alike. Navigating the entrance to the bay through islets and rocks was treacherous for inexperienced pilots (see figure 2.1). Tides were and still are among the highest in all of Europe, thus keeping large vessels from entering the harbor at low tide. Whenever Malouin merchants pleaded for the reinstatement of their erstwhile privilege as a free port, they were met with the same counterarguments as to why such a preferential treatment should be denied. In contrast to the other great ports, Saint-Malo, so it seemed, lacked an economically fertile hinterland with sufficient demand for imported goods and supply of wares to be exported. Even if such a hinterland existed, then Saint-Malo also lacked the river or canals necessary to reach those markets. Whereas Bordeaux had the Garonne, La Rochelle had the Charente, Le Havre and Rouen had the Seine, and Nantes had the Loire, Saint-Malo merely had the Rance, which was navigable only up to Dinan.[11] It also did not help that road connections with other marketplaces in Brittany and Normandy, and certainly with Paris as well, were poor. Contemporaries thus complained that "the post only comes by the Caen road on Tuesdays and Saturdays and by Rennes on Thursdays; so if one fails to catch the post, there are delays."[12] To put this complaint in perspective, note that traveling from Paris to the Breton capital of Rennes by horse and carriage took a full eight days in 1765, at about forty-three kilometers per day. The slightly shorter journey from Paris to Caen still lasted five days, with another day and a half to get from Caen to Coutances in Normandy, which lies about halfway en route to Saint-Malo. One gets the sense, then, of a relatively isolated (or at least provincial) place rather than a central hub of international trade. How, then, did the Malouin merchants brave the obstacles of economic geography and turn their town into one of the most significant ports in early modern France?

TRADITIONAL PILLARS OF COMMERCE

Focusing solely on the lack of accessible and productive marketplaces within the immediate reach of Saint-Malo betrays the fact that the waterways along the Breton and Norman seaboard offered natural routes for the exchange of wares between local ports and beyond. The position of Saint-Malo in its surrounding economic geography was far more ambivalent than the supposed lack of hinterland markets may suggest. Although questionable road conditions may have made journeys to some inland fairs and towns a daunting task, exchanging goods through the *cabotage* (coastal shipping) was among the mainstays of Malouin merchants since the Middle Ages. The *caboteurs* transported a wide range of agricultural products, such as oils, wine, cider, salt, fruits, honey, and wheat. Malouin shipping was embedded in a network of local ports reaching from Carteret and Granville in lower Normandy to Cancale, Saint-Briac, Saint-Brieuc, Binic, Paimpol, Morlaix, and others in northern Brittany, and further down to the southern Breton coast (see figure 2.3). Together, they formed the zone of the *petit cabotage*. One indicator of the strength of bonds between seafarers within this coastal port network is that 95.5 percent of the captains who served on vessels fitted out by Saint-Malo merchant traders and whose place of residence can be identified were recruited from towns in Brittany or lower Normandy.[13] Coastal shipping, however, was not limited to this zone of local commerce in Brittany and lower Normandy. It extended southward to Bordeaux and Bayonne, and northeastward to Dunkirk and Rouen, thus granting Malouin merchants access to the Paris basin through the river Seine.

Traditionally, a considerable share of the outbound shipping from Saint-Malo concerned highly valuable Breton linens. As André Lespagnol has pointed out, the port was ideally placed at the heart of a geographic triangle that encompassed the major region of French textile manufacturing at the time, reaching from Brest in northwestern Brittany to Cholet near the Loire river and onward to Rouen in Normandy (see again figure 2.3). As noted, the conditions of road traffic were often challenging. But apparently, the exported linens commanded such high sales prices at their destinations that they more than compensated for the additional cost and effort of road transportation from their production sites to Saint-Malo.[14]

Turning our gaze toward the sea, we recognize yet another hinterland, not land-based, but rather seaborne, which connects Saint-Malo to the Channel Islands of Guernsey and Jersey, to the ports along the English and Irish coasts, and to the Dutch provinces. Indeed, economic growth from the export of linen

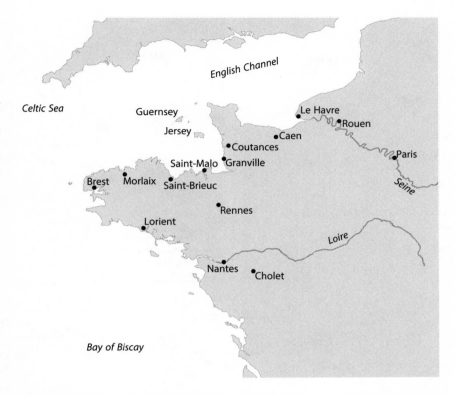

FIGURE 2.3 Location of Saint-Malo among ports and trading centers in Brittany and Normandy.

out of Saint-Malo benefited greatly from shipping to the British Isles. The linen trade continued to prosper until the onset of war led the French crown to prohibit the trade with England. The rise and fall in linen exports is reflected in the number of draperies that were licensed in Saint-Malo: they increased substantially from thirty-two establishments in 1624 to seventy-one in 1650, only to decrease back to thirty-two by 1702, when the War of the Spanish Succession opposed England and France.[15]

To put these observations in perspective, the three panels in figure 2.4 document the scale of shipping out of and into the port of Saint-Malo at the height of its commercial success in the period from 1681 to 1720. The figures compare the number of ships and their tonnage in the various seaborne trades that formed the traditional pillars of Malouin commerce in this period. The share of the *petit cabotage* and French coastal shipping beyond Brittany and lower Normandy (i.e., from Dunkirk in the north to Villefranche in the south) varied quite a bit over

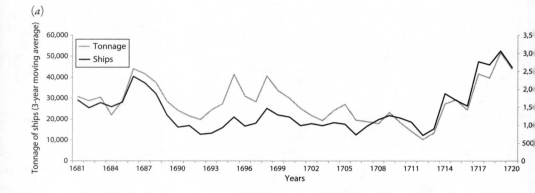

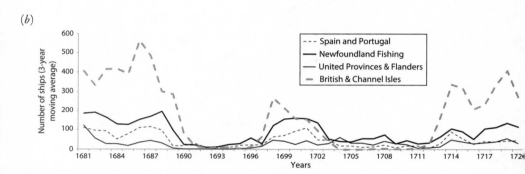

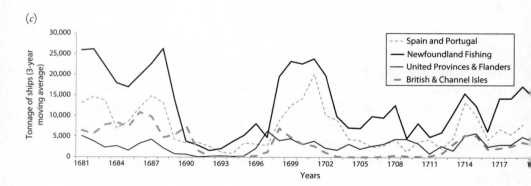

FIGURE 2.4 Statistics of Saint-Malo shipping, 1681–1720: (*a*) French coastal trade, departures and arrivals; (*b*) foreign trade, ship departures and arrivals; and (*c*) foreign trade, tonnage departures and arrivals.

Sources: All trade statistics are taken from Delumeau (1966). Additional information on French shipping to and from Portugal comes from Labourdette (1988, 649–50).

the years. Together, both types of coastal trade made up anywhere between 39 percent and 92 percent of the total annual movement of ships out of Saint-Malo from 1681 to 1720. Their average annual share among departing ships equaled 72 percent (standard deviation = 16 percent). Considering arrivals at Saint-Malo, the portion of coastal trading ranged from 69 percent to 98 percent (86 percent on average; standard deviation = 8 percent). Within foreign commerce, traffic to the United Provinces and Flanders accounted for a modest 3 percent of departures and 1 percent of arrivals, on average. Exchanges with England, Wales, Scotland, and Ireland and the Channel Islands were more salient. Again on average, 13 percent (standard deviation = 10 percent) of all vessels departing from Saint-Malo in a given year were destined for the British Isles, and 8 percent (standard deviation = 6 percent) of those arriving had sailed from ports across the Channel.[16] Thus, despite its less-than-ideal road and river connections, Saint-Malo was far from being a peripheral port, tucked away on some remote islet. Quite to the contrary, it offered an ideal gateway for the northern Breton textile production. At the same time, it served as an entrepôt for provisions and valuable agricultural products destined for consumption in interior centers, such as the Breton capital of Rennes, the most important urban market within reach of Saint-Malo.[17]

The two other traditional strongholds of Malouin commerce—Newfoundland fishing and Spanish trade (figures 2.4b and 2.4c)—emerged with European exploration in the New World and the ensuing opening of new trade routes across the Atlantic.[18] The first recorded expeditions of Breton mariners to the rich cod-fishing grounds around Newfoundland date back as far as the first decade of the sixteenth century. The presence of fishing ships from Saint-Malo in these waters was documented as early as 1519. Long-distance cod fishing expanded rapidly, spurred by increasing demand for salted fish by an urban clientele in northern France and especially in Catholic southern Europe where consumers observed dietary restrictions during religious seasons.[19] By 1580, no less than five hundred vessels, which translates into about twelve thousand seamen and a total tonnage of about forty thousand, undertook the journey into the North Atlantic. Saint-Malo was not the only port that fitted out fishing vessels for Newfoundland, but it quickly rose to become a dominant one.[20]

Fishermen from other ports preferred to make their catch off-shore at *le grand banc de terre-neuve* (Grand Banks of Newfoundland). The size of an average fishing vessel was between fifty and sixty tons, carrying about fifteen or sixteen fishermen. The method of bank fishing was the *pêche errante* (wandering fishery), where the fish were prepared and salted on board while they were still fresh. The name *morue verte* derives from the practice of preserving cod in this manner (green fishery in English). In contrast, Saint-Malo's staple export commodity was the *morue sèche* (dried cod). The fish were caught, brought ashore, split and air-cured until they were ready for transport to mostly southern European markets. Because of this practice, it was also called the *pêche sedentaire* (sedentary fishery). The Malouins directed their efforts to fishing in the bays of southern Newfoundland—the *Chapeau rouge* and the *Baie de Plaisance*—and along the northern coast, also known as the *Petit Nord*, which offered smaller size cod with excellent drying properties. Dried cod fishing employed much larger ships than the green fishery, ranging between one hundred and two hundred tons on average, and equipped with fifty or even more men. The ships were not really fishing vessels, but rather were used for transportation. They carried up to twenty small chaloupes that were assembled on site and formed the actual fishing boats, which were manned by about three fishermen each. Peasants from the hinterlands of Saint-Malo, whose main activity consisted of preparing the catch ashore, accounted for another share of the crew. Consequently, partnerships of merchants in the business of cod fishing armed two kinds of vessels. The larger ones, up to two hundred tons, brought the preserved fish to European marketplaces, and the smaller ones, about forty to fifty tons, carried the workers and materials back to their home ports.

Dried cod fishing quickly turned into a commercial enterprise, producing the commodity in great quantities. Estimates suggest that an able fisherman may have retrieved up to 184 fish on a good day, yielding 13,800 fish during a campaign of two and a half months. Anything less than a daily return of at least one hundred fish per person would have been considered a failure. The fishing fleet left Saint-Malo each spring to stay around Newfoundland into the summer. As noted, the ships did not return immediately to Brittany, but rather they sought to meet the *saison de commerce* to deliver their catch directly to marketplaces in the Mediterranean, including Lisbon, Cadiz, Malaga, Barcelona, Marseille, Genoa, Livorno, and Civitavecchia. Having sold their catch, they typically turned into cargo carriers moving between various local ports as far as Crete and the Barbary coast. On the return leg of this triangular voyage, they would bring valuable wares such as oils, soap, wine, salt, and cotton back to Saint-Malo. It usually took eighteen months or longer before the sailors would see again the shores of their hometown.[21]

How did long-distance fishing compare with other types of trade that the Malouins engaged in? Figure 2.4b illustrates the importance of the Newfoundland cod fisheries, which, on average, accounted for about 30 percent (standard deviation = 16 percent) of all annual shipping in foreign commerce that left or entered the port of Saint-Malo in the period from 1681 to 1720 period. As mentioned earlier, even within the same trades, the size of ships employed varied substantially. Hence, any comparison of the salience of different trades cannot rest solely on the sheer number of trafficking vessels. Yet, even when variation in ship size is taken into account (as shown in figure 2.4c), the average annual tonnage of 12,671 (standard deviation = 7,712) in the cod fisheries still represented 45 percent of the average annual tonnage of 28,191 (standard deviation = 15,597) committed to foreign trade at large.[22] Cod fishing was the "heavy lifting" of Saint-Malo shipping, providing its very foundation. As André Lespagnol has suggested, being a sailor from Saint-Malo nearly always meant being employed on a *terre-neuvier*.[23] Newfoundland fishing fueled an entire supply industry, such as shipbuilding, the making of cords and sails, and the provision of victuals and sufficient amounts of salt for the preservation of cod. It thus ensured business for the *caboteurs* who brought these goods from other ports into Saint-Malo. In turn, the city's residents benefited from the inflow of luxury items through the triangular trade. As such, the fishing trade may not have given rise to immense riches or spectacular opportunities for upward social mobility. Yet, year after year, it provided a steady return that eventually helped to float much riskier enterprises. Finally, the testing conditions of Newfoundland fishing voyages served as an ideal training ground for generations of sailors from Saint-Malo, earning them their high reputation of being the best seamen in all of France.[24]

Next to the age-old *cabotage* and the "bread-and-butter" business of cod fishing, it was the trade with Portugal and Spain in particular that provided the third traditional pillar of Saint-Malo's maritime commerce. Once again, figures 2.4b and 2.4c illustrate how the scale of shipping to and from the Iberian Peninsula compared with other trades that Malouin merchants engaged in. On average, exchanges with Portuguese and Spanish ports accounted for about 16 percent (standard deviation = 10.4) of all vessels engaged in foreign trade that departed from and arrived at Saint-Malo in any given year between 1681 and 1720. Likewise, the average annual tonnage of trade vessels (7,178 tons; standard deviation = 4,817) committed to the commerce with Spain and Portugal represented a full 25 percent of the average annual tonnage that the Malouin merchants fitted out in foreign trade at large.[25]

The foundation of the Spanish trade was twofold. On one hand, the Spanish connection had its roots in the triangular routes of the *terre-neuviers* who, as we learned earlier, first delivered their cargo of dried codfish to the ports of Bilbao, Lisbon, Alicante, Barcelona, and other markets in the Mediterranean. On their return voyage to Brittany, they loaded Andalusian agricultural goods such as oils, dried fruit, and wine for consumption at home. Their itinerary followed the traditional lanes of long-distance coastal shipping beyond the borders of the French realm. On the other hand, a novel and direct trade route to Spain had emerged by the seventeenth century that closely resembled the same *grand cabotage*, so well-established since medieval times. The resemblance becomes blurred once we consider the kinds of vessels the Malouin merchants employed in their direct trade with Spain. The typical vessel was a frigate of about two hundred to five hundred tons, designed for plying the waters at highest speeds. Even though the journey took little more than two or three weeks, the trading ships usually were escorted by warships or heavily armed themselves such that a 450-ton vessel would carry not only forty well-trained soldiers next to its eighty seamen, but also up to forty cannons. Furthermore, they usually traveled in convoys of five to ten ships, well prepared to defend themselves against potential attacks, with Barbary coast pirates being an incessant menace. Their routes may have resembled those of the traditional coastal traders, but the appearance of the *flottes d'Espagne* that set out from Saint-Malo seemed to have more in common with men-of-war than with regular merchantmen.[26]

Convoys were complex and costly to organize. Ships sailed at slower speed when in a convey than on their own. Given the elaborate protection efforts, something must have been worth protecting. What made the direct exchange with Spanish ports so valuable to Saint-Malo's merchants was its role as the gateway to the lucrative colonial markets in Spanish America. Earlier in this chapter, I alluded to the flourishing export of Breton linen and other woven cloth from Saint-Malo to the British Isles. The quality of these luxury textiles was coveted just as much by the colonial elites in Spanish America and demand increased accordingly. By the 1680s, about three-fourths of the exports of linen to the Americas, amounting to 16 millions *livres tournois* (*lt.*), came from French ports, Rouen and Saint-Malo being the two most active ones.[27] The increasing demand overseas was not limited to wares produced in the manufactories of Vitré, Rennes, and Quintin, which all were within the relative vicinity of Saint-Malo. Textiles woven in lower Brittany, lower Maine, and upper Normandy as well as canvases, cloths, and fine laceworks from as far away as Lyon, Puy, Amiens, and Reims all filled the cargo bays of merchant ships that departed Saint-Malo en route to Spain and eventually found their way to consumers in the American colonies. During the seventeenth century, Saint-Malo thus established itself as a premier port for the export of French cloth.

On their return leg, the Malouin merchantmen carried the traditional range of wines, fruits, and oils from southern Spain. They also brought home valuable colonial goods, such as vicuña wool, tropical woods, indigo, and cochineal, the latter two used to derive dyes for coloring fabrics. Above all, however, the fleets of Saint-Malo transported that most treasured of all colonial commodities—silver from the mines of Mexico and Peru, either as bullion or minted into pesos and piastre coins. Indeed, it was in this role as one of the principal French ports of entry for American silver that Saint-Malo and its merchant community gained much of its economic fortune in the seventeenth century. As André Lespagnol aptly noted, on their departure to Spain, the ships from Saint-Malo essentially formed cloth fleets that turned into silver fleets upon their return voyage. In addition to their direct benefits from the Spanish colonial trade, the Saint-Malo merchantry profited from the fees they were able to charge other French traders who relied on the long-term expertise of the Malouins in organizing well-armed convoys for the secure shipping of their wares to Spain. Saint-Malo thus filled a central intermediary role in the commerce with Spain, both as a hub for the distribution of metropolitan luxury goods and colonial commodities and as a specialist provider of secure and timely transportation for other French traders. Each year between 1660 and 1702, Malouin merchants fitted out ten to twenty ships for commerce with Spain, which clearly outnumbered the one or two ships that departed from Dunkirk, the two or three ships from Le Havre, and the four or five ships from Marseille within the same period. On the eve of the eighteenth century, the Malouin merchants sent close to twenty ships per year on their way to Cadiz alone, the central Spanish outport to the colonies. About the same number of ships returned to Saint-Malo each year, amounting to an average annual tonnage of 3,500 to 4,000 tons. Estimates suggest that about 55 percent of the total value of the Franco-Spanish commerce at the end of the seventeenth century was thereby centered on Saint-Malo.[28]

On the Spanish side, the transatlantic commerce with the New World rested on an elaborate institutional system, the *Carrera de Indias*. It coordinated and controlled all shipping of merchandise across the Atlantic from Cadiz to the colonial settlements of New Spain and New Granada as well as the bullion carrying fleets back to Spain. A French memoir dating from 1691 on "the commerce with the West Indies through Cadiz" provides a detailed description of its twofold organization.[29] Each year, a squadron of ten galleons, each heavily armed with soldiers and up to fifty-two cannons, made its way from Cadiz to the ports of Cartagena and Portobello in present-day Colombia and Panama. Their round-trip journey back to Cadiz took about one year. Every summer, another convoy of about sixteen merchant vessels, each amounting to five to six hundred tons and carrying up to thirty-two cannons, was scheduled to depart Cadiz, escorted by two well-armed ships-of-war. The ten largest merchantmen sailed to Veracruz in present-day Mexico, whereas the smaller ones separated from the convoy to reach Trinidad, Curaçao, Havana, San Domingo, and Campeche. They sought to arrive at their destinations before mid-September to avoid the northern winds. Their entire journey, including the return leg to Cadiz, took about thirteen months. The Portuguese organized similar annual convoys that departed Lisbon in the spring to reach their Brazilian settlements in Rio, Bahia, and Pernambuco. We should be reminded, however, that the annual schedule was a prescribed ideal. Both natural hazards and recurrent military confrontations interfered and delayed the actual shipping seasons.

In theory, at least, the Hispano-American commerce was a monopoly right, granted exclusively to merchants who were Castilian nationals, or Portuguese subjects in the case of commerce with Brazil. When such legal restrictions encountered economic realities, however, it became evident that Spanish manufacturers alone were hardly able to satisfy the colonial demand for European merchandise, the thriving export of linen from Brittany being just one exemplary case. Consequently, the cargo filling the holds of merchant ships en route to the New World was not restricted to products of exclusively Spanish origin.[30] Because direct trading with the American colonists would have been punishable as an illicit activity, European merchants sought alternative ways to circumvent the strict regulations, customs inspections, and duties of up to 23 percent. Where foreign merchants were sufficiently skilled in the art of bribery, Spanish officials were prepared to turn a blind eye. Another solution was to hire a local agent, an *ami fidèle*, also known as a *cargador* or *metedor*. Local agents acted as brokers between their European seller principals and colonial customers. They would board the ship at the start of its journey in Cadiz, accompany the precious cargo, and sell it at the destination in, say, Cartagena, and finally return to Cadiz with colonial commodities and bullion. Ideally, vice could be turned into virtue, and the hiring merchant would benefit from his agent's superior knowledge of trade opportunities, market schedules and local price setting in Cartagena and other marketplaces. Leaving aside the additional challenge that their brokerage activity was semi-legal at best, it entailed the same kind of commitment problem that strains principal–agent relationships in similar settings of long-distance trade. The local *cargador* agent and his French merchant principal may agree *ex ante* about the terms of their transaction—what goods should be sold where and when, plus what share of the profits the agent will receive for his services. But because his intimate insight into local markets and complex official regulations clearly favors the agent, incentives for opportunistic behavior arise, and he may no longer feel committed to the initial agreement. What potentially contained opportunism and facilitated successful collaborations between foreign merchants and their Spanish agents were trust-based relationships, established and nurtured through repeated dealings over a long period of time.[31]

But how were these long-term collaborations among trusting partners established? Closeness tends to support the creation of social capital, and it was no different in the case of merchants from Saint-Malo who sought Spanish business partners. The leading families of Saint-Malo set up *comptoirs*—trading posts— of their merchant houses in Cadiz and other cities, such as Sevilla, San Lucar, Malaga, and Alicante. Family members then took up residence and directed their business affairs as junior partners in the Spanish ports for a number of years. One prominent case is the trading house of the Magons, a veritable dynasty and one of the most prestigious families of Saint-Malo. Jean Magon de la Lande spent his formative years from 1659 through 1667 in Cadiz, while his brother Nicolas Magon de la Chipaudière stayed even longer from 1659 through 1673, and so, too, did Jean Magon's sons Nicolas Magon de la Chipaudière (1684–1690), who shared his uncle's name, and François-Auguste Magon de la Lande (1698–1706). They, in turn, were followed by the next generation of grandsons Jean-Baptiste Magon (1710–1739), Guillaume Magon de Clos-Doré (1713–1740), Jean-Baptiste Magon de la Balue (1732–1759), and Luc Magon de la Blinais (1733–1750). Note that the Magons, just like the sons of other prominent Malouin families, began their time at the *comptoirs* as young adolescents: Nicolas Magon the Younger was sent to Cadiz at the tender age of fourteen to be trained in the art of merchantry by his maternal uncle Pierre Eon de la Baronnie; his paternal uncle Nicolas preceded him at the age of fifteen; and his own sons Jean-Baptiste, Nicolas, and Guillaume Magon followed their career path at the ages of fifteen and sixteen. The organizational model of the branch offices of Cadiz provided a hands-on apprenticeship—*formation au comptoir*—in which brothers and cousins worked together, and uncles trained their nephews in all the techniques necessary to conduct their business affairs. It was indeed an invaluable schooling that enriched the experience and ensured the reproduction of subsequent generations of leaders of Saint-Malo's merchant dynasties.[32] They used their apprenticeship years to weave networks of close personal ties and trustworthy collaborations with Spanish, Irish, and various French traders. It turned out to be social capital well spent as it allowed the Malouins to gain valuable knowledge about novel business opportunities in the Spanish colonial markets. Consider just one case to illustrate the intricate use of such social networks. In December 1699, nine years past her husband Nicolas Magon de la Chipaudière's *comptoir* experience in Spain, Madame de la Chipaudière was still able to form a business partnership with two resident French merchantmen at Cadiz, Jean Dufaux and Jean Lambert de la Fontaine, to finance the 160-ton *Vierge de Grace*, armed with sixteen pieces of cannon, for the shipping of merchandise to Cadiz. Another prominent merchant entrepreneur from Saint-Malo, Nicolas Piednoir, sieur des Prés, served as guarantor of the contract. Extending his network well beyond Cadiz, Nicolas Magon's uncle and namesake seized opportunities in colonial trade. In 1707, among other business, he invested the substantial sum of 15,000 *lt.* in the voyage of the three-hundred-ton *Le Saint-Malo* on its way to the Spanish West Indies.[33]

In addition, personal contacts with Spanish traders reduced language barriers and helped contend with the idiosyncrasies of the Spanish administration and its regulations. The networks further tightened the bonds between the mother trading houses in Saint-Malo and their affiliated posts in Andalusia. Above all, the apprenticeship years at Cadiz instilled the characteristic collective commitment to commerce (*fidélité au commerce*) and honed the social capital that was so vital to the Malouin merchant community and gave it its competitive advantage.[34]

The Malouins certainly were not the only ones residing in Cadiz. Merchants from Marseille, Lyon, La Rochelle, Paris, and Lille, next to representatives of the Hanse cities, from Flanders, the United Provinces, England, and Ireland all set up ex-patriate colonies in the Spanish port. The trading houses of Saint-Malo, however, had a particularly significant presence in the port. André Lespagnol estimates that some thirty individual merchants from Saint-Malo and about twenty Malouin trading houses resided in Cadiz in the last quarter of the seventeenth century, which accounted for about 40 percent of the French merchant community. A contemporary source dating from December 1700 indicated that they represented 44 percent, that is twelve out of the twenty-seven resident merchants from northwestern France alone.[35] Indeed, the social bonds with Spain seemed to have left such a strong impression that more than a hundred years later, Chateaubriand still evoked the image of twin cities in his *Mémoires*—"the insular setting, the causeway, the architecture, the buildings, the cisterns, the granite walls of Saint-Malo lend it an air of resemblance with Cadiz: at the sight of the latter, I always feel reminded of the former."[36]

WAR AND THE RISE OF NEW OPPORTUNITIES

By the final quarter of the seventeenth century, Saint-Malo's merchant community had established the city as one of France's premier ports for overseas trade. As much as its growing commercial position already read like a success story, the economic peak was yet to come. And when it did come, it shone brightly. But it was not long-term growth, lasting merely some thirty years from the late 1680s until about 1720. Although the foundations were laid with the experience gained in the fishing and Spanish trades, the merchant community of Saint-Malo owed much of its spectacular rise at the turn of the century to the confluence of extraordinary circumstances. Chief among them was the outbreak of war.

Social science historians have long recognized that war was the rule rather than the exception in early modern Europe. For one, the historical period witnessed the rise of the nation-state. Whether motivated by religious rifts, dynastic interests, or territorial expansion, the rivalries among emerging nation-states routinely led to armed conflict between them. Thus, following Charles Tilly's dictum, state-making was inseparable from war-making during this period. What spurred war between nascent states was a military revolution in early modern Europe. It entailed technological innovations, such as the development of firearms and advances in shipbuilding as well as organizational innovations, from the training of soldiers to more efficient provisioning of armed forces and an effective fiscal administration.[37] Their competing commercial interests were just as important as a driving force behind the recurrent conflicts between states. The idea that a country's economic wealth stemmed primarily from a balance of trade that favored exports over imports was central to the mercantilist doctrine of the time. The same doctrine viewed the overall volume of world trade as limited and commercial expansion as a zero-sum game wherein states gained a competitive advantage if they increased their trade at the expense of other countries. It was no different with the so-called Second One Hundred Years' War, when rivalry in overseas trade and colonial interests contributed to the series of conflicts that pitted France and Britain against each other as the two leading commercial powers of the long eighteenth century (1688–1815). It is in this sense that historian Richard Pares remarked that the Anglo-French confrontations in the West Indies boiled down to a war of trade "dictated by the rivalry between one set of sugar colonies and another."[38]

The Nine Years' War (November 1688 to October 1697), alternatively known as the War of the League of Augsburg among French writers, marked the onset of these conflicts.[39] The exact causes of war remain a matter of dispute among historians. Some maintain that it was William III's anti-French stance in foreign policy that pushed England and its allies into war. Others interpret the war as a deep-seated confessional conflict between a Catholic bloc, led by France, and a Protestant bloc, led by England. Still others argue that it was not a war of religion, but in fact one of the first truly modern conflicts. It was a modern war because it was motivated not by long-standing ideologies but instead by shifting interest groups and the political alliances they formed to achieve their aims.[40] Most seem to agree, however, that England, Austria, and their allies formed a broad coalition to contain the hegemonic ambitions of the absolutist French state under Louis XIV. Despite its heavy toll, the war proved to be inconclusive. A short-lived armistice was brought to an end by the outbreak of the War of the Spanish Succession (1702–1713). Once again, Louis XIV faced a broad coalition that rose up against him. This time, the reasons were dynastic politics, and their consequences for the balance of power within Europe. The will of Charles II, the last Habsburg king of Spain, who died childless, favored Louis XIV's grandson, the Duke of Anjou as his heir. For the other European powers, Anjou's accession to the Spanish throne posed the threat of a union of Spain's rich colonial empire and France's territorial dominance within Europe. Both France and Spain would have been reigned by the Bourbons. A renewed alliance, led again by Britain and Austria, thus sought to prevent this union of the two crowns into effectively a single dynastic state. After a decade of fighting, the Treaty of Utrecht eventually brought the war to an end in 1713 and restored the balance of power. On one hand, the claim to the Spanish throne was recognized. On the other, the allied forces under the Duke of Marlborough and Prince Eugene succeeded in containing France's hegemony within Europe. The price that France had to pay for the preservation of its European territory was the loss of American colonies: Acadia, the settlements on Newfoundland, along the Hudson Bay, and the island of Saint Christopher in the West Indies were ceded to Britain.[41]

Locally, both wars had tangible consequences for Saint-Malo and its reliance on maritime trade. The same strategic location facing the English Channel that offered such an advantage for its seabound trading ventures unfortunately made Saint-Malo vulnerable to direct military attacks. Of particular significance were the repeated attempts of the united English–Dutch fleets in the 1690s to destroy the city through massive bombings and the infamous "machine infernale," a vessel filled to the brim with explosives that the English fleet directed toward the port.[42] The contemporary woodcut shown in figure 2.5 depicts the intensity of one of these attacks, the siege of Saint-Malo that took place in November 1693. Unfortunately, for the Malouins, it proved to be but one in a long series of attempts to sack their hometown. Even more than fifty years later, in 1758, during the Seven Years' War (1756–1763), the British government under William Pitt adopted a strategy of raiding the French coast along the Channel to support campaigns on the continent. In June of the same year, an expeditionary force of nearly fourteen thousand men, including heavy artillery and even cavalry, set sail toward Saint-Malo. The British landed east of the walled city, captured nearby Cancale without a fight, and marched toward both Saint-Malo and Saint-Servan, where they destroyed numerous ships anchoring in the harbor. The threat of capture and destruction was real. The British abandoned their objective of raiding Saint-Malo thanks only to bad road conditions, which hindered the transportation of heavy artillery, and the misperception that strong French reinforcements were fast approaching. Yet another attempt to capture Saint-Malo followed only a few months later in September 1758, but it was thwarted again at nearby

FIGURE 2.5 Siege of Saint-Malo by an English fleet in November 1693.

Source: Bibliothèque Nationale de France.

Saint-Cast by well-prepared French defense forces that inflicted heavy losses on the British landing party. The incident eventually became remembered in the collective memory of French history as the *Bataille de Saint-Cast*.[43]

Without doubt, such armed assaults posed an immediate threat upon Saint-Malo and its citizens.[44] In the long run, however, the perhaps more salient consequence of Louis XIV's wars was how much they harmed the lifeblood of the port, its dependence on overseas commerce (for the following discussion, see figure 2.4). The Dutch and the English were the two leading naval powers confronting France in both the Nine Years' War and the War of the Spanish Succession. It therefore does not come as a surprise that direct trade relationships with England, including Guernsey and Jersey, and the United Provinces came to a halt shortly after the outbreak of hostilities. Shipping from Saint-Malo toward English ports dropped dramatically from an average number of 125 vessels in the years before 1689 to an average of merely 13 vessels per year during the Nine Years' War (see figure 2.4b). The sudden decline was not compensated for by greater capacities of the few ships that risked the voyage: average annual tonnages in the trade with the British Isles plummeted from 3,132 tons before the war to 839 tons during the years of conflict (see figure 2.4c). The decreasing shipping to and from English ports hurt the business of Malouin merchants as much as it did because it effectively closed access to a crucial market for the export of fine Breton linen. A similar pattern of decline repeated itself with the onset of the War of the Spanish Succession (1702–1713) as well as in the number and tonnage of ships that sailed to and returned from Dutch ports. Shipping to and from the Channel Islands, lying just eight miles off the French coast, came to a complete standstill between 1703 and 1711—with the exception of three vessels in 1707–1708, one of which came in at a size of merely four tons.[45]

A considerable portion of both wars was fought at sea, with the supremacy of the allied Dutch–English fleets becoming evident over the course of the conflict. As naval confrontations expanded into the North Atlantic, they also had a dampening effect on Saint-Malo's all-important staple trade, the cod-fishing industry along the coast and banks of Newfoundland. Up to 116 fishing vessels—amounting to a total of 14,166 tons—left their home port for Canadian waters immediately before war broke out in 1688, whereas just five vessel (620 tons) did so at the height of the fighting in 1692. Malouin cod fishing recovered in peacetime, but it suffered yet another decline during the 1702–1713 war. To make matters worse, in 1702, Dutch and English naval forces successfully raided the galleon fleet of France's new ally Spain, and thus interrupted the American colonial trade until the treaty of Utrecht ended the war in 1713. It appeared to be the final blow to the ambitions of Saint-Malo's trading houses because, as we saw earlier, a substantial share of their fortunes came from the commerce with Spain, and hence from their indirect access to the lucrative colonial markets in Spanish America.[46]

Exempting the short armistice at the turn of the century, the French found themselves at war for nearly a quarter of a century. But war may sometimes give rise to new economic opportunities, and when they presented themselves, the Malouin merchants were prepared to seize them. The first of these opportunities concerned privateering: the raiding of enemy merchant ships during times of war, or the *guerre de course*, as it was called in French. The dominant strategy of naval warfare under Louis XIV used to be the *guerre d'escadre*—the employment of a great battle fleet that would directly engage and seek to overwhelm the fleets of opposing states to establish dominance in seapower. Once accomplished, naval dominance might then facilitate further campaigns, such as the capture of colonial settlements or the landing of conquering forces at home in Europe. The Sun King's navy enjoyed initial victories against the Dutch and English fleets, and French control of the seas was within reach. Yet, as the Nine Years' War progressed, military defeat, administrative strains, and insufficient financial backing all led the French royal government to adopt an alternative maritime strategy, the *guerre de course*.[47] Its central aim was not to confront and destroy the opposing state's battle fleet, but rather to erode the enemy's flow of returns from trade. The instrument to do so was commerce raiding—the use of well-armed vessels, known in French as *corsaires*, to capture enemy merchant ships and their precious cargo and sell them as prizes, usually, but not always at the corsair's home port. Alternatively, captured merchant ships might be held for ransom.[48] As such, the *guerre de course* was a genuine economic form of warfare. It was waged either by the state's own naval forces or by private merchant venturers, called *armateurs* (shipowners), and their business partners. These merchant partnerships, or *sociétés*, financed and fitted out ships on their own account to seize this opportunity for their profit. During the Nine Years' War and the War of the Spanish Succession, it was also fairly common that private *armateurs* relied on loaning vessels from the French royal navy for their commerce raids.[49] This shows that the two forms of maritime strategy did overlap, were complementary, and indeed were pursued side by side. The important distinction between the *guerre d'escadre* and the *guerre de course* is that the latter policy relinquished an essential prerogative of the absolutist state—its centralized control over the means to wage war—to private interests, at least in part.[50] It is no accident that the term *corsaires* is usually translated as privateers in English, and the *guerre de course* as privateering war, or privateering enterprise, if one wishes to emphasize its entrepreneurial nature.[51] Hence, "the private war at sea," as one of its eminent historians, John S. Bromley, preferred to call it, might be the most fitting description once the enterprise is in private hands. Another important distinction, and still less well known among nonexperts than one might think, is that between privateering and piracy.[52] The casual observer may be led to believe that pirates engaged in behavior that was comparable to the business of privateers. Yet, in comparison, their raids were indiscriminate and considered to be outside of the jurisdictions enforced by princely rulers at the time. Corsairs, or privateers, in contrast, were legally sanctioned by their own sovereign. Upon application, they received a "letter of marque," that is, a written commission that licensed them to attack enemy merchant ships during times of declared war. Furthermore, this authorization extended exclusively to the capture of enemy vessels, whereas the rights of neutral ships were to be respected. In practice, of course, the boundary between piracy and privateering was not always as sharply delineated. Still, royal administrations instated regulations to enforce the commitment of corsairs to stay within the boundaries of the law. For instance, the *Conseil des prises* judged whether or not prizes were just, merchants who headed privateering ventures were required to pay bonds of surety, and privateers faced severe punishment if they transgressed the legal restrictions of their operations.[53]

The private war at sea was precisely what Saint-Malo's merchant elites committed themselves to once the opportunity did arise with the onset of war. Privateering had been a time-honored business in Saint-Malo and even lend the port city its clichéd moniker—*la cité corsaire*.[54] Some historians consider the *course* to be essential to the *esprit malouin*.[55] Indeed, local merchants and seamen had been organizing privateering ventures since medieval times, and they continued to do so throughout the long Second Hundred Years' War, beyond the Treaty of Utrecht in 1713 that closed the War of the Spanish Succession. The motive behind the *course*, its organization, and its consequences for the Malouin merchant community are at the very heart of the present study. I devote chapters 4 and 5 to a detailed account of the historical origins, the legal regulations, the economic organization, the operations at sea, and the eventual benefits of the *guerre de course*. For now, figure 2.6 suffices to offer a glimpse of the scale of privateering enterprise in Saint-Malo during the wars of 1688–1697 and 1702–1713.

The dashed line traces the annual number of privateering commissions issued to merchants from Saint-Malo by the French Admiralty. The solid line shows the annual number of prize ships captured by Malouin corsairs. Here, as well, the counts rely on all surviving prize declarations that were made before the Admiralty.[56] To put these numbers in perspective, figure 2.7 compares the shares contributed by French ports to the privateering campaigns during the wars of 1688–1697 and 1702–1713.[57] The comparison should be taken with a grain of salt. It is notoriously difficult to gather sufficiently nuanced information on variations in the level of privateering enterprise for every relevant French port.[58]

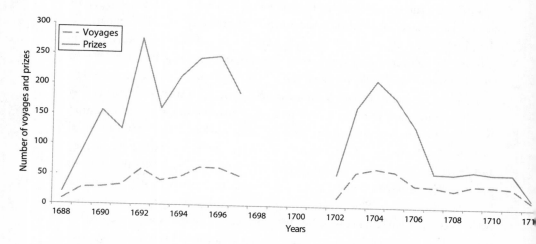

FIGURE 2.6 Privateering enterprise (*guerre de course*) in Saint-Malo during the War of the League of Augsburg (1688–1697) and the War of the Spanish Succession (1701–1713).

Note: The number of voyages refers to the privateering commissions granted by the French Admiralty. The numbers include only vessels that explicitly set out to sea to engage in commerce raiding (*armements en guerre*). Not included are armed merchantmen that carried commissions of *guerre et marchandise*.

Sources: All information on corsair commissions is taken from *AD-IV* 9B408; 9B435, (1)–(3). Data on declared prizes come from *AD-IV* 9B583-585, 587, and from surviving prize dossiers for the years 1688–1713 in *AD-IV* 9B599-622. These archival sources are coupled with evidence collected and printed in Morel (1958) and Martin-Deidier (1976).

The point, then, is not to establish a precise ranking of French ports with respect to their commerce raiding activity. The evidence does suggest that the traders and seamen of Saint-Malo, along with their peers of Dunkirk, contributed the lion's share to the *guerre de course* in this historical period. When we consider the prize tenths that the Admiralty retained, a similar impression emerges (not shown in figure 2.7). Again, the surviving information should be read as but one piece of evidence. Still, Bromley likewise finds that the 10 percent value of prizes captured by corsairs from Dunkirk (331,748 *lt.*) and Saint-Malo (398,200 *lt.*) accounted for more than 50 percent of the grand total of prize tenths (1,356,595 *lt.*) in 1706, a year not untypical during the War of the Spanish Succession.[59]

Armateurs en course and their business partners thus had good reasons to be motivated by the prospect of handsome returns to their investments in privateering ventures. Such spectacular exploits as René Duguay-Trouin's raid of the Portuguese colony of Rio de Janeiro in 1711 may come to mind. The attack of his privateering fleet undoubtedly yielded a sizeable profit, although not the 7 or

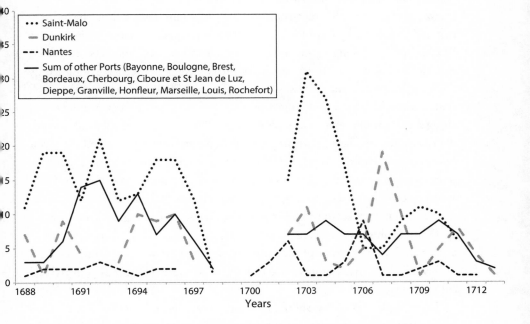

FIGURE 2.7 Privateering enterprise in Saint-Malo compared with other French ports, 1688–1713. The number of corsairs draws on the list of privateering vessels compiled by Demerliac (1995), pp. 294–322.

Note: Demerliac (1995) restricted his list to ships that were larger than one hundred tons, although a few of his entries are of smaller tonnages. Vessels on loan from the French royal navy are not included.

8 million *lt.* that an overly optimistic Duguay-Trouin expected.[60] Certainly not every single privateering voyage turned out to be as audacious and profitable as this particular campaign by Saint-Malo's most famous corsair under the Old Regime. Therefore, one should be careful not to overestimate the average economic benefit and the grander strategic impact of the *guerre de course*. Conversely, the *course* was not merely a poor substitute for regular trading activities in times of war, but rather was a second-best choice in the absence of viable alternatives (see chapter 5). From the point of view of Saint-Malo's merchant investors, the private war at sea complemented both traditional and novel trading opportunities.[61] As we shall read in chapter 7, privateering ventures served as launching pads for those who sought to build their careers in overseas commerce.

The forays of Malouin ships into the South Sea were foremost among the novel trade opportunities that emerged with the onset of war. The *mer du Sud*, as it was known to French contemporaries, referred to the Spanish American possessions along the Pacific coast. What attracted the French to the South Sea was what they perceived as a chance to bypass the monopoly that reserved the Spanish colonial trade for Castilian merchants. The South Sea enterprise implied a new direction, or rather reorientation of the Malouin traders, from the indirect colonial commerce by way of Cadiz toward a new direct exchange with the New World. In fact, seeking entrance into the exclusive colonial markets of Spanish America had been a recurrent agenda for the French. And they were not the only ones. At least since the mid-seventeenth century, English, Dutch, and French traders alike had been pursuing contraband commerce in the Caribbean and along the coasts of present-day Colombia and Venezuela. For the French, including the Malouins, their flourishing colony of Saint-Domingue served them not only as the pivot of the Antilles trade but also as a convenient base for interloping trade in the region.[62] The perhaps even more coveted prize, however, was direct access, without any mediating agents, to the riches of the Spanish Peruvian colonies, and in particular to the silver mines of Potosí. René Duguay-Trouin serves again as an illustrative case. He and his associates reaped a substantial part— estimated at 3 million *lt.*—of the profits from their raid of Rio by shipping some of their booty, such as highly valued textiles, to Peru and selling it directly to local colonial customers.[63]

The true pioneer of the South Sea trade turned out to be one of Saint-Malo's most enterprising *armateurs* at the time, Noël Danycan, sieur de L'Epine. In 1656, Danycan was born into a modest merchant family that had moved from Coutances in Normandy to Saint-Malo at the beginning of the seventeenth century. He began his seafaring career as captain aboard his father's vessels, commanding voyages to Newfoundland, and eventually became one of the many promoters of the traditional cod-fishing route in his own right. Yet the fortunes that made him one of Saint-Malo's most affluent citizens came from a different source. With the onset of hostilities in 1689, Danycan shifted his attention away from Newfoundland fishing, refitted his vessels, financed the construction of new ones, and committed wholeheartedly to privateering enterprise. He apparently never navigated any privateering vessels, but nevertheless, he emerged as Saint-Malo's foremost *armateur corsaire*. Between 1690 and 1697 alone, he armed more than twenty corsairs, amounting to a total of 6,500 tons, and with at least seventy captured prizes recorded to his credit. Several of the prizes that were seized by his corsairs yielded returns of up to 300,000 *lt.*, sometimes even more. Danycan also proved his talent for organizing large-scale enterprises when, in 1696, he entered into a contract with the comte de Pontchartrain who represented the royal government. The contract authorized Danycan to arm an entire privateering squadron consisting of six frigates and an additional fifty-gun warship of the royal navy to raid and conquer all English settlements in Newfoundland.[64]

Eventually, Danycan employed the experience and fortunes he had gained as a leading privateering merchant, and once again, he changed the direction of his entrepreneurial ambitions. This time he turned toward the interloping trade with Spanish America. The concession of exclusive French commerce within both the Indian and the Pacific Oceans, from the Cape of Good Hope to the Straits of Magellan, had been previously granted to the *Compagnie des Indes Orientales*, established in 1664 under the auspices of Louis XIV and his minister Colbert. Unfortunately, when it came to profits, this early incarnation of the French East Indies Company never quite fulfilled its promises. Some of its privileges were ceded to other companies that had been founded subsequently. Hence, in 1698, the comte de Pontchartrain granted the merchants of Saint-Malo the right to establish the *Compagnie Royale de la mer Pacifique*, which was to benefit from a thirty-year monopoly of direct French trade with the islands and coasts of the South Sea. Danycan and a certain Jean Jourdan de Groué, his business partner in Paris, joined forces and became the main investors behind the company.[65] The link between Danycan's previous engagement in the *guerre de course* and his subsequent leading role in the South Sea Company illustrates well the extent to which "the corsair mentality was central to Malouin initiatives overseas," as Bromley has put it.[66] The same close link is evident in the types of vessels that were fitted out for the interloping trade in the South Sea—they were of considerable size (400–650 tons), heavily armed (one cannon for every ten tons), and usually carried privateering commissions as well.[67] Finally, this link was evident in the typical career path that someone like Danycan followed. For Danycan, as for many of his peers in Saint-Malo, the *guerre de course* was a great wartime opportunity, a veritable gateway into the world of international commerce. As we discuss later, this pattern in the unfolding careers of overseas merchants, where their initial privateering activities paved the way toward more ambitious joint ventures, appeared time and again.[68]

But just how worthwhile were the operations of the Malouin traders in the South Sea? One significant challenge to their efforts was the long and arduous passage across the Atlantic, along the Brazilian coast, and onward through the Straits of Magellan to finally reach Chilean and Peruvian shores. The duration of the journey depended on the choice of stopovers, the direction of currents and winds, and the market schedules most favorable for buying and selling wares. On average, voyages could take as long as 218 days outbound and another 177 days for the return leg. For example, the *Phélypeaux*, one of the first ships that Danycan armed for the South Sea Company, left La Rochelle on December 17, 1698, under the command of Captain Jacques Gouin, sieur du Beauchesne. Gouin and his crew entered the Straits of Magellan on June 24, 1699, and reached the Pacific Ocean on January 21, 1700. For much of 1700, they explored various islands, including the Galapagos archipelago, and traded along the Peruvian coast. On their return to France, they passed around Cape Horn on January 13–14, 1701, sojourned at Rio de Janeiro from March 13 to May 12, and finally returned to La Rochelle via the Azores on August 7, 1701.[69]

Perhaps even more important than the considerable distance of the journey and the natural hazards it often implied were the shifting political allegiances between the Nine Years' War and the War of the Spanish Succession. As noted earlier, direct legal trade with the colonies of Spanish America was the exclusive right of Spanish merchants only. Consequently, as we have seen, the principal way for French merchants to exchange their manufactured goods for precious metals and coins from the colonies was the indirect trade through Spanish ports such as Cadiz. Because this indirect trade met with still too many legal hindrances on the Spanish side, in addition to high import and re-export duties and the cost of hiring intermediaries to ship their wares, the French had a natural interest in circumventing the Spanish monopoly. Thus, granting privileges of exclusive trade in the Americas to its own subjects was not really problematic in the eyes of the French crown as long as Spain was a declared enemy or at least an economic rival in the New World. Strictly speaking, any French ventures that directly operated within the South American trade and thereby undermined the Spanish monopoly engaged in illicit interloping. The political constellation changed when Louis XIV's grandson was about to ascend the Spanish throne in 1700, which meant that France and Spain ended up as allies in the ensuing War of the Spanish Succession. Hence, at least until the end of the war in 1713, the maritime policy of the French government in the Americas was rather ambiguous. On one hand, as Spain's ally, and especially given the weakening of Spanish seapower, it fell to the French navy to protect the Spanish colonial empire. On the other, the French still harbored commercial and colonial ambitions of their own, both in the West Indies and in the South Sea.[70]

One implication of this ambiguity in state policy was that the Pacific and Spanish American ventures were more or less clandestine affairs from the beginning. Among the original registers of partnership contracts, one rarely encounters such an explicit declaration of a vessel's destination as in the case of the four-hundred-ton *Le Sage*, which, in 1719, was armed for a voyage "à L'amerique Espagnolle, tant aux costes du nord, que dans Les mers et costes du Sud."[71] Most other contracts kept the direction as vague as "aux costes de l'amerique," "pour le voyage des Isles de l'amerique," or simply "pour aller à l'amerique."[72] One gets the impression that those who ventured to the South Sea carefully avoided revealing that interloping, and hence an illegal activity, was the true purpose of their voyages to these "Isles of America." Likewise, declarations that the ship's mission included privateering ("faisant la guerre et la Course Sur les enemies de L'Etat") figured prominently in these documents even though Dutch or English ships to be taken as prizes were occasional at best, and they alone hardly accounted for the sometimes extraordinary profits the Malouin traders claimed to have made in the South Sea.[73] Once the Chilean coast was reached, the deceptions seemed to have continued. Dahlgren notes encounters with Spanish authorities in which Malouin traders presented fake papers and pretended that their ship belonged to a new company of commerce with China. Once contact with Spanish colonists was established, however, contraband trade began to flourish.[74]

Despite these seeming obstacles, enormous riches could be gained. The prime example is Danycan, sieur de L'Epine, the one person who set off the veritable boom period in the South Sea trade that was to last at least until 1715. Estimates suggest that returns from his engagements in South American interloping amounted to at least 5 million *lt*. In 1701, the *capitation* assessed Danycan's poll-tax at 375 *lt*., classifying him as the highest taxpayer in the entire city. In 1706, he received his knighthood, elevating him to a *chevalier de l'Ordre de Saint-Michel*, one of the highest honors bestowed upon French subjects at the time. His fortunes enabled him to grant each of his daughters a dowry of 800,000 *lt*.. Danycan—perhaps the very image of the *parfait négociant* (the perfect trader) that contemporary economist Jacques Savary had in mind—eventually turned his economic investments into political influence and acquired the office of *conseiller-secrétaire du Roi*, which elevated him to the ranks of nobility.[75]

Danycan certainly belonged to the more illustrious figures of this period. Still, the number of armaments shown in figure 2.8 reveals a comparable preference for South Sea ventures among those merchants who left a less prominent trace in the historical records. Between 1698 and 1724, at least 133 French ships (at a combined tonnage of 46,300 tons) sailed toward the Pacific coast of Spanish America, and presumably engaged in interloping. During the fifteen years between 1701 and 1716, at the height of the South Sea boom, the French dispatched about eight ships per year, on average. Sheer numbers show just how dominant Saint-Malo's merchant entrepreneurs were in the interloping commerce. They clearly took the lead with their promotion of 82 of the 115 (71 percent) French armaments in the 1701–1716 period. Far fewer ventures were initiated elsewhere. Most active beyond Saint-Malo were financiers from Paris who initiated ten armaments within the same period, and promoters from Marseille with seven ventures.[76]

Not only were the manufactured wares to be sold at colonial markets luxury goods, such as finely woven Breton textiles, paper, and wax. Fitting out the ships to carry such valuable cargo all the way to Peru required substantial sums as well. For the eighty Malouin ships during the 1701–1716 period for which such information is available, the investments equaled an estimated 56,575,000 *lt.*. The impressive sum also implies that the Malouins were responsible for mobilizing 72.5 percent of all French investments in interloping expeditions to the South Sea. If we set aside for a moment that some voyages certainly required more capital than others, then we arrive at an average investment of about 700,000 *lt.* per South Sea vessel. Taking the size of vessels into account, the average fitting costs per ton amounted to about 2,177 *lt.*, according to the available estimates for 1701–1719. To raise the necessary capital, the *armateurs* formed share partnerships (*sociétés*) with investors (*intéressés, engagés*, or *associés*) willing to shoulder a proportion of the cost in return for shares (*actions*) in the ventures. Evidence from the registers of partnerships indicates that investors tended to be local residents, yet it was not uncommon for ventures to attract interested parties from across the realm, such as Dunkirk, Paris, Orléans, Amiens, Rouen, Lyon, Marseille, Rennes, Bordeaux, or Brest.[77] Finally, when it came to the profits they achieved, staggering rates of up to 420 percent were not unheard of, even though the median profit rate was closer to 100 percent and losses of an equivalent rate were possible as well, both attesting to the high-risk, high-return nature of the South Sea enterprise. Beyond the gains of individual ventures, the most significant consequence of the South Sea commerce perhaps was the substantial flow of silver bullion and piastres from Peru and Chile into France. Drained of monetary resources by prolonged war, an estimated import of 200 million silver

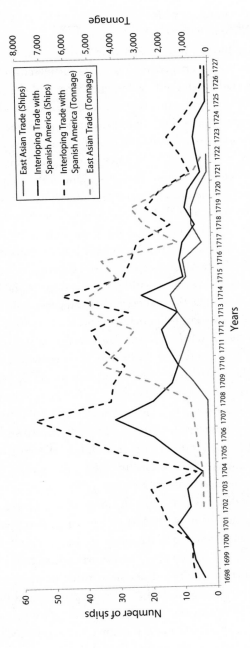

FIGURE 2.8 Saint-Malo ventures to Spanish America and East Asia, 1698–1725.

Sources: All estimates of the number of vessels and their tonnages are taken from Dahlgren (1907) and Lespagnol (1991).

livres between 1703 and 1718 alone surely must have been welcomed by the royal government. As André Lespagnol has pointed out, the South Sea trade thus emerged as an enterprise of nationwide interest, and controlled by the merchant community of Saint-Malo as its center.[78]

Besides privateering and the interloping trade with the Americas, the third commercial opportunity that opened for the Malouin merchant community in this period was the trade with the East Indies, China, and the Arabian Peninsula. The origins of Saint-Malo's involvement in the eastern trades mirrored those of the South Sea Company. Both enterprises were born out of the *Compagnie des Indes Orientales*, founded in 1664, and chartered by Louis XIV's minister, Colbert.[79] As noted earlier, the French East India Company was not exactly blessed with evidence of economic success. Some of the company's peculiar characteristics seem to have been responsible for its shortcomings. For one, the French company arrived late at the scene of Asian commerce. The first Portuguese factory in India was founded as early as 1504; English merchants were trading with India since 1600; and the Dutch East India Company had been established in 1602. The French company thus lagged behind its competitors by at least sixty-two years in experience with organized trade in the East Indies. Furthermore, the French company's organizational form proved problematic for mobilizing capital. Colbert sought to model the venture he envisioned after the successful blueprint of the Dutch *Vereenigde Oostindische Compagnie* (V.O.C.). To the extent that governing and mercantile elites were entwined in the early modern Netherlands, the V.O.C. represented a bottom-up enterprise that grew out of the self-organization of the merchant community. The merchant-founders were not only the major shareholders but also in direct control of their company's commercial policies and strategies. Leading merchants from Amsterdam alone contributed 57 percent of the venture's basic capital. Julia Adams found that at least twenty-four of the thirty-six initial directors of the Amsterdam chamber of the V.O.C. were large-scale merchants.[80]

For his own East Indies project, Colbert adopted the Dutch model of granting the monopoly of trading with Asia to a privileged company, but he replaced shareholder control with royal patronage and supervision, thus limiting the influence of merchant interest in the enterprise. Shareholder meetings were held on an irregular schedule and decisions often made in advance by the minister. Members of the board of directors were appointed by the king and not chosen by the shareholders. The royal government entirely dictated the company's commercial policy. Colbert was apparently convinced that such state control was necessary to avoid the pitfalls and rivalries among merchant groups that had crippled earlier attempts by the French to set up organized trade in Asia. Furthermore, in Colbert's system, overseas trade was seen as a key source of public finance. Because foreign commerce was also subject to intense competition between states, tight control of trading companies became a political necessity for the French state. In contrast to the Dutch as well as the English companies, it was thus the political intervention of the crown rather than the economic initiative of the mercantile community that brought about the French East India Company. The dominance of state over merchant interests meant that a full 45 percent of share subscriptions came directly from the royal family; 19.5 percent from courtiers, assemblymen, and ministers, including Colbert; and another 8.5 percent from financiers—but merchant traders raised a mere 16 percent of the capital. Hence, even though its intended initial capital of 15 million *lt.* was impressive and would place the company at the very top of commercial ventures within France, it lacked a consistent financial backing from the mercantile elites.

On the political side, the company appeared to be a success as the French were able to establish a regular presence in India and on the Île Bourbon (present-day Réunion). Both the Nine Years' War and the War of the Spanish Succession, however, revealed the vulnerability of their company *comptoirs* and colonial settlements, resulting, for example, in the occupation of Pondichéry by Dutch forces between 1693 and 1697. Finally, it also did not help that the company lacked a clear commercial strategy because the merchant elite had no vested interest in the enterprise. All of these conditions contributed to the French East Indies Company's failure to compete with its European rivals in Asia and led to its bankruptcy by the turn of the century.[81]

A strategic alliance between the state-run monopoly and private traders eventually emerged as a solution to the difficulties the company faced. Given its considerable debt, the liquidation and subsequent takeover of the entire company was not desirable to any interested party. It was thus hardly surprising that the initial enthusiasm among private traders was lukewarm at best. To attract their financial commitment, the company subcontracted some of its monopoly rights to private partnerships, similar to the trading privileges it handed to the South Sea enterprise in 1698. The first of these partial concessions was granted for voyages along routes less traveled by the company, such as the commercial exchange with China. The principal promoter behind the *Compagnie de la Chine* was the same Jourdan de Groucé, financier from Paris, who had collaborated with the Malouin merchants Danycan and Magon de la Chipaudière in the westbound *Compagnie de la mer du Sud*. In November 1701, Jourdan's China concession merged with Danycan's South Sea Company. As a result, most vessels on their way to China sailed around Cape Horn instead of crossing the Indian Ocean.

Just as often, the declaration that a ship was bound for China barely concealed that interloping was its true purpose and the coast of Peru its destination. Still, even the fresh funds that flowed to the original company from these two subcontracts were not sufficient to keep it in business.

Another partial lease of company rights to selected private partnerships followed, while the company continued to exist as a formal entity. This time, the directors granted a group of leading merchants from Saint-Malo the permission to trade with specific markets in the East. In return, the company would receive a percentage share (usually 10 percent) in the value of commodities brought back to France. The first of these contracts was signed in November 1707 between the East India Company and the Malouin merchants Martin de la Chapelle and Gris du Colombier. This contract granted them the right to dispatch two vessels for an expedition to the Persian Gulf and the Red Sea to trade in coffee. The voyage opened commerce with Moka (in present-day Yemen) that would become a hallmark of Malouin enterprise in the eastern trades. A number of similar contracts for voyages to the East Indies were sealed in the following years. In July 1712, the company ceded its entire monopoly of trade in the Indian Ocean to the Malouin merchants for the duration of three years. In December 1714, the earlier agreement was renewed and extended into a ten-year contract. By 1715, the Saint-Malo traders finally consolidated their temporary concessions and partnerships into a stable commercial organization that became recognized under its own name as the *Compagnie des Indes Orientales de Saint-Malo*.[82]

Fortunately, the account book of the East Indies Company of Saint-Malo has survived to this day, which allows us to identify its individual directors and main shareholders.[83] Among the venture's twelve directors, only Antoine Crozat did not belong to the merchant community of Saint-Malo. Out of the total 264 shares (*actions*), Crozat held only a single one (*action* number 164), but at a value of 300,000 *lt.*, about 7 percent of the company's total capital of 4.25 million *lt.* A resident of Paris and originally from the Languedoc region in southern France, Crozat was among the preeminent financiers of his time and omnipresent in the commerce with the East Indies as well as Spanish America between 1708 and 1719. Known as "*le riche,*" Crozat contributed not only his substantial financial resources to the company. His Malouin partners in the venture also benefited from his well-connected network at the royal court. Despite his valuable qualities, Crozat found himself in a clear minority position compared with the list of eleven directors from Saint-Malo, which reads like a veritable who's who of the city's merchant trader elite. The lead among them took François-Auguste Magon de la Lande with sixty-six shares and a contribution of 657,000 *lt.*, and François Le Fer de Beauvais with thirty-one shares and 540,000 *lt.*. Even the smallest contribution, from Jean Martin de la Chapelle, amounted to eighteen shares and 136,000 *lt.* Together, the eleven directors from Saint-Malo dominated the company as they held 95 percent of all shares (251 out of 264) and provided 85 percent of the total capital (3.624 of 4.25 million *lt.*). The eleven directors who thus controlled the French East Indies commerce also formed a homogeneous socioeconomic group, representing the merchant elite whom André Lespagnol has called "ces Messieurs de Saint-Malo." Born mostly in the 1670s and 1680s, they belonged to the latest generation of the most respected merchant dynasties whose ancestors had established themselves at Saint-Malo since at least the fifteenth century. It should not come as a surprise that close kinship ties underpinned their business relations. François-Auguste Magon de la Lande and Luc Magon de la Balue were brothers. Both were first cousins of Henri Baude du Val. Pierre Le Fer de la Saudre and François Le Fer de Beauvais were also first cousins. Charles Locquet de Granville married the daughter of Jean Gaubert. Pierre-François Nouail du Fougeray and Julien Eon de Carman were brothers-in-law, and so were Pierre Gris du Colombier and Jean Martin de la Chapelle. It was a tight social network, indeed.[84]

Figure 2.8 shows the expeditions these elite merchants fitted out for the commerce with Asia during the first two decades of the eighteenth century. Between 1709 and 1719, a total of ten vessels amounting to 5,550 tons, including two Dutch prize ships, traveled to Moka to trade in coffee. Two of them also called at an Indian port, and one of the prize ships was retaken by the English. Nine ships thus returned to France with a combined cargo of Arabian coffee weighing an estimated 5,145,000 pounds (*livres-poids*). The much larger Dutch V.O.C. employed nine ships between 1707 and 1716 to import a comparable amount of about five million pounds of coffee. Turning to the core business of their new-won monopoly, the direct trade with India, the Malouin partnerships armed twenty merchantmen (for a total of 8,820 tons) for voyages to Bengal, Pondichéry and Calicut in the years 1707–1719. The ships carried back to Brittany spices, cotton textiles, saltpeter, dyewood, and cowry shells worth an estimated 37 million *lt.* in sales. On their eastern voyages, the Saint-Malo merchant ships typically held commissions of *guerre et marchandise*, permitting them to take Dutch and English ships as prizes. The capture of the two Dutch ships on their way to Moka suggest that they seized this opportunity as well. Considering the outcome of all twenty-six voyages sponsored by the Saint-Malo East India Company in 1708–1720, the partners gained an estimated 50 million *lt.* from sales in return for their investments of about 13 million *lt.* Profits from individual voyages ranged between 49.7 percent for the first expedition to the Indies and 176 percent for expeditions undertaken in

1713–1716. In addition to the East India concession, at least another dozen ships, promoted by *armateurs* from Saint-Malo and totaling 3,580 tons, sailed to Canton in China in 1702–1720, taking either the eastern route or passing along the coast of Peru.[85]

What was it about the merchants from Saint-Malo that made them so successful in the Asian trades? What qualities gave them such a competitive edge compared with their rivals from other ports, such as Nantes, La Rochelle, or Marseille?[86] First, they possessed the technical equipment in the form of a fleet of well-armed frigates and large vessels ranging between three hundred and six hundred tons that have been tried and tested in countless privateering and interloping ventures. Second, with a large pool of highly experienced and seasoned captains, officers, and ordinary sailors, manning their fleet with the best seamen posed no problem either. Third, the fortunes the Malouins had accumulated through privateering and interloping in the Americas provided them with the financial resources to float expeditions that required millions of *livres* in investments. In particular, their control of the flow of American silver into France gave them direct access to the masses of piastres necessary to grease the wheels of commerce in the East Indies and China. Finally, they received a helping hand from the royal government. The Comte de Pontchartrain extended his political support to the Saint-Malo merchants in appreciation of their contributions to his foreign policy, notably the large-scale use of the *guerre de course* and the penetration of the Spanish American commerce.[87]

The result of this turn of events was that a small peripheral port on the northern Breton coast seized control of such a major national enterprise as the Asian trade monopoly. The strategy behind this achievement was similar to that employed in the South Sea commerce. The Saint-Malo merchants clearly recognized that it was not in their best interest to keep pursuing limited subcontracts under the auspices of the royal government. Instead, they were ambitious enough to capture the state-run monopoly of eastern trade, and then to turn it into a powerful private-run company. In contrast to the various companies previously established under Colbert, the merchants, and no longer the state, shaped the decision making within their enterprise and its commercial strategy. What they achieved, then, was a company of their own making, substituting a private-run monopoly for a state-run monopoly. Most important, the Saint-Malo merchants insisted on the preservation of the company's privileges. Their takeover never implied the substitution of exclusive company rights with a free-trade policy, as was the case after the dissolution of the second French East India Company in 1769 (see chapter 7).[88]

THE END OF A GOLDEN AGE?

We tend to associate economic growth with reliable and stable political conditions. The latter rarely benefit from extended periods of warfare. And yet, in one of those strange twists of history, war ushered in Saint-Malo's golden period in overseas commerce. For a good quarter of a century, Louis XIV's last two wars opened extraordinary economic opportunities for the Malouin merchants, turning their hometown into a true hub of global trade. With the onset of war, they captured the Spanish American trade, allowing them to control the flow of silver into France and to extend their business interests into the South Sea. The crown's naval policy of the *guerre de course* encouraged the Malouins to engage in their tried-and-tested activity of commerce raiding. As if the riches gained through interloping and privateering in the western seas were not enough, they secured privileged access to the markets in the East and pioneered the coffee trade with the Arabian Peninsula. In this golden period, roughly between 1689 and 1715, the merchant venturers of Saint-Malo had created a worldwide trading network anchored in northern Brittany and spanning from Cadiz to Peru, from Canton to Bengal and Pondichéry, from Moka to the Île Bourbon and Île de France in the Indian Ocean.

Unfortunately, for Saint-Malo, the political and economic tide began to turn with the years directly following the Treaty of Utrecht signed in 1713.[89] For a place that owed much of its splendid rise in overseas commerce to the unusual circumstances of war, the onset of peace was a serious backlash and brought its economic growth to a halt. For one, the end of war meant the end of privateering enterprise and therefore the loss of revenues from prize sales. The Malouins would have to wait for more than a quarter of a century until the outbreak of the War of the Austrian Succession before they could resume their commerce raiding activities. In fact, it took until April 1744 before the eighty-seven-ton *Le Barnabas* was the first corsair to sail again from Saint-Malo.[90] Furthermore, the end of hostilities saw the restoration of Spanish authority in its American colonies. The capture of five French interloping vessels by a Spanish navy squadron in the harbor of Arica in September 1717 symbolized the end of the lucrative, yet illicit, South Sea ventures along the Peruvian coast.[91] Only two years later, the Malouin merchants lost control of their last bastion, the exclusive access to the eastern trades with China and India, which returned to a state-controlled enterprise. In 1719, John Law, under the new economic policies of his *Système*, revoked all privileges of the *Compagnie des Indes Orientales de Saint-Malo* and transferred them to his newly established *Compagnie perpétuelle des Indes*. The company's headquarters moved as well, from Saint-Malo to Lorient on the Atlantic seaboard, which eventually held a quasi-monopoly as the gateway to the eastern trades.[92]

Whether or not these developments amounted to an economic crisis was a matter of perspective. Quite a few contemporaries saw not much else than decline when they thought of their once-proud hometown.[93] The available evidence suggests that the Malouin merchants did indeed experience an economic stagnation as they were not able to sustain previous levels of overseas shipping. As the estimates for the number of trading vessels in figure 2.9 illustrate, Saint-Malo's shipping in foreign and colonial commerce decreased visibly over the course of the eighteenth century. Slight and brief upswings that came close to previous levels of shipping happened only in the 1750s and again in the 1780s, right before the French Revolution.

The waxing and waning of Saint-Malo's commerce went against the grain of a steady growth in French foreign trade at large. Figure 2.9 complements the information on Saint-Malo with annual data administered by the *Bureau de la balance du commerce* under the Old Regime to show the expansion in French imports and exports, denoted in *livres tournois*, from 1716 through 1780. The point is not a systematic year-by-year comparison of changes in shipping from a single port with changes in the monetary value of imports and exports for an entire country but rather to illustrate two contrasting general slopes. Granted, the surviving eighteenth-century statistics are not always the most fine-grained data. They suffer from a lack of adequate deflation and from selection bias as political interests often motivated what information got reported. Sweeping conclusions are best avoided. Even with these caveats in mind, the broad long-term pattern indicates a surge in French overseas commerce over the course of the eighteenth century, despite some noticeable dips during wartime (especially in 1744–1748 and 1756–1763).[94]

Although its economic performance did not align with France at large, Saint-Malo did not altogether lose its position as one of the leading ports in the French Atlantic Economy. But in the eighteenth century, its merchant elite missed out on some of the opportunities, particularly in the West Indies, that would emerge as the main engines of French economic growth from colonial trade. As we discussed earlier, the Malouins had developed a taste for the kind of swift high-risk, high-return ventures that were particularly attractive under the extraordinary circumstances of war. Danycan's South Sea enterprise and the enthusiasm for the *guerre de course* both are fitting examples. Setting aside their traditional stronghold in Newfoundland fishing, they showed a rather limited interest in the colonial enterprises that generated regular revenues but required long-term investments. In particular, the fortunes gained from the sugar trade

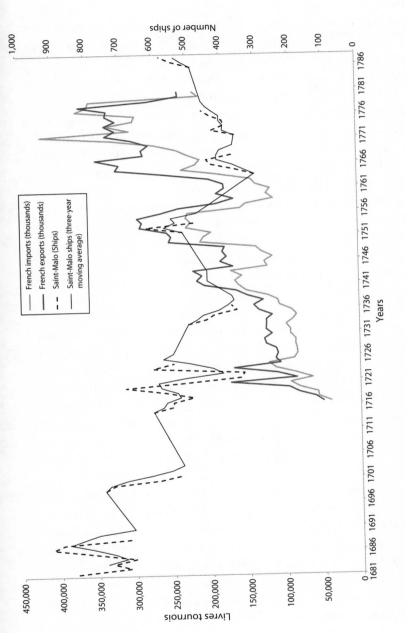

FIGURE 2.9 Trends in foreign commerce, Saint-Malo and France.

Note: The dotted line traces the number of ships from Saint-Malo that were engaged in foreign commerce during years of peace between 1681 and 1787. The thin solid line estimates the trend in Saint-Malo's shipping, using a three-year moving average. The thick light gray and dark gray lines display the overall volume of French imports and exports in millions of *livres tournois* during the 1716–1780 period. The underlying data for French imports and exports were originally recorded by the *Bureau de la balance du commerce* and are printed in Romano (1957).

Sources: All information on Saint-Malo's shipping comes from Lespagnol (1991). The underlying data for French imports and exports come from Lespagnol (1991). The underlying data for French imports and exports were originally recorded by the *Bureau de la balance du commerce* and are printed in Romano (1957).

turned the plantation economy of Saint-Domingue into one of France's most prized colonial possessions in the eighteenth century. Although Saint-Malo was certainly not excluded, traders from the competing ports of Bordeaux and Marseille were the ones who came to dominate colonial trade in the West Indies. Likewise, on the supply side of forced labor for these colonies, merchants from Nantes and La Rochelle controlled much of the slave trade from Senegal, Guinea, and Angola to the Americas. Compared with its rivals, Saint-Malo was relegated to a port of second-order importance (see chapter 7).[95] Consequently, its merchant community was thrown back to its traditional fields of activity, such as the connection with Cadiz. Even here, in their former strongholds, the Malouins faced new challenges. With the end of the Spanish Succession War, the shipping lanes toward Iberian ports were once again relatively safe, and merchants from other ports had no more need for the protection that the heavily armed Malouin convoys used to provide. The negative impact of the Treaty of Utrecht on the Newfoundland fisheries may have been less severe because the exploration of new fishing grounds around Cape Breton compensated for French losses of fishing rights elsewhere.[96]

On the political side, the Saint-Malo elites lost considerable support at the royal court. They no longer benefited from the patronage they used to enjoy under the Comte de Pontchartrain. Additionally, the exclusively Malouin membership of their *Compagnie des Indes* turned out to be its Achilles' heel. Traders from other ports who had been denied access to the company saw little reason to come to its defense when John Law went about revoking its monopoly privileges.[97] In a similar manner, Saint-Malo's merchants, in 1713, 1733–1738, and 1759, repeatedly campaigned for the reinstatement of their erstwhile privileges of a free port, in part to compensate for wartime losses. Every single one of their attempts failed because the elites of competing ports such as Nantes, La Rochelle, and Marseille immediately stymied such claims.[98]

Given these various obstacles, it would take until the second half of the eighteenth century before a new generation of *Messieurs de Saint-Malo* entered the stage. They included such illustrious names as René-Auguste de Chateaubriand and Pierre Jacques Meslé de Grandclos who breathed new life into Saint-Malo's engagement in the East Indies, the slave trade, and, with the outbreak of the Seven Years' War, the *course*.[99] It is a theme we return to in chapter 7.

Few would deny that the historical contingencies that shaped foreign trade were largely beyond the immediate reach of Saint-Malo's merchants. Still, exogenous forces alone were not responsible for the city's spectacular economic rise until the second decade of the eighteenth century, nor should they alone be blamed for its relative stagnation in subsequent years. The reason is simple and comes down to the quality of social organization from within the merchant community. Recognizing new commercial opportunities, such as the South Sea and East Indian trades, and turning them into profitable ventures was not the work of any single entrepreneur, no matter how gifted. Successful commercial ventures in this place and time relied on well-tuned collaborations between ship-owners, neighboring merchants as partners, more distant financiers as investors, experienced captains, and a reliable crew. All of these individuals contributed their particular knowledge, physical assets, and financial resources to the success of their collective enterprise. Whether or not such collaborations worked was contingent on the nature and pattern of social relationships within which the merchant partners were embedded—the various ties of kinship, marriage, previous business partnerships, apprenticeship, and religious allegiance that knitted them together. Which developments in these social relational foundations of Saint-Malo's merchant community facilitated or hindered the local organization of overseas trade is what we turn to next.

CHAPTER 3

SOCIAL SOURCES OF ECONOMIC GROWTH

W hat did the remarkable success of Saint-Malo in maritime commerce rest upon, as long as it lasted? An intuitive response might point to unusually favorable circumstances, both natural and institutional, that benefited the Malouin merchantry in their overseas endeavors. As a seaport, Saint-Malo was indeed strategically well positioned, with the British Isles within reach across the Channel and unhindered access to the main shipping lanes leading across the Atlantic. Unfortunately for the Malouins, the openness of their port to the seas also made it vulnerable to attacks in times of warfare. This latent threat became manifest more than once during the repeated conflicts of the late-seventeenth and eighteenth centuries. As noted, even when armed conflict did not pose an immediate threat to vessels entering or leaving the port of Saint-Malo, the large tidal range and numerous islets strewn across the bay challenged even the most experienced navigators. Despite the availability of nautical charts, contemporaries still recommended relying on local pilots to help them find a safe passage through the coastal waters. To its credit, Saint-Malo boasted a natural harbor, accessible and deep enough for vessels of nearly all sizes to anchor safely—but so did other seaports. With neighboring Solidor, the Malouins possessed an ideal site for a shipyard where the construction of oceangoing ships of up to one thousand tons was not unheard of.[1]

Perhaps even more essential for any comparative advantage over other Atlantic ports was easy access to waterways leading from the coast to inland marketplaces, such as canals and rivers that could be used for the transportation of commodities. Inward shipping from Saint-Malo was indeed possible on the river Rance, but unfortunately no farther than the town of Dinan, where it ended in a cul-de-sac about twenty kilometers upstream. In contrast, it is worth recalling that the merchantry of nearly all French Atlantic ports of some stature profited from closeness to a great river: the Seine linked Le Havre and Rouen to the Paris Basin; the Loire offered much the same for Nantes; traders from La Rochelle relied on the Charente; and the Garonne eased exchanges between Bordeaux and Toulouse in the southwest of the kingdom.

The most obvious natural limitation of Saint-Malo's location was its small size. Save for the narrow strip that made up the Sillon, the city was surrounded by the sea on all sides. As Chateaubriand quipped in his memoirs, the entire rock that Saint-Malo was built on barely matched the size of the Tuileries Gardens in Paris (for a map of the intra-muros old town, see figure 3.1).[2] The first challenge for

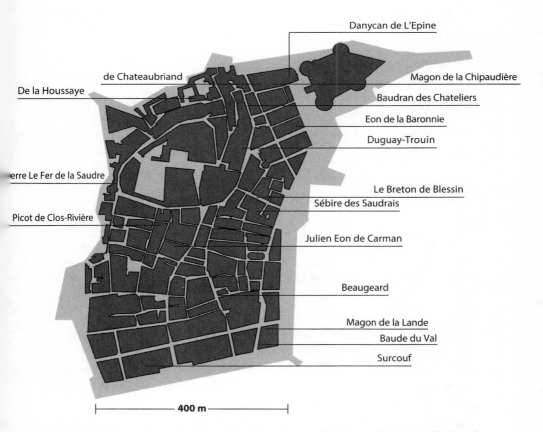

FIGURE 3.1 Map of historical intra-muros Saint-Malo, with places of residence of selected *armateurs*.

Sources: AD-IV C4070, C4086, C4098, C4259, C4262; *AM-SM* CC41; Laurent (1986); Collas (1949a).

TABLE 3.1 Population Estimates of Major Towns in Brittany

	YEAR					
	1667	1696	1770	1774	1789	1801
Saint-Malo	20,000	25,100	18,000	17,925[†]	19,828[†]	19,147[†]
Brest	1,600	9,472	24,600	24,450	33,852	27,000
Dinan	12,000	5,484	6,000	5,975	7,332	4,117
Fougères	16,000	4,388	10,000	6,775	7,093	7,297
Guérande	4,000	5,943	12,000	7,446	6,632	7,336
Lorient			16,000	16,825	18,460	19,922
Morlaix	10,000	7,477	9,512	9,800	10,348	9,000
Nantes		21,513	80,000	48,025	64,994	73,879
Quimper	8,700	4,678	9,500	7,575	6,344	6,608
Rennes	12,000	27,474	42,600	30,075	19,302	25,904
Saint-Brieuc	4,000	5,028	6,600	6,784	6,500	8,090
Saint-Pol	5,740	4,713	5,400	4,950	5,449	
Saint-Servan					8,836	13,000
Vannes	13,200	7,656	10,000	9,150	8,814	8,722
Vitré	12,000	7,152	8,000	10,325	10,850	8,809

Source: Selected entries from Nières (2004, 556–57).
[†] Nières seems to have missed the first digit in these years.

such a cramped place was to accommodate a swelling population that counted close to twenty thousand people during most years of the eighteenth century. Table 3.1 shows that Saint-Malo was densely populated and ranked among the largest towns in Brittany, if we consider the number of residents. Table 3.2 offers a nationwide comparison with other leading towns and ports within the kingdom of France. In its heyday, around the turn toward the eighteenth century, Saint-Malo's population of 25,100 souls was second only to Rennes and Nantes (see the year 1696 in table 3.1). Estimates of urbanization in Brittany for 1693 likewise reveal that 12.8 percent of the Breton urban population lived within

TABLE 3.2 Population Estimates of Major French Towns

	YEAR				
	1600	1650	1700	1750	1790
Saint-Malo	10,500	16,000	23,500	19,000	18,000
Paris	250,000	450,000	510,000	570,000	660,000
Lyon	32,500	67,500	97,000	120,000	146,000
Marseille	45,000	65,000	75,000	88,000	110,000
Rouen	60,000	82,000	64,000	67,500	73,000
Le Havre		6,000		14,000	18,000
Bordeaux	35,000	40,000	45,000	60,000	111,000
La Rochelle	20,000	17,500	21,500	19,000	21,500
Nantes	25,000	35,000	42,500		80,000
Rennes	17,500	36,000	45,000		35,000
Brest		1,000	15,000		30,000
Morlaix	7,500	10,000	10,000		10,000

Source: Estimates compiled by Benedict (1989, 23–24).

the bishopric of Saint-Malo, while 26.1 percent hailed from Rennes and 15.2 percent from Nantes.[3] In addition to the size of its population, another challenge was that the city's natural boundaries posed clear limits to urban development, especially where facilities for commerce and industry—the very lifeblood of the Malouins—were concerned. There was thus much to recommend Saint-Malo as an eminent port for maritime commerce and at the same time little to suggest that it was particularly blessed with geographical assets that offered a comparative advantage.[4]

What they lacked in natural advantages, the Malouin merchant elite may have compensated for by favorable institutional arrangements and economic privileges granted to them. It was not unusual for the crown to confer exclusive trading rights to certain cities and not others. To illustrate, the city of Lyon not only was the center of silk weaving in France but also held a profitable mediating position because all imports of raw silk were required to pass through the city and thus were subject to local custom duties. Dunkirk and Marseille, for their part, benefited from their status as duty-free ports such that incoming goods were exempt from the payment of import taxes. With the royal edict of 1669, the Marseillais merchants likewise enjoyed a de facto monopoly in the trade with the Levant. Because it was a free port, no import duties were levied in Marseille, which attracted unprecedented numbers of foreign merchants to the city. Any other French port that sidestepped Marseille and imported Levantine wares directly had to pay a 20 percent duty. Turning from the Mediterranean to the Atlantic, the merchants of Bordeaux, La Rochelle, Nantes, Rouen, and Dieppe thrived on their exclusive access to the direct trade with the French West Indies. Merchants in other places therefore had little choice but to purchase colonial goods at prices dictated by the privileged ports of entry.[5]

In a similar vein, recall that Saint-Malo's mercantile community benefited from comparable privileges in commerce (see chapter 2 for details). One was the monopoly of trade with the East Indies that Saint-Malo's elite enjoyed in the dozen years between 1707 and 1719. The exclusive trading rights proved to be immensely profitable, but the privilege was short-lived. When John Law revoked the Malouins' concession, few peers from other ports came to their aid, and the privileged enterprise came to an abrupt end.[6] A much older privilege dated to 1395, when King Charles VI issued letters patent that granted Saint-Malo exemption from duties on goods entering and leaving the port. Successive royal governments and dukes of Brittany upheld the tax exemptions and thus guaranteed Saint-Malo's status as a free port. Unfortunately for the Malouin merchant community, the favorable conditions of the decree were not reinstated when the crown granted similar free-trade privileges to the competing cities of Marseille and Dunkirk by the end of the seventeenth century—at about the very moment when Saint-Malo reached its economic peak. The failure to have their erstwhile rights restored despite evidently high returns to trade suggests that privilege alone was unlikely to be responsible for the spectacular riches the Malouin trader elites reaped from overseas ventures. It hardly comes as a surprise that the repeated attempts of Saint-Malo's merchants to have their exclusive trading rights restored were thwarted by their competitors from other centers of seaborne commerce. The arguments against any restoration of trading privileges to Saint-Malo more often than not emphasized the absence of a thriving hinterland, and hence a missing market for imported colonial goods and for the supply of valuable wares to be exported. Whether intended or not, the representatives of rival ports thus linked Saint-Malo's geographic and political economic deficits to prevent the renewal of older rights and the granting of new ones.[7] These limiting conditions remind us of Saint-Malo's volatile role in the French Atlantic Economy. In sum, neither the gifts of nature, nor the privilege-conferring benevolence of a prince sufficiently explain the economic success of Saint-Malo in the late-seventeenth and early eighteenth centuries.

SOCIAL RELATIONAL FOUNDATIONS

Few economic historians of this time and place would deny that success in commerce (or its absence) was contingent on historical conjunctures that opened (or closed) windows of opportunity for maritime traders. The two final wars under Louis XIV were critical moments for the merchant elites of Saint-Malo, as we learned in the previous chapter. Again, we usually do not expect armed conflict to be particularly beneficial for the unhindered exchange of goods, and certainly not in long-distance trade, prone as it was to raids at sea. Yet in the case of the *Messieurs de Saint-Malo*, and perhaps merchant elites in other seaports as well, war gave rise to circumstances that were ripe for profitable opportunities: privateering enterprise, interloping in Spanish America, Danycan's expeditions to the South Sea, and the far-reaching voyages to the East Indies and China. Still, potential for profit-making is one thing, realizing the benefits it promises is something else. However poised for high-risk, high-return enterprises this historical moment might have been, the Malouin merchants required the instincts to recognize new opportunities and the skills to reap the profits on offer.[8]

If we accept this interpretation, where, then, did their ability to adapt to changing circumstances and their sense for new commercial opportunities come from? In what has become the conventional historical account, André Lespagnol has suggested that much of the answer is to be found in the social relational fabric of the merchant elite. Following this established historical narrative, what enabled the Malouin traders to collectively identify and then seize novel opportunities for commerce was neither nature, nor princely politics, but rather their embeddedness in local social bonds that held them together as a merchant community, and it did so even though commerce was first and foremost an enterprise based within individual family trading houses.[9] According to this interpretation, two threads were essential to the weave of their communal ties. First, along a range of demographics, successive generations of leading Malouin families had much in common and little to separate them from each other. Second, this demographic homogeneity coupled with an ingenious set of social relational mechanisms: an apprenticeship system that replenished the merchant elite from within their own ranks, and a partnership system they devised to organize their enterprises in maritime trade.

To unpack these arrangements that served as the engines of Saint-Malo's economic growth, let us consider first the demographic composition of its mercantile community. Given the seaport's prime location on the Breton coast, its citizens felt inevitably drawn to the twin occupations of navigation and maritime trade. Delving into the histories of career choices the Malouin elites made, one finds time and again just how intricately linked trading and navigating were. Various sons of eminent merchant families started their seafaring careers as ensigns and officers on board trading and privateering vessels. Likewise, it was not unheard of that those who earned their laurels as captains, braving the treacherous waters of the North Atlantic, eventually emerged as successful *armateurs* in their own right. As André Lespagnol has pointed out, the lack of suitable occupational alternatives almost certainly contributed to their preference for career paths that were bound for the seas.[10] Saint-Malo did not distinguish itself as a center of manufacturing or royal administration. The few public offices on offer were largely of local significance and therefore of limited appeal to members of the merchant classes who aspired to upward mobility. Where they attained administrative positions, they usually did so without ever abandoning their strong commitment to commerce, their *fidélité au commerce*. Consequently, unlike competing hubs of French seaborne trade, such as Bordeaux or Nantes, that boasted important judicial institutions and offices, Saint-Malo did not witness the rise of an administrative elite of royal officials next to its homegrown merchant elite.[11] For the Malouins, maritime commerce thus remained the foremost source of riches and prestige to be gained.

Trading enterprise as well as municipal governance in Saint-Malo were concentrated in the hands of an oligarchy of eminent merchant families, not unlike other cities that played a leading role in the French Atlantic Economy.[12] Granted, little evidence suggests that the Malouin trader bourgeoisie was a closed elite that barred outsiders from joining their social circles. Instead, migrating mariners and merchants from nearby and foreign places alike were welcomed among their midst. As a result, a good share of those who were engaged in overseas commerce were relative newcomers to Saint-Malo, having settled in the city no earlier than the second half of the seventeenth century. At its core, however, the highest-status Malouin economic elite consisted of well-established merchant dynasties whose ancestries were deeply rooted within the history of their hometown. They included the Baude, Eon, Gouin, Grout, Le Breton, Magon, and Picot families, to name the most prominent ones. In his pioneering work on the Malouin elite during the reign of Louis XIV, André Lespagnol has found that about 47.5 percent of the 160 leading traders in 1701, whom he was able to identify from various sources, stemmed from families that had called Saint-Malo home since 1600. More important, about 52.5 percent of these same leading traders in 1701 descended from distinguished families that had settled in the city before 1600. Another 26.8 percent of this elite group could trace their lineages back to ancestors who had lived in Saint-Malo before 1500. Hence, more than three-fourths of the foremost overseas trading merchants looked back on a rich family history, inseparably tied to their hometown.[13]

We may only speculate to what extent the salience of their locally embedded lineages instilled a strong local identity among the members of the mercantile elite. At the very least, the entries in the poll tax rolls (*capitation*) reveal a clear sense of place when it came to their residential choices. The urban dwellings of most leading trader *armateurs* were concentrated in and around just two neighborhoods of the walled city, the *Quartier Saint-Thomas* in the northeastern part of town, and another in the quarter sandwiched between the *Grande Porte* and Saint-Jean abbey to the east and southeast.[14] On the map of Saint-Malo's intramuros old town (figure 3.1), the townhouses of Danycan de l'Epine and Magon de la Chipaudière illustrate residences in the first *quartier*, while those of Sébire des Saudrais and his repeated business partner Le Breton de Blessin depict the other neighborhood.

In addition to this residential concentration, festivities and public life, ranging from marriages to funerals, in this ardently Catholic town brought the local merchantry together in church. The embittered confessional conflicts between Catholics and Protestants that marred so many early modern communities were noticeably absent in Saint-Malo—for the simple reason that the vast majority of Malouins sided unambiguously with the Roman Catholic church. Religious dissidents, most of them Protestants, were not tolerated among the citizens, and new residents were often required to produce proof of their Catholic faith.[15] For example, one Thomas de Cussy, a merchant arriving from Caen to settle in Saint-Malo, abjured (or was made to abjure) the Protestant faith "entre les mains de frère Zacharie de Ploërmel, Capucin, prédicateur" on November 17, 1685. Another case illustrates that such renouncements were still enforced in the mid-eighteenth century. Paul Amsinck, a Protestant trader originally hailing from Hamburg, Germany, converted to Roman Catholicism on December 21, 1758, at the age of 34, before he took up residence in Saint-Malo as a merchant trader.[16] Further evidence of the tight coupling between commerce and Catholicism, two spheres so obviously dear to the Malouins, is the abundance of vessels named after the Virgin Mary, such as the privateer *La Vierge Marie du Port*

(1710), the one-hundred-ton *La Vierge Sans Maculle* that carried Spanish wine to Stockholm (1704), or *La Notre Dame de la Miséricorde*, a fishing vessel bound for Newfoundland (1740).[17]

It certainly helped cohesion within their community that all faithful citizens, including the most notable families, were organized into just a single parish for the entire city.[18] The cathedral church as the center of cultural and religious life in the city was a mirror image of the *Bourse Commune*—not just a simple market-place by the main gates of town, but the beating heart of Saint-Malo's economic life, where new business deals were arranged and valuable information shared, and where public sales of vessels and auctions of captured prizes were held.[19]

Carefully arranged marriage alliances between leading merchant families helped to cement the relationships they forged in business affairs. Once again, it was André Lespagnol who has traced the marriage choices of fifty heads of the great merchant Malouin dynasties toward the end of the seventeenth cen-tury.[20] The web of conjugal ties that emerges exhibits endogamy above all else. In 90 percent of all marriages, the brides came from other resident families of Saint-Malo, and in 74 percent of all cases, these families had established themselves in the city before 1600. As mentioned earlier, among the higher ranks of Malouin society, not much else beyond the commercial elite existed, which meant that appropriate choices of spouses were to be found exclusively within the merchant elite. Strong endogamy with respect to place, occupational background, and social standing within local commercial society thus was nearly inevitable. With the increasingly entwined kinship bonds that ensued, it was often unavoidable that distant cousins within the same lineage married each other.[21] Once married, their fertility was just as impressive as the expanse of their kinship networks, effectively ensuring the reproduction of the Malouin elite: considering the same sample of fifty leading families, an average of 10.5 children per family were born. As Lespagnol reports, three out of five families had at least ten children, and seven families among them even had fifteen children. At the lower end, in merely two out of fifty families, less than five children were born.[22]

A portrait of a homogenous merchant elite, rich in its past and present ties to the city, emerges from these various impressions.[23] Enclosed by the sea, the dense urban space with its narrow lanes that the Malouins inhabited meant that they hardly could avoid close social intercourse, even if they wanted to. Their social circles were bound to crosscut each other, naturally leading to tightly woven net-works. Their many shared traits were various articulations of the highly cohesive web of social relationships that bound them together, including their devotion to seafaring, and hence their occupational homogeneity; their residential concen-tration, turning them all into neighbors; the zealous Catholicism they shared;

their preference for arranging marriages among the same set of elite merchant families; and their entangled lineages.[24] This is the gist of the conventional historical narrative of the *Messieurs de Saint-Malo*. François-René de Chateaubriand, blessed with a keen sociological imagination, offers us a similar observation of the townsfolk of his birthplace: "Locked up at night in their city by the same key, the Malouins formed but a single family."[25]

How could such an apparently self-contained group of merchants sustain itself and continue to prosper for as long as it did? History suggests that few such communities were able to persist in the long run based on endogamy alone. In the case of Saint-Malo, its trader elite could draw on various sources of replenishment from outside during the late-seventeenth and early eighteenth centuries. From the parish registers, we know that about 24 percent of the port's 7,136 male residents who got married in the 1651–1700 period were born outside of the diocese of Saint-Malo. Most of these men came from neighboring towns and villages in Brittany (8 percent) and Normandy (7 percent), some arrived from other locations in France (6 percent), and few were of foreign origin (3 percent). The composition changed markedly for the 7,474 men who married during the half-century that followed (1701–1750). The shares coming from other parts of France (9 percent) and foreign countries (4 percent) increased only marginally. The city witnessed, however, a substantial surge in migration from nearby communities: a full 20 percent of those on record came from other dioceses in Brittany, and another 19 percent from Normandy took up residence in Saint-Malo. In other words, after the turn of the century, slightly more than half (52 percent) of the male residents documented in the marriage records had been recent migrants from outside of town.[26]

Not every single one of these relative newcomers was a skilled navigator or trader engaged in overseas commerce. But three groups were of particular salience for replenishing the homegrown Malouin mercantile community. First, the continued growth of the port's merchant fleet created an ever-increasing demand for suitable mariners, able officers, and experienced captains. This demand was met by a supply of new seafaring talent that arrived in Saint-Malo from the string of slightly smaller ports facing the English Channel, from Paimpol to Binic, from Pléneuf to Granville. Included in this group were a few ports in the immediate vicinity of Saint-Malo, such as Cancale, Saint-Suliac, and Pleurtuit. The most ambitious among these seafarers used their careers in navigation as avenues to join the ranks of the Saint-Malo *armateur* elite.

The second group stemmed from an altogether different social station. It consisted of the later-born sons—the *fils cadets,*—of the lesser and middling provincial nobility in Brittany. The first-born sons usually inherited two-thirds of their father's wealth, leaving just the remaining third to be divided among all of their younger brothers. Depending on the number of siblings, more often than not, little material wealth would be passed on to them. Left with a noble title, but limited funds for a matching lifestyle, the *fils cadets* sought their fortunes elsewhere, and took to the seas. Some of them turned their efforts to careers in navigation, as officers and captains on board of trading vessels. Others manned privateering ships in the *guerre de course*, more in line with the age-old role of noblemen in feudal society, occupied with fighting. Still others preferred to join share partnerships in trading and commercial ventures. Some among them eventually became *armateurs* in their own right. Thus emerged what contemporary writers such as the abbé Coyer envisioned as a new *noblesse commerçante*. Later, in the second half of the eighteenth century, the most illustrious among these noble sons, dedicated as they were to commerce and the *course* as a means to regain their accustomed social status, was René-Auguste de Chateaubriand, comte de Combourg, father of the much admired founder of the French Romantic movement, yet also a privateering and slave-trading *armateur*. Chapter 7 considers the peculiar role this commercial nobility played in the organization of trading enterprise. Suffice it to say for now that the prospect of riches from trade attracted a fair share of the provincial *petite noblesse* to Saint-Malo.[27]

The third source of replenishment for the Saint-Malo merchantry came in the form of migration of fully formed merchants and traders from places afar, whether French or foreign. Few, if any, particularly high barriers to settle in the city existed, except perhaps the insistence on newcomers being faithful Catholics. For most migrant merchants, it was sufficient to take up residence in Saint-Malo and pay their taxes to pursue their business there. Likewise, any benefits of buying and selling wares under the free-port privilege granted by the crown were not exclusive to long-standing members of the local mercantile community and were extended to foreign traders as well. Only when migrants desired full urban citizenship, with all its rights and privileges, was a formal naturalization procedure required. Drawing once more on the parish registers for Saint-Malo, André Lespagnol has estimated that nearly 20 percent of the local trader elite during the 1680–1701 period can be identified as recent migrants to the city (i.e., about 30 of 160 merchant traders). Who exactly counted as a migrant was a thorny matter for contemporaries, and remains difficult to define today. Apparently, even someone as eminent as Noël Danycan de l'Epine, born in neighboring Saint-Servan and perhaps Saint-Malo's greatest entrepreneur under the reign of Louis XIV, was still treated by some as a second-generation migrant, and this they did despite the fact—or maybe because of it—that his father had moved to the port city from Coutances in Normandy in 1640. Considering just those merchant traders whose families had taken up residence in Saint-Malo since 1600, one arrives at about 40 percent of the entire merchant elite in 1685, about 50 percent in 1701, and about 55 percent in 1710.[28]

Where did these migrant merchants come from, to the extent that their origins can indeed be identified? Overwhelmingly, they used to be residents of villages, ports, and towns in neighboring Normandy (25 percent) and Brittany (34 percent). Particularly close bonds seemed to have existed with the Norman seaport of Granville and the Breton town of Vitré. As a central port engaged in North Atlantic cod fishing—that all important schooling of sailors and navigators alike—Granville contributed to the much-needed supply of experienced seamen for ventures that were fitted out in Saint-Malo. Likewise, Granville's most ambitious *armateurs* may have seen in Saint-Malo a port that offered them even more promising opportunities in overseas commerce. Vitré, in contrast, was a well-established center of cloth manufacturing and trade, and ties between its trader community and Saint-Malo had been close for centuries. It was primarily Saint-Malo that benefited, however, as it attracted much of the entrepreneurial talent that was eager to leave, as Vitré witnessed a severe crisis of its manufacturing industry during the seventeenth century. Beyond Brittany and Normandy, about 17 percent of the new residents had moved from other regions of France, in particular from the western Pays de Loire and southwestern Aquitaine. The final share of about 24.5 percent of the migrant merchants who joined the Malouin merchant community came from foreign countries. Not a single merchant in the business of the northern trade with Scandinavia, Germany, or the Baltic can be found among the various migrants into Saint-Malo. Even more remarkable, few southern European merchants, from Italy, southern France, and the Iberian Peninsula, opted to reside in Saint-Malo.[29] This is remarkable because, as we learned in the previous chapter, Malouin ships regularly satisfied the demand for dried and salted codfish in southern marketplaces, and served as cargo carriers between local ports in the Mediterranean. It also is remarkable because several leading *armateur* dynasties, such as the extensive Magon family, had long maintained their trading posts in Cadiz and other Spanish ports, as gateways to the lucrative colonial trade with Spanish America.

The largest share of foreign merchants came from Flanders, the United Provinces, and the British Isles. By far the most significant group was the colony of Irish émigrés who had been received in Saint-Malo since at least the mid-seventeenth century.[30] They arrived in separate waves, compelled to leave Ireland behind following repeated political and religious conflicts.[31] Some estimates suggest that about one thousand Irish merchants and tradesmen had taken up

residence in Brittany by the mid-1660s.[32] In the case of Saint-Malo, close commercial ties with Galway, Cork, Dublin, Donegal, and several other Irish ports
that had been forged since the sixteenth century were instrumental in facilitating
the influx of Irish merchants and traders. In addition to these long-established
trade routes that turned Saint-Malo into the most important port for Irish merchants, it probably helped that both sides shared the same allegiance to Roman
Catholicism. To those who were forced to flee Ireland for fear of religious per-
secution, Saint-Malo must have appeared as a safe haven. As a result, the small,
but cohesive colony of Irish émigrés found itself well embedded into the local
mercantile community. Their assimilation was evidenced most clearly by several
bonds of marriage between sons and daughters of Irish and Malouin families. In
return, they contributed their fair share to the port's commercial life. The Irish of
Saint-Malo were a particularly strong force when it came to fitting out privateering enterprises during the last two wars fought by Louis XIV.[33] François Browne,
presumably born in France (note his Gallicized first name), but whose father
had arrived from Ireland, contributed as a shareholding partner to at least twenty-two privateering campaigns and two interloping ventures in Spanish America
between 1695 and 1711. Georges Morrogh likewise was a shareholding partner in
at least three different *course* expeditions between 1696 and 1711. In the years that
followed, he continued to hold shares in a number of fishing expeditions bound
for Newfoundland, and in at least two of them, he was the shipowner. Morrogh
came from old Irish stock in Saint-Malo. His father had established himself as a
venerable *armateur* since the 1660s, married into the local Hérisson family, and
acquired the title of *sieur de Saint-Georges*. Thomas Harrington was engaged in
at least four privateering expeditions in 1709–1710. In peacetime, he became an
armateur and fitted out voyages to Newfoundland and the French West Indies
and also shipped various merchandises to northern ports, such as Hamburg and
Gdansk. Belonging to one of the most important Irish families in Saint-Malo,
the captain and shipowner Jacques Walsh (also spelled Wailsh or Welche) organized some five *course* campaigns, including one for *guerre et marchandise*, and
at least one slave-trading venture to the Canary Islands between 1693 and 1703.
His relative, Philippe Wailsh, originally from Dublin, was a shareholder as well
as captain of five privateers from 1693 to 1703.[34]

Granted, any one influx of migrants into Saint-Malo was selective and not
abundant. The successful integration into local society of all three streams of
replenishment from outside—mariners from nearby ports, *cadets* sons of the
middling and lesser nobility, and Irish émigrés—reveals, however, that the merchants of Saint-Malo did not form the tightly closed elite community that their
endogamous tendencies may make us believe. Yet, a cohesive community it still

was, indeed much like the image of an extended single family, sheltered by the city walls, that Chateaubriand would later evoke in his memoir.

Few would doubt that shared religious allegiance, residential concentration, endogamy in marriage choice, a strong local identity, or a shared sense of one's place in a historical lineage were more than suitable preconditions to promote growth in commerce.[35] Still, just because all members of a community were Roman Catholics, or neighbors within a dense urban setting, it does not necessarily follow that they prospered in their commercial undertakings. By themselves, these traits of the Saint-Malo merchant community did not yield economic growth. Hence, this raises the key question: what were the tangible mechanisms responsible for translating this favorable cultural and demographic climate into the economic prosperity that the mercantile elite enjoyed? A major part of the answer lies in two organizational mechanisms that set the sons of the merchant elite on their career paths in seaborne commerce. One mechanism worked through apprenticeship in the art of merchantry and the other through apprenticeship in the art of navigation. The two pathways differed in some respects, yet both instilled a strong collective commitment to commerce (*fidélité au commerce*) among each new generation of traders and helped to ensure the remarkable persistence of the Malouin merchant dynasties.

The first pathway consisted of a long-term apprenticeship in the trading posts (*formation au comptoir*) that the Saint-Malo magnates maintained in foreign ports, most prominently in Cadiz, Sevilla, Malaga, and Alicante on the Iberian Peninsula. In the previous chapter, I considered the forms this apprenticeship took, drawing on the example of the extensive Magon family. Recall that the sons who were sent to the *comptoirs* to be schooled in the art of commerce began their careers at a young age, typically when they were just between fourteen and sixteen years old. Their professional training included all technical aspects of conducting the business of maritime trade. More important, these aspiring merchants met numerous occasions for enriching their social capital. They forged close and lasting relationships with traders of all nations, which led to further business opportunities and valuable knowledge about the workings of local markets. These networks helped to strengthen the central role the trading houses of Saint-Malo played in the exchange with the Spanish colonies in the Americas that was anchored in the Andalusian ports.[36]

Because the attraction of the sea was ever present in a port city like Saint-Malo, sending their sons on board ships to prepare them for their future careers must have been another natural choice for the heads of merchant families. André Lespagnol has estimated that some 50 of the 160 members of the Malouin mercantile elite had learned their craft by pursuing the path of navigation (*voie de la navigation*). It was not only the sons of eminent families who took this route; learning the skills of navigation also allowed hopefuls of lower standing within Malouin society to rise into the leading mercantile circles. Again, apprentices typically made their first steps in seafaring at a very young age, as ensigns and petty officers on vessels bound for the fishing grounds around Newfoundland, the West Indies, or the Mediterranean. One such apprentice who pursued this path was Noël Danycan, who became one of Saint-Malo's most reputed merchant *armateurs* through his South Sea ventures (see chapter 2). Danycan first took to the sea at the tender age of fifteen, and within two years, he had gained sufficient experience in navigation to be entrusted with his first command as captain. Thus, at just seventeen years old, he found himself at the helm of one of his father's ships on its way to Newfoundland's coastal waters. Similar cases include François Le Fer de Beauvais and René Duguay-Trouin, who both entered service at the age of sixteen. Others, like René Moreau de Maupertius or Pierre Jolif, were even younger when they embarked on their first voyage at the age of fourteen. Their practical experiences were complemented by a curriculum in mathematics and the theoretical foundations of navigation at the *Ecole d'Hydrogrophie*, founded at Saint-Malo in 1673. What they had in common with Danycan was their remarkably quick promotion to captain, again at a fairly young age. Duguay-Trouin as well as Danycan's youngest brother, Joseph, received their first commands when they were just nineteen years old. Lespagnol has suggested that their fast promotion was not always the result of merits earned at sea. The main motive appears to have been dynastic interest, the continuation of one's lineage in the commercial elite. Hence, the early promotion to captain was owed to the wish of elite families to elevate their sons as quickly as possible into a professional position commensurate with their status in Malouin society. Still others, like Pierre Jolif at age fifteen, or Luc Magon de la Balue at age seventeen, did not take command of merchant vessels, but rather embarked on trading voyages to destinations in the Antilles or Peru as their particular apprenticeships. Under the tutelage of experienced overseas traders, they were entrusted with merchandise to be sold at colonial marketplaces. Just like their navigating peers, they gained invaluable hands-on experience in shipping; and just like their peers in the *comptoirs* in Cadiz, they became well versed in Spanish as well as in handling the idiosyncrasies of Spanish administration, and they built contacts in far-away markets that proved to be valuable once they sponsored trading voyages under their own responsibility. No matter which particular route these fledgling merchant traders took, their apprenticeships tended to last for a considerable duration. Noël Danycan, for example, spent seventeen years at sea before he began to rely on his then-vast stock of knowledge and experience to focus entirely on his entrepreneurial career as an *armateur*. Among his peers, even twenty to twenty-five years spent in seafaring were not unheard of.[37]

Once concluded, what did these rather long apprenticeships amount to? Above all, it left a new generation of ambitious traders deeply ingrained with an appreciation of the craft of commerce—what has been variously called a "culture of commerce," a "trader culture," or a "veritable fidélité au commerce."[38] This shared dedication to the trader's world featured a number of distinct aspects. The first was a question of dynastic succession for the most eminent merchant families. Through the apprenticeships at *comptoirs* in foreign ports, or aboard ships that sailed for distant destinations, the distinctive expertise in seaborne trade would be passed on from one generation to the next. It thus appears to have been taken for granted that the sons trained in the same maritime and mercantile craft as their fathers and grandfathers before them, a succession that ensured the reproduction of the family-run trading houses.[39]

Second, the collective commitment to commerce stood as a cultural expression of the underlying social networks that held together local society as a cohesive community of like-minded traders. Direct evidence is rarely at hand, but the close ties the Malouin merchants had forged as neighbors, kinsmen, and devout Catholics, as well as through their shared local identity, probably did not hurt when it came to recommend one's son for the position of an apprentice clerk at, say, a cousin's *comptoir* in Cadiz, or as a junior officer on board of a privateer fitted out by another relative or neighbor. Likewise, the ubiquitous matrimonial bonds among the Malouin merchant families suggest that they solidified the relationships built by former business partners in their joint enterprises.

Then, finally, there was the practical training that prepared the apprentices for their role as merchant *armateurs* in the not-so-distant future. It was what today we would call professionalization. Through hands-on socialization, the hopeful young Malouins gained their expert knowledge and were schooled in the technical skills necessary to recognize promising business opportunities. They learned to evaluate information coming their way, the trustworthiness of their business contacts, and how to negotiate with them. As Daniel Roche put it: "What made a good businessman was a reputation for competence and skill. . . . This kind of knowledge was acquired mainly on the job. . . . Business knowledge was a matter of observation, expertise, and flair gained through contacts with other people."[40] In sum, the apprenticeship system entailed a distinct social logic. It was a logic that linked the cohesive social structure the Malouin merchants were embedded in with that characteristic "entrepreneurial spirit" that permeated every aspect of their lives.[41] Herein lies the key to understanding the prosperity of Saint-Malo's mercantile elite.[42]

STATUS ATTAINMENT AND RELATIVE DECLINE

Now that we know what nourished Saint-Malo's growth in commerce, we can examine what developments brought about its economic crisis by the 1720s and spelled the end of its golden period. Even though histories of success tend to be favored, the waning of this once-thriving port city did not go unnoticed by historians. The most influential account of this chain of events remains the one put forward by André Lespagnol. In what has become the established historical narrative, Lespagnol attributes much of the decline in Saint-Malo's fortunes to sociodemographic shifts within the merchantry.[43] A series of exogenous events certainly shaped the prospects of local merchant communities, in Saint-Malo and similar seaports. The end of war in 1713 spelled the end of privateering enterprise; it also meant the end of the lucrative interloping trade with the colonies in Spanish America. With the resignation of the Comte de Pontchartrain, the Malouin merchants also lost an important strategic connection to the royal court; and, in 1719, John Law revoked Saint-Malo's monopoly in the East Indies trade and transferred it to his newly established trading company.

Few historians would brush aside these developments in external conditions, most of which were beyond the immediate control of the local merchantry. Lespagnol is just as careful in considering the change in circumstances. Still, the lion's share of his explanation for Saint-Malo's decline rests with changes within the merchant community, namely, social mobility and a dramatic upward shift in the lifestyle of the leading trader families. According to the poll tax rolls for 1701, 1710, and 1720, the enormous sums that were forthcoming from their prospering enterprises turned at least a dozen heads of merchant families into millionaires, and at least another thirty-five traders had acquired a taxable wealth of 400,000 *livres tournois* (*lt.*) or more.[44] To be sure, some *nouveau riche* could always be found, such as Italian immigrant Natale Stefanini. Originally coming from Livorno, he had settled in Saint-Malo sometime during the 1690s.[45] Arriving with moderate means, he rapidly made a fortune of up to 400,000 *lt.* from his engagements in privateering partnerships and South Sea ventures and as the *armateur* of at least one voyage "a la Coste de guynéé," presumably as a slave trader. Unfortunately for him, he lost most of his wealth just as quickly. By the time of his death in 1724, he left merely 56,000 *lt.* to share among his heirs and creditors.[46] In contrast to Stefanini and similar social climbers, the majority of the merchant elites came from old money. The returns to their investments in the *course* and overseas trade did more to accelerate the accumulation of wealth that previous generations of their lineages had initiated in the seventeenth century. As the latest generation of merchant dynasties, including the Magon de la Lande, Magon de la Chipaudière, Picot de Clos-Rivière, Baude du Val, Baudran des Chateliers, Hérisson des Chesnais, Le Fer de Beauvais, Eon de la Baronnie, and Locquet de Grandeville, not to forget Danycan de L'Epine, these trader elites represented the often-mentioned *Messieurs de Saint-Malo.* Their riches placed them on an equal footing with royal ministers in their political dealings, and with the country's most influential financiers, such as Antoine Crozat, in their business partnerships.

With prosperity came higher aspirations. As their surnames and titles suggest, these mercantile elites sought to rise into the very ranks of the nobility.[47] Leaving behind the narrow cobbled lanes of the walled city, they built themselves stately manor houses, the *malouinières,* in the surrounding countryside. They indulged in the consumption of luxury goods suited to an aristocratic lifestyle. Carefully arranged marriage alliances of their daughters with sons of the Breton aristocracy were enabled by substantial dowries. They sent their sons to colleges in the capital to prepare them for prestigious careers in the royal administration rather than having them apprenticed at the *comptoirs* in Cadiz or as navigators on board ships. Concerning their own prospects, the heads of these Malouin elite families gradually turned away from shipping and trade, and instead reinvested their capital in landed property and the purchase of offices that came with letters of ennoblement.[48]

Hence, following this conventional narrative, a distinct social logic endogenous to the merchant elite was just as responsible for the crisis of Saint-Malo after 1715 as the shifts in the external economic and political climate. To the extent that Malouin merchant elites sought to extract themselves from the world of commerce and shipping, and succeeded in immersing themselves into the world of the nobility, they eroded the social foundations that made their ascent possible in the first place. Notably, they wore down the social cohesion of their community, based as it was on recurrent business partnerships; their mentality of a *fidélité au commerce* that had become second nature; and the replenishment from within through the vocational training of their sons and nephews in seafaring and trade. Thus, decoupling not only themselves but also their offspring from the world of commerce was probably even more consequential than all the noble titles they acquired, their collections of fine silverware and delicate china, or the sumptuous interior decors of their mansions. There were both exemptions and variation: some elite merchants committed only a small fraction of their wealth to landed property, while others remained firmly planted in the business of overseas trade until the end of their days. Still, the conclusion that André Lespagnol and other historians before him have drawn is that much of the decline of Saint-Malo in the early eighteenth century resulted from a process of excessive status attainment and an ensuing implosion of the merchant elite.[49]

MERCHANT ELITE STRATIFICATION

This narrative of status attainment and elite implosion is the core of the accepted historical explanation of Saint-Malo's declining role in the French Atlantic Economy. The argument and the social mechanism it suggests certainly are plausible, and available evidence seems to lend support as well. Nevertheless, a few important caveats remain. Addressing them is central to a better understanding not just of the particular historical developments at Saint-Malo but also of elite relationships and the emergence of merchant networks at large during the early modern period of mercantilism.[50]

One caveat points to an apparent paradox in the strategic behavior of the Malouin merchant elite. Granted, the esteem and lifestyle of aristocrats must have been attractive to prosperous members of the merchant classes who longed for higher ranks in the social status order of the Ancien Régime. Yet even if they coveted upward mobility into the nobility—why would they leave behind, even undermine, the social relational foundations that enabled their commercial accomplishments in the first place?[51] Just as puzzling, why would they pursue their "flight to the top" at the very moment of their greatest success in the world of commerce?[52] A good starting point to disentangle the seemingly paradoxical behavior is to consider the composition of the merchant trader elite. If the rise into the nobility was so powerful as to be one of the main reasons for the implosion of the group as well as the relative decline of Saint-Malo's economic performance, then all, or at least a sufficiently large number, of merchants should have extracted themselves from their bourgeois background at about the same moment. Such a concerted upward mobility, accomplished as it was within a relatively short period of time in the early eighteenth century, presupposes that they all shared similar interests and aspirations. It also presupposes enough social cohesion for them to act upon this similarity and coordinate their activities. Common interests and aspirations, in turn, usually stem from similarity in the social standing of these merchants, and hence the role they played in local society. In other words, the implication is that the Malouin urban elites shared equivalent positions within the structure of social relationships that mattered—such as kinship and matrimonial ties among families, bonds based on neighborhood, and in particular, the partnership ties they formed in their joint business ventures. The conventional historical narrative of Saint-Malo's waning thus leads us to envision a single, unified trader elite whose members acted en bloc when it came to pursuing their interests and aspirations. Here we have arrived at the next caveat: upon closer inspection a different picture emerges, which suggests that in Saint-Malo's commercial society, as in comparable historical settings, elites seldom constitute a single, coherent group, but rather sort themselves into different, sometimes even competing, interest groups and factions.[53]

To be sure, the leading *armateur* families did have much in common. Recall that they resided within the same neighborhoods. Their ties of religious allegiance were virtually indistinguishable, as they were all fervent Catholics. They also kept similar positions in the kinship network because endogamy dictated their marriage choices. Likewise, apprentices at sea and at trading posts were chosen from within their midst. Even those migrants who, like the Irish, stayed and made Saint-Malo their new home tended to share at least some of these same characteristics and relationship patterns, which smoothed their integration into local society. Still, the Malouin merchants differed markedly in one essential dimension of social space—that is, their wealth, which in turn defined their economic status in local society. Positioning with respect to wealth was essential because it shaped the one activity at the very heart of their identity as overseas merchants, namely forming the partnerships necessary to float and maintain their trading ventures.

The perhaps most useful source for understanding the wealth distribution is the *capitation*, or poll tax, for Saint-Malo and its neighboring communities. The origins of the *capitation* are to be found in the relentless competition between the emerging fiscal-military states of early modern Europe.[54] State-building more often than not meant territorial expansion so that waging war against competing princely state-makers was unavoidable. The pursuit of military ambitions was costly, and while credit was available to the king, his commitment to honoring his debt was not always credible. This situation prompted monarchs to keep finding new means of extracting taxes. Louis XIV established the *capitation* in 1695 to finance the immense costs incurred by the French army during the War of the League of Augsburg (1688–1697). The *capitation* was temporarily abandoned with the end of war in 1697 but was reinstated in 1701. In fact, another direct tax, the *taille*, had been in place as a regular annual payment since the early thirteenth century.[55] It generated little revenue, however, because nearly every person of some privileged stature who did not till the soil—whether clergymen, nobles, royal bureaucrats, or petty officials in the provinces—was at least partially exempted. The result was effectively a redistribution of funds from the lower to the upper ranks of the Ancien Régime. As a universal tax, the *capitation* was radically different because it was an attempt to drain the fountain of privilege:[56] without exception, the tax was to be levied on every single one of the king's subjects, ranging from the "Monseigneur le dauphin" in the first class, who was to contribute 2,000 *lt.*, down to foreign sailors serving on privateering and trading vessels in the lowest class, who paid 1 *lt.*[57]

I next focus on *capitation* rolls that document the head taxes collected from the residents of Saint-Malo in the year 1701.[58] These rolls are ideally suited to examine variation in wealth among the local trader elites at precisely the moment when they enjoyed the peak of their prosperity in maritime commerce, and hence when opportunities for upward mobility presented themselves. The 1701 *capitation* also offers the earliest complete information on their taxable wealth for my period of interest. In the form it was established in 1695, the capitation imposed a fixed classification of taxpayers into twenty-two classes, each subdivided into several ranks, based on the social status order of the Ancien Régime. The first and highest class was divided into twenty ranks, from the Dauphin down to the *fermiers généraux* (officers who ran the general tax farm). Ranks in this first class paid 2,000 *lt.* in taxes. Other classes, such as the twentieth, consisted of up to sixty-two specific ranks, from lieutenants and ensigns of the infantry down to surgeons who served on merchant and privateering ships. A tax of 3 *lt.* was imposed on the ranks in this class. In other words, the *capitation* was a nominal tax, not directly proportional to one's actual revenues, yet meant to reflect the wealth that could be expected of someone who occupied the corresponding position in the status hierarchy.[59]

For my purposes, the one challenge with these tax records is that the members of the urban merchant elite, that is, the *armateurs* and *négociants* whom Lespagnol has called the *Messieurs de Saint-Malo*, were not explicitly listed as such in a taxation category of their own. The upper half of the tax system was filled with the high nobility, positions in the military, and high-ranking officers in the royal administration. Categories that were not directly connected to the state did not appear until rank fourteen (*banquiers expéditionnaires en cour de Rome*) and rank fifteen (*banquiers et agents de change*) in the tenth class. It was only with the eleventh class, and a tax burden of 100 *lt.*, that members of the merchantry were listed, namely *marchands faisant commerce en gros* (wholesale merchants) at rank thirteen.[60] Many of the prominent overseas traders of Saint-Malo, however, were

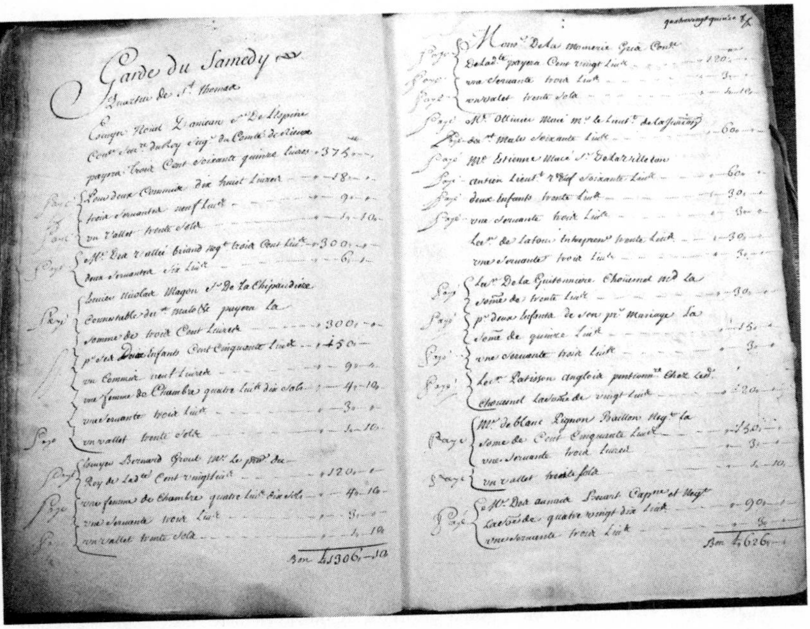

Garde du Samedy
Quartier de St. Thomas

FIGURE 3.2 Extract from poll tax rolls for Saint-Malo, 1701.

Source: *AM-SM* CC41.

not assigned to this or another merchant rank in the *capitation* system. No clear-cut category of *négociants* or *armateurs* seems to have existed in the *capitation*.

Figure 3.2 shows a typical entry from the 1701 *capitation* tax rolls for Saint-Malo.[61] The surviving rolls consist of handwritten sheets, folded into 105 folios, and leather-bound into a single tome. Listed in this excerpt are residents of the *Quartier de St. Thomas*, one of the two preferred intra-muros neighborhoods of the merchant elite, noted earlier. The first entry on the verso in this example is "Escuyer Nouël Danican, Sr. De L'Espine," whose exploits we have encountered before (as with most other names in the records, the spelling of Noël Danycan varied to some extent). In 1701, at the height of his trader career, he paid 375 *lt.* in taxes, placing him firmly in the upper echelon of the city's taxpayers (see figure 3.3). Following Danycan's servants and valets is the entry for another well-known overseas trader and *armateur*, "Escuier Nicolas Magon Sr. De La Chipaudiere" who was assessed at 300 *lt.* What follows is again a list of the other members of the household.[62] At the end of the facing recto, note also how "Mr. de blanc Pignon Baillon" is referred to as a "neg.t," meaning *négociant*,

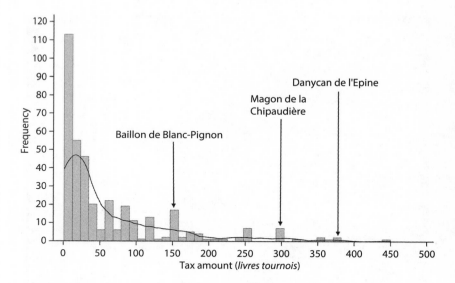

FIGURE 3.3 Variation in wealth within the Saint-Malo merchant elite (poll tax rolls, 1701).

Note: The graph shows the distribution of tax payments for all individual merchant *armateurs* and partners ($n = 368$) who could be identified unambiguously within both the 1701 *capitation* for Saint-Malo and the voyage partnership registers.

Sources: *AM-SM* CC41; *AD-IV* 4E5277-5278; 4E5343; 4E5364; 9B165-176; 9B587.

but the 150 *lt.* he was required to pay placed him in the ninth class, that is, above the highest-ranking merchant category in the eleventh class. Similarly, "Mʳ Des aunais Bezart" is listed as a "Cap.ⁿᵉ et Neg.ᵗ," meaning *capitaine et négociant*. Contemporaries thus must have had some idea what a *négociant* was, but a corresponding category by that name is nowhere to be found in the tax system.[63]

Consequently, although both Noël Danycan and Nicolas Magon were among Saint-Malo's most renowned merchant magnates at the time, neither was explicitly referred to as a *négociant*.[64] One reason could have been tax exemptions for those engaged in maritime commerce. But the fact that they were included in the rolls, albeit not as overseas traders, lends little, if any, support to the exemption idea. The alternative, and more likely, explanation is that they were assessed according to more prestigious functions they fulfilled other than being overseas traders.[65] The lesson is that focusing just on those elite members who were explicitly labeled as *négociants* is likely to yield selectivity and downward biased results with respect to the amount of taxes paid. This selection would exclude the most important and most affluent elite *armateurs* who also held highly prestigious offices—and they often held them precisely because they had been so successful in their trading enterprises. In sum, the official classification of the fiscal hierarchy is of limited help if it is our goal to identify the members of the merchant trader elite and evaluate where they stood in the wealth distribution.

To address these limitations, I rely on a sample of trader elites who appear both in the *capitation* rolls and in the registers of voyage partnership contracts (*actes de société*). Alternative solutions may exist, yet the advantage of this matching procedure is that it selects individual traders based on their observed participation in the share partnerships that they formed to organize long-distance voyages. Because it relies on tangible behavior, this measure avoids mere ascription to some abstract category or class. Recall that the *armateurs* and their investment partners organized their share partnerships to spread the risks associated with long-distance trade and to raise the funds necessary to cover the costs of fitting out their vessel, including victuals and wages for the captain, pilot, officers, and sailors. Additionally, sharing the costs for any single venture freed up funds to sponsor others at the same time.[66]

The matching of tax and partnership records yields a sample of 368 individual *armateurs* and their shareholding partners. Figure 3.3 plots their wealth distribution, according to the amount of taxes they paid in 1701. The histogram and kernel density demonstrate the inequality in wealth among the Malouin merchant traders, based on their poll tax levied in 1701. The resulting pattern reveals a skewed distribution, partitioned into a relatively large group of traders of modest means, taxed at less than 50 *lt.*, followed by a group of middling traders who paid between 50 and 100 *lt.* in taxes. Next came a third layer of well-to-do *armateurs* who reached tax payments ranging between 100 and 200 *lt.*, exemplified by Baillon de Blanc-Pignon. Finally, we find the small, truly elite layer of the most affluent and highest-ranking *haut négoce*, who, like Magon de la Chipaudière and Danycan de l'Épine, were taxed at anywhere between 200 and 450 *lt.*[67] It was this latter exclusive circle whose members, with their extraordinary riches, gave rise to the merchant dynasties of the Eon, Magon, Baude, Le Fer, and Danycan lineages that led Saint-Malo's commercial society. They were the ones who not only had the ambition, but most important, the financial means to adopt an aristocratic lifestyle and eventually to rise into the ranks of the Breton nobility.[68] My point, then, is twofold. First, the *capitation* distribution clearly confirms that a single, unified elite hardly existed at the time when Saint-Malo's commercial success peaked. Instead, we find pronounced elite stratification when it comes to their wealth, despite all the cultural attributes and social ties they otherwise shared. Second, because not everyone among what may still be called the trader elite was a millionaire, few could actually afford to leave commerce behind and seek entry into the aristocracy.[69] Consequently, if the merchantry did not achieve widespread upward mobility, then the excessive status attainment that undoubtedly was pursued by some could hardly be responsible, by itself, for the implosion of the merchant elite at large and for the economic crisis of Saint-Malo.

THE *COURSE* AS ORGANIZATIONAL LINCHPIN

I next consider the consequences of such elite stratification for the organization of commercial ventures, that is, the core activity that defined them as merchant traders. One consequence was that variation in financial abilities translated into variation in the number and types of trading enterprises that they could engage in. Ventures in different trades varied vastly in the funds necessary to furnish a ship and its material supplies, from cloth for sails, ropes, and spare wooden planks to cannons, powder, and ammunition. Funds were also needed to recruit the captain and crew, and to pay for their wages and victuals. To illustrate, the sixteen associates in the partnership for the two-hundred-ton trading vessel *Le Joyeux*, destined for "les Isles d'amerique Espagnolles" in 1709, contributed share values of 2,600, 3,300, 4,222, and 5,000 *lt.* at the lower end, coupled with share values of 12,000, 30,000, 60,000, and up to 153,510 *lt.* at the upper end. To the extent that these contributions suggest the cost of arming the ship, long-distance trading expeditions, such as the one undertaken by the *Joyeux*, were rather expensive propositions for the middling investor. For comparison, the lowest-known contribution to the privateering campaign of the seventy-ton *Bonne Fortune* in 1702 amounted to just 150 *lt.*, and even the largest known contribution was no more than 4,000 *lt.*[70]

Unfortunately, it is notoriously difficult to retrieve reliable information on such fitting costs for a large number of trading and privateering enterprises. Table 3.3 reports systematic evidence on the costs to arm 130 individual ventures from the registers of partnership contracts, supplemented by information published by Lespagnol in his monograph on the *Messieurs de Saint-Malo*.[71] A comparison of these findings confirms that organizing long-distance trade required the mobilization of substantially greater sums: more than eight times the average cost per ton of routine fishing ventures, and still more than six times the average cost per ton for commerce raiding campaigns of *corsaires*. Hence, purchasing shares in either Newfoundland fishing voyages or in privateering campaigns was apparently possible for members of all merchant strata, even for those traders

TABLE 3.3 Fitting Costs of Voyages in Major Trades, 1682–1725

	NUMBER OF VOYAGE PARTNERSHIPS	COSTS PER TON (IN *LIVRES TOURNOIS*)				
		MEAN	STD. DEV.	MEDIAN	MIN.	MAX.
Newfound-land fishing	36	171.56	79.22	172	8	320
Course	26	212.88	76.22	227.5	6	335
Spanish trade and *long cours*	68	1,433.21	939.19	1,403	15	3,866
Total	130	839.76	922.18	279	6	3,866

Sources: AD-IV 4E5277-5278; 4E5343; 9B165-168; 9B587; Lespagnol (1991).
Note: The category *long cours* includes ventures to China, India, Spanish America, the West Indies, Guinea, and South Sea interloping. Fitting costs are not deflated because the distribution of voyage partnerships across years in the 1682–1725 period follows a similar pattern for all three branches of overseas enterprise.

whose commitments were restricted by modest funds. In contrast, this cost comparison also suggests that opportunities for investment in long-distance trade entailed much higher barriers to entry for those groups with middling and lower financial abilities among Saint-Malo's mercantile community. Given the large sums required as starting capital, the high-risk and potentially high-return adventures into the South Sea, or toward the promising markets of India and China, seemed to have been the preserve of Saint-Malo's most potent entrepreneurs.

No matter how rich in resources some of them may have been, the *armateurs* generally did not attempt to float their enterprises single-handedly. As we have seen, to mobilize the capital necessary to sponsor their trading voyages, shipowners sought business partners (*engagés* or *associés*) who would buy shares (*actions*) in the projected enterprise. The shares usually equaled between a half and one-thirty-second of the monetary value of all contributions to a venture. In some cases, they were divided into ever smaller proportions, down to 1/256 of the sum of all shares.[72] Thanks to these subdivisions, shares of lower value could be resold more easily to interested third parties.[73]

Beyond capital mobilization and risk reduction, the creation of share partnerships for vessels (*sociétés de navire*) offered opportunities for younger traders to put into practice the expertise, detailed knowledge, and skills they had acquired during their apprenticeships. They also provided a tangible social organizational nexus that had the potential to connect partners from the various strata of the Malouin merchantry within a collective undertaking. Great *armateurs* like Danycan de l'Epine routinely sponsored a multitude of enterprises at once, both as initiators of their own ventures and as shareholding *associés* in the partnerships of their peers. Yet again, for every Danycan or Magon, flush as they were with money, one could find numerous merchants of more humble means who could afford only to invest in a limited number of low-cost voyages. Thanks to the system of share partnerships, even those with more limited funds than a Danycan or Magon were in a position to become investors and to diversify their contributions, however small, across more than just a single lucrative enterprise. They usually achieved such diversification—or polyvalence, as Lespagnol and other historians have called the phenomenon—by simultaneously taking out smaller shares of one-sixteenth or one-thirty-second in multiple enterprises. For example, between 1,500 and 2,000 *lt.* were usually sufficient to acquire a one-sixteenth interest in a standard Newfoundland fishing campaign. In other words, the potential for cohesion across the various elite strata existed through the organizational device of share partnerships. In the long run, however, extensive polyvalence in investment interests became primarily a tool in the hands of the richest overseas entrepreneurs, the *haut négoce*.[74]

The link between variation in fitting costs and variation in wealth is well reflected in the different branches of commerce, including the *course*, that merchants engaged in, depending on their standing in the taxation hierarchy. In table 3.4, I rely on evidence from the 368 Malouin merchants I identified unambiguously in both the partnership records and in the 1701 *capitation* records for Saint-Malo. To distinguish merchant strata, I opted for a parsimonious partition of these cases into three groups, according to the amount of poll taxes they were required to pay: below the median tax paid (less than 30 *lt.*) to capture the lower end of the ranking; between the median and the seventy-fifth percentile of the observed payments (30–90 *lt.*); and any value above the seventy-fifth percentile (more than 90 *lt.*).[75] To put these amounts in perspective, the median of 30 *lt.* corresponds to the sixteenth class in the *capitation*, which included shopkeepers or merchants who traded grain, wine, and wood. Below them, assessed at 20 *lt.*, we find captains of merchant and privateering vessels that carried twenty or fewer cannons. The middle group included privileged wine merchants in the fourteenth class (50 *lt.*) and bourgeois residents of larger urban centers who could live off their private income in the thirteenth class (60 *lt.*). Finally, the high-ranking group entailed wholesale merchants (*marchands faisant commerce en gros*) in the eleventh class (100 *lt.*).[76]

TABLE 3.4 Taxpaying *Armateurs* and Their Investments in Major Trades

TAXPAYING RANK	NUMBER OF INDIVIDUAL MERCHANTS	NUMBER OF INVESTMENTS IN BRANCHES OF OVERSEAS TRADE[†]						NUMBER OF INVESTMENTS PER MERCHANT		
		CABOTAGE	NEWFOUNDLAND FISHING	COURSE	SPANISH TRADE	LONG COURS	TOTAL	MEAN (SD)	MEDIAN	MAX.
Low (percent)	172 (46.74)	22 (5.88)	147 (39.30)	156 (41.71)	21 (5.61)	28 (7.49)	374 (100)	3.041 (3.378)	1	23
Mid (percent)	100 (27.17)	4 (0.86)	145 (31.18)	217 (46.67)	31 (6.67)	68 (14.62)	465 (100)	5.970 (6.975)	4	35
High (percent)	96 (26.09)	9 (1.20)	177 (23.66)	358 (47.86)	70 (9.36)	134 (17.91)	748 (100)	10.771 (10.948)	6	45
Total (percent)	368 (100)	35 (2.21)	469 (29.55)	731 (46.06)	122 (7.69)	230 (14.49)	1,587 (100)	5.853 (7.714)	3	45

Sources: AM-SM CC41; AD-IV 4E5277-5278; 4E5343; 4E5364; 9B165-176; 9B587.

Note: Included are all individual merchant *armateurs* and partners ($n = 368$) who could be identified both in the 1701 capitation for Saint-Malo and the voyage partnership registers. The calculation of the mean number of investments per merchant includes investments for which information on the branch of trade is missing. Consequently, dividing the total number of investments reported in the table by the number of individual merchants yields lower means than those shown in the table (e.g., for the low taxpaying rank, $374/172 = 2.174 < 3.041$).

Low rank, if tax < 30 *livres tournois* (less than median tax payment)

Mid rank, if tax = 30 – 90 *livres tournois*

High rank, if tax > 90 *livres tournois* (greater than seventy-fifth percentile of tax payments)

[†] chi ($df = 8$) = 114.5503; $p = .000$

Precisely because many merchants diversified their investments, spreading them across a number of different partnerships, the same individual taxpayers may have contributed to more than one voyage and more than one branch of commerce. The right-hand side of table 3.4 documents the scale of investments per individual merchant. A pattern emerges that is consistent with other findings presented so far. Merchant partners in the lower taxation rank invested in three ventures, on average. Their peers in the middle range invested in about twice as many, and those in the highest rank invested in more than three times as many enterprises. The same positive association between poll tax paid and the number of investments holds, whether we consider the median number—to account for skewness in the distribution—or the maximum number of voyages sponsored. The ninety-six merchants in the highest rank represented the smallest group, yet they sponsored the largest number of ventures. In contrast, the 172 merchants in the lowest rank formed the largest group, yet they sponsored the smallest number of ventures. As expected, the level of engagement in maritime trade increased with wealth, as merchants gained the financial means to purchase shares in partnerships.

Finally, we may ask: what branches of commerce did the merchants in different taxpaying ranks invest in? The pattern in the center of table 3.4 also aligns with previous results. To ease interpretation, I have arranged the branches of commerce from left to right according to their increasing fitting costs. Merchants who ranked at the lower end of the taxation scale (below 30 *lt.*) focused their interest on ventures to the left-hand side of the table, that is, the relatively low-cost coastal trade (*cabotage*), and in particular, fishing voyages to Newfoundland and privateering campaigns. Together, these three branches accounted for 87 percent of their investments, whereas these merchants showed only limited interest in costly long-distance expeditions or the commerce with Spain. For merchants in the middle-ranked group, interests shifted to the right-hand side of table 3.4. The number of investments in Newfoundland fishing was still substantial, but the *course* was the primary focus of their attention. Their enthusiasm for the mundane *cabotage* was lukewarm at best. Instead, merchants in this group became more interested in a sizeable number of the high-cost, high-return *long cours* ventures as well as the Spanish trade. Moving to the highest-ranking taxpayers, investments in the coastal trade continued to be few, and relatively speaking, engagements in Newfoundland fishing were at their lowest. Together, the two branches accounted for barely a quarter of all of the partnerships that these most affluent traders sponsored. In contrast, this group displayed the greatest enthusiasm for privateering enterprise, as well as for the more costly, yet potentially more rewarding, Spanish and long-distance trades.

In sum, the members of the merchant community of Saint-Malo certainly had much in common when it came to their social relations and cultural leanings. As merchants, however, commerce was their natural habitat, and it was their engagements as traders that defined their identity. Within this economic realm, they differed markedly, most notably in their taxable wealth, and thus in their ability to sponsor trading and privateering voyages. Naturally, the most affluent merchants preferred enterprises that may have been costly, yet promised substantial gains in return. Those with modest means focused their efforts on more affordable investments in "bread-and-butter" trades that offered lower, yet steady, returns.

I am not the first to note that the Malouin merchants differed in their financial abilities. My point, however, is not merely an existence proof of elite stratification. The more general lesson is that local elites, here as in comparable settings, rarely consisted of a single, unified bloc whose members shared equivalent positions in the networks that mattered and thus supposedly shared similar interests and behaviors. Instead, we typically find that elites sorted themselves into different, often competing, factions. In the case of Saint-Malo, much of the sorting was based on economic positioning. We also know that social cohesion, and in particular the propensity to form associations, was vital to the prosperity of the Malouin merchant elite.[77] If cohesion was so critical for the formation of partnerships, and yet the merchant community splintered into different strata that were far from structurally equivalent, we have to wonder how they could bridge the economic differences that separated them. This is precisely the place where an organizational linchpin would provide a platform to mediate between these elite strata and integrate them into a collective enterprise. An organizational linchpin within the network of voyage partnerships thus is comparable in its role to brokers and mediators who forge indirect ties between two or more otherwise unconnected persons within their social networks. Through this bridging function, both facilitate and contribute to cohesion. This particular historical setting is a case in point to illustrate the workings of such linchpin organizations. The evidence in tables 3.3 and 3.4 suggests that the clear candidate for a linchpin role in the organizational network of Saint-Malo was the *course*. No matter how we look at the results, privateering ventures consistently occupied a middle ground between the lower and the upper end of the distribution, whether considering the cost to arm individual ventures (table 3.3) or looking at the correlations with poll tax payments or the sheer number of investments (table 3.4). The relatively low fitting costs that privateering campaigns incurred made them attractive to merchants with fewer funds. Compared with other branches of commerce, the nature of the *course* was apparently more democratic, in the sense that these partnerships tended to offer various small shares for an investment.

In this historical context, as elsewhere, people acted on such incentives so that privateering ventures attracted greater numbers and a more diverse social composition of shareholding partners than most other regular trade ventures.[78] At the same time, the prospect of potentially immense returns stirred the interest of more affluent trader elites. Indeed, the *course*, with its promises of both profit and glory, seems to have been the one enterprise that elicited commitments from almost every corner of the local commercial society. In particular, in table 3.4, the *course* consistently attracted the largest number of investments from members of all three taxation ranks. Relative to other kinds of ventures, the *course* thus had the greatest potential as a linchpin organization uniting traders from various strata in a collective enterprise, and allowing those with fewer resources to attach themselves to those who were more affluent. Hence, the *course* enabled both merchant strata to take on even more ambitious enterprises in the long run.[79] Chapter 7 examines precisely this launching pad role of the *course* for the unfolding of individual merchant careers in commerce. The flipside of this organizational linchpin—that is, its weakening, erosion, or disappearance—may well have proven to be disastrous for that vital social cohesion among the various trader elites, and ultimately for the economic prospects of a port city like Saint-Malo. Substantively, then, if we want to understand the waxing and waning of such a central port in the early modern French Atlantic Economy, I propose a shift in attention from the motives and excessive status attainment of a few leading merchant traders to a question of endogenous organizational change. In a nutshell, when ventures like the *course* offered an organizational platform for mediation between different merchant groups, social cohesion was likely to ensue. That same cohesive social fabric was just as likely to unravel once the linchpin organizations between merchant strata were absent. Before turning to direct empirical evidence for the mediating linchpin role of the *course* in chapter 6, we first will familiarize ourselves with the historical origins of privateering enterprise, in particular, how it was organized along the lines of venture partnerships (*sociétés*) in France under the Ancien Régime.

CHAPTER 4

THE *COURSE*

Its Origins and Organization

I n chapter 2, we caught a glimpse of the nature of the *course*, or privateering enterprise, as a wartime opportunity. But what exactly did it mean when ship-owning traders and their business partners armed a vessel for a privateering campaign, "pour faire la Course Sur les Ennemies de L'Etat [*sic*]?"[1] At this point, it is useful to consider the historical origins of the *course*, its legal regulations, and its organization by local *armateurs* and their business partners. Eighteenth-century legal scholar Georg Friedrich von Martens has defined the *course*, or privateering as

> the expeditions of private individuals during war, who, being provided with a special permission from one of the belligerent powers, fit out at their own expense, one or more vessels, with the principal design of attacking the enemy, and preventing neutral subjects or friends from carrying on with the enemy a commerce regarded as illicit.[2]

Further attempts at defining corsairs and privateers, the *guerre de course* and privateering enterprise are legion. In his comparative study of the *guerre d'escadre* and the *guerre de course* as strategic means of seapower under the reign of Louis XIV, Geoffrey Symcox has emphasized the extent to which the *course* was a decentralized instrument of naval warfare. As privateers took the lead, control naturally moved from royal authority into the hands of private entrepreneurs. Accordingly, Symcox notes that

> the *course* is essentially a form of economic warfare, and it is admirably adapted to being waged by privateers licensed by the state; the prizes that they take

reward them for their investment and for the risks they run. In privateer warfare, the economic interests of the individual shipowners (or *armateurs*) will naturally take precedence over the wider interests of the state. [. . .] An individual shipowner or captain is licensed by the state to attack its enemies, wherever they may be found. His activities are thus legitimised and sanctioned by the state, and it is the possession of a "letter of marque" or commission from a recognised authority that distinguishes him from a pirate.[3]

Other scholars have resorted to entries in reputable national dictionaries. We may follow the lead of historian Richard Pares who referenced the *Oxford English Dictionary*, which defines a privateer as "an armed vessel owned and officered by private persons, and holding a commission from the Government, called letters of marque, authorizing the owners to use it against a hostile nation, and especially in the capture of merchant shipping."[4]

Setting aside differences in nuance, the essential ingredients of these various definitions tend to be the same. To summarize, as its expression in English— privateering—indicates, the *course* was primarily an enterprise undertaken and paid for by private parties for economic gains. Exceptions did exist, but the *course* was less often the preserve of public, princely, or state action. Furthermore, it was bound by legal regulations, including the provision of a commission, enforceable rules of conduct, and the judgement of captured vessels and cargo as just prizes by specific courts. All of these provisions separated the commerce raids of *corsaires*, or privateers, from the illicit pursuits of pirates for whom apparently there were no bounds. Those who—at least in the minds of their opponents—did not distinguish between ally, neutral and foe, when attacking their prey were treated as pirates. As bandits at sea, they operated entirely on their own accord, outside of local laws and typically without sanction by a sovereign. In contrast, the target of the *course* was limited to enemy vessels and illicit trading of neutrals, which meant that it was considered a legal activity only during times of declared war.[5]

An even deeper understanding of the nature of the private war at sea may be gained if we turn our attention toward its historical roots. Countless films, novels, and historical epics grant center stage to corsairs, pirates, privateers, *flibustiers*, and *Barbaresques*, more often than not conflating these terms. Little may distinguish one from the other in the popular mind, with all of them conjuring romantic images of swashbuckling heroes and dramatic sea battles. History, in contrast, paints a more fine-grained portrait of these various forms of exploits at sea. As naval historian Nicholas Rodger has reminded us, distinct meanings are attached to these words, which themselves are embedded in their particular place and time.[6]

One historical trace of the words *course* and *corsaire* leads us back to the religiously tinged conflicts that pitted Byzantium, the Ottoman Empire, and western Christian maritime powers against each other in the late medieval and early modern Mediterranean world. In this setting, we encounter the Muslim corsairs of the Barbary coast. The *Barbaresques*, as they were called in French, supplemented the Ottoman navy and, at the same time, mounted attacks on Christian trade shipping on their own account, launching them from their North African bases at Tripoli, Tunis, and Algiers. Some historians debate whether they should be considered pirates, rather than corsairs.[7] In as much as they were authorized by the Ottoman government and constrained by the rules of conduct it enforced, the *Barbaresques* indeed were corsairs, in the sense of legally bounded raiders at sea. Their counterparts on the Christian side primarily were the Knights of Malta. Originally one of the religious military orders established during the Crusades, the Knights Hospitaller of Saint John of Jerusalem were granted the island of Malta by the Holy Roman Emperor Charles V in 1530, following their expulsion from their erstwhile seat on the island of Rhodes. The knights evolved into the leading Christian corsair force that confronted the Barbary corsairs who threatened Spanish shipping and outposts in the Mediterranean. At the same time, the Maltese corsairs continued their lucrative business of preying on the trading vessels that traveled along the Levant on their routes from Egypt to Constantinople. The Maltese Knights may be considered corsairs because they were held accountable for their actions by the Grand Master of the Order, the political ruler of Malta.[8] Against this Mediterranean backdrop, we thus find variants of the word *corso* to have been in common use, as in *il corso* in Italian, *faire la course* in French, or *korsan* in Ottoman Turkish, whereas *pirata* in Italian or *pirate* in French were apparently known, but much less commonly used, by contemporaries.[9] Some historians have suggested to reserve the term *corso* for the Mediterranean conflict between Christian and Muslim corsairs and to distinguish this pursuit both from piracy as an illicit activity and from the *guerre de course*, or privateering war, that is, as a form of naval warfare, in which the state permits private entrepreneurs to participate for profit, yet at their own expense and placed within the bounds of law.[10]

Moving beyond the specific Mediterranean setting of the *corso*, the link between the state and private *armateurs* points to the first of three more historical sources of privateering enterprise—namely, the employment of corsairs as auxiliary forces besides the ships of the regular royal navy.[11] In the beginning of the early modern period, when royal fleets were just about to emerge as the kingdoms they supported began to expand, reliance on privately funded and armed vessels looked like an economically sound way to supplement regular naval forces.

In particular, once undermining the commerce of competing states had become a priority of wartime strategy, privateers appeared to be an indispensable instrument to uphold trade blockades whenever regular ships of the royal navy were preoccupied with other duties or were ill-suited to chase merchant vessels that had managed to escape through enemy lines. The enlistment of privately outfitted vessels blurred the boundary between public war, waged by kings and fledgling states for military purposes, and private war at sea for commercial purposes. One consequence was that "privateers had sometimes acted as the Royal Navy, and at other times the Royal Navy had been lent for privateering."[12] The combination of public and private naval warfare further implied that the "essential distinction between a king's ship and a privateer was financial; a ship armed with private capital was a privateer, even if she might be a vessel on hire from the fleet."[13]

A second source of what became privateering enterprise was the right, or rather custom, of reprisals as it had been practiced in Europe since medieval times.[14] In French, this practice was known as the *droit de Représailles*. To illustrate, imagine a merchant trader of Saint-Malo whose ship, along with his valuable cargo of, say, Breton linen, had been robbed by an English vessel during peacetime. Our Malouin trader may have first appealed to an English court that this was an act of unlawful robbery at sea. Most likely, he would have been unsuccessful in getting a just treatment in the foreign court. As a subject of the French king, he nevertheless could have applied to his own sovereign for a letter of marque and reprisal (*lettre de marque et de représaille*). Once granted, the letter would have entitled our trader from Saint-Malo to seek redress by fitting out a private vessel and then to seize as much property from subjects of the English king as needed to recover his losses. Before such a letter was granted, any aggrieved party—in this case, the Malouin trader—needed to produce before the nearest judge of the Admiralty sufficient evidence concerning the value of his ship and the goods that had been taken. Two points are important as they emphasize how clearly the original concept of reprisals differed from the concept of the *course*, or privateering, as introduced by the definitions at the start of this chapter. First, to be considered an unlawful robbery, for which a letter of reprisal was warranted, the event must have taken place during peacetime, and not during war ("les Vaisseaux et autres Effets auront été pris ou arrêtés hors le fait de la guerre").[15] Second, the right of reprisal was a widely recognized legal instrument for aggrieved individuals to recover personal losses. As such, it prevented the escalation of a private conflict between robber and robbed into an armed public conflict between kingdoms or states. Only later, during the sixteenth and seventeenth centuries, did the original meaning of the letter of marque change. What had been a license of reprisals for private losses during peacetime evolved into a commission for private *armateurs* to arm vessels for raiding any enemy ships during times of declared public war. These later privateering commissions may have been called letters of marque and reprisal, but any requirements to document the actual losses one had suffered were nominal at best.[16] The unfortunate consequence is that we find two kinds of letters of marque in history, with two rather distinct meanings attached.[17]

A third source of the *course* and privateering was the extension of the concept of reprisals to the arming of merchant vessels. The primary objective of these ships was long-distance trade, while seizing prizes was only a secondary aim of their enterprise. The *armateurs* of these armed merchantmen took out commissions for two main reasons.[18] The first reason was self-protection. Entirely peaceful trade at sea was the exception rather than the rule, even in times of nominal peace and the absence of armed conflicts between states. Assaults on trading vessels were thus common occurrences, and their owners were well advised to have them armed in case the defense of cargo and ship was necessary. The second reason for carrying commissions was that a successful self-defense of a merchantman might have resulted in taking the attacking vessel as a prize. Without a proper *course* commission, however, the *armateur* of the merchant ship and his business associates had no legal title to any prize captured by their captain and his crew. The *armateur* therefore had good reason to register a prize-taking commission before his vessel left port.[19] In the case of these armed merchant ships, the commissions were called *guerre et marchandise*, which translates roughly as war and trade. Note also that the sequence of prize-taking events was reversed with the advent of the *guerre et marchandise* commissions. The original notion of reprisals entailed an *ex post* reasoning, essentially a compensation for losses a trader had suffered in the past. In contrast, the *guerre et marchandise* commission was meant, at least initially, as an *ex ante* assurance of rightful gains that might arise in the future, following the attacks of pirates, enemy war ships, or privateers.[20] What further distinguished these armed merchantmen from proper corsairs was the payment of wages to the seamen on board.[21] In return, crew members were not entitled to a share of the potential prize money (although it was not unheard of that some of them received a part of the proceeds as an additional reward). Their peers who served on private men-of-war usually did not receive wages (although some did), but one-third of the net prize value, once all administrative fees had been deducted. In addition, some merchant *armateurs* were prepared to offer their seamen advances to compensate for delays in the official adjudication and liquidation of prizes.[22]

In sum, commerce raiding in our period of interest came in three different guises. One was the *guerre de course*, as it was sometimes pursued by regular navy ships alongside their primary objectives, such as engaging the enemy's warships, maintaining blockades, and defending their merchants' trade. Second, proper corsairs were privately outfitted men-of-war that engaged exclusively in the *guerre de course* during times of declared war. The third type, as we have seen, were armed merchantmen that usually were instructed by their owners to priv- ilege trade. Yet, they also carried commissions of *guerre et marchandise* to seize prizes in a legal manner should the opportunity arise.

The popularity of arming both corsairs, pure and simple, as well as *guerre et marchandise* ventures suggests an alignment of interests between the early modern state and its emerging merchant classes.[23] Where royal policies of com- merce were driven by mercantilist principles, the ruler of a maritime power like France would have preferred the export of French goods and manufactures over imports of foreign wares to strengthen the country's economic wealth. Following the same mercantilist view, the overall volume of trade was regarded as limited, leading to a zero-sum game of commercial expansion in which a state gained a competitive advantage if its government increased the trade of its merchants at the expense of competing powers. It is thus little surprising that armed conflicts between early modern states often were born out of commercial rivalries.[24] When state-building monarchs adopted mercantilist strategies, privateering enterprise offered an ideal instrument of economic warfare.[25] Directed as its raids were against foreign commerce, the *course* was ideally suited to the ruler's interest in eroding the enemy's export trade. Furthermore, waging war in the seventeenth and eighteenth centuries quickly drained the king's coffers[26]—all the more rea- son for the royal government to encourage *armateurs* to fit out private men-of- war at their own expense, and at a limited cost for the state. To be sure, for the *armateurs* and their business partners, the *course* resembled a lottery rather than a steady flow of returns to investments. Yet, the scale of privateering in places like Saint-Malo reveals their preference for the *course* as a welcome opportunity to render profits in times of war, when otherwise routine branches of trade were interrupted.[27] Hence, the *course* became an enterprise for which the interests of rulers and private merchants came into alignment.

This is not to say that privateering was devoid of any costs to the state, nor that corsairs and ships of the merchant and royal navy fleets did not compete with each other. Some of the more persistent complaints leveled against privateers concerned prize money and the shortage of suitable ships and skilled seamen.[28] Recall that ships of his majesty's navy were allowed just as much as private parties to take prizes should the opportunity arise, although it was not supposed to be their main task.[29] Given that prize money was an important source of income for naval officers, it seems safe to assume that competition from privateers in the prize game was not met with much enthusiasm. Along similar lines was the complaint that privateers would empty the market for the best ships, a competition that must have been felt particularly hard in times of war when losses of vessels increased. Finally, it was not uncommon that corsairs were accused of luring able seamen away from service in the royal navy as well as from the merchant marine. Competition from privateers thus supposedly fueled a notorious manning problem of the navy. Historians, however, have noted that privateering did very little to augment the manning problem of the French navy. During the Seven Years' War, far fewer trained sailors were attracted to the *course* as has been assumed previously. At worst, the lure of lucrative service on private men-of-war imposed some rather limited strains on the recruitment of able seamen for French merchant ships. Likewise, some vessels that were intended for merchant shipping may have ended up in privateering campaigns. In general, *armateurs* at leading trading ports, such as Bordeaux, La Rochelle, and Lorient, showed little interest for the *course*. Even in that hotbed of privateering, Dunkirk, it attracted primarily foreign sailors and elements from the less desirable corners of society, but rarely French classed seamen.[30] Despite these various arguments against and in favor of the *guerre de course*, the sheer number of corsairs that were fitted out in Saint-Malo and other ports attest to its lasting appeal among the merchantry.

THE HISTORY AND MEANING OF PARTNERSHIPS

Good reasons thus existed for merchant *armateurs* to be drawn to the *course*. Practically speaking, we have to ask how they went about organizing a commerce raiding venture. In chapters 2 and 3, we discussed that the private shareholding partnership was the instrument of choice for merchants to float privateering and long-distance trading enterprises alike. The Malouins under the Ancien Régime were not the first to rely on partnerships as the preferred means of financing their seafaring ventures. In ancient Rome, the *societas* constituted one of the earliest forms of partnership contracts. Byzantine and Islamic traders alike pooled resources as associates to co-sponsor long-distance ventures, and so did the merchants of Venice, Amalfi, Genoa, or Marseille when they established their maritime trading firms during the Commercial Revolution of the Middle Ages.[31]

The historical precursors to the voyage partnerships as they were practiced in early modern Saint-Malo and other French ports came in various guises. Two contractual arrangements, the *commenda* and the *compagnia*, were particularly instrumental for the growth of trading networks in late-medieval Europe. Widespread among traders in the medieval Mediterranean was the use of the *commenda* contract, called *collegantia* in Venice, and known in other places as *societas maris*. Most likely, this type of contract was a blend of business techniques borrowed from manifold sources, such as the Greco-Roman *societas*, the Byzantine *chreokoinonia*, the Jewish *'isqa* financial partnership, and the Muslim *qirad* contract.[32] The *commenda* entailed a two-sided contractual arrangement between, on the one hand, one or more partners, known as *commendatores*, who invested their capital in the venture and remained in place, and, on the other hand, one or more traveling partners, known as *tractatores*, who carried out the partnership's business in markets overseas, using the invested capital. The partnership was usually set up for the short-term purpose of a single trading voyage across the Mediterranean, which routinely took several months to complete. In its unilateral form, the *commenda* was an early case of the division between capital and labor because only one side of the partnership, the investing *commendatores*, provided the capital, whereas the other side contributed local knowledge of distant markets, trading, and perhaps navigation skills. Accordingly, the *commendatores* bore full liability for the loss of capital and, by the conclusion of the voyage, received three-quarters of the profit. Apart from the potential loss of their time and efforts in the event of an unsuccessful venture, the traveling *tractatores* bore no liability for losses of capital. In the case of successful business, they received one-quarter of the profit for their services. In the bilateral *commenda*, as early evidence from eleventh-century Venetian sources attests, the *tractatores* also contributed capital to the venture, usually half of the amount supplied by the *commendatores*. Consequently, both parties shared liabilities for any loss of capital in proportion to their investments such that *commendatores* bore two-thirds of losses and *tractatores* bore one-third. Any profit was divided equally between the two parties in a bilateral *commenda* arrangement.[33]

One can see why the *commenda* was favored as a flexible instrument for maritime commerce in this place and time. A trading voyage usually included an outbound leg toward some destination and an inbound leg when the ship returned with imported commodities. Drafting separate contracts for each voyage thus made sense. The short-term contract of the *commenda* also offered an opportunity for both parties in the partnership to test their mutual commitment in case they had not collaborated before. Trust thus had a chance to grow within a limited undertaking before both partners were prepared to continue the business relationship.[34] Likewise, the division of ownership and management into shares in the venture was an appropriate way to spread the risks inherent to traveling and trading across the seas.

Away from the coast, merchants who sought their fortunes in overland trade used a different form of partnership contract, known as the *compagnia*.[35] As a number of scholars have suggested, the *compagnia* was originally a family-based enterprise wherein close relatives—father, sons, and brothers—shared nearly everything: their bread (*cum panis* in Latin), their household, and their business interests. Real estate owned by the family helped members to secure credit and capital for investments in trade. In contrast to the short-lived *commenda*, the typical *compagnia* was a long-lasting enterprise, modeled on family lineage. Successive generations of the same family renewed their *compagnia*'s contract and maintained control of its capital and organization. Because they shared strong bonds of kinship solidarity, all partners were prepared to contribute both capital and labor to their venture and to share both the risks and liabilities their business activities entailed.[36]

Similar trading-houses could be found elsewhere across Europe, but the *compagnia* was initially the predominant form of business contract in the interior cities of Tuscany, such as Siena, Lucca, Prato, or Florence.[37] Because direct access to maritime commerce often proved difficult, the concentration of capital within such family-run firms was probably instrumental in gaining a foothold in Mediterranean trading networks. As they prospered and grew, the *compagnia* firms eventually came to include non-kin associates as business partners, and preferably those with substantial capital and competence to contribute. The well-documented case of Francesco di Marco Datini, the great medieval merchant of Prato, and his various enterprises is a prime example to show that business partners more often than not resided in places as far-flung from Tuscany as Bruges, Barcelona, Avignon, Montpellier, Genoa, Majorca, or Valencia. Datini's diverse business activities thus revealed that merchants sought to cast a wide net that entangled their agents, associates, and clients, and yet the *compagnia*'s hallmark—joint and unlimited liability of all investing and managing partners—remained intact.[38]

Putting aside their differences, both contractual arrangements, the maritime *commenda* and the land-based *compagnia*, offered considerable efficiency gains precisely because they were organized as partnerships, and in particular, when they included partners who operated in distant trading centers. Without such associates, a merchant would have to travel on his own to sell his wares in far-away marketplaces. The financial resources to organize his business, the time and risk of travel, and the costs of transacting in often little-known markets would have been the merchant's own responsibility. Quite literally, putting all of one's eggs into a single basket ran the risk of losing one's entire wealth. In contrast, having one or more business partners offered the advantage that the capital, knowledge, and complementary skills necessary to float a venture could be pooled. Likewise, within partnerships, the risks of long-distance trade were shouldered by more than just a single merchant. The division of labor between those who invested the capital and those who did the trading enabled ambitious enterprises that neither partner could have undertaken in a profitable manner without the others. The pooling of resources through partnerships also expanded opportunities for trade because merchants could spread smaller amounts across different businesses and markets, and thus diversify their activities.[39] Francesco di Marco Datini once again serves as an exemplar. From his Tuscan base, he directed his numerous business ventures across the continent, dealing (1) in money as a merchant-banker; (2) in the trade of wool from England; (3) in the import of jewelry, blades, and leather from Spain; lambskins from Sardinia; spices from the Levant; and precious metals, sandalwood, and slaves from the Balkans and the Black Sea; and (4) in the export of Tuscan cloth, cotton veils, silk, and other luxury wares to Paris and Avignon. In the words of Iris Origi, the international trader in the vein of Datini "was prepared to take great risks, but diminished them by spreading them over the widest possible field; he acquainted himself with foreign languages and foreign ways, adapted himself to the needs of foreign markets, was both merchant and banker, dealt simultaneously in both wholesale and retail trade."[40]

Such variety and spread in commercial undertakings was not the sole preserve of medieval merchants like Datini. Even today, similar business strategies can be found in the diverse investment portfolios of multiasset funds. Likewise, Origi's portrayal is just as fitting for early modern Saint-Malo, whose merchant *armateurs* preferred to distribute their capital across multiple trading and privateering ventures and did so with multiple partners. Recall the numerous expeditions to the Canadian cod-fishing grounds; the South Sea, East Indies, and West Indies sugar islands; and the African slaving outports. Note also the privateering cruises that were launched and sponsored by Magon de la Lande, Magon de la Chipaudière, Danycan de L'Epine, and later Grandclos Meslé, Le Breton de Blessin, and Sébire des Saudrais, to name a few among the Malouin mercantile elite.[41]

Organizing ventures as partnerships did not merely encourage the expansion of trade through risk-sharing and an efficient pooling of resources and skills. Unfortunately, it also created incentives for opportunistic behavior, especially in long-distance undertakings for which effective means to contain fraud often were limited. Once the traveling partner had set sail, he had an incentive to pursue his own interests, which did not necessarily align with those of his merchant investors who stayed behind in their home port. First, he could have just fled with all the capital and commodities entrusted to him by his partners. Second, even if he did proceed with the trading transactions as planned, he could have exploited his information advantage when it came to local knowledge about far-flung marketplaces: he could have misreported the true balance of gains and losses upon his return, and then filled his own pockets at the expense of his partners. Third, he could have engaged in similar fraudulent behavior, yet this time he might have colluded with one of the principal investors in betraying the remaining partners. Further scenarios can be imagined, but most readers probably recognize the situation as an instance of the familiar principal-agent relationship.[42] At its heart lies a commitment problem. Again, in the case of medieval and early modern voyage partnerships, merchants could not expect immediate returns on their investments in a venture because it took ship and crew weeks, months, and sometimes even years to reach their destination and then return to their home port. In addition, monitoring agents over great distances proved to be exceedingly difficult. It follows that considerable trust had to be placed into the traveling partner's good intentions while en route. Bilateral trust was probably a necessary, but not sufficient, ingredient of long-distance venture partnerships. In some circumstances, written contracts offered a more suitable remedy for agency problems. Before their ship's departure, the partners thus would underwrite an agreement that spelled out rights and obligations and that regulated how the proceeds of the venture would be distributed among the partners. Still, the empirical evidence, then and now, suggests that even the most well-thought-out contracts would have limits, leaving loopholes for agents to exploit them for personal gain. The critical issue was how credible each partner's commitment to the terms of the agreement really was. If partners were unable to commit in a credible manner, the probability of opportunism increased at the cost of decreasing trust. Consequently, with commitment unresolved, investors refrained from entering partnerships, and transactions were bound to fail.[43]

The important challenge, then, for our traders was how they could reap the efficiency gains of partnerships and, at the same time, rein in the potential for opportunistic behavior. When simple mutual trust and bilateral contracts were not sufficient, more effective enforcement was in order. In various historical settings, formal institutional arrangements, run by large companies, the state, or its princely equivalent, were put in place to curtail malfeasance in the organization of overseas trade. As a case in point, the success of late-medieval Venice as a commercial power was supported by a public-order and reputation-based institution for contract enforcement.[44] The Venetian state relied on tight administrative controls to gather reliable information about merchant behavior, which enabled government authorities to sanction contractual breach. At the same time, it offered economic rents lucrative enough for merchants to comply with the Venetian legal system. When merchants or their agents breached contracts, they faced the threat of severe legal sanctions and, perhaps even more damaging, risked the loss of their reputation with the authorities, and hence access to the rents the Venetian Republic generated. The case of medieval Venice is far from unusual. The chartered joint-stock companies that emerged in seventeenth-century Europe adopted comparable institutional deterrents to similar agency-related hazards in long-distance trade. Illustrative evidence comes from the English Hudson's Bay Company and the Royal African Company.[45] Again, assessing the true effort of their employees in distant ports was a considerable challenge for the governing bodies of both companies. Just as thorny was the reliability of trading information they provided for the company headquarters. In response, both companies built an attractive salary into the contract with their agents. The contract's key element, however, required agents to post a bond of security once they were hired. These institutional measures made it costly for an agent to lose his job. Coupled with tight monitoring that even included private correspondence, these measures created strong incentives for agents to refrain from opportunism.[46]

In other settings, it was less a reliance on such formal institutional remedies that kept agency problems at bay, but rather informal arrangements that imposed social control of economic transactions through tightly knit community networks. One illustration comes from Janet Landa's work on southeast Asian markets for rubber.[47] The middlemen who directed sales in these markets preferred exchange relationships within ethnically homogeneous communities whose members were bound to each other by shared "rules of the game"—a preference that helped them to reduce contract uncertainties and transaction costs. Further back in history, economic historian Avner Greif has identified a similar private-order reputation-based enforcement mechanism among the Maghribi (or Geniza) merchants, also an ethnically and religiously homogeneous group of Jewish traders in the medieval Mediterranean.[48] To deter opportunistic behavior, the Maghribi embedded bilateral business partnerships within their cohesive community network.[49] With any breach of contract, an agent thus risked losing his reputation as an honest partner as well as his exclusion from any future business within the entire Maghribi coalition network. The resemblance to the Venetian case is clear, yet what substituted for public-order enforcement was private-order network governance. Of course, fast and reliable information flows about the behavior of business partners were essential for such reputation-driven and network-based enforcement to work. The Geniza merchants maintained a vast correspondence with each other over long distances, touching on investment decisions, shared experiences in different marketplaces, and evaluations of the performance of business associates, bestowing a good (or bad) reputation upon them.[50]

Many of the same elements in dealing with the challenges of agency problems also can be found in the *commenda* and *compagnia* partnerships. Just like the Maghribi merchants, Francesco di Marco Datini, was an avid letter writer. He corresponded frequently both to instruct his business partners abroad and to receive valuable information in return that would prepare him for an otherwise-unforeseen turn of events that could affect his business.[51] Likewise, loyalty, reliability, and trustworthiness all were desirable qualities that *commendatores* were looking for in their traveling partners.[52] What better way to ensure that these qualities were met than to choose partners from within one's own local community network? Indeed, evidence from medieval Marseille, a well-established trading port at the time, reveals that recruitment into *commenda* contracts selected heavily on fellow Marseillais citizens or partners from nearby towns.[53] In chapter 6, we will learn that the merchant elite of Saint-Malo shared the same localist preference in the choice of venture partners.

The central insight from these various cases is that contract enforcement through network governance rests on embedding the ties that link partners within a venture into the broader social networks of their merchant community—networks founded on kinship, friendship, and bonds among neighbors and those who share occupation, religion, and a strong sense of place: in short, precisely the kinds of qualities expressed within Saint-Malo's mercantile elite (see chapters 2 and 3). The empirical evidence further indicates that network-based enforcement works best within densely connected and cohesive communities. Cohesion implies transitivity and triadic closure: a friend of a friend is a friend; my neighbor's neighbor is also my neighbor; a former business partner of my current business partner is someone I am likely to partner with in the future.[54] Cohesion also implies that community members are linked through multiple relationships at once.[55] The resulting redundancy in ties ensures that the community's existence is resistant to outward mobility—say, a prominent *armateur* who leaves Saint-Malo behind for an influential position at the royal court—or the death of prominent individual members. It does so because alternative pathways within the network compensate for any missing links that result from members leaving the community. Together, triadic closure and redundancy create a fertile ground for cooperation, such as the formation of partnerships for seafaring ventures. At the same time, both structural conditions are instrumental for social control: they facilitate monitoring the behavior of partners; they quickly spread information about illicit behavior; and they enable sanctioning it as deemed necessary. Hence, potential agency and commitment problems within partnerships could be contained through network governance.

It is worth emphasizing how deeply encoded with social meaning venture partnerships and other contractual market ties were in medieval and early modern Europe. Few scholars would dispute that contemporary traders were motivated by self-interest in enlarging their wealth. To the extent that they were channeled by wider community networks, economic ties also contributed more than their fair share to the cohesion of the social structure they were embedded in.

Far from corrupting a community's moral and social fabric by imposing cold-blooded cost-benefit calculations onto personal relationships, as critics both left and right have long suspected,[56] business ties were imbued with merchant sociability and thus formed important building blocks of local society. Further supporting evidence that economic relations served as capstones of social structure comes from a number of recent studies in economic sociology that rely on historical data sources. For medieval Genoa, Van Doosselaere shows that ties seemingly formed purely out of business interests—credit arrangements to finance trading voyages and insurance contracts to protect investors from unforeseen losses—played a pivotal role in consolidating the collective identity and political power of the Genoese merchant oligarchy.[57] Padgett and McLean trace how the organizational logic of forming partnerships in business rippled through Renaissance Florentine society and emerged as a model for social organization in multiple spheres of life, from arranging marriages between families to building alliances across political factions.[58] Elsewhere, I have shown how brokerage in economic relationships of extending personal credit served to bind local factions in Revolutionary New England that later aligned with the emergent national parties.[59]

A similar understanding of economic relationships as inherently communal bonds was echoed in the nature of merchant partnerships in Ancien Régime France, and hence in Saint-Malo. This understanding was rooted in a natural-law conception of the human condition, which stipulated that joining together in brotherly love, general friendship, and mutual obligation is an essential trait of human nature. From this fundamental sociability, all institutions of society emerged naturally, so the proponents of natural-law theory have argued. The prevalence of the family and friendship as core social institutions in most cultures known at the time was taken as direct evidence for the universal tendency to form relationships. Built on the model of kinship and friendship, partnership (*société*) was another institution that reflected the natural principles of human sociability. Thus, "the traditional partnership was conceived as an association of equal, interdependent brothers united to promote their mutual advantage," implying a "model of the *société* as the embodiment of fraternal charity." When venture partnerships formed among kin as business partners, they were seen as a natural extension of the family and strengthened its ties. Merchant endeavors were thus "infused with a spirit of brotherly love" and their *sociétés* "best epitomized merchant virtue."[60] The same principles extended to partners who were not family members, with the mutual loyalty and trust of friendship as the equivalent of brotherhood.[61] It follows that the professional association between business partners was largely indistinguishable from their personal relationships as both entailed strong personal bonds of interdependence and equality.

As the eighteenth century wore on, the traditional model of commercial cul-ture and sociability came under threat from new forms of organizing venture associations. The introduction of limited liability with the *société en comman-dite* offered the benefit of separating ownership and management, but it carried the potential to erode the defining principle of interdependence among equals because some partners shouldered a greater risk of losses than others. A perhaps even greater challenge came from the *société anonyme* and the *société en comman-dite par actions*, even though they were not yet fully established as legitimate forms of association. Both forms, and variants thereof, sought to attract investors by offering not only limited liability but also the purchase of negotiable shares in the enterprise (see the following discussion on partnership formation). What effectively amounted to shareholder governance would have spelled the end of the traditional model as it decoupled ownership from any particular associates and their personal relationships.[62]

Beyond these new organizational forms, one more lingering question touches on the structural basis of cohesion: how could sociability *within particular* part-nerships give rise to a well-integrated and cohesive merchant community at large? If we take the citizens of Saint-Malo as exemplary cases, then the historical data indicate that their venture partnerships, in trade or privateering, were indeed at the very heart of their *collective* identity as seafaring merchant elites. In the tra-ditional model of commercial culture, however, the strong notion of sociability seems to have been bestowed primarily, and perhaps even exclusively, on relation-ships among associates *within* partnerships. In the ideal image, friends and family joined in the pursuit of a shared undertaking. Yet, even in a town of a manage-able size such as Saint-Malo, it seems unlikely that all members of the merchant elite maintained partnership ties with everyone else at the same time. The social structural challenge is how segmentation into numerous islands of strong within-partnership solidarity, separated from each other by just as many structural holes, can be avoided. As noted earlier, community-wide network cohesion is greatly beneficial for an efficient organization of trade and the monitoring of oppor-tunistic behavior. That a view that divides the world of commerce into friends (read: associates) and those who are not friends (read: foes) has deficits when it comes to societal integration did not escape the attention of the Scottish Enlight-enment thinkers, who were the contemporaries of our Malouin merchants. As sociologist Allen Silver has shown, Adam Smith and other classic liberals sug-gested instead that the distinction between informal friendship and instrumen-tal market ties in commercial society opened up social space for the integrative role of neutral strangers, connected by relationships of universal sympathy rather than by exclusivist bonds of exchange. In Enlightenment understanding, these strangers are neither allies nor foes, "but authentically indifferent co-citizens—the sort of indifference that enables all to make contracts with all." The existence of strangers therefore did not erode, but rather supported the moral fabric of commercial society and its social cohesion.[63] The ideal of "strangership" focuses on a particular role occupied by individuals in commercial society, but it mirrors the bridging work of organizational linchpins discussed earlier.[64] Both promote cohesion through mediation across otherwise-separate groups, getting the balance right between the benefits of loyalty and trust within partnerships and the advantages of well-integrated community networks at large.

SHIP AND CREW

Moving on from normative prescriptions to the practicalities of partnership organization, the first key step was for the *armateurs* to attract investors willing to support the planned venture as shareholding partners (*associés, intéressés*, or *consorts*). Consider the prospectus for their *armement en course* that a certain Jean-Baptiste Michel Hippolyte Marion and one Louis Marie Marion, sieur de La Brillantais published in 1780 (see figure 4.1).

It was not the only instance in which the two brothers joined as *armateurs*: together, they established themselves among Saint-Malo's most eminent trader entrepreneurs in the latter half of the eighteenth century, having initiated several privateering and slave-trading ventures.[65] They seized the opportunity opened by the American Revolutionary War to outfit the frigate *La Duchesse de Polignac*. It was not uncommon for ships formerly employed by their owners in, for example, the South Sea trade or North Atlantic fishing to be repurposed for privateering cruises.[66] The brothers Marion, however, praised their vessel as having been carefully purpose-built over several months and designed specifically for plying the waters at the highest speed. The ability to outpace a prize ship was obviously an essential quality in any worthy privateer and of a greater value than firepower. Hence, if in doubt, too many heavy cannons that would slow down the privateer were usually avoided.[67] With a size of 450 tons, and armed with twenty-six cannons, plus an assortment of swivel guns and blunderbusses to be used when boarding a prize ship, the *Duchesse de Polignac* counted among the larger (top ten percentile of tonnages) and more forceful (top twenty percentile of cannons) corsairs that were put to sea at Saint-Malo during the wars between 1688 and 1783.[68] The bivariate plots in figure 4.2 provide an impression of the range of sizes and weaponry to be found among Malouin privateering vessels.[69] Rather

ARMEMENT
EN COURSE,
A SAINT-MALO,
DE LA FRÉGATE
LA DUCHESSE DE POLIGNAC,

De 106 pieds de quille, 120 pieds de longueur abfolue, & 30 pieds 6 pouces de bau.

ARMATEURS, MM. MARION & BRILLANTAIS MARION freres.

CAPITAINE, le fieur GUIDELOU.

CETTE Frégate, conftruite depuis plufieurs mois, porte en batterie 26 canons, dont 10 de douze, & 16 de huit, & fur fes gaillards, 4 de fix, & 8 obufiers de 12; en tout 38 bouches à feu, non compris les pierriers, efpingoles & autres menues armes dont elle eft fuffifamment pourvue. Elle fera armée de deux cens quatre-vingts à trois cens hommes d'équipage.

Ce Vaiffeau, bâti pour la plus grande marche poffible, eft mâté, fon gréement caplé, & les Armateurs font pourvu de tous les articles néceffaires à fon armement, de manière qu'ils peuvent fe flatter de le faire fortir auffi-tôt que la Société fera remplie; ce qui ne doit pas tarder, puifqu'il refte peu d'Actions à placer, la majeure partie l'ayant été à Saint-Malo même, par la confiance qu'on a dans cet Armement.

Le fieur Guidelou, Capitaine de cette Frégate, a donné l'année paffée les preuves les plus fatisfaifantes de la capacité fur la Frégate LE MONSIEUR, qu'il commandoit à la premiere courfe, pendant laquelle il a triple le capital de l'Armement, & mis en France plus de 500 prifonniers; ce qui lui a mérité l'eftime du Roi.

Le fonds de cette Société eft fixé à cent cinquante Actions de deux mille livres chaque, fubdivifées en demi & quarts d'Actions, formant en total une fomme de trois cens mille livres, valeur eftimée de l'Armement, & qui fervin de répartiteur dans tous les cas prévus par l'Article XV de la Déclaration du Roi du 24 Juin 1778, dérogeant feulement les Armateurs à l'Article XXV, qui fixe les avances à donner aux Equipages.

Les fieurs Marion freres, voulant donner à leurs Soufcripteurs toute la fatisfaction poffible, s'obligent de dépofer entre les mains des perfonnes dénommées ci-après, des duplicata de tous les comptes d'Armement, même des liquidations qui feront faites par les Amirautés, au moyen de quoi chaque Intéreffé pourra examiner le tout par lui-même.

On foufcrira chez les mêmes perfonnes, & chaque Soufcripteur fera obligé d'y dépofer la fomme qu'il aura foufcrite, quinze jours après fa fignature, foit en argent comptant, foit en lettres de change, ou autres effets qui n'auront pas plus d'une ufance. On y délivrera des Actions à chaque Intéreffé, & il y recevra fa portion dans les prifes au prorata de fa mife.

Les Maifons où l'on foufcrira font celles de MESSIEURS,

BANQUIERS.

VINCENS, rue Vivienne;
J. COTTIN & fils, & JAUGE, rue de Richelieu;
LE COUTEULX & Compagnie, rue Montorgueil;
J. DUPONT fils, rue des vieilles Audriettes.
PEROUTEAU DELON & Compagnie, rue Montmartre.

NOTAIRES.

DUFRENOY, rue Vivienne;
MARGANTIN, rue Saint-Honoré;
LE FAVRE, rue de Condé.

A PARIS, ...

A VERSAILLES, BLAIZOT, Libraire du Roi & de la Reine, rue Satory.
A ROUEN, ... LE COUTEULX & Comp., LE BOURG Freres, PAPILLON.
A NANTES, ... CANE, MESLÉ & BERNARD, CHARETTE & OZANNE.
A L'ORIENT, GALABERT freres, BONDEVILLE.
A SAINT-MALO, MARION & BRILLANTAIS MARION freres.

Les Armateurs fe propofent de doubler leur Frégate en cuivre, fi celui qu'ils attendent arrive à tems; comme cette opération, en procurant plus de marche au Vaiffeau, occafionnera auffi plus de dépenfe, dans ce cas le répartiteur fera de trois cents trente mille livres.

On croit devoir prévenir le Public que voici la faifon la plus favorable pour la Courfe; que tous les Corfaires, fortis depuis le mois de Novembre, font merveilles; puifqu'il arrive journellement de leurs prifes aux Ports de Breft, Morlaix, Saint-Malo, le Havre & Dunkerque.

Permis d'imprimer & d'afficher, ce 18 Décembre 1780. LE NOIR.

De l'Imprimerie de STOUPE, rue de la Harpe, 1780.

FIGURE 4.1 Prospectus of a *course* venture to be undertaken by the frigate *La Duchesse de Polignac* (printed in 1780).

Source: AD-IV 4Fg67.

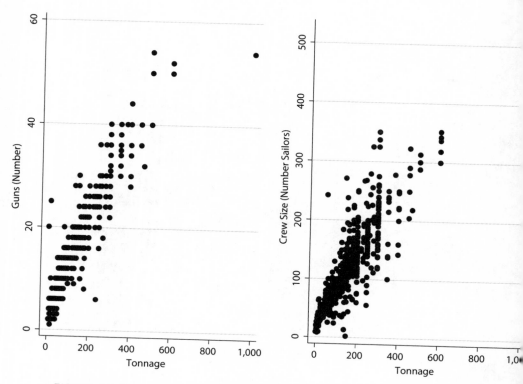

FIGURE 4.2 Tonnage, guns, and crew size of Saint-Malo privateering vessels, 1688–1782.

Note: $N = 563$ ships for the tonnage by guns plot, and $N = 634$ ships for the tonnage by crew size plot (differences due to missing data).

Sources: AD-IV 9B408; 9B435, (1)–(5); Morel (1958); Martin-Deidier (1976).

unsurprising, larger ships tended to carry more guns than smaller ones, revealing a linear relationship between both characteristics.

The same can be said for the manning of privateers from Saint-Malo: larger ships also enlisted a greater number of able seamen than smaller ones. Indeed, according to their prospectus, the brothers Marion and Brillantais Marion prepared to hire between 280 and 300 sailors to run the *Duchesse de Polignac*, once again placing her in the upper echelon of crew sizes. Historians of the *course* have long noted that the size of privateering crews outnumbered that of trading ships of a comparable tonnage. For the port of Nantes, Jean Meyer has estimated that one sailor per ton for a midsize privateer (two to four hundred tons) compared with just one sailor per seven to twelve tons for trading ships fitted out in peacetime.[70] For Saint-Malo, André Lespagnol has suggested that the average ratio of sailors per ton amounted to 0.64, or about three times the average ratio for commerce shipping (the *Duchesse de Polignac* fits this estimate with her ratio of 0.62–0.67).[71] For privateers, it was critical to have a sufficient number of sailors at hand to maneuver quickly when they pursued and attacked potential prey, or when they had to defend themselves (hence, their large crew). Perhaps even more essential, captured ships had to be manned with a prize crew to establish and maintain control on board until a safe French port was reached. That the size of prize crews remained more or less the same, regardless of the size of the privateering vessel, may explain why the ratio of sailors per ton decreased with increasing tonnage: small corsairs at 9 to 15 tons had a ratio of 2.0 to 1.8, slightly larger ones at 30 to 130 tons had a ratio of 0.9 to 1.1, and large ships between 200 and 450 tons had a ratio of just 0.7 to 0.5.[72]

Seamen enrolled for commerce raiding campaigns that were supposed to last for no more than four months.[73] A corsair's *équipage* (crew) consisted of a number of officers, including the first officer, first and second lieutenant, ensigns, and petty officers (*officiers-mariniers*). Among these petty officers were masters in various specialties, such as the first pilot and boatswain. A chaplain also was required for all privateers of one hundred tons or more, as well as a surgeon for crews of more than twenty seamen and two surgeons for crews exceeding fifty seamen. A scrivener (*écrivain*) had the primary duty of taking stock of a captured prize ship and affixing the Admiralty's seal. Next were the able-bodied seamen (*matelots*). Once they were registered as classed seamen by the state, they were officially prohibited from enrolling on a corsair until they had served one year on a royal navy ship and the following two years on a vessel of the merchant marine. Yet, all sorts of loopholes were exploited to defy such regulation, as handsome advances and the prospect of pillages were much more enticing propositions. Exempt from such restrictions were apparently underage crew members: boys (*mousses*) who would become *novices* at age sixteen, and eventually considered to be *matelots* by the age of eighteen.[74]

How much the competition between corsairs and the royal navy created a serious manning problem has been a matter of debate. Apparently, the vast demand for human labor on privateering vessels affected primarily the local supply of able seamen. Each year in 1689, 1690, and 1691, at least 3,600 to 4,000 men were enrolled on privateers—about two-thirds of the entire pool of classed seamen available in the *département maritime* of Saint-Malo. In 1695–1697 and in 1703–1705, the number of men serving on privateers rose to six to seven thousand, this time even more than the total number of classed seamen in the *département* of Saint-Malo. If anything, the shortage was endogenous and had much less to do with competition and interventions from the state. The consequence was that recruitment for the *course* had to cast a wider net: among the less qualified but hopeful (nonclassed young volunteers, invalids, and countryfolk) and even foreigners, Irish refugees chief among them.[75] Still, the overwhelming majority of those hired on Malouin privateering ships came from either Saint-Malo or its immediate vicinity. Registers that document how much individual crew members earned out of the sale of prizes also tell us the towns where they resided. A sample of thirty-six ships from Saint-Malo that campaigned in the years 1756–1757 reveals a fairly homogenous crew composition.[76] Out of 276 *officiers-mariniers*, 105 men were residents of Saint-Malo and another 23 lived in the neighboring suburb of Saint-Servan. Another fifty came from Dinan (less than thirty kilometers from Saint-Malo), and seventy-one officers were recruited from the port of Saint-Brieuc (slightly more than seventy kilometers from Saint-Malo on the northern Breton shore). Among the 864 listed *matelots*, 185 came from Saint-Malo, 23 from Saint-Servan, 274 from Saint-Brieuc, 257 from Dinan, and 68 from Lannion (further West from Saint-Brieuc). Among the seventy-eight *mousses*, most lived in Saint-Malo (thirty-six), whereas nineteen hailed from Saint-Brieuc, and seven each from Dinan and Lannion. Hence, 93 percent of the *équipages* were recruited from just five places, all situated on the northern coast of Brittany.[77] Local homogeneity in composition had its advantages. A well-attuned crew whose members shared a similar social background and sense of place was an invaluable asset in any *course* campaign. Unfortunately, localism could have its disadvantages. Too much familiarity among kin and neighbors could undermine respect for authority, which often enough descended into desertion and mutiny.[78]

The most important person and the one to wield authority on board, including the punishment of unruly behavior, was the ship's captain. He was responsible for recruiting his crew members and submitting the enlistment papers to the Admiralty's office. The 1681 *Ordonnance de la Marine* required that candidates for captaincy had at least five years of experience at sea and successfully passed an exam on the subject of navigation in front of a jury, composed of two masters, officers of the Admiralty, and a professor of the *École royale d'hydrographie*. In practice, however, the *armateurs* of Saint-Malo often preferred to entrust their ship to their sons, and thus they made repeated efforts to have the official regulations amended accordingly.[79]

Essential among a captain's qualities were his navigational and tactical skills as well as his experience in selecting suitable targets, as proven by the results of his prior commands. Indeed, the brothers Marion made a strong case for their chosen captain, le sieur Guidelou. In their prospectus, they conclude that Guidelou's previous exploits were so successful that they were deserving of the king's personal praise (figure 4.1).[80] What the Marions touted was meant to attract potential subscribers to their venture. Yet, it also illustrates an ambivalence inherent to the *course*. As shipowners and merchants, they sought to maximize economic profit and to avoid unnecessary risks that would jeopardize the venture or even their ship. In contrast, corsair captains more often than not held chivalrous ambitions, leading them to ignore risks and not shy away from confronting more powerful adversaries—all in their search for spectacular opportunities that promised honor and glory. Most *armateurs* were probably aiming for a fine balance between audacity and prudence in the choice of their captain. This is not to deny that more daring *armateurs*, such as Magon de la Lande or Danycan de l'Epine, were keenly interested in the fortunes of the *grande course*. They knew full well that the richest prizes were prepared to defend themselves and could rarely be won without some bloodshed, and they selected their captains accordingly.[81]

PARTNERSHIP FORMATION

With an experienced captain recruited, an able crew assembled, and all necessary equipment and victuals prepared, the brothers Marion and Brillantais Marion had readied the *Duchesse de Polignac* for her imminent departure. Their prospectus also shows that marketing skills had to be another *forte* of *armateurs* if they wanted to mobilize subscribers to their venture (figure 4.1). They emphasized that their current season, presumably winter, was ideal for the *course*, as witnessed by the plentiful prizes that had already reached the ports of Brest, Morlaix, Saint-Malo, le Havre, and Dunkirk on a daily basis. The two *armateurs* also urged anyone still hesitant that only a few shares were still left for purchase ("il reste peu d'Actions à placer") because this particular venture had inspired such confidence in other subscribers ("la confiance qu'on a dans cet Armement"). Hence, no time should be lost, as the ship would be ready to sail as soon as all subscriptions would be complete.

The prospectus further details that the capital stock of the *société* amounted to a projected total of 300,000 *livres tournois* (*lt.*), broken down into 150 shares (*actions*) at a value of 2,000 *lt.* each, which could be further split into half and quarter shares (see figure 4.3 for an exemplary *action*). For the sake of full disclosure, the *armateurs* Marion felt obliged to deposit duplicates of all accounts and prize liquidations with their chosen notaries for their shareholders to inspect. It appears that most of the shares were sold directly by the two *armateurs* to

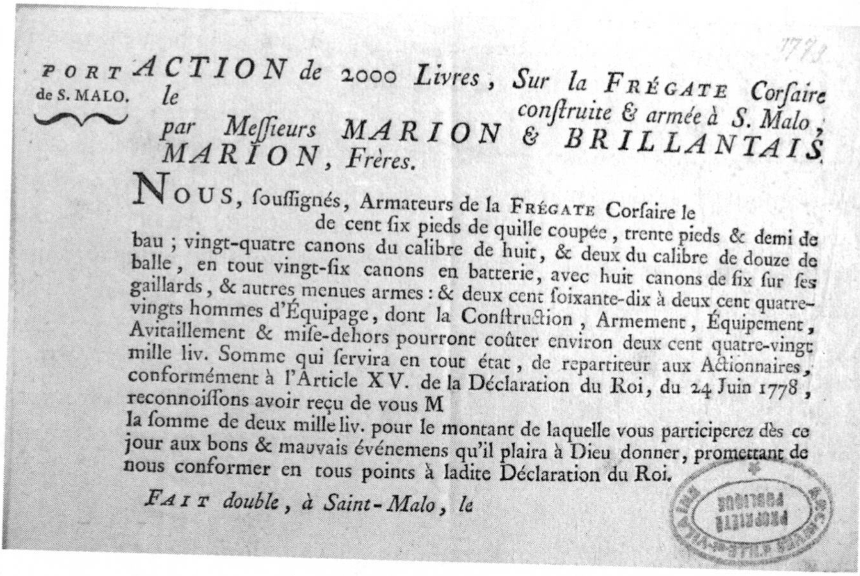

> PORT *ACTION* de 2000 *Livres*, *Sur la* FRÉGATE *Corfaire*
> de S. MALO. le   *conftruite & armée à S. Malo*,
>   *par Meffieurs* MARION & BRILLANTAIS
> MARION, *Frères.*
>
> NOUS, fouffignés, Armateurs de la FRÉGATE Corfaire le
> de cent fix pieds de quille coupée, trente pieds & demi de
> bau ; vingt-quatre canons du calibre de huit, & deux du calibre de douze de
> balle, en tout vingt-fix canons en batterie, avec huit canons de fix fur fes
> gaillards, & autres menues armes : & deux cent foixante-dix à deux cent quatre-
> vingts hommes d'Équipage, dont la Conftruction, Armement, Équipement,
> Avitaillement & mife-dehors pourront coûter environ deux cent quatre-vingt
> mille liv. Somme qui fervira en tout état, de repartiteur aux Actionnaires,
> conformément à l'Article XV. de la Déclaration du Roi, du 24 Juin 1778,
> reconnoiffons avoir reçu de vous M
> la fomme de deux mille liv. pour le montant de laquelle vous participerez dès ce
> jour aux bons & mauvais événemens qu'il plaira à Dieu donner, promettant de
> nous conformer en tous points à ladite Déclaration du Roi.
>
>   FAIT double, à Saint-Malo, le

FIGURE 4.3 Certificate of a share (*action*) held in a *course* venture, worth 2,000 *lt.*

Note: Both the name of the privateering frigate and the shareholder's name were intentionally left blank and still had to be filled in, whereas the ship's size, its weaponry, crew size, and the total fitting and victualing costs (about 280,000 *lt.*) were all itemized.

Source: AD-IV 4Fg67.

interested parties from Saint-Malo proper. The remainder of the shares were offered by notaries and banquiers in Paris, Versailles, Rouen, Nantes, and Lorient (see again figure 4.1).[82] As such, our example *armement* fits well with most other privateering partnerships that were set up at Saint-Malo in this period.[83] In the previous chapter, I considered the extent to which wealth and socioeconomic stratification shaped attraction to the *course*. Recall that it served as a suitable platform to unite a variety of subscribers of rather unequal means. Chapter 6 examines the selection of partners into privateering ventures in greater detail. For now, note that the share of kinship bonds among partnership ties was not as salient as one would perhaps expect. This observation is reflected in the case of the *Duchesse de Polignac*, as the two *armateurs* apparently sought potential partners well beyond their circle of family members. Much like their peers in other Malouin *course* ventures, the brothers Marion recruited their partners primarily from their hometown of Saint-Malo.[84] Yet, as the list of notaries in their prospectus indicates, they also sought to mobilize capital from associates who resided in other ports of Brittany and Normandy as well as in the capital region of Paris and

Versailles. (The increasing geographic reach of partner selection over time can be seen in chapter 6, figure 6.6.)

Within the legal framework of the Ancien Régime, *armateurs* like the brothers Marion had three main options to formally organize their enterprise. A commercial association could, first, take the form of a general partnership (*société générale*), "such that each partner was able to obligate the partnership and was held jointly and fully liable for its debts." The second form was the limited partnership (*société en commandite*). As mentioned earlier, its defining qualities were limited liability and the separation of ownership (capital) and management. In this case, "it was only the general partner who could obligate the partnership and who bore full liability for its debts. The limited partner was not authorized to act on behalf of the partnership and stood to lose only his initial capital investment." Third, by the eighteenth century, the *société anonyme* had gained prominence, "an association of individuals, all of whom have limited liability, whose ownership interest in the business takes the form of negotiable stock certificates, and who participate in corporate governance through shareholder assemblies." Another variant was the *société en commandite par actions*, a hybrid of the limited liability partnership and a more elaborate corporate governance structure, such that ownership was split between associates with limited and others with unlimited liability, and shares in the *société* were again negotiable.[85]

Note that none of these organizational forms were specific to maritime enterprise, be it trade or the *course*, but rather they applied to all private commercial partnerships.[86] The *Ordonnance du commerce*, issued in 1673, spelled out the legal requirements that had to be fulfilled to set up a partnership, whether it was of the general or the limited *commandite* form.[87] Article 1 of the ordinance regulated that all *sociétés* had to be established through a written agreement between the contracting associates, called the *acte de société* in Saint-Malo, as in most other places in France. The contract had to be either notarized or privately signed ("sera redigée par écrit, ou pardevant notaires, ou sous signatures privées"). The ordinance explicitly stipulated that any testimony of oral statements allegedly made by any of the partners before, during, or after the writing of the agreement were to have no bearing on its content. Article 2 required all *sociétés* to have a summary account registered with the appropriate local authorities and posted in a public place for everyone to read. In Saint-Malo, registration usually took place with the local Admiralty's office ("au greffe du siege royal de l'amirauté Etably en Cette ville de Saint-Malo").[88] Documents that lacked the required signatures would not be registered. According to article 3, the summary had to include the names, occupation, social standing and place of residence of all associates, any unusual clauses to the contract, and the starting and ending dates of the partnership ("les noms, surnoms, qualités et demeures des associés, et les clauses extraordinaires, . . . le temps auquel elle doit commencer et finir"). In practice, precise ending dates were exceptional, at least in the Saint-Malo partnership records. Jean Meyer has likewise argued that clauses prescribing such ending dates were illusory because fixing a partnership's dissolution in advance made little sense in most cases.[89] Article 4 stated that any changes in the composition of associates or any addition of stipulations and clauses to the contract were again required to be registered and posted in public. Failure to meet these requirements nullified the contractual agreements between the associates as well as with any of their creditors ("le tout à peine de nullité des actes et contrats passés, tant entre les associés, qu'avec leurs créanciers et ayans cause"). The implication was that the *société* would cease to exist, and the associates would be personally responsible for any claims made against their erstwhile partnership.[90]

The complete set of the 3,250 surviving *actes de société* (more precisely, their summaries for the purpose of registration, plus those documented by notaries) for trade and privateering ventures that were established in Saint-Malo between 1681 and 1792 is the chief data source throughout this volume. Privateering partnerships in particular were known to be organized as *sociétés en commandite*, although it was less a legal obligation to do so than a custom. The *commandite* form with its limited liability appeared to be particularly well suited to garner contributions from the largest possible number of investors.[91] In practice, however, most associations were simply called *société*, without any further distinctions.[92]

Figure 4.4 shows an exemplary *acte de société* of privateering partnerships, registered on November 10, 1707. It is the contractual agreement for the 250-ton corsair *Le Marquis de Thianges*, built in Saint-Malo, armed with twenty-six cannons and manned with 178 seamen (the entry starts at the bottom left, and continues on the top right).[93] Alain Mallet, sieur de la Villestreux, was one of the ship's owners and *armateur* ("proprietaire En partie Et armateur du Navire"). Under the command of Captain François Lair, the *Marquis de Thianges* was fitted out for a privateering cruise against the enemies of the state ("Commandé par le sieur François Lair Capitaine Pour faire La Course sur les ennemis delestat"). What follows is the list of partners (*Interressés*), beginning with Nicolas L'Hostelier, sieur de Lesnaudières, who held one-quarter and one-sixty-fourth of the shares in the venture, and ending with Captain François Lair, who contributed capital for one-sixteenth, and the *armateur* Mallet, sieur de la Villestreux, for one-eighth of the shares (it was far from unusual, and rather common that the captain counted among the shareholding associates). The closing statement declares that this summary document conformed to the *acte de société*, as notarized by the city's

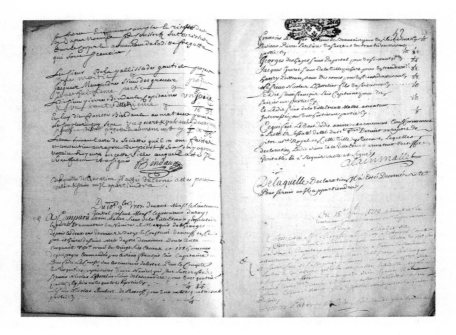

FIGURE 4.4 Partnership agreement (*acte de société*) for the corsair ship *Le Marquis de Thianges*, fitted out at Saint-Malo in 1707.

Source: AD-IV 9B168, ff 51v-52r.

royal notary Pitot on October 12 and that the sieur de la Villestreux indeed was the rightful *armateur*. As such, he also signed the document.

A few more specifics can be gleaned from these partnership agreements. To begin with, it was fairly common to share the ownership of a vessel, and the notion "proprietaire en partie" is a regular sight in the records. For instance, the *société* that financed the voyage of the four-hundred-ton *Le Sage* to Spanish America and beyond in 1719 was headed by three owner *armateurs* ("propriettaires et Coarmateurs"): Gillette Rottou, dame de Grandville; André Lévesque, sieur de La Souctière; and his brother François Lévesque, sieur de Beaubriand.[94] Another case shows that ventures were not always initiated by *armateurs* who were then looking for business partners: in the *société* of the vessel *Le Marin*, for example, the shareholding associates took it upon themselves to nominate and establish one among their ranks—that is, Captain Nicolas Ruault, sieur de la Maisonneuve—as the *armateur* of their joint venture, with all the necessary powers ("ledit Sieur de lamaisonneuve Ruault l'un desdits interressés qui a esté

Nommé et Etably par les autres Ses consorts armateur dudit Navire avec pouvoir a luy de travailler et agir aux armement et Equipement").[95] A similar case was the nomination of Jacques Maugendre, sieur des Grèves, out of the midst of associates, as *armateur* for the corsair *La Legere* in 1705 ("choisy et nommé Entre eux pour armateur").[96]

Turning to the size of partnerships, the registrations of the *actes de société* reveal that privateering ventures counted about nine to ten shareholding partners on average (standard deviation = 12.3), and no more than twenty partners for the vast majority of cases (88 percent). The numbers are virtually the same if we also include *guerre et marchandise* ventures. In contrast, partnerships in regular maritime trades were noticeably smaller, with only three to four partners on average (standard deviation = 4.2), and less than ten partners in 90 percent of all cases. We may interpret this observation as another piece of evidence that the *course*, based on the sheer size of its partnerships, offered more opportunities for joining interested parties from all corners of Malouin society, and thus had a greater potential for delivering social cohesion than other trading ventures.[97]

Gathering partners and distributing all shares could turn out to be a more complex and longer process than planned, in particular, for more elaborate undertakings. Consider the 1,100-ton *Le Duc de Fitz James*, sailing for the Îles de France and Bourbon, the Indies, and China in 1776. Her *armateurs*, Beaugeard and Lesdet, sieur de Segray, registered the first subscription by a certain Le Normand from Paris (presumably a *banquier*) on December 5, 1775. The last contribution was made by J. A. Poupart de Neuflize et fils from Sedan (presumably *banquiers* as well) on August 14, 1776, although the ship had already departed for the East Indies on March 26, 1776.[98] In other instances, shares initially held or purchased by either the *armateurs*, the captain, or early partners were later resold to new entrants into the partnership. The *armateur* of the corsair *L'Union*, armed in 1711, resold a one-sixteenth share each to three new subscribers, a one-thirty-second share each to twelve subscribers, and a one-sixty-fourth share to one more partner—all out of the initial two-thirds he held in his *société* ("En decharge de l'interest"). His captain likewise resold two one-sixteenth shares and four one-thirty-second shares out of his own one-third share to six new subscribers.[99] In the case of the *Bonne Fortune*, another corsair fitted out in 1702, one Jacques Mallon, sieur du Fresne, bought shares in the partnership, only to sell some of them to another merchant investor, a certain Toussaint Cinart.[100] In the *société* of another vessel called *L'Union*, this time fitted out with a *guerre et marchandise* commission in 1704, one of the partners, Desvaux, sieur du Morier, also resold part of his initial share to Jacob Legeard, sieur de la Preveslière, another associate.[101]

It seems safe to assume that the merchant investors who acquired these shares were expecting abundant returns. The *actes de sociétés* also illustrate how their expectations were set straight. Hence, in the notarial papers of the *société* for *Le Sage*, bound for South America in 1719, we find an explicit reminder that all associates should be aware that risks, dangers, and fortune ("risques, perils et fortune") awaited their enterprise in equal measure. Good as much as bad exploits would lie ahead ("bonnes et mauvaises aventures"), and losses were just as likely as profits to be forthcoming ("pertes ou proffit qui pouront arriver").[102]

THE CAMPAIGN AT SEA

Recall that any *armateur* and his associates had to obtain an appropriate commission, or letter of marque, from the local office of the Admiralty where they intended to equip their ship for a commerce-raiding cruise. The document or a copy thereof had to be carried on board during the entire campaign. Figure 4.5 shows an example *guerre et marchandise* commission for the five-hundred-ton *La Paix*, which was issued to a certain Jean Agathange Locquet, sieur de la Lande, in December 1710, at the height of the War of the Spanish Succession. Once again, the commission was to list the names of the *armateur* and captain, as it was personalized, had to be signed, and was not supposed to be transferred to another captain. Also included had to be the name, tonnage, and home port of the vessel. Only subjects of the French king were granted a letter of marque, and obtaining such a commission from another sovereign and engaging in privateering under a foreign banner were treated as acts of piracy. The vessel also had to be in good working order, well-armed, and suitably manned, including a sufficiently experienced captain. To ensure that privateers would not violate the legal boundaries of the *guerre de course*, the registration of the ship at the Admiralty's office also required the *armateurs* to make a security deposit (*caution*) set at 15,000 *lt*. If corsairs caused unlawful damages, or violated neutrals' rights, the *caution* was used to pay for reparations.[103] The amount of the *caution* seems to have remained unchanged since the 1681 royal ordinance was decreed. This same sum applied to corsairs fitted out in Saint-Malo in 1704, 1744, and 1782, and it remained in effect during the French Revolutionary Wars, as documented by the letter of marque registration for the 450-ton privateer *Le Duguay-Trouin* in March 1793.[104]

Weighing risks and opportunities, and with all necessary preparations completed, the *armateurs* and their associates readied their privateering ship to be sent off to sea in search for suitable prizes.[105] We may distinguish three main types

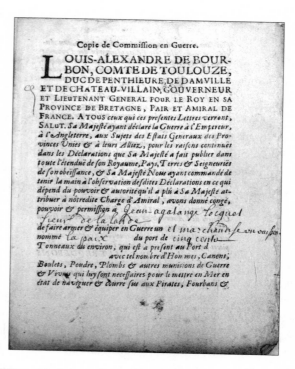

FIGURE 4.5 *Guerre et marchandise* commission to arm the ship *La Paix* of Saint-Malo in December 1710.

Source: AD-IV 9B622.

of corsairs, whose campaigns took place in three corresponding theaters of operation.[106] The first type was the *petite course*, composed of small-scale ships of less than one hundred tons that roamed the Irish Sea, along the Cornish and Devon shorelines, and the Channel Islands. Given their reduced crew size and limited firepower, they took advantage of fog, nightfall, and intimate knowledge of the waters around the British Isles to ambush unexpecting English coastal traders and fishing vessels. Their modest scale meant that the number of partners (usually less than ten) and the sum of their investments were modest as well.

The second type was the classic *guerre de course*, undertaken by midsize frigates between 150 and 400 tons that typically were converted commerce vessels formerly employed in Newfoundland fishing and trading with Cadiz. Corsairs of this type usually chased alone and were deployed in the classic theater of commerce raids, a large triangle that stretched out from the southwestern Irish coast to Brittany and down to the northwestern tip of the Iberian Peninsula. This type of corsairs had been the most prevalent and successful form of the *course* out of Saint-Malo until the English resorted to convoys and armed coastal guards to protect their trade shipping.

The third type has been called *la grande course.* As its name suggests, it was distinguished by the comparatively large scale of the vessels employed and the wide reach of its excursions. It was an oceangoing initiative, where eminent *négociants* such as Magon de la Lande and Danycan de l'Epine took the lead to assemble entire squadrons of four to five frigates of 350 and more tons each, heavily armed with forty to fifty cannons per ship, and manned with about 1,600 seamen. Occasionally, the entrepreneurs received material support from the state, mainly through the loan of ships. Their undertakings were of an aggressive and strategic nature, not shying away from battles to intercept enemy merchant fleets. Their ambitious forays led them as far north as Shetland, Orkney, Iceland, and the Faroe Islands, and southbound to the Strait of Gibraltar and as far as Guinea and Brazil. They preyed on whaling fleets and richly laden cargo ships returning to English or Dutch ports from the East Indies, Russia, and Smyrna. They even ransacked colonial ports, with Duguay-Trouin's raid of Rio de Janeiro in 1711 being but one of the more spectacular expeditions.

To understand exactly what happened at sea, during the corsairs' campaigns, we are fortunate that the royal ordinance of 1681 prescribed that, upon his return, every captain of a privateer was to submit a detailed report of any prize-taking actions to the local representatives of the Admiralty.[107] Thus, I can draw on a 10 percent random sample that I collected from the entire set of surviving captains' reports.[108] A few illustrative cases from these records give us an idea of the range of incidents that unfolded throughout the campaigns.

Leafing through the captains' reports, one quickly recognizes that it was rather uncommon for a privateer to resort to cannon shots and gunfire to seize a prize ship.[109] One among many such cases was the cruise of the two-hundred-ton *Comte de Toulouse*, owned by François Nouail, sieur du Fougeray, equipped with twenty-four cannons, and manned with 138 sailors. This is an example of the classical *course* pursued by the Malouins. Her captain, Robert Surcouf, sieur de la Maisonneuve, reported that he and his crew had sailed past Cap Fréhel on November 30, 1704. On December 9, they chanced upon an English trading vessel of about 130 tons, called the *Catherine of Boston*, just south of Cape Clear off the Irish coast. The *Catherine* was on her way back from Antigua, carrying cargo of sugar, cotton, ginger, and tropical woods. The French corsair took the prize without facing any apparent resistance, manned it with a prize crew, and brought it into the port of Saint-Malo on December 13.[110] A similar case, and fine example of the *petite course*, was the eighteen-ton corvette *Le Gagneulx* of Saint-Malo, armed with just two cannons, and manned with twenty-five seamen. The name of her captain, Darby Sullivan, betrayed his local knowledge of the Irish coastal waters. In the spring of 1712, he and his crew managed to capture three ships without any reported fight: again near Cape Clear, they seized the fifty-ton *Diamond of London*, sailing from Barbados, on April 5; on April 20, inside the Irish port of Dungarvan, they took a thirty-four-ton cargo vessel loaded with charcoal, cheese, and smoked bacon, and another eighteen-ton vessel loaded with beef. All three prize ships were successfully received in French ports.[111]

Certainly, some bloodshed was unavoidable during such encounters. On January 11, 1703, the 150-ton *Le Pierre*, armed with sixteen cannons and manned with a seventy-two-strong crew, left Saint-Malo to continue her *course* along the English coast. On January 22, the French confronted an English vessel of about two hundred tons, which was seized only after a battle that lasted for three hours and took the life of the corsair's first captain, Charles Lossieux, sieur des Saudrais, and apparently left at least another four crew members injured. The report was made by Captain Nicolas Leturas, sieur de la Citté, who was next in command.[112] Others, such as Captain Rouault, sieur des Champs, preferred to avoid such a costly encounter when his corsair *La Marquise de Beringhen* was chased by several English and Dutch warships, forcing him to retreat temporarily from his position near the English coastline.[113]

Not all privateers from Saint-Malo roamed the waters around the British Isles. The eventful expedition of the *Legerre* into the Caribbean serves as a vivid example of *la grande course*.[114] The *Legerre* weighed about 130 tons, was armed with eighteen cannons, and was manned with a crew of 125 seamen. She belonged to Jacques Maugendre, sieur des Grèves, *armateur* from Saint-Malo, and his partners. On May 22, 1706, with Captain Pierre Walsh at the helm, the *Legerre* sailed from Saint-Malo, "in the company of two other vessels, the *Chasseur* and the *Sollide*," to go privateering in the West Indies ("pour aller faire la Course aux Illes de l'amerique"). In September, the small flotilla reached Grenada, continued their cruise along the Isla de Margarita, and onward to the French colony of Saint-Domingue for a layover. On January 6, 1707, the three ships left for their return voyage to France, when "strong headwinds and heavy storms separated and left them to their own devices." The *Legerre* opted for another layover at the port of Santiago on Hispaniola before making for the Caicos Islands: "On the 10th of said month of January, they encountered two English vessels, one armed with 28 cannons, the other with 14 cannons." The French corsair took the larger of the two vessels under cannon fire. After two hours of fighting, the English ship burned down so that "nothing could be saved." The *Legerre* then "pursued the second ship just until nightfall." During the battle that ensued, the *Legerre* "received several cannon shots," and both Captain Walsh and his second-in-command, George Amellot, were "injured by a shot of musket bullets into their thighs," forcing them to retreat again to Saint-Domingue for repairs and fresh provisions. Captain Walsh "found himself incapable of re-embarking," and heeding the surgeons' advice he "remained on land at Petite Rivière." He "handed his commission and the ship's command" to George Amellot. Under the new captain, the *Legerre* sailed off to France on April 1, "in the company of two other ships," both of which soon went their separate ways, leaving her to continue her journey alone. On April 29, at 43°55'N 42°45'W (in the middle of the Atlantic), they encountered the *Mary Madeleine*, a 130-ton English vessel of Falmouth "on her way to Virginia." The Malouin corsair took the prize "without facing any resistance." Among the cargo were "a cask of shoes, two crates of soap, five crates of bottled wine, and two closed caskets of unknown contents" (because they could not be opened), which Captain Amellot had confiscated. He then also took the "English captain and five men of his crew" as prisoners on board of the *Legerre*, "leaving the pilot" and a prize crew of six French seamen on the *Mary Madeleine* "with orders to bring her to the nearest French port." While Amellot and his men continued their journey home, they "encountered several more ships and checked neutrals and others carrying French passports." Finally, the *Legerre* reached Saint-Malo "with thirty-five men still left of her crew." Captain Amellot made his report to the lieutenant general of the seat of the Admiralty at Saint-Malo on May 21, 1707.

CHAPTER 5

RETURNS TO PRIVATEERING

I n the previous chapters, we followed the merchant *armateurs* as they obtained commissions for their *course* campaigns from the Admiralty, acquired and armed a suitable vessel, raised the necessary funds from shareholding associates to finance the venture, and eventually saw their ship off, equipped with instructions for the captain. Any meaningful assessment of the *course* would be incomplete without some consideration of its merits and returns. For example, were its outcomes worth the efforts that went into the planning, funding, and coordinating of the *guerre de course*, both locally, on the ground, in ports like Saint-Malo, and in France at large? To answer this question, we must distinguish the broader strategic merit of the *course* for the state, as an effective instrument of warfare, from any economic benefits that accrued to the private traders who invested in privateering enterprise.

Whether or not the enlistment of privateers in its naval policy was indeed useful for the state's objectives remained a matter of debate well into the revolutionary period. On one hand, advocates of the abolition of the *course* argued that it had proven useless from a strategic viewpoint because it had failed to keep British and Dutch sea power at bay. Opponents of the *course* emphasized that it was at odds with the moral ideals of the French Revolution, stood in contrast to the recently declared universal human rights, and therefore should be banished as an illegal activity. On the other hand, familiar arguments were proposed in its defense. Those who supported the *course* maintained that it served as a lucrative substitute for regular commerce when the latter could not be pursued during times of war. In particular, so the supporters' argument continued, the amount of commerce shipping undertaken by France's enemies offered such lucrative opportunities for French corsairs that they should not be missed. Likewise, and again through a strategic lens, proponents of the *course* pointed out that privateers weakened the enemy's naval strength, both by taking able seamen as prisoners and by seizing vessels as prizes. Finally, an opinion held by many was that the engagement on board corsairs offered French seamen an ideal training and testing ground for any subsequent service in the king's main fleet.[1]

Even in its heyday, during the Nine Years' War (known in France as the War of the League of Augsburg) and the War of the Spanish Succession, French privateering enterprise seems to have generated mixed results.[2] After the failure of the main fleet to project French seapower, the royal government's naval strategy shifted from the *guerre d'escadre* that pitted battle fleets against each other to the *guerre de course* as a war on the maritime trade of France's enemies. The French privateering effort certainly did some considerable harm to Dutch and English seaborne commerce in the late-seventeenth- and early eighteenth-century wars. A few spectacular exploits stood out, such as the raid of Rio de Janeiro by Duguay-Trouin's privateering fleet in 1711.[3] Beyond such outstanding campaigns, however, the *guerre de course* seems to have fallen short of its promise as a decisive instrument in armed conflict that would tip the balance in France's favor. Any wide-ranging success of the *course*, it appears, was hampered by a lack of coordination among privateers, and between them and the king's Admiralty. One important reason was barely concealed: for the *armateurs* who fitted out the vessels, as well as for their business partners, the *course* was first and foremost an economic enterprise. The pursuit of patriotic glory played second fiddle at best. As a case in point, consider once more the call for subscriptions to the campaign of the frigate *La Duchesse de Polignac* in 1780 (see chapter 4, figure 4.1). Granted, it sailed much later than the corsairs under Louis XIV's reign, but there is little reason to believe that the primacy of economic motives among the merchants who sponsored commerce raiding ventures had changed substantially. Having touted their ship's remarkable build and weaponry, the *armateurs*, Messrs. Marion and Brillantais Marion, emphasized the experience and skill of their chosen captain, one sieur Guidelou. The year before he accepted the command of the *Duchesse de Polignac*, Guidelou had been at the helm of the privateering frigate *Le Monsieur*, and quite successfully so. Both shipowners were quick to point out that it was due to Guidelou's gallantry that the investors of said venture enjoyed a tripling of their investment. Clearly, the brothers Marion harbored hopes of similar fortunes for the venture of the *Duchesse de Polignac*: the closing sentence of their advertisement promises that "now is the most favorable season for the *course*" ("que voici la saison la plus favorable pour la Course").[4] This is but one example, yet it illustrates that the principal motivation of privateering merchants was to make money, in the form of returns on their investments. Consequently, what reigned supreme among privateers was competitive individualism, an attitude that probably was not much help in coordinating naval operations against the enemies of the state. As historian Geoffrey Symcox has pointed out, to forge effective coordination between corsairs and the French royal navy, much greater state initiative and especially material support would have been necessary, but the lack thereof was precisely the reason for encouraging the privateering war in the first place.[5]

Robust estimates of the overall impact of French privateering on the progression of war would require systematic data on a much wider scope than a focused study of a single port can offer. Even setting aside such challenges to data collection and scope, my substantive interest is decidedly not in understanding how valuable the *course* was for wielding French naval power.[6] Likewise, an adequate assessment of the profitability of the *guerre de course* for France at large would necessitate systematic longitudinal information on all French privateering ports at the same level of comprehensiveness as I have for Saint-Malo. Instead, my interest is in understanding how and to what extent the social ties forged through the organization of joint *course* ventures helped to bring about the social bonds that held together local merchant communities, such as the one in Saint-Malo. In what follows, I focus on the returns that were forthcoming to the individual *armateurs* and their associates who sponsored the privateering campaigns, next to their engagements in other trading ventures. The substantive reason for doing so, then, is that local returns to privateering can tell us something about the continued incentive and interest the Malouin traders had in organizing *course* partnerships, and, by the same token, how the social ties they formed through these partnerships contributed to cohesion within the merchant community.

THE *COURSE* AS SUBSTITUTE OR COMPLEMENT

Chapter 6 presents systematic evidence that privateering ventures did indeed occupy central positions as mediating linchpins in the organizational network of trading ventures. An important alternative argument implies that whatever prominent role the *course* played in this network, it had little to do with the nature of privateering or its potential to serve as a mediating structural linchpin. Instead, the *course* was no more than yet another potentially lucrative business opportunity that happened to open up in times of war. As soon as war broke out, merchants would have seized the opportunity and invested in privateering ventures. According to this alternative argument, they would have done so rather indiscriminately because regular trades were largely suspended in times of armed conflict. In other words, the *course* offered no more and no less than a welcomed substitute for normal trade during war.[7] There simply was not much else to invest in. If this argument is correct, then it should be little surprising that investors flocked to the *course* under such beleaguered conditions for regular business. Furthermore, if privateering ventures did indeed attract so much interest, then we should also expect them to have filled such prominent positions as bridging nodes in the business network of the merchant community. The substitution argument thus insists that any prominent role of the *course* was not inherent to its social relational nature, but merely the result of exogenous happenstance—such as the outbreak of war—in a given setting.

The substitution argument is obviously important to address because it bears directly on the investment choices and expected returns of *armateurs* and their associates. An extension of the same argument maintains that in great corsair ports like Dunkirk and Saint-Malo, in particular, resident merchants not only substituted the *course* for regular trade, but overspecialized in commerce raiding to such an extent that they neglected promising new opportunities that emerged in other branches of colonial trade. Ultimately, overspecialization led them to lose their competitive edge in comparison to other ports in the French Atlantic economy.[8] Some have gone even further to argue that in contrast to the steady flow of engagements in the Mediterranean *corso*, the Atlantic-bound *guerre de course* was a passing pursuit, bound as it was by the duration of armed conflict. As privateering sparked the interest of enterprising merchants in extraordinary times, it brushed aside ordinary trade. Yet, so the argument continues, it suffered the same fate of diminishing commitments as soon as the fabled riches of the South Sea expeditions became more attractive to investors.[9] One overspecialization replaced another, or so it seemed.

The available evidence, however, tells a different story. For one, the South Sea ventures initiated by Danycan and similar-minded *armateurs* hardly differed from privateering enterprises. In fact, they closely resembled them. These ventures were semilegal at best, as they undercut the official Spanish colonial trade, and more often than not, they were thinly veiled commerce raiding operations (see chapter 2). What differed were their hunting grounds: not the traditional waters off the British Isles and in the North Atlantic, but rather the Spanish and Portuguese colonial possessions in South America. The instructions that merchant investors handed to their captains betray how much the "corsair mentality" motivated their interloping voyages into the South Sea.[10] Because it is a well-documented example, consider once again the partnership contract of the four-hundred-ton *Le Sage*, funded by Gillette Rottou, dame de Grandville, and the two brothers André Levesque, sieur de La Souctière, and François Levesque, sieur de Beaubriand, as the three *co-armateurs*. Recall that they ordered their captain Joseph Girard, sieur du Demaine, to set their ship on its intended course toward Spanish America, "tant aux costes du nord, que dans Les mers et costes du Sud" (what today are the Chilean and Peruvian coasts). Captain Girard carried a commission of *guerre et marchandise*, and in addition to the usual references to expected trading in colonial commodities, the document explicitly states that he should engage in privateering raids against the enemies of the state ("faisant la guerre et la Course Sur les ennemies de L'Etat").[11] Note that the partnership contract had been drawn up in 1719, a year when France, this time as an ally of England, was involved in a set of modest hostilities with Spain.[12] This shows that, where seafaring was concerned, the boundaries between normal trade and the *course*, just as much as those between legal and illicit pursuits, were far from strict and impermeable. It also means that, at least in the case of Malouin enterprises, sweeping assertions that one overspecialized activity replaced another should be taken with more than one grain of salt.

One may argue that anecdotes from a single enterprise make no general pattern. The latter emerges from a systematic quantitative account of the numerous ventures that were launched from the port of Saint-Malo. Such a wider canvas supports the initial impression we may gain from selected cases like the voyage of *Le Sage*. The quantitative evidence confirms the conclusion that the *course* did more to complement rather than to substitute normal trade in times of war. To begin, we may follow the path blazed by the pioneering historian Léon Vignols. He transcribed the number of corsair and trading ventures armed at Saint-Malo between 1706 and 1739 from the registers at the *Archives de port militaire de Brest*.[13] Vignols also distinguished among different branches of seaborne commerce. For my purpose, the comparison of the number of ventures undertaken in privateering and those in regular trades is primarily of interest. Unfortunately, Vignols's list includes only a few years of the War of the Spanish Succession when commissions for the *guerre de course* were granted, namely, in 1706–1712. At least for these years, we can observe to what extent war disrupted normal trade shipping and privateering stepped in to fill the void. In 1706, the Malouins armed twenty-nine corsairs as compared with thirty-nine trading ships. In 1707, twenty-eight corsairs contrasted with fifty-six trading ships. In 1708, twenty-six corsairs and forty trading vessels were fitted out. Only in 1709 did thirty-three corsairs outnumber the twenty-two trading ships. In 1710, we find thirty-five corsairs and forty-three trading ships. In 1711, there were thirty-three ships in privateering and the same number in normal trade. Finally, in 1712, twelve corsairs were clearly outnumbered by sixty-one trading vessels. In other words, the Malouin entrepreneurs continued to fit out trading voyages despite the war, and their privateering campaigns complemented rather than replaced normal trade activities.

Figure 5.1 extends the comparison between privateering enterprise and normal trade voyages in Vignols's data to cover the entire 1681–1792 period. The number of ventures are plotted as they are documented in the voyage partnership registers (*actes de société*) for this period. Light gray bars represent the number of ventures in all regular trades in a given year. Dark bars indicate the number of *course* partnerships. The resulting pattern reveals two clear features. First, normal trade indeed decreased visibly in times of armed conflict, as one would expect

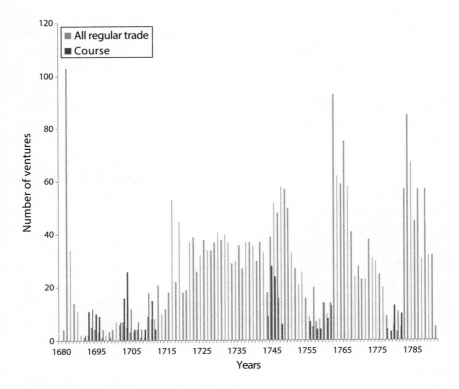

FIGURE 5.1 The *course* as a complement to regular trade.

Note: The chart compares ventures fitted out in regular trades (light gray bars) and ventures armed for the *guerre de course* (dark bars) at Saint-Malo in the 1681–1792 period.

Sources: AD-IV 9B165-9B176; 9B587; 4E5277-4E5278; 4E5343; 4E5364; 1F1914.

given the increased risk of being captured by enemy vessels. Second, whenever war broke out, the Malouins seized the opportunity and armed their corsairs. Note, however, that they continued to invest in normal trade ventures during every single one of the wars in this period. Once again, the evidence suggests that privateering complemented rather than substituted for normal trade in times of war, at least in Saint-Malo. The findings thus support Bromley's argument that the mere replacement of peacetime commerce was never sufficient to create and maintain a successful privateering port such as Saint-Malo.[14] The results imply that there is little empirical basis for the idea that the Malouins overspecialized in either the *course* or the South Sea enterprises. Perhaps they had a greater penchant than others for high-risk, high-return ventures inspired by their corsair mentality, but they clearly let that mentality guide them across a range of commercial endeavors beyond the *course* (see chapters 2 and 3).

The substitution argument is important because it provides an alternative explanation for the central position that the *course* ventures occupied in the Malouin organizational network. That alternative explanation suggests that mere exogenous happenstance—such as the outbreak of war—led merchant traders to divert their investments from regular trade toward the *course*. Hence, when few other opportunities for investment were available besides privateering, merchants inevitably were drawn to the *course*, which in turn resulted in the increasingly prominent role of *course* ventures in the organizational network of voyage partnerships. Because I find little empirical support for extensive substitution of peacetime commerce by privateering, we have little reason to believe that the pivotal network position of the *course* was merely an artifact of circumstances that offered not much else other than privateering for merchants to invest in.

With this understanding that the *guerre de course* attracted the interest of Malouin shipowners and their business partners from various strata as soon as war broke out, we can address the benefits they reaped from the sale of their prizes. Here again, the financial returns to privateering are of interest only insofar as they offer a deeper understanding of the incentives for merchants to become shareholding associates in voyage partnerships. As they joined partnerships, the Saint-Malo merchants formed and strengthened the kind of bonds that contributed to the cohesive weave of their community; and it was this cohesion of their merchant community that proved to be so vital for the success of the Malouins' enterprises in commerce. Because my interest is primarily in the social relational consequences of the *course* for the merchant community, I only briefly refer to the legal procedures that regulated the judgment and adjudication of prizes.

ADJUDICATION AND LIQUIDATION OF PRIZES[15]

Article 17 of the 1681 *Ordonnance de la Marine* stipulated that all corsair captains who seized any prize ships were to transport them, along with any prisoners they had captured, to the port where their privateering ships had been fitted out, unless heavy storms or enemy attacks forced them to make for an alternative port.[16] According to article 21, immediately following their arrival, either the captain or a designated officer was required to appear before the officials of the Admiralty, present their *commission en guerre* and other necessary papers, and render an account of when, where, and under what circumstances the prize was taken.[17] Once all necessary paperwork had been received, officials of the Admiralty went aboard and inspected the prize ship. In the presence of the privateering captain, the captain of the prize ship (or, alternatively, at least two seamen of the prize ship's crew), and any potential claimants to the seized vessel or cargo, the officials drew up an inventory of the captured goods and wares, sealed the ship, and placed a guard on site to deter any thieves (articles 22 and 23).[18]

The next step in the process was to assemble a prize dossier containing a copy of the corsair captain's *commission en guerre*; the prize declaration made to the officials of the Admiralty, as confirmed by two of the principal officers of his crew; any important papers found on board of the captured prize, including their translation into French, where necessary; a report of the inspection of the prize ship by the officials of the Admiralty; and finally a report of the interrogation of the prisoners taken by the corsair.[19] The complete dossier was then submitted to the *Conseil des prises* for evaluation. The prize council was established by a royal decree in 1659,[20] and its regulations and procedures were amended several times, including decrees in 1676, 1681, and 1695.[21] The council members included the Admiral of France, who presided, plus about a dozen prize commissioners, appointed by the crown, the *Secrétaire d'État* of the navy, and the *Secrétaire général de la Marine*.[22] The council convened only during times of war.[23] Its principal purpose was to assess and decide, on the basis of the dossiers, whether prizes were indeed taken in a legal manner, conforming to the regulations set forth in the *Code des prises*.[24] If the council found that a prize had been taken illegally— for instance, without a commission, or by violation of neutral rights—the council members had to decide if the seized ship and its cargo should be returned to their rightful owners, and if any compensation was in order. In addition to the declaration of just prizes, the *Conseil* held the right to sanction privateers and their crew for pillaging and similar transgressions of the regulations that governed the French *guerre de course*. Once the *Conseil* had declared the captured ship and its cargo a just prize (*bonne prise*), said judgment was delivered to the officers who represented the Admiralty locally, as they did in Saint-Malo.[25]

Eventually, upon receipt of the council's judgment, the *armateurs* of the corsair requested the local representatives of the Admiralty to proceed with the sale of their prize.[26] Figure 5.2 illustrates how the public sale of prizes was announced at Saint-Malo, using the case of the prize vessel *Le Georges & Molly* in May 1781.

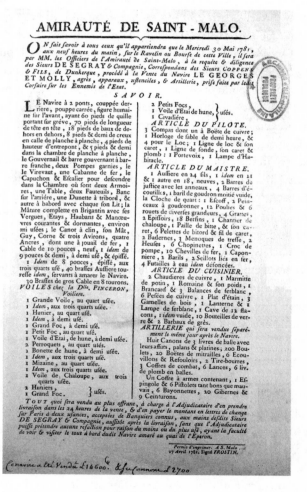

FIGURE 5.2 Announcement of auction of the prize ship *Le Georges & Molly*, at Saint-Malo, May 1781.

Sales took place "sur le Ravelin ou Bourse de cette Ville," close to the main gates of the walled city. The sale of the prize was organized as an auction by the candle, where a short candle was lit and bidding continued until its flame expired. The item on sale went to the last bid that was placed before the candle light went out. Payments by the winning bidders were to be made in notes of exchange accepted by reputable banquiers. All auction payments were handed to the *armateur*— the sieur De Segray in the case of the *Georges & Molly*, which sold for 14,600 *livres tournois* (*lt.*), plus an additional 2,700 *lt.* for the ship's cannons (see the handwritten note at the bottom of figure 5.2).[27] The *armateur* was entrusted by his business partners to keep an account of all proceeds from the auction and to divide them among the associates of the *société* (usually two-thirds) and the crew of the corsair ship (usually one-third). Before any such apportioning could be done, however, various administrative fees had to be paid for. These fees included the costs of unloading and guarding the prize ship; any duties that applied to goods seized by privateers; contributions for disabled seamen who were injured while serving on a corsair vessel and payments to the widows of those who died in service; and diverse fees payable to the courts and for the *armateur's* privateering commission. Finally, the Admiralty was traditionally entitled to a tenth of the prize-money. Settling these administrative fees thus yielded the net proceeds of the prize (*produit net*), which were to be divided among the associates and the crew.[28] The entire process for a single prize concluded the *liquidation particulière*. The *liquidation générale* moved beyond a single assessment and took into account all prizes a corsair captured during the entire commerce raiding campaign. Because this overall assessment included not only the administrative fees, but also initial expenses such as advances paid to the crew, and the fitting and victualling costs for the entire campaign, it provides a clearer idea of the returns to privateering enterprise for the *armateurs* and their business partners.

PROFITABILITY OF THE *COURSE*

For privateering voyages fitted out at Saint-Malo under the Ancien Régime (roughly before 1790), unfortunately, only a few complete liquidation accounts have survived that detail, for the same corsair ship, all initial expenses, advances, and administrative fees, as well as the corresponding sums that resulted from the sale of all prizes seized during the campaign.[29] Despite the lack of a sufficiently large number of such complete accounts, historian André Lespagnol has sought to estimate the cost of arming corsairs during the two final wars of Louis

XIV, relying on scarce evidence from seven privateering ships that were fitted out between 1690 and 1697, and from another dozen vessels that sailed between 1704 and 1710.[30] In chapter 3, I have supplemented Lespagnol's figures with fitting costs for half a dozen additional corsairs that were armed in 1702–1712. I estimated these expenses by summing up the values of shares that the investors contributed to their *sociétés*. The share values, in *livres tournois*, are documented in the notarial records for the voyage partnerships.[31] The combination of Lespagnol's and my estimates, yielding approximate average fitting costs per ton for *course* campaigns in the period 1690–1712, are reported in table 3.3 and discussed in chapter 3.

Moving beyond the wars of the elder Louis XIV, we may wonder how the costs of arming a corsair vessel developed over the course of the eighteenth century.[32] After a relatively long peacetime, from 1714 through 1744, three armed conflicts followed suit in 1744–1748, 1756–1763, and 1778–1783, all of which offered renewed opportunities for French privateers to raid enemy commerce.[33] I again follow the same strategy of estimating the costs of fitting out corsairs from the sum of shares (in *livres tournois*) that the *armateurs* and their business associates invested in a given venture. The underlying assumption likewise remains that the size of investments serves as an acceptable proxy for the actual sums needed to cover the costs of fitting out a private man-of-war. All information on the investments made by the shareholders is drawn from the declarations of voyage partnerships (*actes de société*), as registered by the Admiralty at Saint-Malo.[34] The *actes de société* may not be perfect, but in the absence of complete balance sheets for most *course* campaigns, they constitute the closest we have to a general account of the costs of arming privateers in this period. Table 5.1 summarizes the estimated sum of *livres tournois* invested in *course* ventures as well as the estimated average costs per ton during each of the three eighteenth-century wars.[35] Not unlike price hikes elsewhere, the average costs per ton follow a familiar pattern of rising fitting costs over the course of successive wars. Because the Malouins launched fewer ventures as we move forward from one period of war to the next, resulting in a lower overall number of tons, the total expenses of fitting out privateers decreased as well over time. I am not presenting these estimates for their own sake. Instead, I rely on them to obtain a more fine-grained account of the financial returns to privateering campaigns out of Saint-Malo.

Before we turn to these financial benefits that accrued to individual *armateurs* and their shareholding associates, let us first consider the overall material returns to privateering as well as its losses. In as much as French corsairs were in the business of seizing merchant ships or taking them for ransom, they put themselves at risk of being attacked, captured, or destroyed by enemy ships of

TABLE 5.1 Estimated Fitting Costs of Saint-Malo Corsairs, 1744–1783

	WAR OF THE AUSTRIAN SUCCESSION (1744–1748)	SEVEN YEARS' WAR (1756–1763)	AMERICAN REVOLUTIONARY WAR (1778–1783)
Average costs per ton (*livres tournois*)	190.66	324.62	438.71
(Std. dev.)	(107.77)	(103.58)	(216.05)
Total tons armed	16,365	8,381	4,338
Total fitting costs (*livres tournois*)	3,033,464	2,647,409	2,209,973
Number of ventures	84	70	41

Sources: Observations and calculations are based on venture partnership registers (*actes de société*; AD-IV 9B171–175).
The first period of war (1744–1748) includes one *armement en guerre et marchandise* (*L'Aigle* of Saint-Malo; AD-IV 9B171, ff 31v–32r).
Note: The average costs per ton are calculated based on observed values. Except for three cases, the number of tons per ship are always observed. The total fitting costs are based on observed as well as imputed values, where missing costs are replaced by the mean observed costs per ton. Consequently, dividing the total fitting costs by the total tons armed during a period of war does not equal the average costs per ton, as reported in the table.

war. As noted earlier, robbery and raids were part and parcel of seafaring in the age of sail. Likewise, as they took to the seas, privateers exposed themselves to natural hazards: shipwreck and hence the loss of vessels were not unheard of. It follows that the extent of such material losses, relative to captured prizes, should be taken into account when it comes to the returns to privateering. Table 5.2 thus offers a balance sheet that compares the number of corsair ships armed at Saint-Malo, how many of them were captured or lost, and finally how many prizes and ransoms they took during the five major wars in the hundred years between the 1680s and the 1780s.[36] The findings illustrate once more that the War of the League of Augsburg and the War of the Spanish Succession marked the heyday of Saint-Malo's privateering enterprise, with the largest number of corsair vessels and corresponding tons armed in this earlier period.[37] In the three conflicts that followed, the number of ventures armed at Saint-Malo dropped to between 9 and 22 percent of the numbers we find in the two earlier wars. It also seems that, on average, privateering ships had become smaller and lighter by the onset of the

TABLE 5.2 Material Returns to Saint-Malo Privateering: Prizes, Ransoms, and Losses of Corsairs, 1688–1783

	WAR OF THE LEAGUE OF AUGSBURG (1688–1697)	WAR OF THE SPANISH SUCCESSION (1702–1713)	WAR OF THE AUSTRIAN SUCCESSION (1744–1748)	SEVEN YEARS' WAR (1756–1763)[2]	AMERICAN REVOLUTIONARY WAR (1778–1783)
Number of corsair ventures armed	436	511	88	97	46
Total tons armed	80,230	95,375	16,562	11,570	5,387
Average tons per corsair	184.01	186.64	188.20	119.20	117.10
Number of corsairs lost[1]	69	128	31	26	14
Percent of corsairs lost	15.8	25.0	35.0	27.0	30.0
Total tons lost	9,750	13,547	5,834	3,738	1,639
Total number of prize ships	1,044	683	315	218	136
Average number of prizes per corsair	2.40	1.33	3.58	2.25	2.96
Total number of ransoms	231	203	23	65	40
Sum of prizes and ransoms	1,275	886	338	283	176
Average prizes and ransoms per corsair	2.92	1.73	3.84	2.90	3.83

Sources: For the War of the League of Augsburg and the War of the Spanish Succession, Lespagnol (1991, 382); AD-IV 9B408, 9B435, (1)–(3); for the remaining three armed conflicts, AD-IV 9B435, (4)–(5); Martin-Deidier (1976, 374–419).
Note:
[1] Losses include sunk, wrecked, or captured corsairs.
[2] For the Seven Years' War (1756–1763), Martin-Deidier (1976) reports substantially greater losses of corsairs in her summary tables than she does in her raw data (as included in the appendix to her dissertation). This table therefore shows the summary statistics I obtained, based on her raw data.

Seven Years' War and the American Revolutionary War. Considering the losses, the percentage of corsairs that were sunken, wrecked, or captured increased as well as we move from the reign of Louis XIV to the three wars in the second half of the eighteenth century. We also must consider the outcomes of commerce raiding ventures. It is hardly surprising, of course, that the more corsairs were put to sea, the greater the overall chances were of capturing any prizes—as long as the supply of potential prey remained stable. Because far fewer corsairs were fitted out during the latter half of the eighteenth century, the total number of prizes also decreased over time. The average number of prizes per individual corsair, however, increased between the two earlier and the three later wars. With the possible exemption of the War of the Spanish Succession, the Malouin corsairs appear to have been rather effective in their campaigns, with about two and a half prizes per individual corsair, on average (for a nuanced sense of the distribution of prizes across the years of each war, see chapter 2, figure 2.6, and chapter 7, figure 7.1).

As insightful as these material returns to privateering are, they do not fully tell us what monetary rewards, in *livres tournois*, the shipowners and their shareholding partners could reasonably expect on their investments in the *course*. The proceeds from selling prizes at auction could vary substantially, even within the same year. In the Seven Years' War (1756–1763), to cite just one conflict, the gross proceeds, before fees and duties were applied, could be as low as 687 *lt.* for a 25-ton prize vessel and as high as 509,643 *lt.* for a 130-ton ship, and just about any amount in between these two extremes.[38] Consequently, the sheer number of prizes may hint at how effective the Malouin corsairs were, but offer only a rough sense of the campaigns' financial outcomes. A closer look at the balance sheets of costs and benefits for individual privateering campaigns out of Saint-Malo promises a more fine-grained answer. Building on and extending the earlier efforts of historians J. S. Bromley and Annick Martin-Deidier, André Lespagnol has estimated the overall costs and benefits of Saint-Malo's privateering enterprise during the last two wars fought by Louis XIV.[39] In table 5.3, the first two columns reproduce Lespagnol's estimates. For the War of the Spanish Succession (1702–1713), the results of prize sales can be gleaned from the remittances of the Admiralty's tenth to Paris for ransoms and prize vessels cleared at Saint-Malo.[40] Unfortunately, comparable central registers do not exist for the earlier War of the League of Augsburg (1688–1697). In their absence, historians had to rely on local prize court judgments for ransoms taken, and on surviving dossiers of the sale and liquidation of prize ships and their valuable cargo. Drawing on these documents, previous historical accounts reached a sobering conclusion: for the most part, privateering enterprise out of Saint-Malo seemed to have yielded moderate gains at best, and at worst, spelled a financial disaster for the sponsoring merchants.[41]

TABLE 5.3 Estimated Profitability of Saint-Malo Privateering, 1688–1783

	WAR OF THE LEAGUE OF AUGSBURG [1688–1697]	WAR OF THE SPANISH SUCCESSION [1702–1713]	WAR OF THE AUSTRIAN SUCCESSION [1744–1748]	SEVEN YEARS' WAR [1756–1763]	AMERICAN REVOLUTIONARY WAR [1778–1783]
Number of selected corsair ventures in source			38	24 [1]	22
Average gross proceeds from prize sales (min.–max.)			—	188,356 (3,359–778,459)	—
Average net proceeds (min.–max.)			165,226 (21,240–484,910)	117,860 (2,976–357,216)	96,521 (3,005–466,192)
Average costs (min.–max.):					
Admiralty's tenth			16,523 (2,124–48,491)	—	—
Payments to crew			—	60,654 (2,198–234,946)	—
Administrative fees and duties			—	80,270 (1,236–229,558)	—
Estimated investments made by associates			34,957 (3,150–59,953)	60,093 (1,948–227,234)	57,281 (2,563–285,159)
Estimated average profits (min.–max.)[2]			75,194 (–22,658–303,273)	—	9,901 (–102,531–132,582)
Alternative estimated average profits (min.–max.)[3]			130,269 (–5,388–464,910)	80,115 (–97,386–298,200)	43,491 (–59,860–283,797)

Total number of corsair ventures armed	436	511	88	97	46
Estimated total gross proceeds from prize sales	25,750,000	33,000,000			
Estimated costs:					
Administrative fees	5,150,000	6,600,000			
Payments to crew (wages, advances, share in prizes)	2,288,800	2,933,000			
Total investments made by associates	14,530,000	19,940,000			
Estimated total profits accrued by associates	3,781,200	3,527,000			

Sources: For the War of the League of Augsburg and the War of the Spanish Succession, Lespagnol (1991, 392); *AD-IV* 9B408, 9B435, (1)–(3) for the remaining three armed conflicts, *AD-IV* 9B435, (4)–(5), 9B598 ("Etats des prises amenées et vendues à Saint-Malo"); data appendix in Martin-Deidier (1976); and Collas (1949b) for ventures organized by René-Auguste de Chateaubriand in 1760–1761.

Notes: All monetary values are denoted in *livres tournois*. Net proceeds deduct administrative fees, duties, and payments to the crew from auction sales of prizes. From 1743 onward, the Admiralty's tenth was to be deducted from the net proceeds of all prizes seized during a corsair's *course* campaign, and by 1758, it was abolished altogether. Estimated investments refer to the sum of shares (in *livres tournois*) contributed by the *armateurs* and their associates to a venture. Profits are calculated as the net proceeds, minus any outstanding payments due to the crew, and minus the investments made in the venture (investments are subtracted because each venture usually had a separate *société* of share partners. A *société* usually did not constitute a long-term investment akin to a joint stock that would be used to launch multiple successive ventures, although the exact same associates may have joined in another venture).

[1] For twelve ventures in the 1756–1763 period, information on costs is insufficient to estimate profits. For another three ventures in the same period, information on investments and profits are directly available from the sources, but any information on the gross proceeds from auction sales and administrative costs is lacking. Because fees did not necessarily vary in proportion to gross proceeds, missing information cannot be replaced with estimates from known costs.

[2] For the 1744–1748 and 1778–1783 periods, profits are estimated under the assumption that one-third of the net proceeds still had to be paid to the crew.

[3] For the 1744–1748 and 1778–1783 periods, the alternative calculation estimates profits under the assumption that the crew's share was already paid as advances and thus was included in the investments.

Whatever monetary returns a *course* campaign may have produced, they were swiftly consumed by substantial administrative expenses, and by the share of the pie, usually a third, that was rightfully claimed by the ship's crew. Finally, when considering any surplus left to the *armateurs* and their business partners, the initial investments in their venture would have to be deducted as well.[42]

We may be inclined to accept this interpretation of these sources because it sits neatly with the often-heard lament of contemporary merchants that unfavorable circumstances had befallen their businesses. If, however, their ventures did indeed perform so poorly, then why did the same Malouin merchants continue investing in them? As the historical evidence attests, they continued to fit out corsair campaigns whenever armed conflict offered an opportunity to do so, thus revealing their preferences for privateering enterprises.[43] In other words, the *armateurs* and their associates must have been aware of at least some successful campaigns that served as blueprints for their own undertakings; otherwise, they would have had little reason to believe that their sponsorship was worthwhile. In a similar vein, revisionist historians, such as André Lespagnol, have suggested that earlier accounts underestimated the true returns to privateering for two main reasons.

First, they typically excluded long-distance raiding expeditions such as those operating as far away as in the Indian Ocean or targeting the colonial ports along the South American coastline. The reason for their exclusion is that prizes seized on these journeys usually were adjudicated and sold in faraway ports, and thus they did not find their way into local registers in metropolitan France. Successful long-distance raids matter for an adequate assessment of the results of Saint-Malo's privateering efforts. They matter because they fetched substantially higher prizes than those privateers that preyed on shipping closer to their homeport. Lespagnol found that these extraordinary expeditions into the Indian Ocean and the South Sea yielded about 8 million *lt.* in 1710–1714 alone—that is, in addition to a return of merely 3 million *lt.* from ordinary ventures that pursued the *course classique* in the triangle between the shores of northern Spain, Ireland, and Brittany. The War of the League of Augsburg likewise yielded a number of rich prizes for the Malouins, seized at the expense of their enemies' colonial shipping, and amounting to another 7.5 million *lt.* in the years 1688–1691. The results in table 5.3 reflect these adjustments to earlier calculations of the returns to Saint-Malo's privateering enterprise.[44]

Second, earlier studies leaned toward lower-bound estimates of the financial outcome of the *course* because they assumed that hefty administrative fees of up to 24 percent applied to the gross sales value of prizes. The dearth of detailed accounts is certainly to be blamed. Yet, the few detailed liquidation records of the late-seventeenth and early eighteenth century that have survived indicate a more realistic amount of about 20 percent to be levied on prize sales. Accordingly, this is also the rate of administrative fees reported in the first two columns in table 5.3.

Even more consequential for understanding the true gains to be made from the *course* is how one treats the share of profits that belonged to the crew. Officers and sailors generally were entitled to a third of the net sales value achieved at the auction of a prize. One could consider, as some historians have done, the crew's third just like any other expenses and deduct that amount directly from the net sales value.[45] Had the crew's share indeed been paid in this manner, it certainly would have reduced the gains left to the *armateurs* and their associates by a substantial margin. Surviving accounts of how the proceeds from prize sales were apportioned, however, show that crew members usually received advance payments once they enlisted for a privateering cruise. These *avances* were taken into account when the crew's share was determined at the end of a campaign. It was thus only in cases in which the actual third of a given prize value exceeded their *avances* that officers and sailors were entitled to a bonus payment to make up for the difference—otherwise, they received no further (*néant*) payments.[46] The estimates of the crew's third for the 1688–1697 and the 1702–1713 periods given in table 5.3 also have been adjusted accordingly.

I follow much of the same rationale for the remaining three eighteenth-century conflicts that France was involved in. One difference, compared with Lespagnol's summary calculations, is that I rely on printed and archival sources for individual campaigns to arrive at average returns to Saint-Malo's privateering enterprise.[47] For the four years of the War of the Austrian Succession (1744–1748), information on the Admiralty's tenth has survived for thirty-eight of the eighty-eight privateering vessels that were fitted out at Saint-Malo. Recall that, in 1743, the royal administration changed its policy such that the Admiralty's share in prizes was reduced to a tenth of the net benefit.[48] Hence, knowing the amount of the Admiralty's tenth for individual campaigns permits us to calculate directly the net proceeds from the auction of prizes. The estimated net proceeds could be as little as 21,240 *lt.*, but they also could get close to 500,000 *lt.*, with an average of about 165,000 *lt.*[49] Furthermore, the estimated investments made by the *armateurs* and associates reflect the initial costs of fitting out a corsair vessel, including victuals, weaponry, equipment, and advances paid to the crew. Again, I use the sum of shares contributed by the associates in a *course* venture to estimate these fitting costs.[50]

Finally, knowing the net proceeds from auction sales and the initial investment costs, we can estimate how profitable the Malouin privateering campaigns were during the 1744–1748 conflict. Depending on whether or not one considers advances paid to the crew as expenses that were included in the investments for a venture, two variants can be used to estimate profits. The first variant leads to lower profit estimates because it assumes that the crew's share in the prize value needed to be deducted from the net proceeds. The second variant leads to higher profits because it relies on the assumption that advance payments covered most of the crew's share and that these advances were included in the initial investment costs. As shown in table 5.3, the two alternatives thus yield an upper and a lower bound of estimated profits, ranging from about 75,000 *lt.* to 130,000 *lt.*, on average. Together, they offer a realistic picture because it is not unlikely that some crews participated in the capture of particularly rich prizes, and therefore they did indeed receive payments beyond their initial advances. The calculations may seem a bit involved at first, but the lesson is straightforward. Even though some ventures apparently resulted in complete losses, by and large, privateering enterprises out of Saint-Malo during this period were in fact profitable for the investing merchants.[51]

With the onset of the Seven Years' War (1756–1763), yet another opportunity for privateering arose for the merchants of Saint-Malo. They took advantage of the moment and fitted out at least ninety-seven corsair ventures over the course of the war. Fortunately, otherwise hard-to-find documentation of the detailed costs and benefits of some twenty-four *course* campaigns exists for the first two years (1756–1757) of this particular conflict. For each corsair, the sources include information on the names and sizes of the prize ships captured, the date of their capture, the gross proceeds from their sales, the administrative fees imposed, the amount of the crew's share in the proceeds, and the net proceeds that accrued to the *armateurs* and their share partners.[52] Not included in the account balance are the initial investments made by the associates in each venture. As before, I draw on the sum of share values and estimated costs per ton to calculate these initial costs involved in fitting out a corsair vessel, provided that matching information can be identified in the share partnership records. The estimated averages and ranges for costs and benefits of the campaigns are summarized in table 5.3. Once again, some ventures ended in financial losses. For the most part, however, privateering in the Seven Years' War was profitable for the Malouin shipowners and merchants—at least as far as the cases from the onset of war are concerned.[53]

The American Revolutionary War was the last major conflict that involved France under the Ancien Régime, as it sided with the revolutionary colonists against Britain from 1778 until 1783. For Saint-Malo, it offered yet another window of opportunity for the *guerre de course*. Direct evidence on the net proceeds is available for nearly half of the campaigns undertaken by Malouin corsairs (twenty-two of forty-six).[54] In line with the two previous periods, I calculate the initial investments made by the associates from the sum of shares they contributed to their venture partnerships and the estimated costs per ton, as the size of privateering vessels is known in all cases. Likewise, I include the two variants of assessing profits, by now familiar from the estimates for the War of the Austrian Succession: first, assuming that the crew's share still had to be deduced from the net proceeds of the prize sales, and second, assuming that the crew's share was covered by advances, and thus part of the initial fitting costs. As shown in the last column of table 5.3, the results that emerge look familiar as well. In a few cases, the initial investments outweighed whatever net benefits were achieved, turning the venture into a failure from a business perspective.[55] On average, however, privateering enterprise in this last war period apparently yielded a positive balance for individual campaigns, just as it did during previous conflicts.

What conclusions, if any, may be drawn from these various pieces of insight into the business aspects of the *course*? Financially speaking, was privateering a worthwhile and successful enterprise for the Malouin merchantry? To begin, the fitting costs, and hence the average investments required to float a commerce raiding campaign rose substantially over time: from about 35,000 *lt.* in the 1740s up to 57,000 *lt.* and 60,000 *lt.* during the two wars in the second half of the eighteenth century. This increase occurred even though the vessels deployed for the *course* tended to become smaller over time, as evidenced in the decreasing average tonnage (see table 5.2). Ventures thus became more costly to get them off the ground, as we move from one war to the next.

Perhaps these rising costs were met by corresponding returns that prevented major losses and enabled substantial gains, at least on average. At first sight, both the average net proceeds and the estimated average profits per venture appear to have remained positive throughout. Just as noticeable, however, the levels of net proceeds as well as profits dwindled substantially between the War of the Austrian Succession and the American Revolutionary War.[56] The skeptical view, put forward by earlier historians, that the *guerre de course* was of limited profitability, indeed may be warranted. A few empirical considerations put this interpretation into perspective, however. First, the numbers shown in table 5.3 are lower-bound estimates of returns because they draw primarily on prizes declared before the Admiralty at Saint-Malo, whereas captains of Malouin corsairs routinely carried their prizes into ports other than Saint-Malo.[57] Second, as mentioned earlier, the returns could vary substantially across campaigns, even within the same year. One indication is the wide range between negative and positive values for the net proceeds and profits given in table 5.3. Such volatility suggests that favorable circumstances for successful commerce raids were not systematically related to any particular years. Consequently, some *armateurs* and their associates lost their entire investments. Unfortunate cases in point include the *société* of the corsair *L'Heureux* in 1746, which seized at least three prizes, yielding estimated net proceeds of 52,000 *lt*. What sounds like a formidable return was consumed entirely by initial investments of about 57,000 *lt*. for the large three-hundred-ton *L'Heureux*. Depending on whether or not one considers additional costs for the crew, the corsair's owner, Richard Butler, and his share partners ended up not with a profit, but with a negative balance of an estimated −5,300 *lt*. (or if payments to the crew were still unsettled, −22,600 *lt*.). Likewise, the associates who sponsored the much smaller 140-ton *La Vestale* for its 1744 campaign ran into a deficit of an estimated −4,540 *lt*. (or if the crew's share still had to be accounted for, −16,360 *lt*.), even though the corsair seized at least two prizes worth some 35,450 *lt*. in net proceeds.[58]

In stark contrast, others made impressive fortunes. One may point to one of the earliest *course* campaigns that the sieur Grandclos Meslé sponsored as the owner of the two-hundred-ton corsair *Le Puisieulx* in 1757. The estimated fitting costs of about 65,000 *lt*. that Granclos Meslé and his sixteen associates had to invest were easily outweighed by some handsome net proceeds (i.e., after administrative costs and payments to the crew) of up to 314,000 *lt*. that flowed from the capture and auction sale of at least a dozen prize ships.[59] At the height of the Seven Years' War, a comparable success was achieved by René-Auguste de Chateaubriand with his frigate *L'Amaranthe*, which he purchased for the sum of 32,100 *lt*. Next to his own contribution, Chateaubriand managed to mobilize capital from nineteen associates whose shares in the venture allowed him to cover the 59,016 *lt*. in fitting costs that were necessary to put the *Amaranthe* to sea. Their investment proved to be worthwhile. The *Amaranthe*'s campaign from October 1760 through February 1761 alone resulted in some dozen prizes and five ransoms, and hence a net benefit of 357,216 *lt*., which in turn meant a profit of 298,200 *lt*. for the shareholding partners, a fivefold return on their investment.[60]

These may be but a few of the most illustrious cases, but they invite an alternative interpretation to the overly skeptical view set forth by previous historians' accounts. Consider the following analogy. Seeing that others have won in previous rounds is often enough for a modern-day lottery-player to place her bet, however unlikely a win may be for each individual. Likewise, for the individual merchant and shipowner, it may not have been so important that every single venture was indeed successful and brought home enormous riches. Rather, the mere fact that some expeditions, like that of the *Amaranthe* or the *Puisieulx*, returned in a triumph showed that glittering prizes were a tangible promise, and offered enough of an incentive for others to follow suit and try their hands at the *course*.

More than a few authors have likened the *course* to a lottery, as fortunes certainly could be made, and indeed were made, from such engagements. It is worth emphasizing again, however, that monetary gains were conditional on corsairs not getting captured, lost, or sunken and having seized any prizes to begin with— without prizes, no returns were gained, and again, not every single campaign resulted in the capture of one or more enemy vessels. The *course* clearly was a high-risk, high-return undertaking. With these caveats in mind, the expected profits from commerce raids offered clear incentives to attract the Malouin *armateurs* and their business associates to privateering enterprise. Now that we know that good reasons existed to invest in the *course*, let us turn to the role it played in maintaining social cohesion within the merchant community.

CHAPTER 6

DYNAMICS OF PARTNERSHIP NETWORKS

I n chapter 3, I have shown that the members of Saint-Malo's merchant community did not form a single, unified trader elite. As reflected in the *capitation*, the poll tax records, they were stratified according to their economic standing in the city. Few social science historians would be surprised to find such multiple layering and grouping among merchant elites, even within a place as bounded and small as Saint-Malo. More important are the consequences of this elite stratification for the economic and social cohesion of the local merchant community in Saint-Malo and its vicinity. The Malouin merchants differed in their social standing because they differed in the extent of their wealth, and hence in the amount of financial resources they could invest in trading enterprises. Small-scale shipping along the French Atlantic coastline usually did not require enormous sums of capital. To pick just one, yet admittedly stark example: in 1712, some still moderate 7,000 *livres tournois* (*lt.*) were required for the Malouin *armateur* Claude Girard and his thirteen *associés* (business partners) to ship a charge of sardines on the 150-ton *La Paix* along the coast between Brittany and the Strait of Gibraltar.[1] In contrast, the fitting cost of a staggering 609,878 *lt.* for the four-hundred-ton *Le Comte de Toulouse* on her way to Canton in 1718 illustrates the substantial financial commitment that long-distance trading voyages to China and the East Indies necessitated.[2] Only a select circle of affluent merchant elites was able to raise such large sums. With pronounced wealth inequality among the local merchantry, it would be hardly surprising to find its members engaged in separate clusters of commercial ventures according to financial means. In other words, in the absence of any joint investment and partnership ties that could serve as bridges across clusters, such economic cleavages would have given rise to social fragmentation, thus separating the various elite groups within the merchant community.

Yet, much of the spectacular economic success of Saint-Malo in this historical period seems to have rested on the social cohesion of its merchant community. This dense web of strong social bonds was formed by shared religious sentiments, a strong sense of place, and its history; supported by marriage alignments, kinship, and neighborhood ties; and replenished through selective migration into the community from outside. It was this social cohesion—channeled through apprenticing sons, nephews, and cousins into the arts of commerce and navigation—that nurtured that collective *fidélité au commerce*, a distinct instinct for lucrative trading opportunities that proved to be beneficial for the city's merchantry. What helped to maintain social cohesion among the Malouin merchants despite the clear inequality in wealth, and thus prevented their fragmentation into separate factions? I suggest that bonds forged through joint *course* partnerships facilitated this very social cohesion. To describe their mediating role, I have introduced the notion of *course* partnerships as linchpin organizations that bonded the various merchant groups through repeated collaborations. Because the role of a linchpin organization is inherently relational, it arises first and foremost out of the pattern of relationships within which the merchants are embedded. To be sure, just as their peers elsewhere, the Malouin merchants certainly had good economic reasons for engaging in some partnerships while steering clear of others. Little precluded them from purposefully creating linchpin organizations when forming these partnership ties. For linchpin organizations to work, however, it is not strictly necessary that they were set up intentionally, by design.

The previous two chapters set the scene as we considered the historical origins, the business organization, and the legal regulations of the *guerre de course* in France under the Ancien Régime. With the institutional setting in mind, I now turn to direct empirical support for the linchpin role of *course* ventures within Saint-Malo's merchant network. Two questions in particular are of interest. First, to what extent did privateering partnerships indeed contribute to the social cohesion of the Malouin merchant community? Second, as we know that the commercial success of Saint-Malo waxed and waned over the course of our historical period, did the mediating role of privateering partnerships also change over time?

Before we can plunge into the empirical study of these questions, I will introduce the structure of the underlying network dataset. As it is often the case, such relational data tend to be complex, in particular as they stem from archival sources that are prone to all sorts of lacunae. The network data I reconstructed open avenues for new insights, but they also have their limitations. In the interest of full disclosure, much of the discussion in the following section may be rather technical. Although I will not assume any prior knowledge of social network analysis, readers who do not share an enthusiasm for the likes of matrix transformation and coding decisions on tie strength should skip ahead to the next section.

BUILDING NETWORKS FROM ARCHIVAL RECORDS

Answering both questions just raised requires a systematic analysis of social cohesion within the network of relations among the Malouin merchants over time. What defined the heart of their collective identity were their manifold commercial activities that led them to create a worldwide web of trade relationships, with their home port of Saint-Malo at its center. The importance the Malouins placed on the apprenticeship of their sons and nephews in the arts of trade and navigation further attests to the essential role of seaborne commerce in their lives. If social cohesion among the merchantry should have been expressed in any one place, then it should have been in the networks of partnerships they formed in pursuit of their commercial interests. The rich archival holdings of trade partnership declarations (*actes de société*) are among the most suitable primary sources available to reconstruct these commercial networks.[3] As discussed earlier, the surviving declarations contain comprehensive information about the purpose and intended destination of the planned trading voyage, and the characteristics of the vessel to be fitted out, such as its type, name, tonnage, and size of crew. Recall that these declarations also list the names of the main *armateurs* who typically, although not always, owned the ship and initiated the venture, the name of the captain, and the names of all merchant partners (*associés*) who held shares in the venture, including their places of residence. The size of their shares (e.g., half, quarter, eighth, sixteenth) or the monetary value of their contributions (in *livres tournois*) is often, but not always, included.

I collected this information from all surviving declarations, amounting to 3,250 unique voyage partnerships and involving 6,298 individual shareholders. The latter include the *armateurs*, the merchant investors, and the vessels' captains who were listed among the partners. Depending on the destination of a given voyage and the size of the vessel, the number of affiliates could vary considerably, with the largest venture attracting up to 150 shareholders. On average, about four partners (standard deviation = 6) participated in a voyage. The earliest records of partnership contracts date back to October 1681. The latest entries in my dataset are from February 1792 and thus extend well into the events of the French Revolution. As a general rule, I use the earliest date written on a given document to code the starting date of a voyage partnership.[4] The declarations generally do not contain an ending date that would have limited the duration of a venture.[5]

Drawing on these data, I coded affiliation networks—two-mode or bipartite networks in technical parlance—that connect individual merchants to the ventures of trading voyages in which they participated. Because I am interested in the development of social cohesion versus fragmentation within the merchant community over time, I split these networks into separate periods. Similar to other longitudinal network data that stretch over a long time span, finding the right balance between historical detail and a sufficiently broad view of merchant relationships tends to be a thorny issue. On one hand, an adequate number of discrete periods is necessary to reveal potential changes in network patterns. On the other, any division into periods should not be sliced so finely as to artificially create fragmentation by cutting off observed ties among merchants that otherwise would contribute to social cohesion. Affiliation networks will necessarily show strong local clustering because, by definition, all partners of a given venture are considered to be directly connected to each other.[6] The built-in clustering tendency that yields fully connected, yet isolated, cliques of merchants is thus primarily a result of the underlying data structure. Consequently, partnership ties that bridge across these venture-based cliques are vital for social cohesion to emerge in the first place. Merchants who became serial investors and participated in at least two different ventures were the only sources of these bridging ties. In other words, however time is split, the choice should accommodate as much as possible the engagements of merchants in successive ventures within a given period.

To meet these challenges, I defined period-specific networks that are sensitive to historically meaningful events and that also are based on the observed duration between each merchant's subsequent ventures. The complete network extends from 1681 through 1792, and it includes 2,142 merchants (i.e., 34 percent of the total) who were involved in more than a single voyage. Within this subset of serial investors, each individual merchant participated in an average number of six voyages (standard deviation = 9.069). Their successive ventures were launched about five or six years apart from each other (mean = 5.578 years; standard deviation = 8.199). On the basis of these observations, I distinguished six discrete periods. As summarized in table 6.1, all six periods are characterized primarily by salient historical events, and most significantly, by a long sequence of wars in 1688–1697, 1702–1713, 1740–1748, 1756–1763, and 1778–1783 because it was only during armed conflict that opportunities for privateering emerged.

TABLE 6.1 Choice of Periods

PERIOD	START	END	YEARS	HISTORICAL EVENTS
1	1681	1697	17	War of the League of Augsburg (1688–1697); period begins in 1681 due to left-censoring
2	1698	1720	23	War of the Spanish Succession (1702–1713); Danycan's South Sea Co. established in 1698; height of Saint-Malo's commercial success until 1720; Saint-Malo's East Indies monopoly revoked in 1719
3	1721	1740	20	Prolonged peacetime; relative decline of Saint-Malo's commerce
4	1741	1755	15	War of the Austrian Succession (1740–1748); fighting brakes out in December 1740
5	1756	1777	22	Seven Years' War (1756–1763); new generation of *messieurs de Saint-Malo* emerges; French East Indian trade opened to private traders in 1769
6	1778	1792	15	France enters American Revolutionary War (1778–1783); in 1789/1790, the French Revolution arrives in Saint-Malo

The third period (1721–1740) is an exception, as it witnessed an unusually long peacetime, and thus the absence of any privateering. These periods not only carry historical meaning but also err on the side of social cohesion. Even the two shortest among these six periods lasted for at least fifteen years, nearly three times as long as it typically took individual merchants to engage in successive ventures. Furthermore, because the sources unfortunately do not reveal when partnership ties ended, my choice of period-specific networks likely is biased toward social cohesion among merchants. This bias avoids the problem of arbitrarily cutting off observed ties, and therefore yields lower-bound estimates of social fragmentation in the merchant community.

For each period, I first constructed a binary merchant-by-voyage venture matrix with merchants arrayed in rows and voyage ventures in columns. In the first period (1681–1697), for example, the matrix cross-tabulates 723 individual merchants with 239 trading voyages. Each cell in this matrix reports if a merchant participated in the *société* of business partners who fitted out the vessel for its trading or privateering voyage. I then transformed each of the six period-specific matrices into a symmetric merchant-by-merchant matrix and a corresponding symmetric voyage venture-by-voyage venture matrix. Within each resulting merchant-by-merchant network, pairs of merchants are linked to the extent that they were business partners in the same trade or privateering ventures. Entries are equal to zero in the absence of such partnership relations.[7] Their mirror image can be found in the voyage-by-voyage networks, which document the extent of the interlocks between trading ventures, that is, the number of merchants that each pair of ventures had in common as business partners.

The voyage contract records allow me to distinguish not only between engagements in the *course* and in trade but also between different kinds of trades. The map in figure 6.1 draws on the number of *actes de société* (voyage partnership contracts) in each branch of overseas commerce. It does not come as a surprise that the number of *sociétés* (partnerships) fluctuates substantially across different branches. For ease of visual comparison, the size of each branch is therefore displayed on a logarithmic scale. The resulting map invites us to appreciate the sheer scope of the Malouin network of trade routes and destinations. It spanned the entire globe during the 1681–1792 period—from the coasts of Peru and Chile to Pondichéry in India, and from the plantations on the Îles de France et Bourbon (present-day Mauritius and Réunion) in the Indian Ocean to the fishing grounds around Newfoundland. That such extensive information on the various trades as well as on privateering is available in the surviving documents is not merely a historical accident.[8]

The merchants of Saint-Malo, just as their peers in other port cities, had good economic reasons for simultaneously committing their investments to multiple overseas trading ventures. Initially, the diversification of these vested interests may have been born out of necessity, in particular, to spread and thus to minimize the risk of losses. It did not take long, however, before the Malouins recognized that maximizing the diversity of their investments across multiple trades also improved their chances of making a profit. Notably, members of the leading merchant dynasties who had plenty of funds at their disposal adopted the spread of investments (or polyvalence, as André Lespagnol has called it) as a forceful strategy to multiply their access to lucrative business opportunities.[9] A fine example is Jean Magon, sieur de la Lande (1641–1709), who belonged to one of the most prominent merchant families in Saint-Malo. In my dataset of

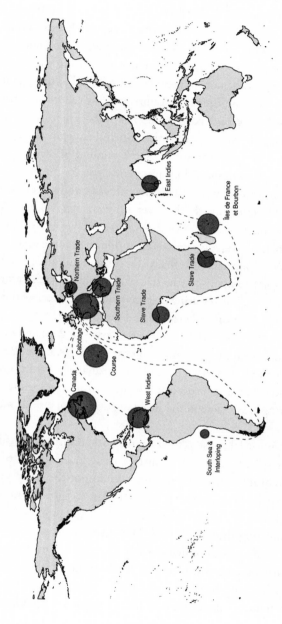

FIGURE 6.1 The worldwide trading network of the Saint-Malo merchant elite, 1681–1792.

Note: The size of circles represents the number of partnership contracts (*actes de société*) for voyages to each destination. For readability, the number of voyages is displayed on a logarithmic scale.

Sources: AD-IV 9B165-9B176; 9B587; 4E1277-4E1278; 4E1343; 4E1364; 1F1914.

voyage contracts, the Magons counted thirty-one individual *armateurs* and traders among their ranks, making them also one of the most active merchant dynasties, next to the likes of the Duguen, Tanquerey, and Potier families. Between 1681 and 1685 alone, Jean Magon de la Lande participated in twenty-five voyage partnerships to Newfoundland, Cadiz, and the Mediterranean; traded in the export of valuable wares to Spanish America, Amsterdam, and Marseille; acted as a commissioner in the cloth trade for French and foreign clients; and became an associate in partnerships formed for the assurance of ships.[10] Upon his death in 1709, Jean Magon's accumulated wealth amounted to nearly 2 million *lt.*, all left to the benefit of his heirs.[11] Because the strategy of the Magons and other families was anchored in the organization of *sociétés*, casting a wide net of investments also meant weaving a wide net of partnership ties, which in turn increased connections among various ventures and ultimately contributed to social cohesion within the merchant community.

The surviving records of partnership contracts reflect precisely this commercial strategy. Using the information on the different trades that merchants were involved in, it is straightforward to append the corresponding ties between merchants and their diverse ventures to the period-specific network matrices. What emerge, then, are time-varying networks of partnerships over 112 years, from 1681 through 1792, for which the content of ties comes from multiple kinds of enterprises. One caveat is that the descriptions of voyage destinations in the original documents varied considerably. Some contained rather generic phrases, such as "destiné pour aller negocier" (quite literally "sent out to trade"). In other cases, the inclusion of the destination, such as "en Guinée," did little to veil the venture's intended business, namely, slave trading.[12] Still other descriptions included much more detailed instructions, as in the case of the four-hundred-ton *Le Sage* whose owners and business associates fitted her out in 1719 for an extended voyage to "L'amerique Espagnolle, tant aux costes du nord, que dans les Mers et costes du Sud et ailleurs ou lesdits associés ont deliberé d'envoyer ledit Navire en guerre et marchandises y vendre, traitter, sejourner et negocier sa ditte cargaison faisant la guerre et la Course sur les ennemies de L'Etat [sic]."[13] The key is to distill the minute characteristics of each case into a limited number of trade categories that allow us to recognize patterns in the organization of overseas endeavors. In what follows, therefore, I classify each of the various voyage destinations and purposes into one of twelve trade categories. A residual category captures voyages that are so specific that they do not fit unambiguously into any of the existing categories.[14] Table 6.2 reports the resulting classification and compares the types of trade and privateering with respect to the number of voyage partnerships, their average size, and the average tonnage of the vessels employed. There are few surprises. Judging

TABLE 6.2 Classification of Trades and *Course* (Privateering Enterprise), 1681–1792

CATEGORY	DESCRIPTION	NUMBER OF VENTURES (TOTAL = 3,250)	PROPORTION	NUMBER OF PARTNERS IN VENTURE			TONNAGE PER VESSEL		
				AVERAGE	STD. DEV.	MAX.	AVERAGE	STD. DEV.	MAX.
0	French coastal trade	589	.181	3.085	3.239	20	60.467	52.047	400
1	Spanish and southern European trade	142	.044	3.669	4.267	22	192.048	98.405	500
2	British Isles and northern European trade	34	.011	1.941	3.946	22	94.538	71.196	320
3	*Pêche* (Newfoundland fishing and Canadian trade)	978	.301	4.353	4.606	31	125.957	75.563	500
4	*Course* (privateering enterprise)	360	.111	9.633	12.306	150	134.806	99.235	630
5	Trade with Saint-Domingue and French West Indies	226	.070	3.434	4.590	42	186.265	102.236	600
6	Trade with China, East Indies, and *Îles de France et Bourbon*	92	.028	5.685	6.998	25	405.143	349.261	1,500
7	African slave trade, Cape Verde, and Canary Islands	93	.029	3.441	2.976	17	172.353	92.942	450
8	Interloping in South Sea and Spanish America	16	.005	6.375	6.840	20	286.000	54.589	350
9	*Guerre et marchandises* (letter-of-marque ventures)	18	.006	8.056	3.404	14	202.667	98.595	400
10	Sale of ships	96	.030	0.604	1.511	9	68.654	58.246	280
11	Long-distance voyages (*long cours*)	12	.004	2.417	2.275	7	123.417	84.321	350
12	Other ventures	55	.017	2.618	3.998	23	125.000	92.985	400
13	Destination or purpose unknown	539	.166	3.438	3.528	25	104.171	86.804	800

Sources: AD-IV 9B165–9B176; 9B587; 4E5277–4E5278; 4E53431; 4E5364; 1F1914.

just by the number and proportion of ventures across all trades, Newfoundland fishing, as Saint-Malo's traditional stronghold in maritime commerce, accounted for nearly a third of all partnerships. Another long-established branch, shipping from port to port along the French coastline, contributed 18 percent of all ventures. Two additional findings reveal once again how dedicated the Malouins were to the *guerre de course*. First, with 360 registered contracts—11 percent of the total—it was the third-largest branch of seaborne enterprise. Not included are the ventures of *guerre et marchandise*, that is, vessels fitted out primarily for trade, yet whose captains carried letters of marque that entitled them to seize prizes should the opportunity arise. Second, the average number of business partners attracted to *course* ventures was up to five times as large as in other trades.[15] Both findings attest to the potential of privateering enterprise to play a mediating role within the merchant community: *course* ventures could hardly provide a platform for network mediation without a sufficient number of merchants engaging in the *course* to begin with.

Finally, the average size of vessels, measured in tons, corresponds to the intended purpose of the voyages. Long-distance shipping of manufactured wares and colonial raw materials to and from destinations, in the East Indies, the Caribbean, or even the Mediterranean, required vessels with sizeable cargo holds. Far smaller vessels were employed for the relatively short distances covered when crossing the English Channel or shipping along the Breton and Norman coastlines.

Beyond the multiple types of trade engagements, another important concern that needs to be addressed is the extent to which the strength and the value of partnership ties mattered for social cohesion among the merchantry. The central question is how much any variation in the values of shares could have shaped the social relational patterns that embedded the members of the Saint-Malo merchantry. The substantive reasoning behind this question is that stronger ties with high-value shares presumably reflect a deeper commitment to the enterprise. Because they had such a vested interest, deeply committed shareholders also had a strong incentive to influence the economic course and political control of said enterprise. Following this argument, any mediating role of privateering in the partnership network may have had little to do with the inherent nature and organization of privateering but a lot to do with the political objectives and strategic choices of the committed shareholders.

As plausible as this reasoning may sound, my foremost interest is to reveal cohesive patterns within the merchant network and to identify the organizational mechanisms that facilitated them. Network patterns rest on the presence versus absence of social relations, and in this regard, considering tie strength has its limitations. Recall that the data consist of affiliation networks, such that, by definition, all partners of a venture are connected to each other. Mutual connections that are derived from these affiliations denote joint membership and are not directed, in contrast to directed ties that reflect, for instance, the buying and selling of goods or the flow of information from a sender to a receiver. Now, imagine that one merchant holds one-quarter of the shares and his business partner holds three-quarters of the shares. What should be the value of their joint relationship? Because the relationship is not directed, the two share values may be combined. We could sum both shares and declare their tie to have a value of one. We could do the same if the two partners both contributed half shares. Similarly, one partner could have contributed one-eighth and the other seven-eighths of the shares. In all three scenarios, the sum of the shares equals one, but we probably would not want to treat them as identical because the equality of contributions varies markedly. Another option is to choose a cutoff value, say at least one-third of the shares in a partnership, to consider a tie. Ties with values below this threshold then would be deleted from the network.[16] Alternatively, one could rely on the distribution of observed tie values, and choose the mean or median value to set such a threshold value without being overly arbitrary in one's choice. Even so, there is yet another drawback. Those merchants who participated in several ventures at once but acquired only low-value shares still maintained multiple relationships with a wide range of partners. Well-connected as they were, these merchants might have been much more critical for community cohesion than their peers who made a few spectacular investments that implied a rather limited number of partner ties. What matters for cohesion in this comparison is the pattern of the network at large, contingent on the presence or absence of relationships, not on their strength. Hence, although they may appear plausible at first, none of these coding suggestions offer an unambiguous and substantively meaningful rule to decide whether a tie is present or absent.

Setting aside these substantive concerns, the idea that the network ties among venture partners should be weighed by share values also has empirical limits. For one, information on the size of shares (e.g., half, quarter, eighth) is missing for 2,987 out of the total of 14,004 investments. No matter which method we would choose to weigh network ties according to their share size, we would have to exclude 21 percent of all investments because the necessary information is not available.[17] Yet, even if such data had survived, an eighth share in a voyage that cost its business partners 25,000 *lt.* to fit it out should probably weigh more than an eighth share in a voyage that took a mere 2,500 *lt.*

to launch. Unfortunately, the exact monetary value of shares (again in *livres tournois*) is known for even fewer cases, 2,256 investments to be precise, and the total fitting cost are rarely stated in the records. So, again, using this information to determine tie weights would ignore as many as 11,748 cases, that is, the vast majority (84 percent) of all investments. Furthermore, only forty-nine investments contain information on both the size of shares and their equivalent value in *livres tournois*. Finally, even if we would consider the 11,017 investments for which information on the various sizes of shares is available, it turns out that the range of these sizes within partnerships was quite narrow. The 11,017 investments were made within 2,072 unique voyage partnerships, and in 94 percent of these partnerships, we can distinguish at most five different share sizes. In 71 percent of the cases we can distinguish just three different share sizes, and in 51 percent, merely two different share sizes are evident. Consequently, if the shares within partnerships differed so little, then it hardly would be necessary to adjust partner ties by their strength. Little would be gained, then, but a lot of information would be lost if the partnership ties were to be weighed by the size or value of shares.

COHESION WITHIN THE MERCHANT NETWORK

The six panels in figure 6.2 enable readers to take a bird's-eye view of the partnership network. This vantage point enables us to visualize the contours of the network and how it evolved over time, using the time periods discussed earlier. Each panel corresponds to one of the six period-specific networks within which the Malouin merchants were embedded. More specifically, the nodes within these graphs represent individual merchants. Solid black nodes refer to merchants who were engaged in a privateering venture at least once during the respective period. This does not imply an exclusive commitment to privateering, however; privateering *armateurs* and their business partners also may have participated in other trading ventures beyond the *course*, and a good number among them did so. What distinguishes those merchants who are shown as light gray nodes within a period is simply that they never joined a privateering partnership and instead dedicated their efforts to other branches of commerce. The size of individual nodes increases with the number of ventures that a merchant participated in. As noted earlier, although 4,156 (66 percent) of all 6,298 merchants in my dataset made only one investment, the remaining 2,142 merchants

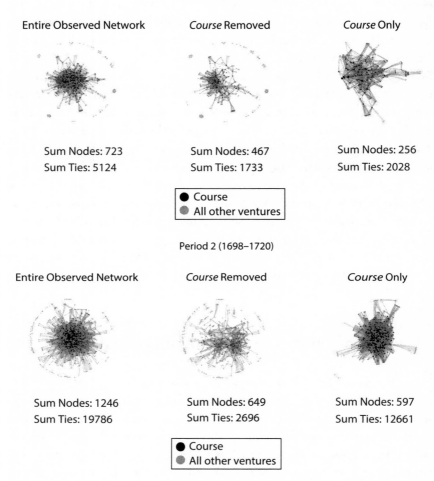

Period 1 (1681–1697)

Entire Observed Network

Sum Nodes: 723
Sum Ties: 5124

Course Removed

Sum Nodes: 467
Sum Ties: 1733

Course Only

Sum Nodes: 256
Sum Ties: 2028

● Course
● All other ventures

Period 2 (1698–1720)

Entire Observed Network

Sum Nodes: 1246
Sum Ties: 19786

Course Removed

Sum Nodes: 649
Sum Ties: 2696

Course Only

Sum Nodes: 597
Sum Ties: 12661

● Course
● All other ventures

FIGURE 6.2 Cohesion and fragmentation in the Saint-Malo voyage partnership network, by period (1681–1792).

Note: The left-hand graph in each panel shows the observed network of partnership ties, derived from joint affiliations of merchants within the same trading or privateering venture. Black nodes represent merchants who were partners in at least one privateering voyage (*course*) within a period-specific network. All other nodes refer to merchants who participated in other commercial voyages, but not in privateering ventures. The graph at the center of each panel replicates the observed graph, with all merchants who participated in privateering ventures removed from the network, together with all their ties. The right-hand graph in each panel shows the privateering merchants and their ties in isolation, detached from the rest of the partnership network. The layout of all three network graphs within each period-specific panel uses the same coordinates. All drawings rely on a force-directed graphing algorithm such that the distance between individual merchants is proportional to the shortest path linking them, variation in the length of ties is limited, and any overlap among nodes and ties is minimized.

Sources: *AD-IV* 9B165-9B176; 9B587; 4E5277-4E5278; 4E5343; 4E5364; 1F1914.

Period 3 (1721–1740)

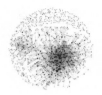

| ● Course | Sum Nodes: 1343 |
| ● All other ventures | Sum Ties: 7544 |

Period 4 (1741–1755)

Entire Observed Network   *Course* Removed   *Course* Only

Sum Nodes: 1330   Sum Nodes: 1002   Sum Nodes: 328
Sum Ties: 8678   Sum Ties: 2452   Sum Ties: 4695

| ● Course |
| ● All other ventures |

Period 5 (1756–1777)

Entire Observed Network   *Course* Removed   *Course* Only

Sum Nodes: 1604   Sum Nodes: 1339   Sum Nodes: 265
Sum Ties: 15049   Sum Ties: 5672   Sum Ties: 5889

| ● Course |
| ● All other ventures |

FIGURE 6.2 (*continued*)

Period 6 (1778–1792)

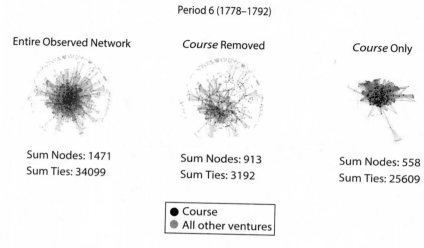

Entire Observed Network

Sum Nodes: 1471
Sum Ties: 34099

Course Removed

Sum Nodes: 913
Sum Ties: 3192

Course Only

Sum Nodes: 558
Sum Ties: 25609

● Course
◉ All other ventures

FIGURE 6.2 (*continued*)

(34 percent) were partners in several ventures, about six on average (standard deviation = 9.074). Because the number of partnerships per merchant varied considerably, ranging anywhere from 1 to 160 ventures (in one extreme case), the size of the nodes is displayed using a logarithmic scale. Without such rescaling, particularly large nodes would dwarf nodes that represent less active traders. The networks are drawn using a force-directed graphing algorithm such that the distance between individual traders is proportional to the shortest path linking them, variation in the length of ties is limited, and any overlap among nodes and ties is minimized.

With these technicalities settled, we can first consider the graphs shown on the left-hand side of the panels in figure 6.2. Each maps the observed web of business collaborations among the Malouin merchants (one display for each period). Even to the untrained eye, the strong concentration of merchants and their relationships into a single dense cluster is immediately recognizable. Some isolated dyads and smaller clusters surround the well-connected core of the network. But they are few and far between. Such a concentration into a single well-connected core is precisely the kind of network pattern we would expect to find if the merchants of Saint-Malo were indeed embedded in a close-knit community. This close-knit community network offered an organizational platform ideally suited to uphold their collective culture of commerce.

As we progress through the six periods, this cohesive social structure remains largely robust. The network in period 3 (1721–1740) appears to be the exception to the rule, as it is visibly more fragmented into multiple disconnected clusters. As such, the wearing away of cohesion in the partnership network coincided directly with the well-documented economic waning that Saint-Malo's merchantry faced during these very same years. Likewise, the increase in network fragmentation corresponded to the one period that witnessed no armed conflicts, a situation that seldom spelled bad news for foreign trade. But it did harm that other lucrative business the Malouins specialized in, the *guerre de course*. No war implied that no legal opportunities were on offer to raid foreign commerce. The absence of privateering partnerships in peacetime thus was systematically related to the weakening of connectivity in the merchant community network. This observation suggests that *course* partnerships, if they were present, indeed played a mediating role. The ties they forged through joint *course* undertakings apparently helped the Malouin merchants to uphold the complex web of affiliations they had built in various overseas trades. Consistent with this argument, cohesion was on the rise again once the outbreak of wars during the last three periods reinvigorated the commitment of French *armateurs* to privateering enterprise.

The impact the presence or absence of privateering had on social cohesion warrants a more systematic study. Even the most well-drawn picture can tell us only so much. Let us therefore turn to the more systematic findings given in table 6.3 to support the initial visual impressions. They offer more fine-grained evidence for the extent of cohesion in the merchant networks. In the table, the first row for each period reports descriptive statistics for the complete network of voyage partnerships. The first two columns of statistics list the number of merchants and the sum of venture partnership ties linking them. The overall size of the network grew substantially over time, from 723 merchants connected through 5,124 ties in the early years (1681–1697) toward 1,471 merchants and a total of 34,099 ties during the final period (1778–1792).[18] In rare circumstances, and usually confined to small-scale shipping, it was conceivable for a shipowner to fit out a voyage single-handedly, and even to command his own vessel. The small number of isolated merchants within each period documents the rarity of these cases. Despite the growth of the partnership network at large, the proportion of isolates among all traders remained negligible throughout, ranging from a mere 0.6 percent during the initial four decades (1681–1720) to a maximum of 3.5 percent in the third period (1721–1740).[19] By definition, a small proportion of isolates means that all other merchants, their investors, and venture partners within this community

TABLE 6.3 Cohesion within the Merchant-by-Merchant Partnership Network, 1681–1792: Effect of Removing *Course* Partnership Ties

		PARTNERSHIP TIES						NETWORK COHESION					
PERIOD	NETWORK	MERCHANTS	TOTAL	MEAN DEGREE	STD. DEV. DEGREE	MIN. DEGREE	MAX. DEGREE	ISOLATES	UNREACHABLE PAIRS (%)	NUMBER OF COMPO- NENTS	MAIN COMP. SIZE	MERCHANTS IN MAIN COMP. (%)	MEAN COMP. SIZE	STD. DEV. COMP. SIZE
1 (1681–1697)	Observed	723	5,124	14.17	19.83	0	234	4	12.82	14	675	93.36	40.17	158.44
	Course ties removed	723	3,496	9.67	17.29	0	209	185	53.32	14	494	68.33	3.63	34.94
2 (1698–1720)	Observed	1,246	19,786	31.76	50.90	0	437	8	8.17	17	1,194	95.83	49.84	238.37
	Course ties removed	1,246	9,335	14.98	26.67	0	202	386	59.30	22	795	63.80	3.05	39.31
3 (1721–1740)	Observed	1,343	7,544	11.23	25.11	0	248	47	37.68	86	1,060	78.93	10.10	91.74
	No *Course*	—	—	—	—	—	—	—	—	—	—	—	—	—
4 (1741–1755)	Observed	1,330	8,678	13.05	21.19	0	199	38	28.30	55	1,126	84.66	14.30	116.55
	Course ties removed	1,330	4,557	6.85	11.03	0	114	237	53.27	60	909	68.35	4.48	52.68

5 (1756–1777)	Observed	1,604	15,049	18.76	36.25	0	380	20	24.77	56	1,391	86.72	21.11	159.25
	Course ties removed	1,604	10,260	12.79	25.23	0	380	187	41.94	58	1,222	76.18	6.55	77.99
6 (1778–1792)	Observed	1,471	34,099	46.36	87.82	0	1,140	14	11.48	28	1,384	94.09	35.02	213.23
	Course ties removed	1,471	11,065	15.04	42.51	0	736	425	58.64	35	946	64.31	3.20	44.06
All periods	Observed	6,298	90,280	28.67	67.76	0	1,544	108	15.36	143	5,794	92.00	25.09	365.59
(1681–1792)	*Course* ties removed	6,298	46,257	14.69	40.02	0	1,140	1,192	45.09	158	4,667	74.10	4.67	126.99

Sources: AD-IV 9B165–9B176; 9B587; 4E5277–4E5278; 4E5343; 4E5364; 1F1914.

Note: Because the underlying data have a panel structure, individual merchants may appear in more than one period-specific network. In contrast, the last two rows treat the network as a cross-section for the entire 1681–1792 period such that individual merchants appear only once. Hence, the sum of merchants over all period-specific networks exceeds the sum of merchants in the complete 1681–1792 network. All component sizes are *n* > 1.

were connected to each other, either directly through joint-trade partnerships, or indirectly through third-party ties.

Beyond an enumeration of such lone entrepreneurs, table 6.3 also includes two indicators that are particularly useful for assessing how cohesive the partnership networks were.[20] Reachability is a first intuitive measure of social cohesion that directly complements the number of isolates. The measure takes all possible pairings of merchants in the network and calculates the proportion of paired merchants who were unable to reach each other, again either directly as cosponsors of the same voyage, or indirectly through ties established by partners' partners. The fewer unreachable dyads in the partnership networks, the more cohesive these networks were. The results in table 6.3 show that the percentage of unreachable pairs could be as low as 8.2 percent (in period 2, 1698–1720), and as high as 37.7 percent (in period 3, 1721–1740). Taking into account all years at once, as a single cross-section from 1681 through 1792, reveals that about 15 percent of all pairs of merchants were unable to connect with each other through their venture partnerships. Given the variation in reachability between periods, these results do not seem to lend themselves to a straightforward conclusion. Viewed from a different angle, however, the vast majority of merchant traders—85 percent of pairs in the entire 1681–1792 period, and up to 92 percent in period 1—were in fact joined through their partnership ties. Seen in this light, the findings suggest that social cohesion was indeed pervasive. The one exception is again the network in period 3, in which privateering was absent and reachability among dyads dropped to 62 percent. To put these numbers in perspective, note that affiliation networks invariably generate a pattern of local clustering that reflects underlying group membership. In this historical case, what defines group membership is the collaboration of merchants in organizing a trading or privateering voyage. Local clusters are thus a defining feature of the kind of networks that the Malouin merchants and their peers formed through their joint enterprises. When connections between such local clusters are lacking, reachability in the network at large will necessarily be reduced as well. The degree of reachability, then, and hence the cohesion we observe within the Saint-Malo partnership network, was greater than the clustering tendency of its underlying affiliation data would lead us to expect.

Measuring the share of unreachable pairs thus supports the visual impression of social cohesion in the network graphs we examined earlier. First and foremost, this is still a dyadic summary measure, aggregating distances between pairs of traders. It reaches its limits when it comes to a more detailed understanding of the pattern of ties that characterizes the network at large. Of particular concern is the extent to which bridges and brokers—presumably through *course* ventures—supported the embedding of the various local clusters of merchants and their partnerships into a single broader community. To answer this question, we need a second indicator of social cohesion, one that considers the number and size of components formed among the Malouin merchants. Substantively, components identify subgroups in a network such that each member of a component is linked to every other member by at least one pathway, again using one's direct contacts and their subsequent contacts.[21] What makes them so useful for measuring cohesion is that these components are mutually exclusive subgroups with no bridges. Consequently, from a bird's-eye view, the topology of a well-connected network will consist of few separate components, and most likely a high concentration of merchants within a single main component. Conversely, within a fragmented network that lacks cohesion, merchants will become dispersed over a large number of distinct components. The results that emerge from the component analysis confirm the initial impression of the network's visual display at successive timepoints. Concentration within the main component was consistently high, ranging from 85 percent to 96 percent of the total number of *armateurs* and their venture partners in each period. The finding once again indicates a tightly woven web of trade partnerships. As before, the one exception was the network in period 3, when privateering opportunities were absent. With just 79 percent of all merchants embedded in its main component, social cohesion within the partnership network was less pronounced compared with all other periods.

As noted earlier, the network graphs also show a number of smaller clusters, detached from and surrounding the central core. The systematic evidence in table 6.3 reveals the same pattern, as reflected in the considerable number of separate components in addition to the dominant main component. Note, however, that the average size of components in all six periods was just a small fraction of the number of merchants we find in the core. Hence, a series of independent clusters did indeed surround the network core. Yet, the number of traders and investors that these enterprises attracted was apparently limited to smaller social circles.

What the evidence so far amounts to, then, is a distinct image of a well-integrated community of *armateurs* and merchant partners, as they committed themselves to overseas commerce as well as to commerce raiding. We may ask how particular this pattern of social cohesion really was. I suggest that a specific organizational mechanism—namely, mediation through *course* ventures—facilitated the rise of the observed network pattern. Alternatively, however, it may well be the case that the observed network structure arises routinely out of economic collaborations, even without any specific mediation mechanism. Unfortunately, few studies of economic partnership networks in similar historical settings exist to offer a reliable benchmark and to permit a systematic comparison. Still, it is possible to examine whether this observed pattern of partnership ties would arise by chance alone. Under this scenario, merchants and investors would have been indifferent as to who their partners were in a joint overseas enterprise. In contrast, social networks that stem from naturally occurring interactions—such as the Malouin merchant network—reflect the fact that people build their relationships around preferences, and not indifference. Given the risks and large investments involved in overseas voyages, merchants in Saint-Malo and elsewhere probably would have preferred to collaborate with kin, friends, neighbors, or others who shared their interests.

I set up two simulations to contrast observed preference versus assumed indifference in business partner choice. The first simulation is a conditional random assignment of merchants to voyage ventures. Both the number of merchants and the number of partnership ties that each individual merchant maintained are the same as in the observed network. Then I reshuffled and randomly assigned voyage IDs to individual merchants. By holding constant the number of voyages per individual merchant, each person's individual level of commitment to overseas ventures is preserved.[22] In the second simulation variant, I applied an unconditional random mixing of merchants and voyages. Using simple random sampling with replacements, I selected and paired individual merchant IDs and individual voyage IDs from the list of observed merchants and voyages. In contrast to the first method, this procedure is no longer contingent on the fixed number of voyages each individual merchant invested in. These steps are repeated until the resulting random edgelist is the same length as the edgelist for the observed network. The results for both simulation setups come from one thousand iterations of randomly generated two-mode networks between merchants and voyages. For the cohesion analysis, I then transformed the resulting random two-mode networks into one-mode merchant-by-merchant networks.[23]

The four box-plot panels in figure 6.3 illustrate the contrast between the one observed merchant network and the one thousand simulated random networks, using the two critical measures for cohesion, the percentage of unreachable pairs, and the percentage of merchants located in the largest, or core component.[24] All four panels point to the same conclusion. First, the percentage of unreachable pairs is consistently greater in the observed network than in the simulated random networks. Second, the percentage of merchants

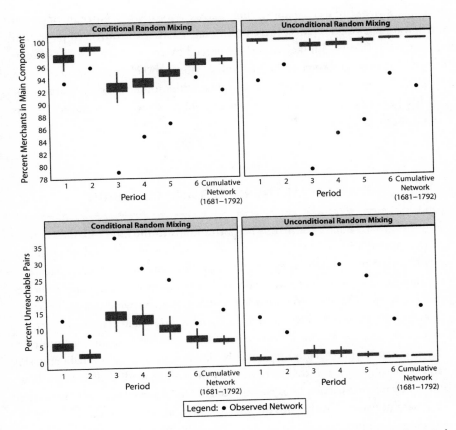

FIGURE 6.3 Comparison of cohesion indicators: observed versus random networks, by period (1681–1792).

Note: Simulation results are obtained from one thousand runs of randomly generated two-mode networks between merchants and voyages. Simulation variant 1 holds the number of ties per merchant constant, and then randomly assigns voyages to merchants. Variant 2 prescribes no tie distribution before randomly matching merchants and voyages. For calculating both cohesion indicators, the simulated two-mode networks are transformed into merchant-by-merchant one-mode networks. In the plots, the boxes enclose the interquartile range of cohesion values for the one thousand random networks. The whiskers extend to cohesion values within one and a half times the interquartile range beyond the boundaries of the boxes.

Sources: AD-IV 9B165-9B176; 9B587; 4E5277-4E5278; 4E5343; 4E5364; 1F1914.

embedded in the core component is consistently smaller in the observed network than under both variants of random assignment of merchants to voyages. Notably, however, precisely because random networks neglect preferences in partnership formation, any distinct pattern is unlikely to emerge. Large random networks invariably tend toward strong connectivity into a single component.

They lack the kind of local clustering that we typically recognize in empirical affiliation networks. Hence, these results suggest that the observed pattern of partnership ties was unlikely to have emerged by chance alone. Some systematic social process, based on an economic choice about where to invest one's funds, apparently gave rise to this particular affiliation network. My argument is that organizational mediation through *course* ventures is the social process in question.

COURSE PARTNERSHIPS AND COHESION

Much of what we have learned so far corresponds to the kind of cohesive network structure that would have arisen if *course* partnerships did indeed occupy a mediating position relative to ventures in other branches of commerce. The findings also seem to be in line with evidence from poll tax records, which indicate that *course* ventures, more so than other trades, attracted a wide array of business partners who varied considerably in their social standing and economic means.[25] Still, these findings remain more or less indirect correlates of the linchpin role that privateering partnerships presumably played in the organizational network. An alternative empirical strategy to identify this role more directly is to ask how much privateering partnerships contributed to the observed connectivity in the merchant network. Turning this question on its head, we may ask to what extent the *absence*, rather than the presence, of privateering partnerships would have eroded cohesion within the merchant community. The main idea is to entertain the counterfactual scenario in which opportunities for commerce raiding voyages were not available to the Malouins.

One observed partnership network meets precisely this restriction—that is, the network in period 3 (1721–1740). During this time, France was not involved in armed conflicts, and hence, the *guerre de course* lay dormant until hostilities broke out again in the 1740s, with the conflict over the Austrian succession. Comparing the network patterns of period 3 and the other five periods listed in table 6.3, this difference is evident. Individual merchants in period 3 have the lowest average degree centrality (11.23; standard deviation = 25.11). At the same time, both the number of isolates (47)—merchants cut off from the rest of the network—and the number of separate components (86) are the largest among all observed networks. When it comes to the two cohesion indicators, we also find the smallest percent of merchants located in the main component (78.9 percent), and the largest percent of unreachable pairs of merchants (37.7 percent). In the absence of privateering, the network in period 3 thus stands out as the one in which merchants were the least connected.

This same empirical condition of absent privateering opportunities is obviously not met in the other five period-specific networks. We may still create a what-if scenario in which the absence of the *course* is mimicked by simply removing its partnerships from the observed networks. To do so, let us return to the network graphs in figure 6.2. Consider the center graphs within the period-specific panels. They demonstrate the impact of removing all merchants from the network who participated as partners in at least one *course* venture during the period in question. Likewise removed are their partnership ties. Hence, we are left with only those merchants engaged in regular trade affiliations, such as ventures established for shipping along the French coasts and to Spain, Newfoundland fishing, or colonial trade. Otherwise, the exact same layout and coordinates as shown in the left-hand graphs are preserved. Under this counterfactual condition, the absence of the *course* has a rather dramatic effect on the network structure during all periods. Structural holes appear where a tightly woven web of partnerships once characterized the merchant community. The core of the network appears much less cohesive and integrated compared with the full observed networks on the left-hand side.

One may further wonder just how cohesive the privateering partnerships were. They could have sorted themselves into separate groups of privateering merchants who only appear to be well connected to observers when they are seen in conjunction with the entire observed network. By themselves, however, they would have looked like numerous small clusters, widely scattered across the entire network, equivalent in their positions perhaps, but cohesive certainly not. Under a different scenario, however, *course* ventures may have combined into a highly cohesive subnetwork onto themselves, with a deep embedding of their members. Once removed from the observed network, these privateering merchants would have left a significant void in the overall organizational network. Turning to the right-hand graphs of the panels in figure 6.2, this second scenario clearly would have been realized empirically. In nearly all cases in which they would have been extracted from the full network, the set of merchants engaged in *course* ventures would have formed a single, well-integrated component.[26] Hence, far from being some disjointed assortment of traders, these privateering merchants were embedded into a coherent group, which was nested within the broader partnership network, much like a pit inside a peach.[27]

As before, the interpretation of network graphs, as revealing as they are, should be supported by more systematic evidence. Consider again the findings in table 6.3. The second row for each period-specific network documents the effect that the removal of privateering partnerships had on social cohesion. I employ the same indicators of social cohesion as I did for the observed networks. Compared with the center graphs in figure 6.2, however, I use a more conservative method to estimate the consequences of removing opportunities for the *course*. In the drawings, I remove merchants who were partners in privateering voyages, as well as all of their ties, from the networks. This procedure most likely returns estimates of social cohesion that are slightly biased toward fragmentation. Imagine, for example, a merchant who participated as a share partner in a privateering voyage and also sponsored a regular trading voyage to Cadiz with another merchant. Once removed from the network, along with all of his ties, he would leave his partner in the Cadiz trading voyage behind as an isolate—unless, of course, that partner is affiliated with another regular trading venture. To avoid this potential fragmentation bias, the procedure in table 6.3 removes only the ties associated with *course* ventures, but it retains all nodes for individual merchants, whether or not they participated in these *course* ventures. By preserving all other affiliations in regular trades, much more of the original observed network is left untouched. Hence, estimating the effect of removing *course* partnerships in this manner is more conservative because it is considerably harder to induce a similar degree of fragmentation as in the network drawings.

Despite these higher constraints, we find again a substantial decrease in social cohesion if the ties associated with *course* partnerships were to be withdrawn from the observed network. Because the number of ties is reduced, a corresponding decrease in the average degree per merchant is hardly surprising. The drop may be less pronounced, as in period 1, when the mean tie degree per merchant decreases from 14.2 to 9.7. Or, it may be more dramatic, as in period 6, where the mean degree falls from 46.4 to 15. As the findings in table 6.3 document, cutting the ties involved in *course* partnerships from the network also results in a sizeable increase in the number of isolates. Traders who participated exclusively in the *course*, and who therefore lacked connections to partners in other types of trades, would be left behind as isolates. At the lower bound, the number of isolates increases from 20 to 187 merchants (in period 5); at the upper bound, it increases from 14 to 425 merchants (in period 6). Cutting *course* affiliations from the network not only multiplies the number of isolated traders but also decouples *armateurs* and partners alike from the central main component, thus reducing its size considerably. The share of partners who organized themselves within the central main component would drop accordingly, at a minimum from 86.7 percent to 76.2 percent in period 5, and most strongly in period 2, from 95.8 percent down to 63.8 percent. The waning of social cohesion is just as visible in the increasing number of unreachable pairs once the *course* ties are omitted from the partnership network. Even in the least dramatic cases, the percentage of Malouin merchants who are unable to connect through their partnership ties increases from 24.8 percent to 41.9 percent (in period 5), and from 28.3 percent to 53.3 percent (in period 4). The more dramatic cases involve changes in the share of unreachable pairs from 11.5 percent upward to 58.6 percent (in period 6), and from 8.2 percent to 59.3 percent (in period 2). Put differently, in four of the five periods in which privateering enterprise was a viable opportunity (i.e., periods 1, 2, 4, and 6), more than half of all pairs of merchants would not have been able to reach each other without any privateering ties in the merchant network.

In sum, the evidence of this what-if scenario reveals that the removal of *course* partnerships and the ties they implied would open structural holes, convert connected individual traders into isolates, and thus undermine the cohesion of the network at large.[28] That the removal of privateering ventures has such a strong fragmenting impact on network cohesion is even more remarkable given that the underlying data structure privileges cohesion. As noted earlier, the duration of each period comfortably accommodates successive investments made by the same individual merchants. Furthermore, voyage partnerships rarely have an ending date included in the source documents, and thus for coding purposes, they last for the entire duration of a period. Both conditions tend to prevent fragmentation and favor connectivity in the network. Both conditions also are amplified when we consider the entire 1681–1792 network as a single period (as in the bottom rows of table 6.3). It is the most conservative scenario, in which neither people, nor their partnerships, ever die, and yet the removal of privateering ties erodes social cohesion: the number of isolates increases from 108 to 1,192 merchants; the share of merchants in the main component decreases from 92 percent to 74 percent; and the share of unreachable pairs increases from 15.4 percent to 45.1 percent. In all cases, even though ample opportunities to maintain cohesion through alternative partnership ties were on offer, cutting out the *course* ties would fragment the network substantially.

One obvious question looms large: would the removal of other types of ties than the *course* have comparable consequences for connectivity? In other words, did something specific about the nature of *course* ventures make them so pivotal, or would the removal of a simple random draw of ties yield the same extent of fragmentation? The box-plots in figure 6.4 address this question directly, in line with the box-plots shown earlier in figure 6.3. The two panels compare differences in network cohesion that result from (1) the removal of *course* ties, and (2) the removal of randomly selected ties.[29] For each period, I use a simple random

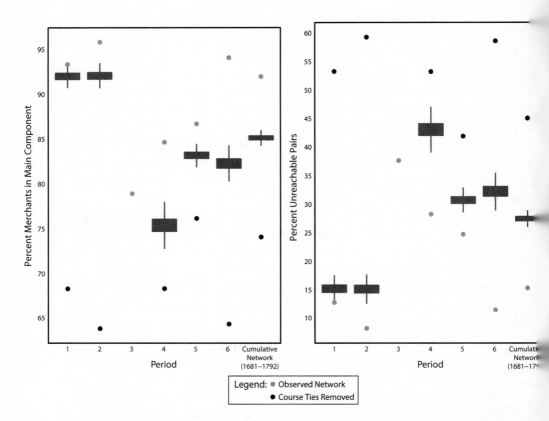

FIGURE 6.4 Comparison of cohesion indicators: effect of removing *course* ties versus removing randomly selected ties, by period (1681–1792).

Note: The two panels compare differences in network cohesion that result from (1) the removal of *course* ties, and (2) the removal of as many randomly selected ties as there are *course* ties (one thousand iterations). Gray markers represent the observed networks and black markers the same networks with *course* ties removed. The boxes capture the distribution of results for the one thousand networks for which the randomly selected ties are removed. For details on the box-plots and the sources, see figure 6.3.

selection to draw the same number of ties as *course* ties, and then remove them from the observed network. I then measure the percentage of merchants in the main component and the percentage of unreachable pairs. For each period, I follow these steps for one thousand iterations. The resulting distributions for the two cohesion measures are shown in the boxes. It is not surprising that cutting ties, no matter their nature, has at least some effect on network cohesion. Yet, both plots clearly demonstrate that the removal of *course* ties consistently reduces network cohesion more than the removal of any randomly selected set of ties.[30]

Once again, opportunities for commerce raiding did not exist in period 3, and hence, any comparison with random selections of ties is not meaningful.

The same critical question can be pushed further. For one, some *course* ties may end up being included in each random draw of ties to be removed from the network. A more direct approach to reveal the role of other kinds of ties in the network is to think about the formation of partnerships as an opportunity structure. If the *course* had not been available for investment, the Malouin merchants and their partners probably would have turned elsewhere for alternative opportunities for trade. Among the most likely candidates would have been the *pêche*, or Newfoundland fishing trade. By its sheer volume alone, with a third of all ventures fitted out in Saint-Malo, the *pêche* was the most prominent among the trading alternatives (see table 6.2). It also was the port's traditional stronghold in maritime commerce, a fairly routine enterprise and natural training ground for merchants and sailors alike. As such, it attracted *armateurs* and investment partners from various corners of the merchant community. The North Atlantic fishing trade thus stood in contrast to high-stakes undertakings, such as the long-distance journeys to South America, India, or China, that were the preserve of the most affluent merchant houses. Hence, if one branch of commerce stood out whose removal from the partnership network might be expected to have consequences similar to the *course*, then it was the Newfoundland fishing business.

The box-plots in figure 6.5 compare how much the *course* and Newfoundland fishing differed in their influence on cohesion in the merchant network. I adopt a similar empirical strategy as before, using once again the two key indicators of social cohesion: (1) the percentage of merchants located in the main component, and (2) the percentage of merchant pairs who were unable to reach each other through their partnership ties. Simply omitting all fishing voyages, and then comparing the effect on the network pattern to the removal of *course* voyages bears little meaning, however. Because there were nearly three times as many fishing ventures than privateering ventures, the former are bound to have a stronger impact by chance alone (see table 6.2). My solution is to draw, for each period, just as many fishing ventures as there were privateering ventures, using simple random selection. To get a distribution of outcomes for the two cohesion measures, one thousand random draws are taken from the set of fishing ventures in each period, and then deleted from the period-specific two-mode affiliation networks. The boxes in figure 6.5 plot the distribution of the two cohesion measures in the one-mode merchant-by-merchant networks once the selected sets of fishing voyages are deleted. For comparison, the figures also include markers for the observed merchant networks, and for the

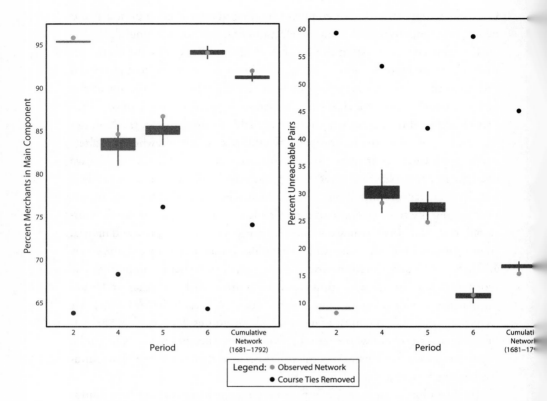

FIGURE 6.5 Comparison of cohesion indicators: effect of removing *course* voyages versus removing *pêche* (Newfoundland fishing) voyages, by period (1681–1792).

Note: The two panels compare differences in network cohesion that result from (1) the removal of *course* voyages, and (2) the removal of as many randomly selected voyages in the Newfoundland fishing trade as there are *course* voyages (one thousand iterations). Voyages are removed from the two-mode affiliation networks, and cohesion indicators are then calculated on the one-mode merchant-by-merchant networks. Gray markers represent the observed networks and black markers the same networks with *course* voyages removed. The boxes capture the distribution of results for the one thousand networks for which the randomly selected fishing voyages are removed. For details on the box-plots and the sources, see figure 6.3.

networks from which I removed the *course* ventures.[31] Once again, a distinct pattern emerges from these plots that confirms my previous findings: whenever the *course* is removed from the network, it clearly induces more pronounced fragmentation than we would see if the same number of fishing ventures were removed. In fact, the outcomes for removing the sets of fishing voyages are quite close to, and sometimes virtually indistinguishable from the cohesion characteristics of the observed network. These findings indicate again that *course* partnerships played a pivotal role in the web of affiliations that held the merchant community together. Apparently, it was a role that other types of partnerships were less well placed to fulfill.

TOWARD MULTIPLEX NETWORKS

Kinship Relations

An important insight from studies of similar settings, both contemporary and historical, suggests that the intersection of multiple networks often creates fresh opportunities for collective undertakings.[32] Consider kinship networks: few historians would deny that kinship was an important pillar of merchant society, whether in Saint-Malo or elsewhere, in early modern Europe.[33] Family bonds certainly contributed a sizeable share when it came to replenishing the Malouin trading elites. For an illustrative case, recall how the eminent Magon family sent their sons, generation upon generation, to the overseas branch of their trading house in Cadiz to have them apprenticed in the arts of commerce. The presence of kinship ties was not limited to the *comptoir.* Seafaring careers likewise unfolded through family ties, as captains took aboard their sons as ensigns, training them in the skills of navigation.[34] It is therefore not farfetched to suggest that kinship relations were just as salient as they informed the formation of voyage partnerships. Put differently, we may ask to what extent it was a preference for collaborating with kinsmen rather than the presence of linchpin organizations that gave rise to the observed network pattern.

Unfortunately, comprehensive, let alone complete, information on kinship relations is limited to some of the most prominent trading houses, including the Baude, Eon, Lefer, Locquet, Porée, Perrée, Magon, or Vincent families. Even if it were available for all cases in my database, with more than six thousand individual *armateurs*, captains, investors, and creditors, strewn over more than one hundred years and more than two hundred different locations, any attempt to reconstruct the full set of kinship relations among each and every one of them would be a daunting and improbable task within the limits of the present monograph. As a suitable alternative, I coded kinship ties through a careful matching of merchants' surnames using both a systematic name recognition algorithm and in-depth case-by-case inspection.[35] This coding yields a kinship network wherein people are connected if they share the same surname. I then identified components in this kinship network as a proxy for families.[36] Nesting the kinship and venture partnership networks within each other allows me to establish to what extent pairs of merchants were linked through ties of kinship as well as economic collaboration.

This coding strategy obviously offers only a proxy for kinship. For not all merchant partners who shared the same surname were necessarily relatives; yet, relatives need not necessarily share the same surname either. Hence, this particular bias may occur in both directions, introducing too much as well as too little identity. Likewise, matching on surnames captures only patrilineal descent. That is, the coding scheme groups uncles, nephews, and cousins along the father's lineage into the same family, whereas it obscures those of matrilineal descent, not to mention godparenthood as a form of spiritual kinship alliance.[37] We have good reasons to believe, however, that these caveats are much less severe than they may seem. First, as André Lespagnol has shown, most trading activities in Saint-Malo were spearheaded by an oligarchy of a few dominant and fervently Catholic merchant dynasties, where responsibilities were handed down from grandfathers to fathers to sons along patrilineages.[38] Second, whatever bias in kinship coding remains, it should have only a limited impact on my inferences about the pattern of partnership ties because it applies equally to all period-specific networks. Third, little empirical evidence exists to suggest that matrilineal cross-cousin ties were particularly prone to serve as bridges between otherwise separate network clusters, such that missing them would obscure a significant contribution to social cohesion.

With these caveats in mind, I find 3,036 unique families that can be unambiguously identified across the entire 1681–1792 period. Although the number seems large at first, it should be emphasized that family components range in size from just a solitary member to groups of up to thirty-one relatives (mean = 2.07; standard deviation = 3.04). In 88 percent of all cases, a family has just three or fewer members. Furthermore, these families resided not only in Saint-Malo, but also in neighboring communities of Brittany and Normandy, in French cities and towns farther way, and even beyond the borders of the realm, in Europe and overseas.

Mapping the voyage partnerships onto the kinship network reveals that merely 1.8 percent of the 90,280 partner ties within the full 1681–1792 period linked merchants who belonged to the same family. Table 6.4 documents that the share of dyads wherein two relatives partnered with each other was not substantially larger within any of the period-specific networks. The percentage varied within narrow bounds, between barely 1 percent in the sixth period and 5 percent in the third period. This focus on dyads across the entire network, however, presumes an opportunity structure for kinship that seems rather unrealistic: in networks of up to 1,600 people per period it is very unlikely that potentially all, or even a

TABLE 6.4 Voyage Partnership Ties Among Kin

PERIOD	MERCHANTS	TOTAL TIES	TIES AMONG KIN IN NETWORK		PROPORTION OF KIN AMONG EGO'S PARTNERS	
			DYADS	PROPORTION OF TOTAL TIES	MEAN	STD. DEV.
1 (1681–1697)	723	5,124	197	.038	.034	.099
2 (1698–1720)	1,246	19,786	343	.017	.026	.091
3 (1721–1740)	1,343	7,544	374	.050	.075	.201
4 (1741–1755)	1,330	8,678	233	.027	.040	.131
5 (1756–1777)	1,604	15,049	203	.013	.019	.085
6 (1778–1792)	1,471	34,099	314	.009	.020	.089
All periods (1681–1792)	6,298	90,280	1,664	.018	.032	.118

Sources: AD-IV 9B165–9B176; 9B587; 4E5277–4E5278; 4E5343; 4E5364; 1F1914; Paris-Jallobert (2000–2004, 2004).
Note: The proportion of kin among ego's partners is not meaningful for solitary *armateurs* (see the number of isolates in table 6.3).

large proportion, shared bonds of kinship. A more plausible alternative considers the number of direct voyage partners for each merchant, and then calculates the share of partners to whom this merchant was bound through kinship. To illustrate, Jean Magon, sieur de la Lande, is listed in my relational dataset with a total of 123 partners, with whom he collaborated to launch multiple voyages during the first period (1681–1697), and about 8.5 percent of his partners also belonged to the Magon family. A quick glance at the results for all merchants listed in table 6.4 reveals that the average share of kinsmen among one's partners was consistently low across all periods, ranging from 1.9 percent in the fifth period to at most 7.5 percent in the third period. Hence, neither of the two alternatives presented in table 6.4 offers particularly strong evidence that kinship bonds did much in terms of influencing economic collaborations at large.[39]

Perhaps asking how much the partnership ties overlapped with kinship ties is in fact the wrong question to ask. Instead, given that *course* ventures made such a salient contribution to the cohesion of the merchant community, we may wonder whether kinship exerted a more indirect influence on the shape of the merchant network. Channeling selection into privateering partnerships would have been one such indirect influence. The idea is that there might not have been anything inherently attractive about the *course* other than the fact that one's relatives had invested in it. Merchants then would have decided to join privateering partnerships because their kin did so first, or because their kin recruited them. Therefore, we may find that partnership ties among kin were indeed more prevalent within *course* ventures than in regular overseas trades. Consequently, kinship would have contributed indirectly to the formation of the partnership network, as a preference for ties with kin drove selection into the *course*, which in turn gave rise to a cohesive network structure.

Accordingly, table 6.5 compares the average degree of kinship homophily between ventures engaged in the *course*, in the *pêche* (Newfoundland fishing), and in other regular types of commerce. I draw on three complementary measures. All three assess the proportion of merchants within a partnership who were related through kinship affiliations, albeit from slightly different angles. If we imagine that each partner also carries a kinship identifier, then the proportion of unique families that contributed two or more partners offers a first indicator of endogamy. A second measure is the proportion of individual partners who shared a kinship tie with at least one other partner within the same venture (although the exact composition of kin ties between partners remains hidden from view). A third measure rests on the proportion of all dyads in a voyage partnership that linked pairs of kinsmen. The outcomes for all three measures thus range between zero, indicating complete heterogeneity with respect to kinship,

TABLE 6.5 Kinship Homophily Within Voyage Partnerships, 1681–1792

	NUMBER OF VENTURES	NUMBER OF PARTNERS IN VENTURE			PROPORTION FAMILIES WITH MORE THAN ONE PARTNER IN VENTURE			PROPORTION PARTNERS WHO SHARED KIN TIES WITH OTHER PARTNERS IN VENTURE			PROPORTION DYADS AMONG KIN IN VENTURE		
		AVERAGE	STD. DEV.	MAX.	MEAN	STD. DEV.	T-STATISTIC	MEAN	STD. DEV.	T-STATISTIC	MEAN	STD. DEV.	T-STATISTIC
Course	360	9.633	12.306	150	.089	.146		.143	.198		.036	.108	
Pêche	978	4.353	4.606	31	.077	.165	−1.1658	.117	.216	−2.0080*	.043	.136	.8977
All other trades	1,912	4.207	3.653	43	.076	.183	−1.2266	.108	.227	−2.7168**	.047	.157	1.2661

Sources: AD-IV 9B165–9B176; 9B587; 4E5277–4E5278; 4E5343; 4E5364; 1F1914; Paris-Jallobert (2000–2004, 2004).
Note: The first *t*-statistic for each homophily measure refers to the means comparison between *course* ventures and *pêche* ventures. The second *t*-statistic refers to the difference between the *course* and ventures in all other trades.

* *p* = .0224; ** *p* = .0033 (one-tailed). All other means comparisons reveal no significant differences.

and a value equal to one, indicating that everyone in a voyage venture had kins-men among their business partners.[40]

The comparisons for all three measures in table 6.5 show that voyages engaged in privateering were not substantially more likely than other types of trading ventures to have their partners selected on the basis of kin relationships. The slight differences in magnitude one finds are not consistent across the three measures. In addition, they are statistically significant only for the proportion of partners who share kin ties with other partners in their venture. Even here, the substantive dif-ferences between 14.3 percent in *course* partnerships, 11.7 percent in *pêche* partner-ships, and 10.8 percent in other trade partnerships are not particularly impressive. The findings certainly do not mean that family ties played no role at all in orga-nizing overseas trade partnerships (they did, as we observed in chapters 2 and 3). Little evidence, however, suggests that the linchpin role of the *course* in the organi-zational network was merely an expression of underlying kinship affiliations that steered selection of merchants into privateering enterprise.

Residence Patterns and Ties to Outside Partners

Beyond kinship, we may wonder how much of an influence the contributions of outside associates and investors had on the Malouin merchant network, and in particular, on the selection into privateering partnerships. Who exactly were these outsiders? Saint-Malo certainly had its share of immigrants from out-side of Brittany and France, most prominently a sizeable Irish community, as described in chapter 3. Their presence in the city is not, however, what I mean by outsiders. I have in mind the shareholders in trade and privateering partnerships who did not reside in the immediate vicinity of Saint-Malo and Saint-Servan. Most hailed from ports and inland towns within Brittany and Normandy. Some included business partners and individual and corporate investors who resided in places across all of France, but particularly in Paris, Rouen, Nantes, La Rochelle, Bordeaux, and Marseille, which for the most part, were bustling trade ports in their own right. Still others made their contributions from locations beyond the borders of the realm, sometimes as far away as Québec, Saint-Domingue, or Pondichéry. Corporate investors typically consisted of family-run banks based in Paris. Illustrative cases include Jean Cottin l'aîné et fils, banquiers, who acquired several shares, ranging from 3,000 up to 140,000 *lt.*, in at least nine separate voyages between 1770 and 1781. Cottin's bank sponsored one privateer-ing cruise (3,000 *lt.*), but all other voyages were bound for long-distance trades with more exotic destinations, such as the îles de Bourbon et France, China, Goa, and other parts of India.[41] Likewise, from 1771 through 1776, Sellouf et Cie, banquiers, invested sums between 4,000 and 56,000 *lt.* in seventeen voyages that were headed for trade with Pondichéry, Mahé, and Goa; the Bengal, Coromandel, and Malabar coasts; and eventually China.[42] Within the records, one even finds absentee owners of ships moored at Saint-Malo who authorized merchants based in the city as their local agents to file the necessary declarations with the Admiralty court and to pay the required fees. Hence, Joseph Fichet Desjardin, a Malouin merchant trader, had the 240-ton *Le Philantrope* constructed at Saint-Malo. The vessel eventually was destined for a voyage to the Americas, and Fichet Desjardin registered it "pour le compte Du Sieur Olive demeurant à Paris" on May 23, 1788.[43] More often than not, however, outsiders figured as ordinary shareholders who committed average sums to voyage partnerships.

I am able to identify citizens of Saint-Malo and its suburb Saint-Servan, and to distinguish them from outsiders, on the basis of information for the place of residence for a total of 3,311 *armateurs*, investment partners, and ship captains— that is, 53 percent of the total set of 6,298 merchants. Much of the residency information is noted directly in the partnership contracts and is listed right after the names of shareholders. Alternatively, this information can be retrieved from the listings of taxpayers within the *capitation* rolls. In some, but unfortunately not all, cases, when such direct evidence is missing, it is feasible to trace the place of residence using parish registers of baptisms, marriages, and burials.[44] The relatively large number of missing cases naturally raises the question of selection bias. Selectivity may be particularly problematic if entire groups of merchants who came from specific locations, and therefore were likely to be closely connected, would be systematically excluded from the analysis, all for the sole reason that their residence is not explicitly stated in the sources. This selection bias, however, turns out to be less severe than it seems. A closer look at some basic cohesion indicators reveals that merchants with unknown residency did not form a uniform and tightly knit group. The greatest number of opportunities for ties among these merchants would have existed in the network that spanned the entire 1681–1792 period. Even here, however, they maintained only an average number of four ties to their partners (standard deviation = 6.37). Likewise, they sorted themselves into a rather large number of 302 separate components, such that the vast majority of pairs among these merchants (85.7 percent) could not reach each other using their partnership ties. If anything, merchants with missing residency information did not cluster among themselves and instead were scattered widely across the entire partnership network. These findings suggest that they did not hail from just a few places that are systematically excluded from the following analysis.[45]

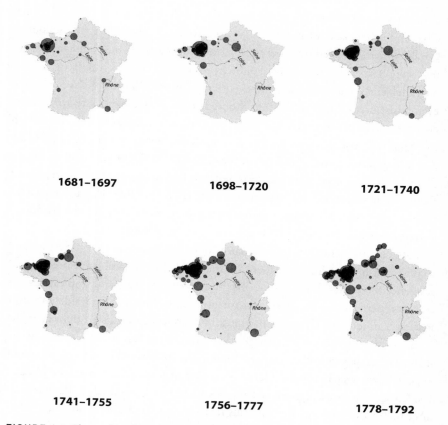

1681–1697   **1698–1720**   **1721–1740**

1741–1755   **1756–1777**   **1778–1792**

FIGURE 6.6 Places of residence of partners in Malouin voyage partnerships: locations within France.

_____

Note: The size of circles (logarithmic scale) corresponds to the number of business partners residing in each location.

Sources: *AD-IV* 9B165-9B176; 9B587; 4E5277-4E5278; 4E5343; 4E5364; 1F1914; C4070; C4086; C4098; C4259; C4262; AM-SM CC 41; Paris-Jallobert (2000–2004, 2004).

Keeping in mind these constraints in the sources, the maps in figure 6.6 show the geographic distribution of shareholding partners in overseas ventures that were organized by *armateurs* in Saint-Malo. France is drawn within present-day's political boundaries (excluding Corsica, as no partner is known to have resided on the island). The size of circles corresponds to the number of shareholding partners residing in each location. Because of the wide range in the number of partners across locations, the plots use a logarithmic scale for ease of comparison.

The six maps suggest three patterns. First, and foremost, they illustrate the local concentration of most business associates. The share of partners who either belonged to Saint-Malo's merchant community, or resided within its vicinity in northern Brittany and lower Normandy remained substantial throughout all six periods. Second, investors coming from outside of Saint-Malo and Brittany resided overwhelmingly in other coastal towns, and a gradual increase in these numbers over time can be discerned. Most of these associates came from Rouen and Le Havre in the north; from Nantes, La Rochelle, and Bordeaux to the west; and from Marseille in the south. This latter observation squares with the image of a commerce-oriented Atlantic France, set apart from a more rural eastern France, a contrast alluded to in chapter 2. The large contingent of shareholders from seaports suggests that they were most likely maritime traders, rather than, say, financiers, grandees at court, or landed gentry who had funds to spare for investments in overseas ventures. This finding also implies that collaborations across important port cities were frequent despite their allegedly intense commercial rivalries over trading privileges granted by the crown.[46] Third, the notable exceptions to this seabound pattern of locations include the prominent roles of Paris, and, to a lesser extent, Lyon. As noted, one reason for this exception was the vested interest that some banking houses, such as Cottin et fils and Sellouf et Cie, both of Paris, or Scheidlin, Finguerlin et Cie, of Lyon, held in large-scale Malouin enterprises that were fitted out for destinations in India, China, or the Americas.[47]

The map in figure 6.7 depicts just how far the Malouin partnership network expanded beyond the boundaries of France. As before, the dominant pool of shareholders was found within France. When it came to international relations, however, the Malouins succeeded in casting a wide net. They attracted associates from thriving centers of commerce across Europe, including Lisbon, Cadiz, Genoa, and Venice to the south; and Amsterdam, London and the Hansa ports to the north. In addition, they found interested parties in places as far away as Québec in Canada, Saint-Domingue in the West Indies, and Pondichéry in India. Table 6.6 summarizes the geographic distribution of associates in Malouin voyage partnerships, and reveals the gradual increase in the share of outside partners from other locations within France.

Once again, in the network that encloses the entire 1681–1792 period—which is conservative in the sense that people never die and ties never decay—we should expect to find the greatest number of opportunities for outside associates to forge relationships among themselves and with Malouin *armateurs* alike. Consequently, in this network, we also should see most clearly how strong an influence these outside investors had on the network structure. Similar to the role of kinship bonds, outsiders may have shaped the pattern of partnerships indirectly

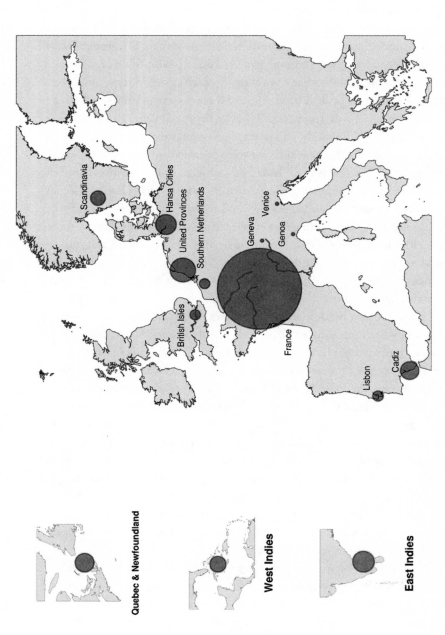

FIGURE 6.7 Places of residence of partners in Malouin voyage partnerships: locations within and beyond France.

Note: The size of circles (logarithmic scale) corresponds to the number of business partners residing in each location.

Sources: AD-IV 9B165-9B176; 9B587; 4E5277-4E5278; 4E5343; 4E5364; 1F1914; C4070; C4086; C4098; C4259; C4262; AM-SM CC 41; Paris-Jallobert (????-????)

TABLE 6.6 Geographical Origins of Associates in Malouin Voyage Partnerships

PERIOD	MERCHANTS WITH KNOWN PLACE OF RESIDENCE N	SAINT-MALO AND SAINT-SERVAN		BRITTANY AND NORMANDY		OTHER REGIONS IN FRANCE		OUTSIDE FRANCE	
		N	PROPORTION	N	PROPORTION	N	PROPORTION	N	PROPORTION
1 (1681–1697)	492	388	.789	68	.138	32	.065	4	.008
2 (1698–1720)	606	458	.756	94	.155	40	.066	14	.023
3 (1721–1740)	628	379	.604	184	.293	58	.092	7	.011
4 (1741–1755)	605	276	.456	212	.350	85	.141	32	.053
5 (1756–1777)	1,108	451	.407	422	.381	215	.194	20	.018
6 (1778–1792)	1,019	480	.471	351	.345	173	.170	15	.015
All periods (1681–1792)	3,311	1,644	.497	1,067	.322	512	.155	88	.027

Sources: AD-IV 9B165–9B176; 9B587; 4E5277–4E5278; 4E5343; 4E5364; 1F1914; Paris-Jallobert (2000–2004, 2004).

Note: Cases with unknown places of residence are excluded (see discussion in main text). Because the underlying data have a panel structure, individual merchants may appear in more than one period-specific network. In contrast, the last row treats the network as a cross-section for the entire 1681–1792 period such that individual merchants appear only once. Hence, the sum of merchants over all period-specific networks exceeds the sum of merchants in the complete 1681–1792 network.

by selecting themselves predominantly into *course* ventures. They then may have been drawn to ventures in other overseas trades, thereby linking otherwise separate partnerships. Under this scenario, it would have been the investment behavior of outside partners rather than any inherent mediating nature of the *course* that lent cohesion to the merchant community. The empirical implication is that privateering partnerships should have attracted a particularly large contingent of outsiders compared with other branches of overseas commerce.

As table 6.7 shows, however, little in the available evidence supports this implication. The table compares the provenance of partners in the *course* with its closest alternative, the Newfoundland fishing trade (*pêche*), and with all other trades. Contributions to all three categories of ventures were not mutually exclusive: one and the same merchant could have held shares in more than one voyage partnership and in more than one branch of overseas commerce at once. The results clearly show that no substantial differences existed in the regional composition of associates between the *course*, the *pêche*, and other trades. This finding holds no matter whether we consider everyone an outsider who resided beyond the city walls of Saint-Malo, or whether we restrict the term to those who were not of Breton or Norman origin. If anything, the share of Malouins and Servannais (65 percent) was larger among *course* partnerships than in any other branch of overseas commerce. This finding attests to the strong local roots of the *course* in Saint-Malo: physical propinquity did matter to our merchant entrepreneurs as they formed their partnerships. It also squares with my argument that the *course* played a central role in maintaining cohesion within Saint-Malo's merchant community. If ties forged through joint *course* ventures were indeed so important for upholding the social fabric in the city, then local merchants forming the majority among the privateers is precisely what we should find.[48] In sum, little systematic evidence suggests that outside associates served as the real conduits of economic collaboration, and they alone were not responsible for the central mediating position of the *course* in the merchant network.

CORSAIRS AS BROKERS

Shared by all the findings so far is a bird's-eye view of the merchant network. Such a vantage point has helped us to recognize the expanse of its lattice work of partnership relations. It has also revealed how the presence and absence of privateering partnerships ties shaped how well connected and embedded the Malouin

TABLE 6.7 Geographical Origins of Associates in Malouin Voyage Partnerships: *Course* and Other Trades Compared, 1681–1792

TYPE OF VENTURE	MERCHANTS WITH KNOWN PLACE OF RESIDENCE	SAINT-MALO AND SAINT-SERVAN		BRITTANY AND NORMANDY		OTHER REGIONS IN FRANCE		OUTSIDE FRANCE	
		N	PROPORTION	N	PROPORTION	N	PROPORTION	N	PROPORTION
Course	1,017	660	.649	217	.213	131	.129	9	.009
Pêche	1,324	845	.638	306	.231	164	.124	9	.007
All other trades	2,255	1,170	.519	713	.316	298	.132	74	.033

Sources: AD-IV 9B165–9B176; 9B587; 4E5277–4E5278; 4E5343; 4E5364; 1F1914; Paris-Jallobert (2000–2004, 2004).
Note: Cases with unknown places of residence are excluded (see discussion in main text). The sum of partners may exceed the total of 3,311 reported in table 6.6 because the same merchants could have been associates in more than one type of venture.

traders and their partners were within the global, or what some may prefer to call the macrolevel, network structure. My claim certainly is not that the role of privateering enterprise is the single factor that explains both stability and shifts in the network's pattern over more than a hundred years. Such bold monocausal claims are best avoided when studying complex social relationships in historical settings. Still, the Saint-Malo merchant network owes much of its observed structure to the presence rather than the absence of affiliations that stemmed from *course* partnerships.

One natural question to ask is whether the central linchpin role of the *course* was visible not only in its aggregate form, within the overall pattern of ties, but also at the level of individual ventures and the positions they held in the organizational network. To answer this question, we need to shift our perspective to a more fine-grained examination of the mediating role that each *course* venture played. Ideally, such a focused view should reveal that *course* ventures were critical for cohesion by acting as a link between two otherwise disconnected ventures, whether engaged in alternative overseas trades or in commerce raiding as well. Granted, little would have precluded ventures other than those operating in privateering to offer the same kind of mediation in the organizational network. Still, following the linchpin argument, we would expect that, on average, *course* partnerships were more likely than ventures in other regular trades to occupy a mediating position. Naturally, each venture's mediation potential was contingent on the portfolio of ties its partners brought to their collective enterprise. Consequently, it is worth emphasizing that any such positioning of a venture in the organizational network is first and foremost an opportunity; seizing and acting on it depended on the individual merchants involved and their strategic choices.

A suitable relational measure of linchpin positions in the organizational network needs to identify mediating ventures that are placed between otherwise disconnected ventures. It also needs to distinguish among the different branches of maritime commerce that each individual partnership engaged in. The measure of brokerage roles is particularly well suited to this task.[49] As illustrated in table 6.8, this measure takes as its starting point the most elementary form of brokerage: an open triad in which one node mediates between two disconnected nodes, thereby offering an indirect link. In the present case, the nodes represent ventures in the organizational network of partnership ties. Ovals around nodes and around the pairs of nodes represent the distinct branch of maritime commerce the voyage partnerships belonged to, such as, among others, Newfoundland fishing, colonial commerce, the Spanish and Mediterranean trades, or privateering enterprise. The top black nodes mark voyage ventures positioned in a brokerage

TABLE 6.8 Brokerage Roles in the Voyage-by-Voyage Network: *Course, Pêche* (Newfoundland Fishing) and Partnerships in Other Trades Compared, 1681–1792

	NUMBER OF VENTURES	ITINERANT BROKERAGE				LIAISON BROKERAGE				GATEKEEPER BROKERAGE			
		MEAN	STD. DEV.	MEDIAN	T-STATISTIC	MEAN	STD. DEV.	MEDIAN	T-STATISTIC	MEAN	STD. DEV.	MEDIAN	T-STATISTIC
Course	360	1,056.66	3,185.48	116		3,135.79	9,472.56	390.5		2,082.82	4,128.96	576.5	
Pêche	978	180.87	596.88	5	-8.2198	794.25	2,567.46	25	-7.0616	1,149.66	3,220.51	67.5	-4.3399
All other trades	1,912	228.64	782.85	1	-9.8967	758.50	2,661.04	5	-9.2175	287.50	934.87	4	-16.8679

Sources: AD-IV 9B165–9B176; 9B587; 4E5277–4E5278; 4E5343; 4E5364; 1F1914.

Note: Brokerage roles adapted from Gould and Fernandez (1989). For details of measurement see text in chapter 6. Top nodes refer to brokers. Gray shades and ovals reflect different branches of maritime commerce that venture partnerships engaged in. The first *t*-statistic for each brokerage role refers to the means comparison of *course* ventures and *pêche* ventures. The second *t*-statistic for each brokerage role refers to the difference between the *course* and ventures in all other trades. All means comparisons reveal significant differences at $p < .0000$ (one-tailed).

role. For each of the three brokerage roles—itinerant, liaison, and gatekeeper—the measure calculates the number of times a given venture bridges a structural hole separating two other ventures.[50] It does so by considering all pairs of other ventures that the brokering venture is connected to through joint partnership ties. As a result, three cumulative brokerage scores are available for each individual venture, one for each of the three brokerage roles. Table 6.8 reports both means comparisons and median scores for *course* partnerships, for the *pêche* (Newfoundland fishing) as Saint-Malo's most prominent trade, and for partnerships in all other trades.

A crisp pattern emerges from the evidence: in all three roles, whether we consider average or median scores, *course* ventures consistently exhibited a greater number of brokerage opportunities than either fishing partnerships—most likely the closest alternative—or ventures in any of the other regular trades. The means comparisons show that the contrasts are statistically significant as well.[51] Perhaps the most instructive findings are those for the itinerant and liaison roles. They document just how much the *course* contributed to the cohesion of the Malouin organizational network by bridging between otherwise decoupled ventures in a variety of different trades. As the means comparisons attest, ventures in other areas of maritime activity apparently were not as well placed to facilitate cohesion to a similar degree.[52] For the organizational network, these findings thus confirm the structural advantage—at least when it comes to cohesion—of *course* partnerships over alternative enterprises (an advantage seen in figure 6.5) in the network of bonds among individual merchants.

One potential caveat stems from the observation that investors in the Malouin *course* ventures tended to outnumber their peers in other types of trading partnerships. With respect to average partnership sizes, about ten partners in *course* voyages and about eight partners in mixed *guerre et marchandise* (letter-of-marque) enterprises contrasted with merely three to four partners in other kinds of trading voyages (see table 6.2). Likewise, a third (126 out of 380) of the largest partnerships—those in the ninetieth percentile, with ten and more partners—were organized in pursuit of privateering opportunities. The caveat is that, by chance alone, wherever a large number of share partners participated in a voyage venture, connections to other ventures, and hence opportunities for brokerage tended to multiply as well. Indeed, the correlation between the number of partners in one's venture and the number of partnership ties to other ventures is not negligible ($r = .65$). Thus, it might have been sheer size, and not any genuine social relational or organizational quality specific to *course* ventures, that placed them into their linchpin positions. By the same token, if linchpin positions indeed were not related to the substantive nature of the ventures that occupied them, then just about any other class of trading ventures could have played that mediating role, provided they were of a sufficient size.

Size dependence would be particularly problematic if some exogenous selection mechanism that had little to do with the particular interests of the Malouin merchantry determined the number of partners in a given venture. An example would be the contrast between large joint-stock companies that, by their very nature, were designed to attract many shareholders, and small private partnerships for which contributions came mostly from close and more distant kin. Whatever the preferences of shareholders, any private partnership would have been unlikely to ever include as many contributors as a joint-stock company. Yet, no such exogenous selection existed in this historical case: all ventures invariably were of a single type, namely, private share partnerships. This means that the relatively large size of many *course* partnerships reflects how attractive they appeared to merchants from varied backgrounds, echoing the findings from chapter 3. If that is so, then the mediating linchpin position of *course* ventures was not a chance meeting, but rather a—not necessarily intended—consequence of the investment preferences of the Malouins *armateurs* and their partners.

To conclude, the evidence clearly suggests that *course* partnerships played a vital role for upholding the social fabric of the merchant community. The evidence not only is clear but also consistent, whether viewed from various vantage points, or across a range of different measures. Fulfilling their positions as structural linchpins, *course* ventures contributed an important share to the cohesion of the Malouin merchants' network. A significant number of ventures that had been set up for all kinds of overseas trading voyages would have been decoupled had it not been for the mediating role of *course* partnerships. More often than not, these privateering partnerships were unmatched in their linchpin organizational role by collective enterprises in other branches of maritime commerce.

CHAPTER 7

THE RISE OF *NEW MEN*

T he ups and downs of Saint-Malo's role in maritime commerce are what make it a particularly attractive case for studying the development of economic networks over time. Its peculiar trajectory was not one of steady economic growth, but rather one of unexpected turns and detours. Recall that Saint-Malo used to be a fairly traditional fishing port, accustomed to coastal shipping, and home to seafarers whose trading ambitions for the most part went only as far as the shores of Spain. Its remarkable growth in overseas commerce came with the Sun King's renewed ambitions in foreign politics. The ensuing dynastic conflicts among European powers created the wartime opportunities for the *Messieurs de Saint-Malo* to amass enormous riches from high-risk (and sometimes high-return) colonial, interloping, and privateering enterprises.

So much for the upswing in Saint-Malo's economic development in the early modern period. By the 1720s, however, its decline was just as remarkable as its growth in the preceding years. The negative trend is visible in the downward slope of overseas shipping from Saint-Malo, as seen in chapter 2, figure 2.9. Likewise, it appears that the number of most active overseas traders in the city decreased from about 150 in 1710 to a meager 50 in the 1740s.[1] Recall that the account put forward by historian André Lespagnol has emerged as the most widely accepted explanation of this decline relative to other French ports (see chapter 3). The main insight of his explanatory narrative is that, above and beyond any exogenous changes, Saint-Malo's economic growth and decline both followed social logics inherent to the merchant community.[2] The political and economic circumstances that once were so favorable to the commercial enterprise of the Malouin merchantry certainly may have shifted. The absence of armed hostilities until the 1740s meant that no more wartime opportunities existed; patronage ties to the royal court were cut loose; and monopoly privileges in the East Indian trade were revoked. Although these exogenous shifts cannot be denied, Lespagnol insists that a distinct endogenous dynamic was primarily responsible for the waning of Saint-Malo's role in overseas trade. He suggests that the *Messieurs de Saint-Malo*, building on the extraordinary returns to their trading enterprises, aspired to higher positions in the social order and developed a taste for an aristocratic lifestyle. Emulating the nobility, they became avid book collectors, built mansions in the surrounding countryside, and bought landed property and the noble titles that came with it. Generous dowries enabled the richest merchant families to marry their daughters into the established nobility of Brittany. As a result of their excessive status attainment, apprenticeships at sea were no longer seen fit for a nobleman's son. They deemed it more appropriate for their heirs to be educated at colleges in Paris that would prepare them for prestigious offices in the royal administration. Because the apprenticeship system used to ensure that sons would follow their fathers' footsteps into trade, the new preference for administrative careers undermined the reproduction of the merchant dynasties. The *Messieurs* as well as their offspring thus gradually retreated from the world of trade and melted into the world of the Breton nobility.[3] In doing so, their flight to the top spelled an end to the traditional *fidélité au commerce* and unraveled the social fabric that had enabled their economic success in the first place.

As plausible and well documented this historical account is, a few puzzling questions remain. In chapter 3, I pointed to the apparent paradox that these elite families sought to escape their social roots at the very moment of their greatest success, turning their backs on the same social networks that were so instrumental in generating their wealth in the first place. To understand this seemingly puzzling behavior, it is worth remembering that elites rarely form a single unified group. Like their peers in comparable places, members of the Malouin elite distinguished themselves according to their divergent interests as well as differences in financial means and sources of wealth. This observation naturally leads to a follow-up question: how was social cohesion among the merchantry possible in the face of such multiple interest groups? Asking where cohesion originates is a key question because collaborations in voyage partnerships among the various Malouin trading houses provided the organizational platform necessary for their economic success. We have already seen that much of the answer lies in the mediating role of partnerships the Malouins forged through their joint privateering enterprises, and in particular, how they helped to connect a complex web of multiple affiliations.

In what follows, I consider a related question that appears to be just as puzzling. If our *Messieurs de Saint-Malo* were indeed so successful in their flight to the top echelons of society, uprooting themselves and their offspring so thoroughly from their mercantile origins, then why do we see the emergence of a new generation of Malouin trader elites by the 1760s?[4] The names that come to mind include the likes of the Surcouf brothers, Blaize de la Maisonneuve, La Fontaine Le Bonhomme, Pottier de la Houssaye, Meslé de Grandclos, de Chateaubriand, Beaugeard, and de Segray—all of whom were just as illustrious as the first generation of *Messieurs de Saint-Malo.* On the face of it, their accomplishments as traders and *armateurs* were remarkably similar to those of Magon de la Lande, Magon de la Chipaudière, Picot de Clos-Rivière, Locquet de Grandeville, and Danycan de L'Epine during Saint-Malo's earlier golden period. Assuming that all anchoring in the world of commerce and shipping was indeed cut off decades earlier, where did the *new men* come from? How did they achieve their standing as such eminent members of the mercantile class? As it turns out, understanding how these new trader elites entered the stage, pursued their careers, and filled the vacancies left by the first generation also reveals much about the micromechanisms that underpinned the network pattern identified in chapter 6.

OPPORTUNITIES FOR A NEW GENERATION

The new cohort of *armateurs* did not arrive on the scene fully formed. Mirroring the experience of their predecessors under the reign of Louis XIV, armed conflict and economic competition among the major European powers shaped the fortunes of these aspiring entrepreneurs in maritime trade. Once again, although these economic and political circumstances constrained some commercial interests, they also gave rise to fresh opportunities for the *new men* of Saint-Malo. History repeated itself, it seemed—an impression that held particularly true for the persistent Anglo-French rivalry throughout the long eighteenth century.[5] The conflict came to a temporary halt with the Treaty of Utrecht in 1713. Its terms and conditions reflected the scale of French defeat during the War of the Spanish Succession (1702–1713) and Britain's rise as the supreme naval power. The loss of considerable possessions in Canada, notably Newfoundland and Acadia, and in the West Indies appeared to have dispelled much of the colonial ambitions in the Americas that the French might have harbored. Lost as well to the hands of the British was the *Asiento*, the exclusive right granted by the Spanish crown to sell enslaved Africans to the Spanish colonies in America.[6]

Viewed from a different angle, France may have emerged as the true beneficiary of the Treaty of Utrecht.[7] For one, the trading privileges and territorial claims the British had gained to make further inroads to the west of the North American continent were rather difficult to enforce, especially where the Iroquois Nations who settled the lands were concerned. Likewise, their discovery and exploitation of the rich fishing grounds around Cape Breton compensated the French for the limits the treaty had imposed on their rights along the Newfoundland coast. Southward, the growth in sugar production on Martinique and Guadeloupe made the loss of Saint-Christopher in the West Indies more than bearable. Ceding the *Asiento* was not as dramatic as it might have seemed because French traders routinely failed to deliver the quantities spelled out in the contract. Few would deny that the scale of power tipped in favor of British interests whereas the French possessions in the Americas from Louisiana to Québec resembled but a strewn patchwork. As elusive as the French Empire may have been, however, its colonists and traders braved the formidable challenges imposed by the terms of the 1713 treaty.[8] The nearly three decades of peacetime (1713–1740) that followed did in fact witness a considerable growth in French colonial commerce, certainly in no small part because of the thriving economies of the West Indian sugar islands of Saint-Domingue, Martinique, and Guadeloupe (see the discussion in chapter 2 and figure 2.9).[9]

The conflict between France and Britain was not quelled, however, and peace turned out to be no more than an episode that soon gave way to another round of armed hostilities. In the Americas, both an intense competition over the sugar trade in the West Indies and a growing colonial population in Virginia pushing into the Ohio and Mississippi valleys quickly escalated. Westbound British traders not only contested the French economically, but also posed a threat to the carefully woven network of alliances with resident Indian Nations that the French had crafted along the interior frontier.[10] Not before long, the two opponents were embroiled in the Jacobite Rebellion (1745) on British soil and in the dynastic War of the Austrian Succession (1740–1748) that involved nearly every European power of note. A brief eight-year interlude following the Treaty of Aix-la-Chapelle eventually led to the Seven Years' War (1756–1763) that once again pitted France and Britain against each other, this time on a truly global scale. On European battlefields, an Anglo-Prussian alliance confronted the combined forces of Austria, France, and Russia. In North America, the struggles wherein French and British colonists and their respective native allies opposed each other came to be known as the French and Indian Wars.[11] Meanwhile, entangled as they were in shifting coalitions with rival local rulers during the

Carnatic Wars (1746–1763), the English and French East India Companies vied with each other for political influence and economic control on the Indian subcontinent. Related theaters were found in Germany, Senegal, and the southern Iberian waters from Gibraltar to Lagos, and Havana.[12]

The Return of Privateering Enterprise

Much of this global war was decided by seapower.[13] A pivotal reason why Britain ultimately emerged victorious was her naval supremacy. The British were able to take such swift command of the ocean because they combined a well-designed deployment strategy and an effective fiscal-military state to extract the taxes necessary for funding the Royal Navy.[14] As in previous contests, part of France's response entailed the encouragement of *armateurs* and seamen to engage in the *guerre de course*.[15] To be sure, not every port in metropolitan France was equally enthusiastic about the prospects of privateering enterprise.[16] Among the Malouin merchantry, at least, the renewed opportunity appears to have fallen on fertile ground. Witness, for one example, the reaction of Luc Magon de la Blinaye (1715–1794) who directed the long-established trading house of the Magon family during the second half of the eighteenth century. In his correspondence with his business partners, Magon regarded as inevitable the oncoming conflict with England as early as January 1755. In a letter to his partner Chauvel, resident of Le Havre, he expressed his worries about the harm that the hostilities will do to commerce. Consequently, he turned to privateering as a recourse. In August of the same year, Magon informed another investor, a certain Mme de la Moizière, that he and other partners were prepared "to take an interest in the *course*" because "there is no doubt, with war on its way to be declared, that we will arm *corsairs* here" in Saint-Malo.[17] Magon was not alone in his turn toward the *course*, as demonstrated in figure 7.1 by the number of Malouin vessels that were readied for commerce raiding. The *armateurs* of Saint-Malo had a similar reaction once France entered the American Revolutionary War against Britain (1778–1783) to side with the cause of the rebels.[18] As figure 7.1 shows, their efforts may not have reached the same levels as during the late wars of Louis XIV, the heyday of Malouin privateering enterprise. Once again, however, war opened a window of opportunity for a fresh generation of aspiring merchant entrepreneurs in Saint-Malo to rely on the *course* as a trampoline for their careers.[19]

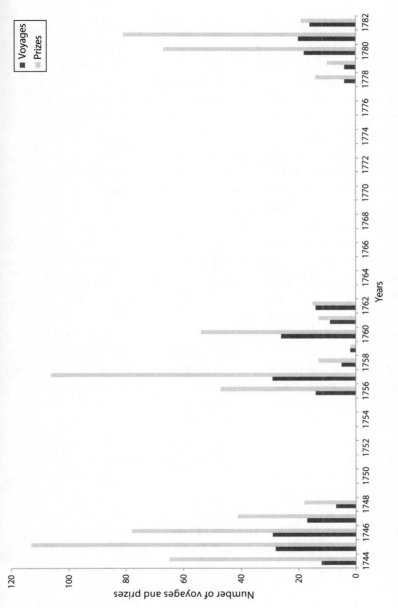

FIGURE 7.1 Privateering enterprise (*guerre de course*) in Saint-Malo during the War of the Austrian Succession (1740–1748), the Seven Years' War (1756–1763), and the American Revolutionary War (1778–1783).

Note: The number of voyages refers to the privateering commissions granted by the French Admiralty. The numbers include only vessels that explicitly set out to sea to engage in commerce raiding (*armements en guerre*). Not included are armed merchantmen that carried commissions of *guerre et marchandise*.

Sources: Information on corsair commissions is taken from *AD-IV* 9B43s, (4)–(5). Data on declared prizes come from *AD-IV* 9B591; 9B598, and from surviving prize dossiers in *AD-IV* 9B623-639. These archival sources are coupled with evidence collected and printed in Martin-Deidier (1976).

Trade with the East Indies

A second occasion that helped to usher in the cohort of *new men* was the reopening of the French East Indian commerce to private traders by 1769. Recall that the first installment of the *Compagnie des Indes*, instigated by Jean-Baptiste Colbert in 1664, was marred from the very start by an imbalance of private merchant interest and the political agenda of the state. Colbert sought to model the French company after its Dutch counterpart, but its administration and strategic decision making were turned on their heads: not bottom-up private shareholder interests, as in the case of the Dutch V.O.C., but the top-down political will of the royal government dictated the endeavors of the French East Indies Company. The belief that French colonial trade was still insufficiently established seems to have guided Colbert's approach, and thus, it would benefit from firmer encouragement by the state, using the regulated company form, until it could become self-sustaining.[20] Because their commercial interests were poorly represented in the company's strategic management, the response of the merchant communities was far from enthusiastic when it came to making any substantial financial commitments. The organizational and financial deficits were further coupled with the vagaries of war, which did not spare the French colonial outposts and trading comptoirs from attacks, mainly by British forces. Facing bankruptcy in the first decade of the eighteenth century, the company first subcontracted, and eventually fully bestowed, its exclusive trading rights with Asia to a group of influential *armateurs* from Saint-Malo. By 1712, private traders thus appeared to have gained the upper hand in the leadership of the *Compagnie des Indes*. Note, however, that the Malouin takeover of colonial trade in the East Indies, between 1707 and 1719, fully preserved the spirit and practice of a commercial monopoly and did not imply its replacement by free trade.[21] For such a comparatively small place as Saint-Malo, its merchants dispatched a substantial number of at least twenty-six vessels (nearly twelve thousand tons) to Pondichéry, Bengal, and Moka in the few years between 1708 and 1719. For an estimated 12.6 million *livres tournois* (*lt.*) in fitting costs, the 48.25 million *lt.* from the sale of colonial goods that the ships brought back to France yielded a handsome return. At least another eleven vessels (totaling 3,580 tons) were bound for Canton between 1702 and 1718. Their merchant fleet thus testified to the entrepreneurial spirit of the Malouin trader community.[22] No wonder that the newly won monopoly in the trade with Asia counted among the main sources of Saint-Malo's wealth during the port's golden period of overseas commerce (see chapter 2).[23]

The often-strained character of the relationship between private merchant interest and state power once again came to the fore by 1719, when the monopoly of Saint-Malo's East Indies Company was revoked. By 1716, John Law, the Scottish financier and monetary reformer in the service of the Regent of France, had begun to introduce his *Système* to solve the debt crisis that followed Louis XIV's vast war-related expenses. Law's economic policy combined the creation of a royal national bank that was to issue paper money with the establishment of an encompassing trading company that was to control all monopolies of French commerce in both the western and the eastern hemispheres. In 1719, Law thus absorbed the trading privileges of the existing Malouin East Indies Company into this newly established *Compagnie des Indes*, merging it with both the *Compagnie d'Occident*, also known as the Mississippi Company, set up in 1717 to spur colonial development in Louisiana, and with the slave-trading *Compagnie du Sénégal*. Under the umbrella of his *Système*, Law sold shares in this combined company complex in return for government certificates issued by his new royal bank. At the prospect of enormous riches to be gained from the Louisiana colony, the trading value of company shares rose steadily and speculation thrived. As his Mississippi scheme required ever more funds, and being steadfast in his belief that more money in circulation would support economic growth, Law began to issue an ever-increasing volume of certificates. The inevitable happened in 1720, when what went down in history as the "Mississippi Bubble" did burst. The collapse resulted from a combination of rising inflation, the realization on the part of shareholders that promises of precious metals to be reaped from the Louisiana colony remained unfulfilled, and an ensuing devaluation of company shares. With the liquidation of the *Système*, it took the remains of the East Indies Company until 1731 to disentangle itself from Law's enterprises and to shed any remaining liabilities, including the monopoly trade of enslaved Africans to the West Indies and the return of the Louisiana colony to the crown. Nevertheless, after a decade of administrative and financial reorganization, the *Compagnie des Indes* emerged like the proverbial phoenix, coming back from the ashes, and indeed was able again to compete with its Dutch and English rivals in Asian markets.[24]

The considerable organizational changes the company's administration underwent between 1723 and 1731 did not mean that private enterprise suddenly came to dominate its operations. At this point, the *Compagnie des Indes* remained a vehicle for exerting royal power in the realm of commerce, just as much as the rivalry between merchant shareholders and representatives of the crown persisted within its organization. The assembly of shareholders certainly was not without influence on the course of action the company would take, including, at least on paper, the election of the board of directors. Most candidates for the positions were recruited from within the trading communities of the French Atlantic port cities. An illustrative case is René Moreau, sieur de Maupertius (1664–1746), a successful former privateering and interloping captain and *armateur*, who turned to a career in politics in 1706, when he was elected as a deputy for Saint-Malo to the *Conseil du commerce*. He was also elected as a director of both the *Compagnie d'Occident* (1717–1719) and the *Compagnie des Indes* (1721–1723).[25] Ultimately, power within the governance of the company rested with the crown as its principal stockowner, whereas any leverage in the hands of directors remained limited. The election of Maupertuis notwithstanding, seats on the board of directors typically were appointed by way of royal order until 1764. Likewise, the crown wielded its authority through the *contrôleur général* and the royal *commissaires* who supervised and, when they saw fit, vetoed the company's financial decisions, commercial operations, and any political dealings in India.[26]

The company and its monopoly position were thus firmly reestablished after the turbulent years under John Law's leadership. At the same time, the merchant communities of the Atlantic port cities that were excluded from the company's benefits continued to challenge the very principle of the chartered company and its exclusive trading rights as being ill suited to commerce with the eastern world. As early as 1700–1701, deputies of these port cities in the Council of Commerce voiced their concerns in a series of memoirs. Among them, La Motte-Gaillard, the representative from Saint-Malo, advocated for "a complete freedom of trade" for his city's commerce to flourish. Contemporary memoirs written by his peers from other port cities were full of similar arguments, all leveled against privileged trading companies, about how they manipulated prices and prevented both open competition and the growth of French colonial settlements.[27] Hence, the long-standing rivalry between private trader interests and the economic policies of the crown found a new expression in the guise of an opposition between monopoly and free trade.[28] Indeed, we find the same critique of mercantilist policies, and the exclusive trading rights of the *Compagnie des Indes* in particular, mirrored in pamphlets and polemics throughout the eighteenth century. Some writers saw little difference between the monopolies of domestic artisan companies and those of foreign trade companies, criticizing both for their alleged abuse of commercial privilege and what these days would be considered rent-seeking. Eventually, the very concept of monopoly came to be seen as an expression of despotism, and hence the abuse of political power under the Ancien Régime. By the 1750s, the *Compagnie des Indes* faced incessant attacks, now coming from within the inner circle of economic policymakers at the royal court. Intendants and controllers general alike condemned the company's misalignment with the spirit of commerce and its financial mismanagement, in particular, its reliance on continued borrowing. The debate then spilled out beyond the shareholder assembly and turned into a genuine crisis that caught the interest of the press and general public, and motivated the Physiocrats to side with the company's critics.[29]

The loss of colonial possessions in India in the aftermath of the Seven Years' War (1756–1763) further aggravated this crisis. The Treaty of Paris that ended the war spelled the end to grander ambitions of a French colonial empire on the Indian subcontinent. The trading activities of the company were thus constrained to a handful of *comptoirs* located within the enclaves that the French retained in India.[30] In August 1769, with mounting critiques at home and the loss of colonies afar, the King's Council finally suspended the monopoly rights of the *Compagnie des Indes*, effectively opening French commerce with the east to private enterprise.[31]

Given their historical ties to the East Indian trade, it does not come as a surprise that the Malouin merchant *armateurs* were among the first to seize this renewed opportunity (see figure 7.2). Notably, however, private trade was never truly excluded under the umbrella of the chartered East Indies Company.[32] Similar to the English East India Company, when captains of merchantmen journeyed between Indian and Malayan ports on their own private account and thus helped to weave a trading network that eventually served the company, the French *Compagnie des Indes* permitted, and even encouraged, private initiative in the *commerce de l'Inde en Inde* (i.e., the regional country trade between local Asian markets).[33] What explicitly changed after 1769 was the expansion of private enterprise beyond the confines of the Indian Ocean to include the exchange of goods between Asia and France. This institutional change offered the new generation of *Messieurs de Saint-Malo* a second opportunity, after privateering, to advance their mercantile careers. As figure 7.2 illustrates, even when the company monopoly was still in place, from 1719 onward, the Malouins certainly did not refrain from arming trading vessels for the East Indies. Beginning in 1769, with the suspension of the monopoly, the number of vessels fitted out in Saint-Malo surged, which was accompanied by a similar rise in Asian shipping in France at large.[34]

The Malouins as Slave Traders

Finally, trading in enslaved Africans—known as *la traite des Noirs* by French merchants—offered a third business opportunity for the *new men* of Saint-Malo to build a career.[35] Obtaining the true number of Africans that were captured

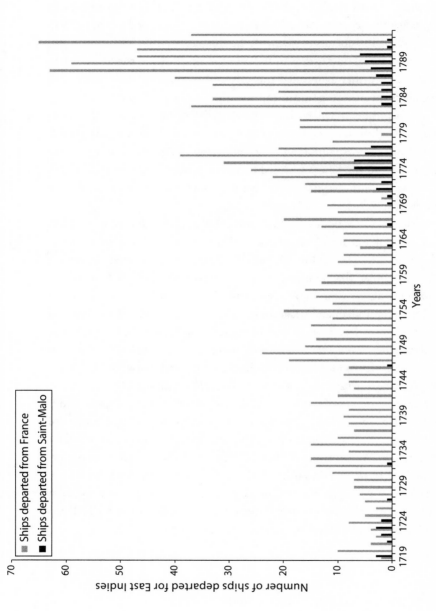

FIGURE 7.2 East Indies trade: Departures from France at large and from Saint-Malo, 1719–1793.

Note: Destinations for departures from France include the Mascarenes Archipelago (present-day Mauritius and Réunion), Moka (present-day Yemen), Pondichéry and Bengal in India, China, and voyages beyond the Cape of Good Hope whose exact destination is unknown.

Destinations for vessels armed at Saint-Malo also include Goa, Mahé and the Malabar Coast, the Coromandel Coast, and Chandernagor on the Indian subcontinent, as well as Mozambique.

Sources: Haudrère (2005, vol. II, 810, 857), 4D-IV (28B-6/1, 2 B 2 . . .

and deported to plantations in the Americas and the Indian Ocean remains a thorny task.[36] Estimates from what is currently the most comprehensive database indicate that Britain took the lead in the transatlantic slave trade for much of the eighteenth century. Imports into the sugar islands in the West Indies amounted to 1.98 million Africans. Another 117,000 were forced to work in British North America, in colonies that would later become the United States (see table 7.1).[37] British slavers were followed closely by Portuguese traders who sought to meet the demand for manual labor in Brazil (1.93 million captives), by the French (about 915,000), and the Dutch (399,000), whereas the Danish West Indies held the smallest share (60,000). Much of the same distribution held when it came to organizing the shipping of enslaved Africans to destinations in the New World. Estimates show that 8,837 vessels intended for the slave trade sailed from British ports during the 1681–1792 period. At the same time, French *armateurs* fitted out an estimated total of 3,358 ships for slave-trading expeditions from their ports, followed by the Portuguese (2,296 vessels), and the Dutch (1,038 vessels).[38]

Just like their European competitors, the French relied on forced labor to sustain production within their plantation colonies.[39] In the West Indies, tobacco proved to be relatively easy to grow, even under varying climatic conditions, and thus became the crop of choice for seventeenth-century French settlers to export to Europe. Precisely because tobacco could be produced just as easily elsewhere, its market value soon declined, urging colonists to seek alternatives. In Louisiana, under the scheme of John Law's company (at least as long as it lasted), the colonial production of tobacco was heavily promoted and subsidized. On the islands of Guadeloupe and Martinique, planters cultivated ginger, cocoa beans, and coffee for refinement and consumption in Europe as well as cotton and indigo to be used for fabrics and dyes. Cotton and coffee were likewise grown in Cayenne (French Guiana), next to roucou (annatto), a seed-based red dye. The jewel in the crown of France's colonies was Saint-Domingue. As elsewhere in the Caribbean, colonists on the island received handsome revenues from the export of cotton, cocoa, and indigo, all of which continued to fetch high prices on European markets. Much of the planters' wealth, however, stemmed from the cultivation of sugarcane, which emerged as the most important New World commodity of the eighteenth century.[40]

The vast plantation estates established in the colonies prospered on the basis of a large manual labor force. Neither the relatively small indigenous population nor the limited number of indentured European servants who had arrived during the seventeenth and early eighteenth centuries were sufficient to produce enough sugar, chocolate, coffee, and similar tropical imports for the insatiable appetite of European consumers.[41] The French islands thus required an ever-increasing slave population to meet the growing demand for labor and to maintain an

TABLE 7.1 Estimated Slave Imports into Overseas Colonies

YEARS	FRANCE	SPAIN/ URUGUAY	PORTUGAL/ BRAZIL	GREAT BRITAIN	NETHERLANDS	NORTH AMERICA/ UNITED STATES	DENMARK/ BALTIC	TOTALS
1681–1690	11,028	1,825	76,197	85,631	35,035	554	2,767	213,037
1691–1700	7,139	0	143,667	89,600	24,011	1,465	17,360	283,242
1701–1710	19,363	0	156,674	125,870	30,162	96	2,582	334,747
1711–1720	47,303	0	177,048	137,796	18,810	1,552	529	383,038
1721–1730	63,133	0	184,214	186,170	27,012	4,322	1,366	466,217
1731–1740	82,389	0	180,016	201,537	23,970	14,144	843	502,899
1741–1750	99,382	0	193,516	142,918	33,791	9,997	2,382	481,986
1751–1760	84,398	251	193,638	210,937	36,432	19,043	6,797	551,496
1761–1770	117,243	3,383	191,713	294,609	53,439	31,183	5,255	696,825
1771–1780	143,652	0	193,583	253,491	42,542	21,049	5,524	659,841
1781–1790	240,456	425	237,078	247,466	13,710	13,820	14,868	767,823
Totals	915,486	5,884	1,927,344	1,976,025	338,914	117,225	60,273	5,341,151

Source: Eltis (2016).
Note: Estimated numbers refer to disembarkments of slaves in the colonies.

TABLE 7.2 Estimated Slave Imports into French Colonies

| DESTINATION | YEARS | NUMBER OF SLAVES SHIPPED | |
		ALL NATIONAL CARRIERS	FRENCH TRADERS
Americas:			
Saint-Domingue	1681–1790	731,328	723,706
Martinique	1681–1790	146,839	124,742
Guadeloupe	1681–1790	34,499	9,988
Guiana	1681–1790	11,658	10,523
French Caribbean unspecified	1681–1790	11,561	3,901
Louisiana	1681–1762	7,577	7,215
Mascareignes (Indian Ocean):			
Île de France and Île de Bourbon	1670–1769	—	50,985–54,726
	1770–1810	—	160,572–184,355

Sources: Eltis (2016) for imports into colonies in the Americas (slaves disembarked). For imports into Louisiana, see also Pritchard (2004, 13). France ceded Louisiana to Britain and Spain by the end of the Seven Years' War (1762). For slave shipments to the Mascareignes islands in the Indian Ocean, see Allen (2015, 18–19), who reports estimated ranges of slave exports from Eastern Africa, Madagascar, and India.

adequate level of colonial production.[42] Africans purchased and enslaved along the Senegal, Gambia, Benin, and Guinea coasts in West Africa were shipped across the Atlantic and sold on the French sugar islands in the Caribbean, in Guiana and Louisiana (see table 7.2).[43] Note that the French slave trade was not limited to the Antilles, Guiana, and Louisiana. Plantation economies comparable in their organization to those in the New World existed on the Mascarene Islands (*Mascareignes*)—the Île de Bourbon and the Île de France—in the Indian Ocean. To furnish a sufficient labor force for these islands, an accompanying eastern slave trade with a supply of captives from Madagascar and Mozambique, and to a lesser extent from India, developed as well (see table 7.2).[44]

The available historical evidence reveals that the Atlantic ports of Bordeaux, La Rochelle, Le Havre, and, above all, Nantes formed the center of French slave-trading enterprise during much of the eighteenth century.[45] Figure 7.3 shows the relative contribution of the leading port cities. The chart traces the overall rise in the number of slave-trading expeditions registered in French ports, employing the same six periods between 1681 and 1792 identified in chapter 6. The involvement of the Malouin merchant-*armateurs* in the *traite des noirs* was certainly far from negligible. In relative terms, however, the commerce was not as prominent in Saint-Malo as it was in rival ports along the French Atlantic. Until the early 1750s, the Breton city never ranked higher than fourth place among French slave-trading ports—despite its previously strong showing in other colonial trades. During the heyday of the slave trade in the second half of the eighteenth century, Saint-Malo began to trail even farther behind its competitors.

Even a lesser role of Saint-Malo in the slave trade appears to be an observation that is hard to swallow. The thought of Malouin seafarers as unscrupulous slave dealers does not sit particularly well with the romantic image of the walled city as the home of swashbuckling privateers that tends to fill the pages of popular histories.[46] Even if we take the salience of the slave trade seriously, it is difficult to determine just how attractive this particular traffic really was for the Malouin merchant community. It was rare for partnership contracts drawn up for overseas ventures to mention explicitly that the slave trade was the intended purpose of the voyage. Out of the entire set of 3,250 partnership records that survived from the 1681–1792 period, merely five contracts did so.[47] In 1719, we find the 120-ton flute *Le Don de Dieu*, fitted out by its owner Pierre Des Vaux and his three shareholding *associés*—all residents of Saint-Malo—for a voyage "a la Coste de Guinée pour la trocque et traite des noirs" and onward "de la aux isles de lamerique française [*sic*]."[48] Two years later, in 1721, the *armateur* François de la Motte, sieur de la Villejosselin, assembled seven business partners to finance the voyage of the two-hundred-ton *La Sainte Famille* to the Guinea coast, also to pursue "La Trocque des Noirs" and bring their cargo to "Lamerique française [*sic*]."[49] In 1730, Guillaume Jolif, sieur du Clos, owner of the 160-ton *L'hirondelle*, gathered the support of two Malouin partners and two merchants who resided on the Caribbean island of Martinique to organize yet another venture for "La Traite des noirs."[50] Remarkably, one has to skip ahead forty-six years before finding another overt reference to the slave trade in the partnership records. In 1776, the *L'Aimable Victoire* sailed into the Indian Ocean to engage in "la traite des noires au Mozambic" and transport them to the "isles de france et Bourbon [*sic*]."[51] Another fifteen years later, in 1791, the brothers Marion of Saint-Malo, with their

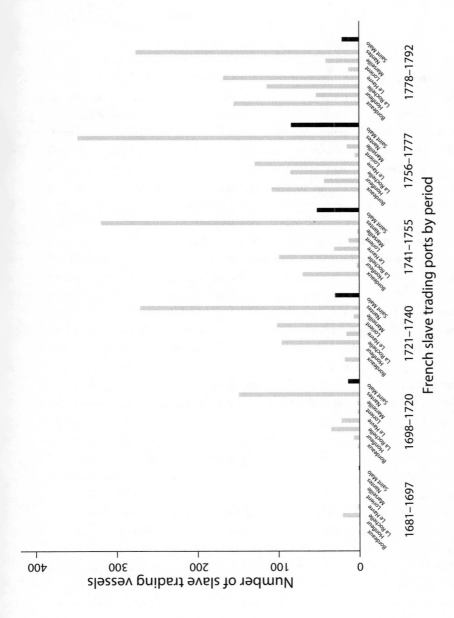

FIGURE 7.3 Leading ports in the French slave trade, 1681–1792.

Note: The chart reflects the number of vessels fitted out for slave trading expeditions and registered in French ports.

Source: Eltis (2016).

partner Duguen and associates from Saint-Malo and Nantes, dispatched the 150-ton *Les Deux Fanyes* "pour la traite des noirs à la Côte d'Affrique [*sic*]."[52]

Only a handful of contracts may have survived in the Saint-Malo partnership records that contain such unambiguous references to the *traite de Noirs*. Yet, the available documents allow us to gain some insight into the financing of a slave-trading venture.[53] Consider, for example, the preparations undertaken in 1776 for the voyage of the just mentioned *L'Aimable Victoire*. Much like the *sociétés* in the *course* and other maritime commerce, ship-owning *armateurs* formed voyage partnerships with shareholding associates to pool the necessary funding. They had to recruit an experienced captain and an able crew of sailors to navigate the vessel. Victuals ("vivres de l'Equipage") were needed for the sailors as well as advance wages equivalent to four months of service ("quatre mois d'avances à l'Equipage"). Maintenance and repairs required hiring carpenters and furnishing wooden materials. The surgeon's equipment ("les articles du chirugien") had to be paid for. Coins and other valuable items ("piastres et Cargaison"), presumably all useful in prospective transactions, were among the cargo to be loaded. In the case of the 169-ton *L'Aimable Victoire*, these and various other expenses equaled a total of 200,751 *lt.*[54] This sum was roughly comparable to the fitting costs of other long-distance ventures armed at Saint-Malo earlier in the eighteenth century: between 197,000 and 304,000 *lt.* were needed for large privateering vessels of 300–350 tons, and for trading ships of about 200–350 tons that were armed for interloping in the South Sea or journeys to Canton in China.[55] Later, in the 1780s, similar fitting costs can be found for various voyages to the Antilles (169,552 *lt.*, on average) that the *armateurs* Solier and Company organized in Marseille.[56]

These records, then, provide fine-grained knowledge about the funding and organization of a small number of slave-trading voyages. Other partnership contracts seem to lack such detailed information. Plenty of ventures documented in the partnership sources, however, did not specify the slave trade as their intended purpose, but they nevertheless shared the same routes as those five declared slave-trading expeditions. Within our period of interest, from 1681 through 1792, a total of ninety-three vessels set out from Saint-Malo to reach destinations in Africa or nearby islands. The vast majority among them—eighty-three vessels— sailed for the coasts of Guinea and Senegal in West Africa, and thence across the Atlantic to the American plantation colonies. Eight ships traveled to the Cape Verde and Canary Islands, and another one made its way to the Île de France and the Île de Bourbon in the Indian Ocean. The record of one further vessel mentions only an indistinct "côte d'Afrique" as its destination.[57] Their intended journeys thus offer good reasons to count these ventures among the African slave-trading expeditions that set out from Saint-Malo.

Turning to the individual merchant entrepreneurs who took it upon themselves to arm these expeditions, we recognize a sizeable share of the *new men* among the leading slave traders of the port city. Indeed, the peak of the slave trade in Saint-Malo during the second half of the eighteenth century coincided with the rise to prominence of a new generation of *Messieurs de Saint-Malo*.[58] Because their commitment to seafaring commerce lay at the heart of their identity and defined who they were, table 7.3 lists leading representatives of this emergent merchant elite with an eye to their wealth and their various trading activities.[59] Several among them were avid slave traders, including Le Bonhomme de la Fontaine, Sébire des Saudrais, and Ledet de Segray as well as Beaugeard, the Surcouf brothers, and Meslé de Grandclos. None of them were specialists, however, who focused their business activities exclusively on the slave trade.[60] Considering all Malouin slave-trading merchants, beyond this uppermost group, table 7.4 shows that they cast a wide net when it came to their investments in overseas trade. Within the partnership documents, 271 merchants held an interest in a slave-trading venture. Most of them (193 merchants, or 71 percent) participated in more than just a single partnership. Only a few concentrated all their efforts in successive slave-trading expeditions. The vast majority (183 merchants, or 95 percent) of these serial investors spread their interests widely across different branches of maritime commerce.

The same pattern of multiple engagements in a variety of trades that we find among the slave traders at large was also shared by the leading *new men* within Saint-Malo's merchant elite.[61] It was not uncommon to hold investments in more than forty separate venture partnerships over the course of one's merchant career (see table 7.3). Some, like Meslé de Grandclos, Guillemaut des Peschers, and Fromy du Puy financed up to 88, 92, and 153 enterprises, respectively. None of these traders remained silent partners. Instead, more than once, they played active roles as *armateurs* who instigated the partnerships, owned the ship for the planned voyage, and typically floated the lion's share of the required capital. Beyond their interest in the slave trade, the *new men* immersed themselves in nearly all branches of overseas commerce available: from the tried-and-tested cabotage, Spanish trade, and Canadian cod fishing to the lures of the West Indies and the high-risk, high-return voyages to the East Indies and China. The complex web of affiliations that emerged from concurrent and sequential investments does not make it any easier for us to understand how salient the slave trade really was among the merchant entrepreneurs of Saint-Malo, compared with their other activities. It does emphasize how much this new generation followed in the footsteps of the old generation of *Messieurs de Saint-Malo* in seeking careers based on what some historians have called functional polyvalence.[62] Recall that polyvalence refers to the strategy of investing in multiple voyage partnerships at the same time, often entwined through the same shareholding partners. This strategy granted them flexibility to pool profits from previous ventures for reinvestments elsewhere, spread risk across a diverse portfolio, and adapt quickly to changing economic and political circumstances. Chief among such external changes was the outbreak of war, which led to renewed opportunities for privateering enterprise. With the onset of the Seven Years' War and the American Revolutionary War, it is no surprise that the new *Messieurs de Saint-Malo* seized the opportunity to arm vessels for the *course.* Every single one among them, from Chateaubriand to the Surcouf brothers, and from Le Bonhomme de la Fontaine to Robert de la Mennais, took part in commerce raiding, just as their predecessors Danycan, Duguay-Trouin, and the elder Magon de la Lande did during the late wars of Louis XIV.

The fortunes the new *Messieurs* made through their successive trading activities are also reflected in the poll tax (*capitation*) they were required to pay. The right-hand columns in table 7.3 draw on Saint-Malo's poll tax rolls for selected years, from the Seven Years' War to the eve of the French Revolution, when the new Malouin elite was at its prime. If their documented tax returns are anything to judge by, the traders who belonged to this rising elite counted among the more affluent burghers of their city.[63] With just two exceptions, Guillemaut des Peschers and Saint-Marc in 1763, their *capitation* quota fell squarely within the top ten percentile of taxpayers, no matter what years we consider. By 1789, Guillemaut des Peschers, at least, had moved up the ranks, both in the merchant community and in the tax classification, with his wealth now assessed at 213 *lt.*[64] His status attainment does not appear to have been unusual. His peers Sébire des Saudrais, Pottier de la Houssaye, le Bonhomme de la Fontaine, Coquelin de la Tiolais, and Robert de la Mennais were all rated at a higher tax quota in 1789 than in the 1763 *capitation* roll, thus indicating their increased means.[65] The 1789 *capitation* further reveals that twelve of the sixteen new elite *armateur-négociants* listed in table 7.3 were among the top 5 percent of taxpayers in Saint-Malo. The most illustrious among them, someone like Pierre Jacques Meslé de Grandclos (who paid 1,000 *lt.*), or Fromy du Puy (assessed at 444 *lt.*), or Pierre Louis Robert sieur de la Mennais (who paid 320 *lt.*) even reached into the highest echelons of the local social order.

As in similar settings of the time, economic and political elites in Saint-Malo tended to overlap. This was no different with the new generation of *Messieurs*, as their economic standing in the merchant community translated into positions of political influence. Most of them assumed public offices within the municipal administration of Saint-Malo, often filling multiple positions.[66] At the highest

TABLE 7.3 Leading *New Men* Among Saint-Malo's Merchant Elite

	VENTURES			NUMBER OF OVERSEAS TRADES INVESTED IN								POLL TAX PAYMENTS (*CAPITATION*) IN *LIVRES TOURNOIS*				
	TOTAL	AS *ARMATEUR*	AS INVESTOR	*COURSE*	SLAVE TRADE	*CABOTAGE*	SPANISH TRADE	PÊCHE	FRENCH WEST INDIES	INDIAN OCEAN/ CHINA	OTHER TRADES	1763	1766	1767	1788	1789
Pierre Jacques Meslé sieur de Grandclos	88	33	55	14	9	10	2	34	7	4	8				700	1,000
Pierre Beaugeard	53	37	16	3	3	6	1	11	3	20	6	112				
Surcouf frères	62	18	44	17	3	11	1	18	6	1	5	72			280	355
Guy Jean Sébire sieur des Saudrais	70	29	41	10	4	8	2	17	6	14	9	33				160
Robert Servan Pottier sieur de la Houssaye	52	27	25	6	1	9	1	15	11	1	8	81				151
Jean-Baptiste Hippolyte le Bonhomme sieur de la Fontaine	28	11	17	12	5	3		6		1	1		100	80 (300 in 1768)		
René Auguste de Chateaubriand	19	13	6	7	3		1	5	2	1	1	130				
François Guillaume Leyritz	45	12	33	25	2	4	1	8		1	4					133
Jean-Baptiste Michel Hippolyte Marion	27	11	16	4	3	6		8	2	1	3					
Louis Marie Marion sieur de la Brillantais	29	11	18	6	3	8		6	2	1	3					

(*continued*)

Joseph Alain Fromy sieur du Puy	153	38	115	13	37	7	61	4	3	28	444
Benjamin Dubois	52	35	17	14	12		15	1	5	5	
Auguste Jean Guillemaut sieur des Peschers	92	19	73	17	18	5	31	4	1	16	21
											213
Jean Coquelin sieur de la Tiolais	28	21	7	6	6		8	1		7	33
											56
Louis Blaize sieur de la Maisonneuve	44	16	28	9	13		14		2	6	222
Joseph Fichet sieur des Jardins	29	13	16	9	2		11	2		5	62
Urbain Jacques Raoul Canneva, l'aîné	26	16	10	8	3	1	12		1	1	80
Louis François Robert sieur de la Mennais, père	55	33	22	16	7	1	19	7		4	120
											151
Pierre Louis Robert sieur de la Mennais, fils	41	15	26	5	13	2	8	4	3	6	320
Isaïe Louis Ledet sieur de Segray	39	25	14	5	2	1	4	3	21	1	107
Jean Julien Bodinier	24	11	13	5	6		7	2	1	3	
Jean Mathieu Auguste Saint-Marc, fils	22	15	7	3	2	1	12	2	2	2	24
										50	44
Louis Jean Marie Harrington	12	4	8	3			6		2	1	
										130	200

Sources: For trade and *course* investments, *AD-IV* 9B165–9B176; 9B587; 4E5277–4E5278; 4E5343; 4E5364; for poll tax payments (*capitation*), *AD-IV* C4086; C4098; C4259; C4262; Sée and Lesort (1911). The tax amount for Chateaubriand in 1768 is mentioned by Collas (1949a, 52). Identification of *new men* draws on leading *armateurs* and slave traders as reported by Roman (2001, 58–59).

TABLE 7.4 Multiple Partnerships of Saint-Malo Slave Traders, 1681–1792

PANEL A. ALL SLAVE TRADERS	NUMBER OF TRADERS		NUMBER OF VENTURES				
	N	PERCENT	MEAN	STD. DEV.	MEDIAN	MIN.	MAX.
Partner in single venture	78	28.78					
Partner in multiple ventures	193	71.22	14.09	15.82	8	2	88
Total	271	100					

PANEL B. SLAVE TRADERS IN MULTIPLE VENTURES	NUMBER OF TRADERS		NUMBER OF VENTURES					NUMBER OF DIFFERENT TRADES				
	N	PERCENT	MEAN	STD. DEV.	MEDIAN	MIN.	MAX.	MEAN	STD. DEV.	MEDIAN	MIN.	MAX.
Partner in slave trade only	10	5.18	2.5	0.85	2	2	4					
Partner in multiple trades	183	94.82	14.72	16.00	8	2	88	4.42	2.23	4	2	11
Total	193	100										

Sources: For both panels. *AD-IV* 9B165–9B176; 9B587; 4E5277–4E5278; 4E5343; 4E5364.

level of town governance, the *corps de ville*, Meslé de Grandclos, Pottier de la Houssaye, and Robert de la Mennais served as *échevins* (aldermen) along with the mayor on the executive committee of Saint-Malo. All three filled the supporting offices of *assesseurs*, as did Guillemaut des Peschers.[67] Le Bonhomme de la Fontaine and Marion took on leading roles in the communal assembly as *prieur consuls*. Sébire des Saudrais acted as one of the *administrateurs de l'Hôtel-Dieu*.[68] Still others were elected as representatives of corporate bodies to the municipal assembly. These representatives included Marion de la Brillantais for the professional corps of architects and constructors, Blaize de la Maisonneuve for the group of overseas traders, Fichet des Jardins for the officers of the *milice bourgeoise*, and le Bonhomme de la Fontaine who is listed as a *deputé des corporations* in the sources.[69] Beyond communal politics, Robert de la Mennais, son of the *échevin* just mentioned, was appointed *subdélégué de l'Intendant* in the 1780s.[70] At Saint-Malo, Jean Julien Bodinier held local offices as *juge baillif des eaux*, as *receveur général des droits de navigation*, and he represented the group of *armateurs* at the city council. Within the national political arena, Bodinier rose as a notable figure who served as the alternate representative for the *sénéchaussée* of Rennes at the Estates General of 1789, and as a delegate for the *département* of Ille-et-Vilaine at the Revolutionary Legislative Assembly of 1791–1792, the *Conseil des Cinq-Cents* of 1795–1799, and subsequent national assemblies under the Directory, the Consulate, and the First Empire.[71] Venality existed as well. Sébire des Saudrais, for instance, bought his office as *secrétaire du roi*, a rather nominal position that nevertheless came with handsome privileges, such as the prospect of ennoblement and access to otherwise closed circles at court that proved useful for advancing one's career.[72]

Now that we have an idea who the *new men* were who stepped to the fore by midcentury, we may wonder how they attained their position. How did they build their careers, and what were the consequences for the local merchant community at large? To answer both questions, let us consider two protagonists among them: René-Auguste de Chateaubriand and Pierre-Jacques Grandclos Meslé.[73]

A COMMERCIAL NOBILITY

Setting aside culinary delights, most probably associate the name Chateaubriand with the leading light of French Romanticism, author of the *Mémoires d'Outre-Tombe*, and one of Saint-Malo's most famous sons, François-René de Chateaubriand (1768–1848). Yet, it was his father René-Auguste de Chateaubriand, comte de Combourg, who restored his family's erstwhile status within the higher circles of the Breton and French aristocracy. Born on September 23, 1718, René-Auguste was the second son of François de Chateaubriand de la Villeneuve, seigneur des Touches, and Perronnelle Lamour, dame de Lanjégu. His parents' titles suggest a solid aristocratic stock. Indeed, the Chateaubriands counted among the oldest Breton noble families. They claimed a direct lineage to a certain Brien or Brient I, baron under the Duke of Brittany, who established the *seigneurie* and was said to have distinguished himself in the Battle of Hastings in 1066. With the passing of time, the family's name changed from Brien to Briant or Briand. As the barons settled in their château, their fief eventually became the barony of Chateaubriand. In the long list of illustrious ancestors, Geoffroy, baron de Chateaubriand, followed his oath of allegiance and joined King Saint-Louis during the Seventh Crusade. Through marriage, the Chateaubriands were even related to the royal families of England and Spain.[74]

Unfortunately for René-Auguste, not much of the former glory and wealth were left by the time of his birth. For one, he belonged to a mere *cadet* branch of the main Chateaubriand de la Guérande lineage because his grandfather was but the second son of his great-grandfather, Jean de Chateaubriand de la Guérande (1631–1711).[75] What appears to be a simple matter of birth order, placing the *fils aîné* (first-born son) before the *fils cadet* (younger son), had vast consequences for the property of noble families. The inheritance laws in place at the time prescribed that the first-born son should inherit two-thirds of his father's holdings, whereas the remaining third should be divided among the younger sons. The same principle applied to the next generations of sons and grandsons. The consequence was an unhealthy division of property into ever-smaller shares, until little was left for the "cadets des cadets," in the apt words of Chateaubriand, than to quarrel over some rifles and a hunting dog ("d'une canardière et d'un chien de chasse"). The rules of succession thus led to an impoverishment of *cadet* nobles relative to their older brothers, and the process accelerated with every new marriage and its offspring. It probably did not help that these younger sons clung to their honorary titles, such as "chevaliers hauts et puissants seigneurs." Paired with a tangible loss of wealth, their infatuation with pedigree and titles only served to deepen the contrast between their aristocratic identity and the harsh economic reality they faced. René-Auguste de Chateaubriand embodied the impasse reached by the "cadets des cadets" of the lesser and middling nobility. He had to share the third of an already small inheritance left by his father with his two younger brothers, leaving him with a meager annual income of about 550 to 800 *lt*. Therefore, we may appreciate the extent to which he felt humiliated at the loss of his accustomed station, and why he was so dedicated to reclaiming his privileges and rank among the noblemen of Brittany. According to his son's famous literary portrait, the one single passion that drove him throughout his life was his surname ("une seule passion dominait mon père, celle de son nom").[76]

Enlistment in the royal navy offered one escape route for poor middling nobles from Brittany and other provinces. For many, however, the additional cost of living at the Brest naval base, acquiring an officer's uniform, and purchasing the required military equipment proved to be prohibitive. The world of commerce and overseas trade promised an alternative opportunity to regain their lost prosperity, and with it the means to pursue a lifestyle worthy of a young aristocrat. When the abbé Coyer published his pamphlet *La noblesse commerçante* in 1756, he sought to encourage young noblemen like Chateaubriand to leave behind the now-useless insignia of their status and seek new glories in maritime trade (see figure 7.4). What the abbé had in mind when he prescribed a career in commerce was not just individual gain and the recovery of fortunes the *cadets* had lost ("Devenez, par le commerce, des Dieux tutélaires pour vos femmes & vos enfans [*sic*]"). His vision for the members of the emerging commercial nobility was that through their collective efforts, they would breathe new life into the economy and contribute to the common good of the French nation ("Devenez, pour la Patrie, les nourrissiers des terres, la vie des Arts, le soutien de la population, l'appui de notre Marine, l'ame de nos Colonies, le nerf de l'Etat, les instruments de la fortune publique").[77] Despite its verve, the abbé's plea was not met with much enthusiasm. For many nobles, participation in commerce was frowned upon and not deemed commensurate with their sense of station in the Old Regime's social order. They feared the loss of prestige and privileges if they joined the ranks of a commercial nobility. Conversely, to the extent that it pursued mercantilist economic policies, the royal government had an interest in stimulating the participation of the nobility in overseas trade. In a series of edicts in 1669 and 1701, and again in 1767, Louis XIV and Louis XV declared commerce an honorable undertaking that was vital to the prosperity of the state. The crown assured all noblemen that engagement in maritime trade would not result in the derogation of their social position and privileges. Despite such encouraging royal policies, many aristocrats refrained from entering the world of commerce and even disapproved of it. Theirs was a world that revolved around the stewardship of their *seigneuries*, a culture in which noble status, privilege, and wealth all derived from the tangible property of land—not from the fleeting fortunes of trade.[78]

In regions along the French Atlantic seaboard, with their long-held traditions of fishing and maritime trade, the prospect of high returns from commerce fell

Qui sert ce vain amas d'une inutile gloire? Boil. Sat. V.

FIGURE 7.4 Frontispiece of *La Noblesse Commerçante* by the abbé Coyer, published in 1756.

Note: The engraving captures a young nobleman—supposedly a *fils cadet*—as he is about to step from his accustomed station as an aristocrat into the world of commerce: he casts backward a melancholic glance at his coat of arms and letters of nobility, left on the ground and reduced to mere symbols of a once glorious past, while he has set one foot onto the plank of a trading vessel, loaded to the brim with wares, thus alluding to the riches that await those who invest in commerce.

Source: University of California Libraries.

on more fertile ground among the lesser nobility. The lure of the sea was always present in provinces like Normandy and Brittany. Saint-Malo, in particular, provided an economic environment that was ideally suited for a commercial nobility to emerge. Generation upon generation of merchant elite families who had made the port city their home as far back as the late-fifteenth century laid claim to a noble heritage, and yet at the same time, found it natural to devote themselves to seaborne commerce. Several members of well-established Malouin lineages, such as de la Haye, Pépin de la Broussardière, Martin de la Chapelle, Artur de la Motte, or the Ecuyer Boullec de la Villeblanche, became ship captains, co-owners of ships, *armateurs*, and even *corsaires* over the course of the sixteenth and seventeenth centuries. Likewise, at least fifteen resident merchant nobles played an active role as *armateurs* in launching a total of fifty-four privateering expeditions from Saint-Malo between 1688 and 1715.[79] Brittany and Saint-Malo, in particular, proved to be a hotbed of the commercial nobility.

Later, around midcentury, René-Auguste de Chateaubriand took a similar road and sought his fortunes in the world of commerce. Two principal options were available for new entrants to this world: (1) a merchant apprenticeship in trading posts abroad, such as the Malouin *comptoirs* in Cadiz; or (2) training in navigation within the merchant marine (see chapters 2 and 3). René-Auguste opted for the latter and took to the sea. His enrollment papers indicate that he served first as an ensign on at least two voyages to Newfoundland between 1739 and 1741. His promotion to lieutenant and another six voyages followed. The War of the Austrian Succession opened opportunities for Chateaubriand to take part in a number of privateering campaigns, first as lieutenant and then as second-in-command on the corsairs *l'Assomption* and *le Tigre*. In 1747, at age twenty-nine, he passed the captaincy exam and finally received his commission. His first command followed soon, for the 280-ton *le Blancfort*, owned by the Malouin *armateurs* Pétel and Dufresne, sailing for the West Indies as a letter of marque vessel. Eventually, he turned to the vibrant port city of Nantes where his social network included close ties to another eminent mercantile aristocrat, Antoine Espivent de Villeboisnet, whose eldest son, Pierre Antoine, became his trusted friend. Between 1754 and 1757, Chateaubriand thus stood at the helm of a number of vessels sponsored by the Espivents and other Nantais merchant *armateurs*, some destined for Saint-Domingue, whereas others were slave-trading expeditions to West Africa. As a result of his service, he gained first-hand navigational skills, forged a personal network rich in valuable and influential contacts, and made a fortune of about 30,000 *lt.*, enough to establish himself at Saint-Malo as an *armateur* in his own right.[80]

Chateaubriand's lieutenant on board of the *Blancfort* was none other than Pierre-Jacques Meslé de Grandclos, who, after the Seven Years' War, would emerge as Saint-Malo's most important overseas trader. His beginnings in maritime commerce were humble, as was his rural family background. Ten years younger than Chateaubriand, Pierre-Jacques followed a similar career path in navigation, enlisting as an ensign at the tender age of thirteen. At twenty-four, and having served as an officer on just fourteen voyages, he received his first command as captain in his own right. At the time of his marriage in 1753, Meslé de Grandclos had already earned some 25,000 *lt.*, as he benefited from holding shares in the ventures that he commanded. Unlike Chateaubriand, Meslé did not come from a rich aristocratic heritage. His grandfather Étienne began as a pilot for Newfoundland cod-fishing ventures, and left no more than 5,000 *lt.* to his family. His father, Jacques Meslé, started his career as a captain, also on board of fishing vessels in the North Atlantic, yet he had built a fortune of 10,000 *lt.* by the time of his marriage at age thirty-four. Their careers over three generations illustrate the rise to prominence within the trader elite of Saint-Malo, which no doubt was helped along by marriage arrangements with venerable merchant dynasties.[81] The gradual ascent of the Meslés further demonstrates the two-sided recruitment and meaning of the commercial nobility—assuming we do not take the abbé Coyer's view of this group as literally the sole preserve of indigent aristocrats. Among the group's ranks, we find both the offspring of the lesser and middling nobility who sought in commerce a means to reclaim their erstwhile status, and the representatives of an emerging bourgeoisie, many of whom used the wealth they achieved through maritime trade to lay claim to their own ennoblement. The merchant elite of the *noblesse commerçante*, in Saint-Malo and elsewhere, thus formed a new composite class of "bourgeois-nobles" that blurred the boundaries of societal rank that otherwise separated the nobility from the upper echelons of the trader world.[82]

THE *COURSE* AS LAUNCHING PAD FOR TRADER CAREERS

As they turned from commanding ships in the service of other merchants toward their own prospects as *armateurs*, Pierre-Jacques Meslé de Grandclos and René-Auguste de Chateaubriand filled the void left by the older generation of *Messieurs de Saint-Malo*. They did not, however, immediately join the higher strata of Saint-Malo's merchant society. Not unlike modern-day internal labor markets, in which new entrants typically start at lower positions and await opportunities for promotion until vacancies open in higher-ranked jobs, both Meslé de Grandclos and Chateaubriand gradually worked their way up before reaching their leading roles within the merchant community.[83] What, then, was their starting point as they became *armateurs* who fitted out their own ships? If we were to characterize the essence of the career paths that both the Comte de Chateaubriand and Grandclos Meslé pursued as shipowners, then it was their early commitment to privateering enterprise that held the key to their considerable success. In making this commitment, they followed in the footsteps of predecessors like Noël Danycan de L'Epine, perhaps the greatest *armateur corsaire* during Saint-Malo's golden age (see chapter 2). As André Lespagnol has shown, the privateering ventures Danycan undertook were his entry ticket into the world of international commerce—his very own "trampoline" into the upper ranks of the Malouin trade elite.[84] For Chateaubriand and Meslé de Grandclos, their engagement in the *course* likewise served as a launching pad that propelled their careers as *armateurs* in overseas trade. In 1756, the twenty-eight-year old Meslé de Grandclos first joined his father's *sociétés* in fitting out voyages. By 1762, he had established himself as an *armateur* in his own right. He had done so at the height of the Seven Years' War, which offered him plenty of opportunities to launch privateering operations out of Saint-Malo to prey on British ships in the Channel and beyond. Particularly profitable to him and his associates proved to be the three-hundred-ton *Le Mesny*, joined by the fifty-ton *L'espérance*, that he both armed "en Course sur les Enemies de l'état."[85] Alain Roman estimates that his commerce raiding exploits earned Grandclos Meslé considerable returns of about 300,000 to 500,000 *lt.* by the end of the war. He promptly used this sum to finance the trading house he established in Saint-Malo. Over the following three decades, he and his business associates fitted out a total of 166 ships to pursue all manners of commerce.[86] What the *Mesny* was for Grandclos Meslé, the 90-ton *Villegénie* and the 150-ton *Amaranthe* were for Chateaubriand. He, too, recognized the opportunities for privateering during the Seven Years' War. In 1759, he bought and armed the corsair *La Villegénie* on his own account, with the sieur Leyritz fils, a certain sieur du Rouvre, and the Villeboisnets (father and son) as his associates in the ship's *société*, and his younger brother Pierre Anne de Chateaubriand, sieur du Plessis, as his trusted captain. In 1761, he bought the smallish fifty-ton *Le Vautour*, and the frigate *L'Amaranthe*, which was ideally suited for the *guerre de course*, with her build and the ability to carry up to eighteen cannons. Together, their privateering campaigns were tremendously successful and yielded dozens of prize ships and just as many ransoms. By the end of the Seven Years' War, Chateaubriand had amassed a fortune comparable to Grandclos Meslé's, estimated as well in the range of 300,000 to 500,000 *lt.* With the *Amaranthe* easily repurposed as a slaver, he used a good share of this sum to float several slave-trading expeditions to Guinea as well as new ventures to Newfoundland and even the East Indies.[87]

As the *course* resembled a lottery more than anything else, it did not generate huge returns on a regular basis. When it was successful, plunder and profit went hand in hand. Danycan reinvested the extraordinary profits from his privateering raids to finance his forays into the South Sea and marketplaces in China. Similarly, for Chateaubriand and Meslé de Grandclos, the sheer monetary returns from their commerce raiding expeditions certainly played no small role when it came to the launch of voyages in other branches of overseas trade.[88] The profits gained from the *course* thus helped to breathe new life into their ventures to the French Antilles, the East Indies, and the Newfoundland cod fisheries as well as their slave-trading expeditions to the coasts of Africa.[89] Not only did the high-risk, high-return "corsair mentality" inspire their campaigns in commerce that followed suit, as John Bromley has observed.[90] Perhaps even more important for the question of social cohesion, *armateurs* like Meslé or Chateaubriand drew on the tried-and-tested business relations they had built in their initial *course* ventures to join forces once again in subsequent trading enterprises. Figure 7.5 illustrates how the privateering partnerships he had forged during the Seven Years' War (shown as black ties, accumulated from 1759 through 1762) gave rise to René-Auguste de Chateaubriand's personal network of business collaborations in the years that followed. The sequence of affiliation networks showcases how the activities expanded from privateering (black ties) into various branches of overseas commerce (dark gray ties). They ranged from traditional cod-fishing ventures around Newfoundland to the slave trade in Guinea and Mozambique and voyages to the West Indies. The network images also show that when their enterprises attracted new shareholders, opportunities arose for *armateurs* like Chateaubriand to forge bonds between both old and new business partners (in figure 7.5, past collaborations retreat into the background as light gray ties). We thus may think of someone like Chateaubriand or Meslé de Grandclos as a skillful *bricoleur* of social structure whose ties with partners at hand embedded them in the wider network of the Saint-Malo merchant elite.[91] Readers familiar with the social psychological roots of social network analysis will recognize this as a process akin to transitive closure within triads such that mutual affection and trust, shared interests, and preferences yield strong ties within groups of three people: a friend of a friend is a friend, and a former business partner of my current business partner is likely to be someone I would do business with in the future (see chapter 4).[92] In the trading world of Saint-Malo, this meant that two formerly unrelated merchants were likely to join in a future partnership because both had previously collaborated with, say, Chateaubriand or Grandclos Meslé, in separate trading ventures.[93] By initiating this veritable enchainment of past and present partnerships, as shown here in Chateaubriand's extended personal business network, the *course* facilitated transitive closure among the Malouin merchant elites.[94] As their investment careers began to evolve into diverse portfolios of trades beyond the *course*, they eventually helped to maintain cohesion within the merchant community at large, whether intentional or not. The wide range of business ties that followed from these ventures, including their undertakings in privateering, enabled these *armateurs* to mediate between their merchant partners who were embedded in otherwise separate networks.

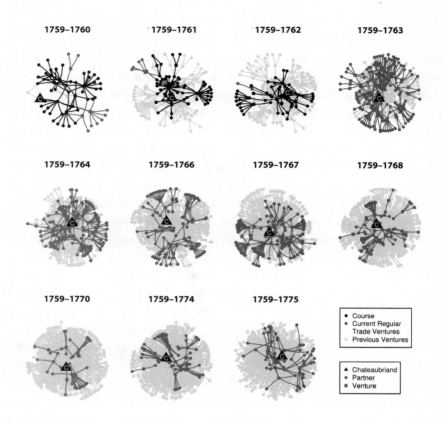

FIGURE 7.5 Growth of Chateaubriand's network of share partnerships.

Note: The two-mode graphs, linking merchants to partnerships, show all ventures initiated by René-Auguste de Chateaubriand as *armateur* to the extent that they are preserved in the partnership contracts. The black triangle marked with a "C" denotes Chateaubriand's own network position. Included are all cumulative ties that are up to two steps removed from Chateaubriand, thus taking into account ties among his partners' partners. The positions of nodes and ties are drawn using the force-directed Kamada-Kawai algorithm. The layout is optimized separately for each period-specific network.

Source: AD-IV 9B173-175.

MEDIATION IN MULTIPLE NETWORKS

The personal histories of René-Auguste de Chateaubriand and Pierre-Jacques Grandclos Meslé serve as exemplars of their kind. As rich in historical detail as they are, however, they beg the question to what extent their lesser known peers in the merchant elite followed suit and showed similar patterns in their investment careers. More precisely, we may wonder how systematic, beyond just a few anecdotes, the link really was between initial engagements in the *course*, on one hand, and subsequent opportunities for network mediation and closure, on the other. Likewise, how pronounced was this same link in those alternative career sequences that were composed exclusively of regular trade ventures and thus lacked any investment in privateering partnerships? To answer these questions we must examine some additional statistics. Once again, the registers of voyage partnerships, both with the Admiralty and in notarial records, provide the most suitable data source to examine this link between career structures and mediation in the merchant network.[95]

I focus on serial investors only—that is, merchants who participated in at least two successive voyage partnerships. The complete network of affiliations that I coded from the original voyage partnership declarations includes 2,145 merchants with multiple investments—that is, 34 percent of the total 6,298 merchants listed in the records. The reasoning behind the restriction to serial investors is twofold. First, just like modern-day patterns of occupational mobility where people move from one job to another, the very idea of a career in this historical setting also implies successive steps from one trading or privateering venture to another (figure 7.6 shows examples of shorter observed career trajectories that emerged out of repeated investments). Hence, any systematic comparison of investment careers is meaningful only for *armateurs* or shareholders who participated in at least two successive ventures. Merchants who joined no more than a single trading voyage hardly made a career for themselves in this business. Second, only those merchants who participated in multiple ventures could possibly have brokered between their former and present business partners, which then might have led to closure among them. In contrast, whoever took part in just a single venture had little to offer as a broker because all of his or her partners already would have been fully connected to each other by virtue of their joint membership in this particular venture.

Furthermore, if investment careers that evolved from initial *course* ventures did indeed provide a vehicle for mediation that was not limited to any particular cohort of Malouin merchants, then such a general mechanism should account for cohesion in the observed partnership network across all years. In what follows, I therefore consider the career sequences of all serial investors for the entire window of observation, from 1681 through 1792, and not just for the generation of *new men*.[96]

With these considerations in mind, table 7.5 compares four broad career trajectories that overseas traders pursued as they sponsored their multiple enterprises. The first typical sequence, shown in column (1), groups merchants who had a vested interest in various regular trade partnerships but never in the *course*. They made up a little under two-thirds of all serial investors ($n = 1,268$). Accounting for the remaining third ($n = 877$), the three other career paths, listed in columns (2) through (4), include all *armateurs* and their partners who participated at least once in a privateering venture. The distinction between privateering merchants and those who abstained from *course* ventures and instead concentrated their efforts in regular trades follows directly from my central argument and the evidence provided thus far—namely, that the *course* promised the greatest potential as a structural linchpin in the merchant network. Tables 7.5 and 7.7 provide further systematic evidence in support of this argument, using a range of different indicators. For comparison, both tables also show how our two exemplary cases (René-Auguste de Chateaubriand and Pierre-Jacques Grandclos Meslé) fared along these indicators (see table 7.5, columns (5) and (6); table 7.7, columns (5) and (6)).

Before we turn to these findings, a further distinction within the group of privateering merchants is warranted. Recall the idea that organizing *course* ventures opened a first opportunity to enter the market of overseas trade. In present-day parlance, their initial engagements in commerce raiding kickstarted these rookies into building a career and establishing themselves as successful traders and *armateurs*. Once returns from the capture of prize ships were forthcoming, so the argument continues, these aspiring merchants began to broaden their ambitions and invested in other branches of overseas commerce. Not everyone who eventually opted for such a mixed investment strategy made their first steps in the business of commerce raiding. Hence, 337 merchants who indeed did begin their careers with a *course* venture (table 7.5, column (3)) may be distinguished from the 381 merchants who made their debut elsewhere before trying their hands at privateering (table 7.5, column (4)). Naturally, still others committed themselves exclusively to privateering enterprise, without any further attempts to seek opportunities elsewhere in commerce (table 7.5, column (2)). Only a minority shared such a limited preference: just 159 among the serial investors did nothing but privateering, in contrast with the clear majority of 718 merchants whose investment choices reveal a preference for a diverse portfolio that took in both privateering and a host of regular trades.

The important point is the link between the linchpin role of the *course* within the network of ventures, as it attracted interest from all corners of the merchant community, and those careers that initially centered on the *course* before they embraced a diverse array of activities. Effective mediation, and eventually cohesion in the merchant community, rested on *armateurs* who assembled a diverse portfolio of investments. Many began with *course* ventures, yet ultimately became

TABLE 7.5 Sequence Patterns of Merchant Investment Careers in *Course* and Trade Voyage Partnerships, 1681–1792

		EVER INVESTED IN COURSE			EXEMPLARS OF NEW MEN	
	[1]	[2]	[3]	[4]	[5]	[6]
	NEVER INVESTED IN COURSE	INVESTMENTS IN COURSE ONLY	INVESTMENT CAREER STARTED WITH COURSE	INVESTMENT CAREER STARTED WITH REGULAR TRADE	RENÉ-AUGUSTE DE CHATEAUBRIAND (1718–1786)	PIERRE-JACQUES MESLÉ DE GRANDCLOS (1728–1806)
	MEAN (STD. DEV.)/ PROPORTION	MEAN (STD. DEV.)/ PROPORTION	MEAN (STD. DEV.)/ PROPORTION	MEAN (STD. DEV.)/ PROPORTION		
Length of investment career						
Years	12.623 (15.148)	2.849 (4.628)	19.923 (17.653)	26.268 (18.613)	16	31
Number of voyages invested in	3.681 (3.141)	2.843 (1.581)	9.632 (12.398)	11.819 (15.049)	19	88
Concentration of sequence patterns in investment careers						
Number of different patterns in career sequences observed	469	8	249	313	—	—
Number (proportion) of merchants with unique career sequences	373 (.294)	1 (.006)	226 (.671)	288 (.756)	—	—

(continued)

Number (proportion) of merchants who shared most common career sequence	199 (.157)	99 (.623)	24 (.071)	19 (.050)	—	—
Diversity of investment portfolio						
Years until first trade change	10.074 (12.729)	—	8.098 (10.271)	10.202 (11,387)	4	2
Spread of different trades over sum of voyages invested in	.226 (.227)	—	.360 (.159)	.354 (.163)	.263	.102
Number of trade changes over entire career	2.165 (1.756)	—	5.623 (6.955)	6.924 (8.221)	10	52
Total merchant investors (proportion of all serial investors)	1,268 (.591)	159 (.074)	337 (.157)	381 (.178)		

Sources: AD-IV 9B165–9B176; 9B587; 4E5277–4E5278; 4E5343; 4E5364; 1F1914.
Notes: Results include only serial investors (i.e., merchants who held shares in at least two voyages).

steeped in multiple partnership networks at once—precisely the kind of career paths that Grandclos Meslé and Chateaubriand exemplified.

The mere distinction of these four broad career trajectories offers little more than a first glimpse of the likely candidates for network mediation. For a better understanding, more systematic and fine-grained indicators are needed. One simple measure of varying patterns in careers is their length. Whether or not network mediation was intentional, building bridges between otherwise disconnected partners was possible only if the mediating *armateur* participated in multiple ventures. The number of investments tended to correlate with career length. Merchants with longer careers usually were the ones who had a stake in several ventures. Hence, longer careers opened more opportunities for these merchants to act as brokers in the partnership network. As table 7.5 shows, merchants who participated in at least one *course* venture, alongside their commitments to other trades, did indeed stay within the business for about seven to fourteen years longer than their peers who refrained from privateering altogether and contributed exclusively to other regular trade voyages. As telling as the number of years spent in the business is, experience as a seasoned trader could lead to successful brokerage only insofar as it was coupled with multiple voyage partnerships. Again, on average, merchants who pursued a mixed strategy that combined privateering and regular trade partnerships participated in about ten to twelve ventures over the course of their careers. In contrast, those who never invested in the *course* participated only in about four partnerships. In other words, judging just by the length of their careers in maritime commerce, privateering merchants were indeed well placed as potential brokers within their networks.

Careful readers will have noticed that those merchants who invested solely in privateering enterprise and turned their back on regular trades had considerably shorter careers—merely three partnerships in about as many years. This finding suggests that the course was likely to offer considerable opportunities for network mediation, but only if it was coupled with other partnerships in regular trades.[97]

A long time spent in the business of maritime commerce and a large number of ventures suggest potential for mediation. It was a diverse portfolio, combining privateering and various trade interests, that enabled bonds between partners and bridges across otherwise separate clusters within the partnership network. Once again, to understand such diversification, it helps to think of merchant careers as the sequential ordering of successive participations in overseas ventures. The graphs in figure 7.6 illustrate variation in the types of investments using examples of observed merchant careers from my database. To distinguish between types of investments—that is, the successive states in career sequences—I use the classification of ventures into privateering and thirteen trade categories introduced in chapter 6. In fact, Malouin merchants pursued a range of different patterns in these career sequences. If diversity in successive investments indeed held the key to effective brokerage, then we should consider the composition of merchant careers. The indicators in table 7.5 show that the group of traders who never invested in the *course* displayed the largest number of different patterns in their career paths ($n = 469$). This result seems to run against the grain of much of the evidence discussed thus far. A closer look at the concentration of particular patterns, however, corrects this first impression. Only about 29 percent of all 1,268 traders who never held a stake in privateering enterprises pursued a unique career sequence. In stark contrast, among the 718 merchants who combined privateering and regular trade partnerships, between 67 percent and 76 percent displayed distinct career patterns of their own. Precisely because so many did not share the same careers, the latter necessarily must have been diverse in their composition. Considering the reverse picture, the percentage of merchants who shared the most common career sequence was more than twice as large among traders who never invested in the *course* (16 percent) as compared with those who adopted a mixed strategy that combined the *course* and regular trades (between 5 percent and 7 percent).[98] We do not gain much insight from examining the composition of careers among those who committed themselves exclusively to privateering. Almost two-thirds pursued the same trajectory—that is, two successive *course*

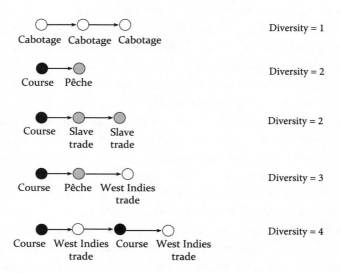

FIGURE 7.6 Illustrations of observed investment career sequences.

partnerships. Little variation could exist, and where it did, it came entirely from differences in the number of ventures.[99]

A more fine-grained set of measures captures changes in the composition of careers. As before, figure 7.6 offers illustrations, using cases in which merchants began with the *course*, switched to Newfoundland fishing (*pêche*) or to the slave trade for their next partnership, and then turned perhaps to the West Indian trade. Such diversity in one's investment portfolio likely created opportunities for bridging and brokerage. Where they seized the opportunities, the mediating merchants, intentional or not, contributed to the overall cohesion in the partnership network. Did this window of opportunity open faster for those who started their careers as *armateurs* in the *course*, as it was the case with the likes of Grandclos Meslé and Chateaubriand? The results in table 7.5 suggest that it did: it took eight years, on average, for merchants who made their first investment in the *course* to branch out into other regular trades, whereas others needed about ten years before they added a venture in a different trade to their portfolio.[100]

Moving beyond the first transition in a given career, it should have mattered how many different branches of maritime commerce were covered by the partnerships that a merchant invested in over his lifetime. If diversity did indeed facilitate mediation, then the spreading of one's partnership ties across many different trades should have been more promising for bridging ties than a concentration of one's activities in, say, just Newfoundland fishing—even if one was a partner in a fair number of cod-fishing voyages. In line with previous results, a comparison of the average spread ratios in table 7.5 reveals that merchants who participated in both privateering and regular trade voyages boasted greater diversity in their portfolios (.360 and .354) than their peers who focused on regular trade engagements alone (.226).[101] This measure lacks, however, a better sense of the timing of changes, or for lack of a better term, the rhythm inherent to career sequences. For example, using the spread measure, the top sequence in figure 7.6 consists of one type of trade over three voyage partnerships, resulting in a score of .333. The second sequence, with its switch from the *course* to the *pêche*, would result in a ratio equal to 1 (two trades spread over two voyages). The fourth sequence would yield the same ratio of 1, although its three voyages entailed three different types of activities: the *course*, followed by the *pêche*, and finally an engagement in the West Indian trade.

For an alternative measure of portfolio diversity, I consider the number of successive changes from one trade to another over the course of a merchant's investment career. For example, the first career sequence in figure 7.6 yields a diversity score equal to 1 because this merchant stayed within the coastal trade (*cabotage*) for all of his three voyage partnerships. The next two sequences both result in a diversity score of 2 because both merchants changed directions once: (1) from a first participation in the *course* to the *pêche*, and (2) from the *course* to the slave trade. Note that one additional partnership in the slave trade does not imply a change in interest, and thus does not contribute to the measure. The fourth career pattern shows three successive partnerships in three different branches of maritime commerce and, therefore, yields a diversity score of 3.[102] The final case, with its repetitive pattern, exhibits the kind of rhythm in career sequences I referred to previously. In this case, investments were made in only two areas, privateering and the West Indian trade, but this merchant continued to switch between the two, thus resulting in a diversity score of 4.

Returning to table 7.5, the results for this diversity measure lend further support to the argument that the *course* provided an organizational platform for mediation in Saint-Malo's partnership network. On average, merchants who partnered both in privateering and regular trades shifted their interests between six and seven times over the duration of their careers. Their behavior indicates a greater willingness to explore new grounds and potentially to forge additional ties with new partners. In contrast, merchants who never considered the *course* as an investment made only about two such shifts in their entire careers. Their behavior indicates that they were much more conservative when it came to seizing new opportunities and expanding their network of business partners.[103]

Figure 7.7 throws the contrast between these investment behaviors into even sharper relief. For each of the four typical career trajectories in table 7.5, the subgraphs plot the diversity of portfolios by the length of careers. Each dot depicts the observed career of an individual merchant contained in the dataset. The differences in the length of investment careers that I have pointed to earlier are immediately visible. The graphs also confirm that longer careers went hand in hand with diverse sets of partnerships. For comparison, imagine a forty-five-degree line crossing each subplot. Observations falling directly onto this baseline indicate cases in which each additional venture that a merchant joined would have been in a different branch of commerce than the previous venture. Hence, maximum diversity would result from repeated switching between kinds of activities, whether in privateering or in regular trades. Observations in the top left panel represent merchants who had multiple investments in various regular trades, but never in the *course*. Very much in line with the evidence discussed earlier, the lumping of cases in coordinates close to the origin suggests that most of these careers were relatively short and limited in their diversity. Observations in the top right panel include those dyed-in-the-wool privateers who never made any commitments outside of the *course*. As noted earlier, because they were wedded to commerce raiding ventures, what little variation existed among them

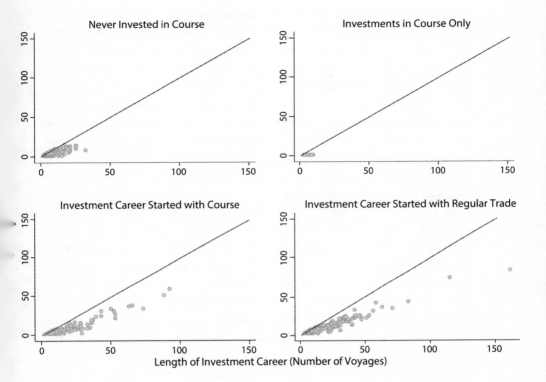

FIGURE 7.7 Four typical investment patterns among Malouin merchants: differences in portfolio diversity and length of investment careers.

Sources: AD-IV 9B165-9B176; 9B587; 4E5277-4E5278; 4E5343; 4E5364; 1F1914.

came entirely from differences in the number of ventures. In stark contrast to these two types—pure traders and pure privateers—the two bottom plots depict those merchants who combined their interests in privateering and regular trades within a mixed strategy. Their cases are more spread out along the forty-five-degree line, thus emphasizing how multifaceted their activities really were compared with the other two career trajectories.[104]

The onset of the first partnership in privateering separates the cases in the two bottom panels of figure 7.7. The left-hand side shows the 337 merchants who were most akin to the prominent examples of Chateaubriand and Grandclos Meslé, because they began their endeavors with the *course* as the launching pad for their later career in maritime commerce. The right-hand side shows the 381 merchants who made their first steps as partners in some regular trade, and only later participated in one or more *course* partnerships. If indeed it was primarily the *course* that attracted merchants from a broad variety of social strata and inspired them to partner in new ventures that were equally varied, then these latecomers should have developed a taste for diversity during or after their first *course* partnership, but not earlier, in one of their regular trade ventures. Pushing this argument further, we may wonder to what extent it was really the *course* that opened the opportunity for merchants to seek diversity in their investments. Perhaps it had more to do with the self-selection of merchants who happened to have a preference for a mixed investment strategy. Some of them might have then seen it fit to add a privateering partnership to their portfolio, whereas others invested elsewhere to assemble a similar mixture.

As plausible as the self-selection alternative may sound, at least two pieces of evidence suggest that portfolio diversity was indeed born out of, or at least facilitated by engagements in the *course*. First, if a fully formed taste for diversity was all that was needed to yield the observed career patterns, with any organizational benefit the *course* had to offer mattering very little, then we should see hardly any difference between pure traders and those merchants who began with trade partnerships and later combined them with privateering. A clear difference between these merchants across various indicators of diversity is precisely what the results in table 7.5 and the plots in figure 7.7 (top left and bottom right panels) demonstrate. Given that the inclusion of the *course* in their careers is the single activity that distinguished these two groups of merchants, it suggests that privateering partnerships, rather than mere self-selection, provided an organizational platform that was ideally suited to assemble diverse investment portfolios.

Second, upon closer inspection, we find that most of the 381 *armateurs* and investors who began their careers with a regular trade partnership could hardly be considered real latecomers to the *course*. For 63 percent ($n = 240$), it took only their second or third partnership to change direction from regular trade to become a partner in a privateering venture. More than 80 percent ($n = 309$) had joined a privateering partnership by their fifth voyage, at the latest. In most cases, then, the diversity we observe in their portfolios did not precede but rather followed from their engagements in the *course*.

Note, however, that diversity in investments was first and foremost a promise that pointed to the potential for building bridging ties.[105] How then did diversity in investments translate into social cohesion? The anecdotal evidence gleaned from the two cases of Chateaubriand and Grandclos Meslé implies that cohesion in their local networks emerged through transitive closure. Both men continued their collaborations with former partners and also recruited new ones, while their past and present partners began to collaborate in ventures of their own. Where this enchainment of past and present partnership relations extended throughout the merchant community, it paved the way for cohesion within the Malouins' network at large. Together, network closure and enchainment worked as a plausible micromechanism. The question remains as to how representative prominent figures such as Chateaubriand or Grandclos Meslé really were. Can we observe the same structural mechanism at work among other *armateurs*, who were similarly positioned and shared much of the same career pattern, beginning with the *course*? Answering this question requires adequate network indicators that allow us to evaluate the degree to which ties with previous partners were maintained, how well positioned potential brokers were, and finally how much transitive closure really existed across the multiple partnership affiliations.

Turning first to continued partnerships, table 7.6 clearly demonstrates that, on average, pairs of business partners within privateering undertakings were much more likely than partners in regular trade ventures to have continued their collaboration. We know, however, from the network analysis in chapter 6 that shareholders in *course* ventures tended to outnumber their peers in regular trade voyages (about ten versus four contributing partners, on average).[106] Little could be gained if the greater numbers attracted to the *course* were all strangers. Even if we set aside this caveat, and weigh the results by the total number of dyads in each voyage partnership, we still find a greater proportion of ties linking repeated partners within *course* ventures than in regular trading enterprises. Continued collaborations entailed the benefits of trust-filled relationships, such as shared experience, mutual reliability, and the exchange of valuable information. Just as important, especially for the question of privateering's contribution to social cohesion, bonds among longstanding partners served as a secure anchor, while new contacts were recruited to join one's personal network. If the creation of ties between former and current partners was of any interest, then continuing one's tried-and-tested collaborations certainly must have been of some help.

We next consider how well positioned as potential brokers the privateering *armateurs* were, such that they could create bridging ties across multiple affiliations. Particularly valuable for this task were those who assumed the role of hubs in the voyage partnership network—that is, merchants who were well-connected not only because they had many contacts but also by virtue of having collaborated with partners who also were well-connected to many others.[107] Consider the findings presented in table 7.7. *Armateurs* who followed the path of a Grandclos Meslé or a Chateaubriand, and thus combined *course* and regular

TABLE 7.6 *Course* Voyages as Organizational Platform for Repeated
Partnerships and Transitive Closure, 1681–1792

	COURSE VOYAGES (N = 334)	REGULAR TRADE VOYAGES (N = 2,039)	*T*-STATISTIC (ONE-TAILED)
	MEAN (STD. DEV.)	MEAN (STD. DEV.)	(*P*-VALUE)
Number of repeated partner dyads	17.147	4.985	−8.9670
	(43.498)	(17.465)	(.0000)
Proportion of repeated partner dyads	.336	.280	−2.7738
	(.318)	(.346)	(.0028)
Number of transitive partner ties	120.615	57.220	−6.9365
within voyage partner-ship	(195.516)	(112.324)	(.0000)

Sources: AD-IV 9B165–9B176; 9B587; 4E5277–4E5278; 4E5343; 4E5364; 1F1914.
Note: Results include only serial investors (i.e., merchants who held shares in at least two voyages).
The means comparison for transitive ties considers only voyage partnerships that entailed such transitive partner ties. Consequently, the number of *Course* voyages reduces to $N = 247$, and the number of voyages in other trades reduces to $N = 1,176$.

trade partnerships during their careers, scored two times, sometimes even three times, as high on hubness than pure traders or pure privateers. Bear in mind, however, that hubness as a measure is based on the number of one's partners as well as the number of one's partners' partners. Therefore, we may suspect that higher scores resulted primarily from the fact that *course* ventures routinely counted more interested parties among their ranks than other enterprises in regular trades. In other words, the results may indicate merely size differences, and not any genuine organizational advantage of the *course* that placed privateering *armateurs* into brokerage positions. Differences in size, however, also revealed investor preferences. In some sense, privateering was not unlike a modern-day

TABLE 7.7 Hubs and Transitive Closure in Partnership Networks, 1681–1792

| | [1]
NEVER INVESTED IN COURSE | EVER INVESTED IN COURSE | | | EXEMPLARS OF NEW MEN | |
| | | [2]
INVESTMENTS IN COURSE ONLY | [3]
INVESTMENT CAREER STARTED WITH COURSE | [4]
INVESTMENT CAREER STARTED WITH REGULAR TRADE | [5]
RENÉ-AUGUSTE DE CHATEAUBRIAND (1718–1786) | [6]
PIERRE-JACQUES MESLÉ DE GRANDCLOS (1728–1806) |
	MEAN (STD. DEV.)/PROPORTION	MEAN (STD. DEV.)/PROPORTION	MEAN (STD. DEV.)/PROPORTION	MEAN (STD. DEV.)/PROPORTION		
Hubness (eigenvector centrality)	.003 (.020)	.002 (.003)	.009 (.032)	.007 (.016)	.005	.054
Number of transitive ties among partners	3.795 (11.485)	31.692 (64.966)	95.843 (225.146)	132.633 (257.040)	104	1,060
Number in top twenty-fifth percentile	3	25	85	146		
Number in top tenth percentile	9	102	277	404		
Local density of transitive ties among partners	.016 (.035)	.032 (.032)	.025 (.026)	.031 (.026)	.078	.029
Total merchant investors (proportion of all serial investors)	1,268 (.591)	159 (.074)	337 (.157)	381 (.178)		

Sources: AD-IV 9B165–9B176; 9B587; 4E5277–4E5278; 4E5343; 4E5364; 1F1914.

Note: Results include only serial investors (i.e., merchants who held shares in at least two voyages). Hubness increases to the extent that a merchant is connected to other well-connected merchants in the voyage partnership network. This eigenvector centrality is calculated for the one-mode merchant-by-merchant projection of the two-mode affiliation network between merchants and ventures. Using the two-mode projection yields results with roughly comparable magnitudes, the main difference being even weaker eigenvector centrality scores for merchants who never invested in the *course*, and even weaker scores for merchants engaged in the *course*. A transitive tie exists between two partners of a given merchant if the latter shared ties with both partners within some earlier ventures whereas the two partners shared no such prior partnership ties. For details, see text in the section "Mediation in Multiple Networks."

lottery—ticket prices for entry (read: shares in partnerships) were relatively low and expectations of glittering prizes (read: prize ships loaded with valuables) were high, even though complete losses were not unheard of.[108] In other words, merchants in Saint-Malo and other places most likely were drawn to privateering for rather good reasons.

What remains to be addressed systematically is transitive closure within partnership networks. If one pivotal social relational foundation of cohesion existed in the Malouin merchant community, then it was transitivity among one's erstwhile partners. A high degree of closure among one's past and present partners essentially was an expression of successful mediation, with the enchainment of partnership relations accomplished.[109] Technically, I measure transitive ties as follows. I first consider all partners who were directly connected to a given merchant (*Ego*) through joint sponsorship of a venture. A transitive tie existed between two of *Ego*'s partners *i* and *j* if the following conditions were met:

- at least one tie between *Ego* and *i* existed before the tie between partners *i* and *j* formed; and
- at least one tie between *Ego* and *j* existed before the tie between partners *i* and *j* formed; and
- no tie between *i* and *j* existed before or when the tie between *Ego* and *i* formed; and
- no tie between *i* and *j* existed before or when the tie between *Ego* and *j* formed.

Accordingly, what matters for the outcome is not simply a count of the ties among shareholders within a given partnership. Because we are dealing with affiliation networks, full closure would result by definition. A genuine process of transitivity over time among previously unrelated partners is important. Note that it was not strictly necessary that *Ego* was included in the voyage partnership, wherein merchants *i* and *j* bonded eventually through transitivity.

Table 7.7 provides descriptive statistics for the number of transitive ties among the partners of each merchant. Any such count is contingent on the number of partners a merchant had. More partners meant more opportunities for the formation of transitive ties. For this reason, I include the local density of transitive ties within a merchant's personal network. The results are consistent with the findings thus far. Considering both the number and the local density of transitive ties, *armateurs* who had a vested interest in privateering clearly outperformed their peers who were pure traders.[110] The contrast is particularly stark for merchants who resembled our two exemplars Chateaubriand and Grandclos Meslé, and for whom the *course* served as a launching pad for their subsequent careers, as well as for those who began in regular trades before they entered privateering. Merchants who pursued either of these two career trajectories enjoyed significantly more transitive relationships among their partners than did the pure traders or the pure privateers.[111]

As is often the case with positions of influence, the distribution of this indicator of successful mediation is rather skewed. Focusing just on those *armateurs* whose partners were most inclined to closure, a familiar pattern emerges. No matter whether we consider the 25 percent or the 10 percent highest scoring *armateurs* in each of the four career types, those with at least one foot in privateering enterprise consistently experienced more transitive closure among their present and past partners compared with the pure traders.

At a first glance, the results for the local density of transitive ties appear to be less clear-cut. It seems to amount to very little if merely 2.5 percent to 3 percent of the relationships among one's partners were transitive. Recall, however, that it also takes little—only one bridging tie—to connect two otherwise separate clusters of one's former partners, and only two bridging ties to render the bond even stronger through redundancy. Thus, being relatively rare is the nature of such bridging ties. No role would have remained for bridging ties or brokers if connections between network clusters were ubiquitous.

The evidence indicates once more that privateering ventures were well suited as catalysts for mediation, local closure, and eventually cohesion in the merchant community network at large. Nevertheless, one caveat is left, and it is similar to the case of portfolio diversity addressed earlier. We may ask whether the tendency toward network closure had perhaps little to do with the *course*, as an organizational platform for forging relationships and mediating in multiple networks. Even without presumed local brokerage on the basis of *course* partner ties, transitive closure might have happened anyway, as it often did in historical communities that became similarly tight knit as Saint-Malo. Bonds of kinship, a strong local identity, and a hotter sort of Catholicism come to mind as potential sources. Few would deny that these were important influences. In yet another alternative scenario, closure might have arisen as a result of the self-selection of merchants who preferred partnerships that were likely to yield transitivity. Indeed, more often than not, these merchants had good reasons to seek transitive closure as soon as they committed their returns from privateering to uncertain long-distance trades. Close bonds with one's business partners held the promise to offer mutual assurances and to exchange reliable information with trustworthy partners that turned plain uncertainty into foreseeable risk. Little of this safety net was necessary for the tried-and-tested coastal trade or Saint-Malo's other strongholds in Newfoundland fishing or the Iberian trades. When it came to the exploration of new and far-away opportunities, however, the Malouin merchants had a clear economic incentive to select themselves into partnerships that led to transitive closure.

Recall that the self-selection counterargument played a similar role in explaining the composition of diverse investment portfolios. An important difference exists between these two scenarios. It certainly was conceivable for an *armateur* to weigh alternatives, and based on a strategic choice, to assemble a varied portfolio of ventures. In contrast, transitive closure among one's erstwhile partners was not just a matter of personal strategic choice. It involved at least two other parties. Former partners also made informed decisions about the relationships they preferred. It thus seems considerably harder to imagine that *armateurs* could control the formation of ties that were at least one step removed from their direct contacts.

Likewise, in contrast to the self-selection argument, another finding demonstrates that the emergence of transitive closure was closely related to the *course* as a specific organization. Returning one last time to table 7.6, we see that privateering partnerships, on average, entailed more than twice as many transitive ties than any other kind of regular trade partnership. Local closure, and ultimately social cohesion in the merchant community at large, indeed seem to have been facilitated and upheld through partnerships in the *course*. In the end, however, this historical setting would not be the first in which the relationship between organizational opportunities and strategic self-selection was endogenous. As much as *course* ventures attracted interests from a variety of merchant strata and eased bonding among them, so too did it also take skillful *armateurs* to seize the opportunities for mediation across the multiple networks that the *course* offered.

CHAPTER 8

THE COMING OF THE REVOLUTION

Privateering enterprise spurred the renewal of Saint-Malo's mercantile elite at two critical moments, at least, during the port city's eventful history between the 1680s and the 1780s. The first moment came at the height of Saint-Malo's commercial boom around the turn of the eighteenth century, which also marked the final years of Louis XIV's reign. The second arrived at the tail end of the same century, with the dawn of the French Revolution. Historical events like these usually do not arise by themselves. They are the result of the collective effort of individual people, embedded as they are in their particular circumstances and a web of affiliations. Granted, whether the collective consequences of people's individual behaviors are of their own choosing is a different matter. As this book is meant to show, however, studying their experiences and relationships not only offers a lens that sharpens our view of the social fabric that held together the merchant community in this time and place. It also teaches us a lesson or two about the local organizational foundations that supported early modern traders as they explored new markets overseas and expanded their network of commerce.

With this understanding in mind, let us revisit the exploits of some of the protagonists we have encountered in this historical narrative. Of particular interest is how these *armateurs-négociants* fashioned their careers out of the manifold enterprises they undertook, and how, by the same token, they affirmed their standing within the merchant elite community. Their trajectories serve as exemplars that illustrate the development of the merchant community at large. If one were to single out an exemplary figure to represent the first critical moment, when Saint-Malo's economic thrust reached its peak in the late-seventeenth and early eighteenth century, one would have to look no further than to Noël Danycan, sieur de L'Epine. Danycan, we may recall, came from a humble background as the son of a petty merchant from Normandy who had settled in Saint-Malo in the early 1600s.[1] His initial steps as a captain and promoter of Newfoundland fishing expeditions swiftly gave way to a brilliant career as an *armateur corsaire* of more than twenty highly successful privateering ventures in the Nine Years' War alone. What followed close on the heels of a short period of peace was the War of the Spanish Succession. As we learned earlier, Danycan lost no time to seize this new opportunity. Even before the outbreak of hostilities, he reinvested the profits gained from the previous *guerre de course*, repurposed his ships, and turned his entrepreneurial skills to the establishment of the South Sea Company. The latter was a barely concealed scheme of plunder, privateering, and illicit interloping trade with the Spanish colonial ports in South America. Although Danycan never quite managed to escape his status as a newcomer, and remained an outsider in the eyes of more than a few of his peers among the urban patriciate, the fortunes he made from his several endeavors elevated him into the highest socioeconomic ranks of Saint-Malo's merchant community.[2]

In his role as a leading *armateur*, Noël Danycan crossed paths more than once with members of the well-established Magon family. Jean Magon de la Lande, one of Saint-Malo's most important promoters of commerce and the *course* alike, was among his illustrious business partners in the trade of Spanish colonial goods.[3] Jean Magon's younger brother, Nicolas Magon de La Chipaudière was not only Danycan's neighbor in the *Quartier de St. Thomas* but also joined him as one of the major forces behind the South Sea enterprise.[4] François-Auguste, one of Jean Magon's eight sons and eventual heir to the title of de la Lande, followed a pathway not unlike Danycan: he, too, started out as an *associé* in privateering ventures during the War of the Spanish Succession.[5] François-Auguste then used his experience and gains from the *course* as a launching pad for an immensely successful career as an *armateur* and investor in a wide range of enterprises, from harvesting the Canadian fishing grounds to trade with Spain and Portugal, and from the slave trade along the Guinea coast to commerce with the French West Indies. Most notably, he became the most potent investor and a director of the *Compagnie des Indes Orientales de Saint-Malo*.[6]

If we treat the paths taken by Magon de la Lande and Danycan de L'Epine as instances of a general pattern within the merchant elite, then two important observations emerge from their experience. First, they, and often others like them, began their careers with engagements in the *course*. Certainly, both Magon de la Lande and Danycan de L'Epine were among the most affluent and visible members of the merchant community, and not everyone had the means or was willing to take up privateering enterprise when the opportunity arrived. For those who did, however, it routinely served as a launching pad toward a lasting and successful career in maritime trade. Second, sponsoring multiple ventures in a variety of trades at once—what French historians have called "polyvalence"—was another hallmark of Danycan, Magon, and their peers within the Malouin merchant elite.[7] As emphasized throughout this book, privateering was very much a high-risk, high-return undertaking that required *armateurs*, investors, and captains who were prepared to take such risks. To the extent that the *course* served as a gateway into the wider world of commerce, Saint-Malo's *armateurs* carried their "corsair mentality" into subsequent ventures in which they exhibited a similar taste for ambitious, yet risky, campaigns, such as the trade with the East Indies or the South Sea project.[8]

My argument in this book follows directly from these two observations: as our merchants launched their careers with privateering ventures, and then branched out into other trades, they united their erstwhile partners from separate prior campaigns and joined them in new ones. In so doing, they set in motion an enchainment mechanism that supported social cohesion through partnership ties within the merchant community. Because the organization of commerce, and privateering as well, was a collective effort, the resulting cohesive social networks proved to be instrumental for the Malouins in setting up new partnerships and seizing new business opportunities. Likewise, cohesive networks served them well as an organizational platform to meet the challenges of outside threats to their city and community in times of armed conflict.

Elite formation was an integral part of this process. Through the unfolding of their careers, a novel role emerged among the *armateurs-négociants*, an image aligned with the ideal of the *parfait négociant* that Jacques Savary had in mind, characterized by a strong commitment to commerce, or *fidélité au commerce*.[9] In short, the historical moment at the end of the seventeenth century witnessed the rise of a professional identity of the elite merchant *armateurs* as a socioeconomic group. It seems that those whom historian André Lespagnol has called the *messieurs de Saint-Malo*, with their manifold enterprises on an increasingly grander scale, were the very expression of this new role and identity.[10]

As noted earlier, the second historical moment of elite renewal came in the latter half of the eighteenth century, leading up to the French Revolution. This was a time marked by the Seven Years' War and the American Revolutionary War, and hence the resurgence of privateering. It also entailed the reopening of the French East Indies trade to private entrepreneurs as well as a stronger commitment of the Malouins to the slave trade between Africa and the sugar plantation islands in the West Indies and the Indian Ocean. These developments offered new opportunities that a younger generation of *armateurs-négociants* from Saint-Malo lost little time to exploit.[11] These *new men*, as I have called them, pursued career paths that looked remarkably similar to those followed by the older generation of Magon, Danycan, and their peers. Mirroring the latter's experience, Pierre-Jacques Meslé de Grandclos, René-Auguste de Chateaubriand, and others like them among the *new men* opted for the lottery of the *course* as their entry ticket into the field of maritime commerce. Whenever profits from privateering campaigns were forthcoming, as they were for Grandclos Meslé as much as for Chateaubriand, they enabled these *armateurs* to mobilize capital for their subsequent, often cost-intensive and grand-scale ventures to the French Antilles, the East Indies, and China, and slave-trading expeditions to the coasts of Guinea and Mozambique. In other words, among the rising *new men* of Saint-Malo's merchant community, the returns to early engagements in privateering enterprise once again laid the foundation for successful careers that embraced a variety of different trades. These *new men* shared a taste for "polyvalence" when organizing their various ventures. As illustrated by Chateaubriand's growing partnership network, they likewise brought their past and present business partners into the fold to form new collaborations.[12] Like the members of the earlier generation, the embedding of the *new men* in successive partnerships thus helped to maintain social cohesion within the wider network of Saint-Malo's merchant community.

For these *new men*, pursuing a profitable career in commerce was not only a matter of forging business partnerships but also as much about advances in their social standing. Their experience was not uniform. As a second-born son of an illustrious family of the Breton nobility that was rich in history and pride, yet relatively poor in financial means, someone like René-Auguste de Chateaubriand wholeheartedly committed himself to his ventures for one primary reason— that is, the returns from his investments in the *course* and commerce permitted him to regain a position and way of life that matched his aristocratic pedigree. Chateaubriand was thus the embodiment of the *noblesse commerçante* that the abbé Coyer had in mind. Others, like Grandclos Meslé were similarly strong-minded and determined in their ambitions, yet an inverse logic led them to climb the social status ladder: coming from rather modest merchant backgrounds, the fortunes they made from maritime trade promised upward mobility into Saint-Malo's urban oligarchy. Their socioeconomic trajectory thus closely resembled the path taken by the likes of Danycan, Magon, and their peers of the earlier generation of the Malouin merchant patriciate. Theirs was a nobility born out of commerce rather than a world of commerce peopled with impoverished nobles.[13]

Considering the history of Saint-Malo's merchant traders from the late-seventeenth to the late-eighteenth century, it would be too strong to conclude that their various activities, and privateering in particular, led to class formation in the same way that we think of modern-day social stratification. Still, much of the evidence I have presented suggests that, at least, the commitment of successive generations of *armateurs-négociants* to the *guerre de course* played a critical role in the rise and renewal of their identity as a genuine urban elite and, indeed, a commercial nobility.[14] Any meaningful identity implies a social relational sense of the boundaries that separate group members from others who are considered outsiders. Elite identity shows the same pattern of inclusion and exclusion. In most historical settings, claims of belonging were hotly contested. Rare are the instances in which an elite forms a single unified group, and we tend to find cleavages between competing and even opposing elite factions instead. More often than not, elite politics meant elite conflict. Early modern Saint-Malo was no exception. Tensions between local factions of the established urban patriciate and the *new men* eventually would surface once the turmoil of the French Revolution had reached the city.

NEW MEN AND THEIR POLITICS IN HISTORY

If one takes a closer look at comparable cases in history, it turns out that the *new men* of Saint-Malo were neither the first nor the last up-and-coming elites who were committed to defend their interests in the face of political opponents. The involvement of upwardly mobile *hommes nouveaux, gente nuova*, or *new men* in power struggles that gave rise to political change is a pattern familiar from other settings.

One case in point is the part played by the *gente nuova*, or *novi cives*, in the recurrent conflicts between various elite factions in late-medieval and early Renaissance Florence. A central fault line ran between an oligarchic patriciate on one side and said *gente nuova* on the other. In a place where social rank and political power were determined by the prestige of one's family, the old guard of the patriciate consisted of members of the most-established and wealthiest families who took pride in a long lineage of ancestors who had been dominating the Arno city's civic and political life for generations. Challenging them economically and politically were the *gente nuova* whose rise to prominence in business as well as in the Signoria, the city's highest governing body, were of a fairly recent nature. As immigrants and newcomers from obscure backgrounds, these *new men* were parvenus who began their careers as low-ranked guild members before they made their fortunes in international trade. What they lacked in prestige, they made up for in ambition. One figure, familiar from an earlier chapter, was Francesco di Marco Datini. He exemplified the determination of these *new men*, as a self-made business man who set up his own international trading firm that served markets from Tuscany to Avignon and Catalonia. At the same time, as historian Gene Brucker has noted, Datini's entire demeanor, his insecurity, avarice, and distrust of others, expressed the structural vulnerability of the *gente nuova*: sandwiched between an urban aristocracy, to whose status they aspired, and the lower strata of artisans and shopkeepers, from whom they sought to uplift themselves.[15]

In the political arena, this cleavage between oligarchs and social climbers was mirrored in the contention concerning eligibility for public office, and hence control of the institutions of communal governance. Much of the conflict was couched in terms of Guelph versus Ghibelline animosities so familiar to late-medieval political strife. The conservative, or oligarchic side, led by the Parte Guelfa, asserted that officeholding should remain restricted to honorable members of long-established elite families, whereas recent immigrants and anyone suspected of Ghibelline sympathies should be excluded from government. The liberal side insisted on an inclusive policy when it came to communal offices. Unsurprisingly, this democratic opposition to the patricians attracted most of the *gente nuova*.[16] For some historians, the sheer ambition of these *new men* to reach the highest echelons of the social hierarchy turned them into a dynamic force of Florentine political history.[17] Others have interpreted their political actions as being shaped by their vulnerable structural position between the oligarchic elite and the lower artisan strata. Anxiously longing for any inclusion, the *gente nuova* thus were all too willing to became fervent followers of the Medici who co-opted them into their patronage network.[18]

We likewise recognize the rise of *new men* in the political developments under way in both Tudor and Stuart England. In the first instance, we are dealing with the skillful administrators whom Henry VII, first of the Tudor kings, relied on in support of his robust style of royal government. Councilors and ministers like Edmund Dudley, Richard Empson, Reynold Bray, Thomas Lovell, or Henry Wyatt took a decidedly more active stance in the affairs of royal governance than the *gente nuova* in the Florentine case. Bray, the son of a mere surgeon, became Treasurer and Chancellor of the Duchy of Lancaster. Empson, who was trained as a lawyer, headed the Council Learned in the Law and was responsible for executing the king's rigorous fiscal policies. Dudley, who worked closely with Empson, held various judicial offices, was Speaker of the Commons, and eventually served as President of the King's Council. Lovell, likewise a lawyer and from a minor Norfolk gentry family, was eventually named Chancellor of the Exchequer and Treasurer of the King's Chamber. Not only were these royal administrators blamed for the perceived tyranny of Henry's regime, especially when it came to taxation. It was also the fact that these men so close to the king were not of great noble stock, but "caitiffs and villains of simple birth" that irked their opponents.[19] Hence, what the early Tudor *new men* shared with their Tuscan equivalents is the now-familiar pattern in which humble backgrounds gave rise to men of ambition, both in their professional and their political careers.

About 150 years later, in Stuart England, this pattern reappeared as the country edged toward civil war.[20] In the years before 1642, the parliamentary Puritan leadership that opposed the king's personal rule had forged an alliance with radical Puritan citizens in London. This coalition eventually succeeded in overthrowing London's old oligarchical order. It took military control of the City, and forced King Charles I to flee his capital. The success of this oppositional alliance was not inevitable because its activists had to bridge several divergent interest groups. The key to this success was the organization of the opposition's membership network. The radicals recruited their leading activists from London's domestic traders, second- and third-tier merchants, artisans, and shopkeepers. The Revolution also brought *new men* into power, several of whom belonged to aspiring colonial merchants, such as Samuel Vassall, Maurice Thompson, and Thomas Andrews, who challenged the established merchant oligarchy of the City. Like the *gente nuova* or the Tudor *new men* before them, these new merchants came from unassuming ranks of the middling sort. As they lacked the pedigree and connections to gain access to the rich Levantine and East Indian trades, then dominated by the loyalist merchant oligarchy, these new merchants turned their ambitions to the American colonial plantations as a second-best choice. By the early 1640s, the new merchant elites were steeped in multiple networks at once and occupied a structural position from which they could broker political mobilization. They were linked, on one hand, to the City radicals, artisans, and shopkeepers through their shared social origins and joint political activities, and were connected, on the other, to Puritan lords and members of the national parliamentary leadership through their colonial collaborations in the New World.

This detour into Italian and English political history is not meant to be a distraction from the narrative, but rather to emphasize the similarity and continuity of relational patterns across otherwise different settings. The common thread in all of these cases is the emergence of an upwardly mobile group of *new men* of often modest origins whose members struggled against, or at least competed with, an entrenched old guard elite for privileges and material resources. The tension in their relationship usually became manifest in times of political upheaval. An essential element of these conflicts was the formation of a political identity among the *new men* that complemented their emergent professional identity, formed through careers in the world of commerce.

ELITE CONFLICT IN REVOLUTIONARY SAINT-MALO

Political change in its most radical guise also reached Saint-Malo with the coming of the French Revolution. Blood reportedly was shed as early as January 1789, when bands of young bourgeois Malouins, clad in their corsair garb and armed with pistols, muskets, and boarding axes, mobilized to aid the students of Rennes in violent clashes with young noblemen. With the taking of their city's château, the Malouin radicals even had their own little Bastille moment. In August 1789, the municipal authorities ordered all nobles and their property to be put under the "safeguard of the Nation." In 1791, the troubles continued with outbreaks of antifeudal revolts in the countryside, aimed at the properties and land titles of ennobled representatives of the old order, such as Baude de la Vieuville of Châteauneuf. In October 1793, as the Revolution had progressed to the Terror, the Committee of General Security ordered the arrest of the leading *armateurs* of the Magon family and their associates on charges of counterrevolutionary conspiracies. The most prominent and wealthy among them ended up in front of the Revolutionary Tribunal in Paris. Eventually, Luc Magon de la Blinaye, Jean-Baptiste Magon de La Balue, Nicolas Magon de la Villehuchet, and Jean-Baptiste Magon de Coëtizac were executed in the summer of 1794.[21]

Of the two figures who accompanied us throughout the narrative of the previous chapter, one, René-Auguste de Chateaubriand, was spared a similar ordeal as he had spent his final months at his château de Combourg where he died on September 6, 1786.[22] The other, Pierre Jacques Meslé de Grandclos, experienced the ambivalent situation that so many of his peers among the Malouin *armateurs-négociants* found themselves in. He certainly harbored sympathies for the new order. For one, Meslé de Grandclos did not hail from the traditional aristocracy, and his was a title of merit, not a birth right. He also had good reasons to be critical of the political imbalance under the Ancien Régime, which denied merchants and traders like himself their due influence, in line with their economic weight. In addition, Meslé de Grandclos was prepared to serve in several offices under the new revolutionary regime. In November 1790, he was appointed as one of six commissioners to draft a report on the abolition of slavery. In December 1790, together with his peer Sébire des Saudrais, he acted as a delegate of the Malouin community in Paris to lobby (unsuccessfully so) for the creation of an additional *département* in Brittany, with Saint-Malo as its intended administrative center. From 1786 through January 1789, he had already served as an alderman (*échevin*), and in 1790, he was counted again among the twenty-four elected *notables* of the municipal government, was in charge of the city's public water supply and fire pumps, and was appointed as *juge consul* in criminal justice cases. Finally, he had tens of cannons from his own trading vessels repurposed as artillery for the defense of Saint-Malo against an imminent assault by counterrevolutionary Vendée forces.[23]

For all intents and purposes, Meslé de Grandclos seemed to be a typical member of the rising mercantile classes who stood on the side of the patriotic cause, as they overwhelmingly did in other port towns of Brittany.[24] His many deeds of public service were recognized by some, but not all, however. Clear and quite literal warnings, uttered by Le Carpentier, the infamous agent of the Terror in Saint-Malo, threatened that the heads of rich *négociants* would roll next.[25] In December 1793, Meslé de Grandclos was put under arrest at his home by police commissioners of the Convention. He managed to escape and joined the numerous émigrés among Saint-Malo's elites, only to return to France in 1795.[26]

Who, then, were the representatives of the new political elite in Saint-Malo, that assumed positions of power in the early days of the Revolution? As André Lespagnol has demonstrated, the emergent "bourgeoisie patriote" was composed of two groups, distinct in their occupations, yet coming from similar social backgrounds. One group was the "bourgeoisie des talents" whose members included lawyers, notaries, physicians, and others who came from the liberal professions, as well as, unsurprisingly in a port city, sea captains. The second group was the "bourgeoisie d'entreprise," which included precisely those merchants introduced earlier as the *new men* in Saint-Malo's merchant community.[27] Following Lespagnol's lead, they can be identified from the lists of salient political offices. Among the commissioners charged with the assessment of the poll tax in late 1789 were the signatures of La Fontaine Le Bonhomme and Blaize de Maisonneuve, both eminent *armateurs-négociants* of the new generation.[28] In the spring of 1789, in an unprecedented effort of public consultation, each French town was supposed to submit a *cahier de doléances*, essentially a collection of grievances and demands that its townsfolk had voiced.[29] The delegates at Saint-Malo's municipal assembly nominated eight commissioners to draft the *cahier*. Inclusion on this list was another indication of who took a leading role in municipal politics. With Etienne-Eusèbe-Joseph Huard (*armateur*), Blaize de Maisonneuve (*négociant*), and Jean Bodinier (*armateur*), the merchant traders of the *new men* generation figured once again prominently among the commissioners.[30] A third list consists of the twelve delegates that were given a mandate to represent Saint-Malo at the assembly of the Third Estate in Rennes in April 1789. Nominated were again Huard, Bodinier, Blaize de Maisonneuve, and La Fontaine Le Bonhomme, in addition to Lecoufle, père (*négociant*), Sébire des Saudrais (*négociant*), and a certain Danycan, l'aîné (*capitaine navigant*).[31]

These representatives of the new order were indeed *hommes nouveaux* who seized the opportunity to turn their rising socioeconomic standing into political influence and authority. Notably, the proponents of this revolutionary bourgeoisie who took over control of municipal politics in Saint-Malo mostly emerged from humble social origins, with family names that meant little in the social hierarchy before this time. Even someone like Blaize de Maisonneuve, who achieved considerable political clout and wealth as an overseas trader, was a social climber and self-made businessman who began his career as a simple trader clerk from Paimpol-Plounez.[32] If anything, these revolutionary *new men* formed a "bourgeoisie plébéienne" that stood in stark contrast to the old merchant elite of Saint-Malo whose members had held the real power in the city for generations.[33] The latter refer to the great prestigious merchant dynasties, including the Baude, Eon, Gardin, Grout, Lefer, Locquet, Magon, Moreau, Porée, and their peers whose histories we followed earlier in this book. Together they constituted a veritable urban patriciate whose ancestors had established themselves at Saint-Malo since the beginning of the seventeenth century. The members of this oligarchic elite, often ennobled, owed their immense wealth in no small part to benevolent connections to the royal court. Recall, for instance, how a benefactor like the comte de Pontchartrain was instrumental in securing exclusive trading rights for the South Sea and East India companies of Saint-Malo.[34] We have also witnessed how they sought to elevate themselves into the nobility, through strategic marriage alliances, the acquisition of extensive landed property, and the adoption of a lifestyle worthy of the rural gentry. Theirs was indeed an aristocracy born out of fortunes in commerce.

Thus, it is no wonder that the two factions of the Malouin merchant elite—the old guard of the patriciate, and the *new men* of the plebeian bourgeoisie—were bound to confront each other with the coming of a new political and social order. Much of what the patricians had achieved was through tight alignment with the old regime. Unfortunately for them, at the very moment they had reached the summit of their aspirations, the Revolution toppled the principles upon which the established rank order was founded—being an aristocrat suddenly became the most devalued and least coveted social status. In contrast, the *new men* stood only to gain from the new regime, or so it seemed.[35]

THE END OF THE *COURSE*?

The question that looms large, given this elite conflict, is whether the integrative pull of privateering enterprise had lost its grip on the Malouin merchant community in the revolutionary years. In the previous chapter, drawing on the enterprises of Chateaubriand and Meslé de Grandclos, I traced how building personal networks of partnerships in the *course* gave rise to social cohesion among the merchantry at large. Compared with earlier times, however, why could the extent of cohesion yielded through the *course* no longer be sustained into the early revolutionary years?

For one, what seems to have been lost in the revolutionary period is the successful translation of this socioeconomic cohesion, stemming from commercial and especially privateering partnerships, into meaningful cohesion within the field of politics. Likewise, the *course* could fulfill its role as an organizational linchpin that held together the various elite factions only as long as their members were willing to participate as partners in privateering ventures. One explanation, as historians have long noted, thus points to the observation that the *armateurs* of the established merchant elite had developed a taste for the life as landed gentlefolk and had begun to turn their backs on such enterprises. Indeed, and with all the lacunae of the *actes de sociétés* records in mind, one finds that merely four of seventy-seven *armateurs* (5 percent) engaged in the *course* during the Seven Years' War and the American Revolutionary War can be unambiguously identified as members of the great families that André Lespagnol counts among the merchant patriciate of Saint-Malo.[36] The proportion doubles (to 10.5 percent) when it comes to associates in privateering ventures, and not just the shipowners who directed these enterprises. Twenty-nine partners from families of the *haut négoce* still remains a modest number compared with the total of 276 partners from all socioeconomic backgrounds.[37] In other words, the evidence suggests that, in the long run, proponents of the old guard did indeed pull out of privateering partnerships, and this retreat had been largely accomplished by the eve of the Revolution. Their withdrawal certainly did not help with any bridging the *course* might have offered across the emerging political cleavage between the two elite factions.[38] Whatever degree of cohesion was maintained within the partnership network, it apparently did not map any longer onto the salient political alignments.

Two lessons can be drawn from these findings: one substantive historical and the other more general. First, recall that, from a long-run historical perspective, privateering enterprise was not always at the heart of Saint-Malo's economic development. As discussed at length in chapter 2, the two traditional pillars of Malouin commerce in early modern times were the Newfoundland fishing trade and the commercial exchange with Spain.[39] The provision of armed convoys to other traders was another prime occupation of the Malouins. It was not until the late-seventeenth century that arming for the *guerre de course* began to play a central role for the maritime traders of Saint-Malo. The *course* reached its apex during the latter half of Louis XIV's reign, and yet we also know that it was eventually abolished, de facto after 1815, and de jure with the declaration of Paris in 1856.[40] To the extent that social cohesion within the merchant community was just as important at earlier as well as later times, it is conceivable that, given the unavailability of the *course*, bonds forged in other activities stepped to the fore and played the role as organizational linchpins. Whether or not such substitution was successful, is a different (and primarily empirical) question.[41] I do not mean to suggest any singularity of the *course* in the creation of community cohesion. Beyond our case at hand, then, a second more general lesson can be gleaned. Whenever we seek to understand the sources of cohesion in similar historical or contemporary settings, we have to look for structural and functional equivalents to *course* partnerships if we are to identify comparable linchpin organizations. What privateering offered in Saint-Malo was most likely provided by other collective undertakings in other places.

So, did all of these developments spell the end of the *course*? This is not the place to discuss what consequences the Revolution had for local society in Saint-Malo, its maritime commerce, or the French Atlantic Economy at large. What we do know is that, with war once again on the horizon by 1793, privateering enterprise had lost little of its attraction as an investment opportunity for the *armateurs* and as a path to fame and glory for the corsair captains.[42] As long as the corsair mentality and its dreams of riches and glory persisted, it continued to cast its spell on the Malouins. Thus, in May 1793, citizen Michel Delastelle armed the corsair *Le Tigre* of Saint-Malo and hired Dugué, aîné as his captain. His armament was only one of the first in a long row of others that were to follow during the Revolutionary and Napoleonic Wars. On May 18, 1793, fitted with eighteen cannons and 143 sailors on board, the *Tigre* set off from Cape Fréhel for her campaign.[43] Whether the sun was setting as she sailed toward the horizon, we do not know.

APPENDIX TABLES

APPENDIX TABLE A.1 Comparison of Observed Merchant-by-Merchant Partnership Network with Simulated Random Networks, 1681–1792

PERIOD	NETWORK	MERCHANTS	PARTNERSHIP TIES						NETWORK COHESION					
			TOTAL	MEAN DEGREE	STD. DEV. DEGREE	MIN. DEGREE	MAX. DEGREE	ISOLATES	UNREACHABLE PAIRS [%]	NUMBER OF COMPONENTS	MAIN COMP. SIZE	MERCHANTS IN MAIN COMP. [%]	MEAN COMP. SIZE	STD. DEV. COMP. SIZE
1 (1681–1697)	Observed	723	5,124	14.17	19.83	0	234	4	12.82	14	675	93.36	40.17	158.44
	Conditional random: Simulation Means (Std. dev.)	723 (0.00)	4,981.49 (33.83)	13.78 (0.09)	18.48 (0.51)	0 (0.03)	222.01 (14.84)	6.12 (2.00)	5.09 (1.58)	6.03 (2.09)	704.32 (5.89)	97.42 (0.81)	63.30 (17.92)	206.36 (28.50)
	Unconditional random: Simulation Means (Std. dev.)	624.56 (7.74)	4,279.05 (63.50)	13.70 (0.26)	8.28 (0.31)	0.66 (0.55)	50.23 (5.56)	0.46 (0.66)	0.36 (0.45)	1.29 (0.54)	623.44 (7.81)	99.82 (0.22)	438.41 (179.81)	216.63 (206.69)
2 (1698–1720)	Observed	1,246	19,786	31.76	50.90	0	437	8	8.17	17	1,194	95.83	49.84	238.37
	Conditional random: Simulation Means (Std. dev.)	1,246 (0.00)	19,052.88 (121.17)	30.58 (0.19)	44.26 (0.77)	0.01 (0.12)	409.06 (31.65)	3.65 (1.73)	2.11 (0.81)	5.20 (2.07)	1,232.79 (5.14)	98.94 (0.41)	157.23 (65.21)	430.74 (78.93)
	Unconditional random: Simulation Means (Std. dev.)	1,150.14 (8.22)	12,757.69 (114.58)	22.19 (0.26)	12.67 (0.32)	1.47 (0.72)	79.57 (8.08)	0.08 (0.29)	0.02 (0.08)	1.02 (0.15)	1,149.99 (8.20)	99.99 (0.04)	1,089.69 (178.84)	82.76 (244.61)
3 (1721–1740)	Observed	1,343	7544	11.23	25.11	0	248	47	37.68	86	1,060	78.93	10.10	91.74
	Conditional random: Simulation Means (Std. dev.)	1,343 (0.00)	7,418.47 (39.11)	11.05 (0.06)	16.02 (0.41)	0 (0.00)	173.79 (17.72)	24.47 (4.11)	14.16 (1.7)	33.02 (4.96)	1,244.26 (12.34)	92.65 (0.92)	23.65 (2.69)	164.72 (10.76)
	Unconditional random: Simulation Means (Std. dev.)	1,167.88 (10.40)	5,436.14 (73.25)	9.31 (0.15)	5.90 (0.17)	0 (0.03)	37.63 (4.16)	6.82 (2.53)	2.04 (0.71)	3.31 (1.54)	1,155.90 (10.75)	98.97 (0.36)	126.73 (46.00)	375.46 (62.99)

4 (1741–1755)	Observed	1,330	8,678	13.05	21.19	0	199	38	28.30	55	1,126	84.66	14.30	116.55
	Conditional random: Simulation Means (Std. dev.)	1,330 (0.00)	8,422.63 (84.67)	12.67 (0.13)	20.29 (0.57)	0 (0.00)	217.33 (26.66)	17.69 (3.41)	12.84 (1.75)	29.55 (4.56)	1,241.59 (12.48)	93.35 (0.94)	28.54 (3.39)	181.39 (12.32)
	Unconditional random: Simulation Means (Std. dev.)	1,148.59 (10.31)	5,539.14 (74.27)	9.65 (0.15)	6.09 (0.18)	0 (0.03)	38.97 (4.42)	5.49 (2.27)	1.78 (0.69)	3.10 (1.43)	1,138.33 (10.74)	99.11 (0.35)	149.51 (59.38)	404.02 (73.43)
5 (1756–1777)	Observed	1,604	15,049	18.76	36.25	0	380	20	24.77	56	1,391	86.72	21.11	159.25
	Conditional random: Simulation Means (Std. dev.)	1,604 (0.00)	14,356.52 (129.48)	17.90 (0.16)	35.56 (0.82)	0 (0.00)	439.21 (34.44)	23.86 (4.02)	10.16 (1.41)	26.94 (4.68)	1,520.32 (11.91)	94.78 (0.74)	32.05 (4.02)	214.36 (14.81)
	Unconditional random: Simulation Means (Sst. dev.)	1,435.88 (10.87)	8,487.32 (94.62)	11.82 (0.16)	7.23 (0.18)	0.02 (0.15)	46.61 (4.53)	3.53 (1.82)	0.82 (0.40)	2.06 (1.02)	1,430.01 (10.98)	99.59 (0.20)	304.69 (163.59)	630.33 (141.69)
6 (1778–1792)	Observed	1,471	34,099	46.36	87.82	0	1140	14	11.48	28	1,384	94.09	35.02	213.23
	Conditional random: Simulation Means (Std. dev.)	1,471 (0.00)	28,733.94 (616.72)	39.07 (0.84)	74.85 (1.93)	0 (0.00)	967.40 (65.71)	11.26 (2.68)	6.83 (1.26)	18.76 (3.94)	1,419.87 (9.59)	96.52 (0.65)	50.29 (8.39)	261.48 (23.03)
	Unconditional random: Simulation Means (Std. dev.)	1,324.19 (10.13)	10,753.90 (106.07)	16.24 (0.2)	9.62 (0.25)	0.58 (0.52)	61.58 (6.39)	0.58 (0.77)	0.18 (0.21)	1.26 (0.50)	1,323.02 (10.18)	99.91 (0.11)	897.94 (387.36)	483.39 (433.17)
All periods (1681–1792)	Observed	6,298	90,280	28.67	67.76	0	1544	108	15.36	143	5,794	92.00	25.09	365.59
	Conditional random: Simulation Means (Std. dev.)	6,298 (0.00)	87,849.79 (422.47)	27.90 (0.13)	62.32 (0.86)	0 (0.00)	1,454.10 (112.19)	66.27 (6.69)	6.21 (0.55)	60.47 (7.31)	6,099.40 (17.86)	96.85 (0.28)	49.99 (3.91)	542.92 (22.61)
	Unconditional random: Simulation Means (Std. dev.)	5,875.75 (18.27)	44,527.61 (211.32)	15.16 (0.09)	8.88 (0.10)	0 (0.00)	62.51 (5.10)	6.05 (2.41)	0.30 (0.12)	2.29 (1.12)	5,866.97 (18.62)	99.85 (0.06)	799.74 (334.67)	2,121.91 (399.01)

Note: See table 6.3 for a description of the observed network. See chapter 6 for a description of the two variants of simulated random networks.

APPENDIX TABLE A.2 Cohesion Within the Voyage-by-Voyage Network (1681–1792): Observed Network, Removal of *Course* Voyages, and Removal of Randomly Selected Voyages Compared

PERIOD	NETWORK	VOYAGES	PARTNERSHIP TIES					NETWORK COHESION						
			TOTAL	MEAN DEGREE	STD. DEV. DEGREE	MIN. DEGREE	MAX. DEGREE	ISOLATES	UNREACHABLE PAIRS (%)	NUMBER OF COMPONENTS	MAIN COMP. SIZE	MERCHANTS IN MAIN COMP. (%)	MEAN COMP. SIZE	STD. DEV. COMP. SIZE
1 (1681–1697)	Observed	239	3,392	28.38	32.02	0	150	15	15.29	3	220	92.05	13.28	51.59
	Course voyages removed	191	2,400	25.13	30.67	0	136	15	21.74	4	169	88.48	10.05	38.49
	Simulation Means (Std. dev.)	191 (0.00)	2,167.89 (164.87)	22.7 (1.73)	25.64 (2.28)	0 (0.00)	118.92 (8.13)	14.58 (2.12)	17.78 (2.59)	2.47 (0.81)	173.21 (2.74)	90.68 (1.44)	11.38 (1.44)	41.96 (3.24)
	P	—	—	—	—	—	—	33.50	7.80	0.40	5.50	5.50	—	—
2 (1698–1720)	Observed	398	11,016	55.36	55.55	0	278	21	13.12	4	371	93.22	15.92	73.98
	Course voyages removed	280	3,508	25.06	28.65	0	135	24	23.46	6	245	87.50	9.33	44.51
	Simulation Means (Std. dev.)	280 (0.00)	5,439.37 (356.75)	38.85 (2.55)	39.11 (2.71)	0 (0.00)	192.99 (15.94)	18.32 (2.58)	15.52 (1.99)	3.08 (1.09)	257.37 (3.03)	91.92 (1.08)	13.28 (1.64)	55.73 (4.01)
	P	—	—	—	—	—	—	0.90	0.00	0.10	0.00	0.00	—	—
3 (1721–1740)	Observed	684	6,501	19.01	31.55	0	218	114	41.10	19	525	76.75	5.14	45.42
	No *Course*	—	—	—	—	—	—	—	—	—	—	—	—	—
4 (1741–1755)	Observed	629	6,649	21.14	25.05	0	154	79	31.14	14	522	82.99	6.76	54.01
	Course voyages removed	546	3,464	12.69	14.63	0	101	82	37.42	16	432	79.12	5.57	43.52

Simulation Means (Std. dev.)	546 (0.00)	5,007.34 (190.81)	18.34 (0.70)	21.77 (0.93)	0 (0.00)	132.27 (7.19)	73.80 (3.53)	33.46 (1.59)	12.83 (1.87)	445.39 (5.34)	81.57 (0.98)	6.31 (0.25)	47.77 (1.46)
P	—	—	—	—	—	—	0.50	0.40	2.50	0.40	0.40	—	—
5 (1756–1777) Observed	767	18,379	47.92	58.28	0	414	63	22.33	13	676	88.14	10.09	77.41
Course voyages removed	697	13,966	40.07	48.82	0	316	63	25.41	15	602	86.37	8.94	68.03
Simulation Means (Std. dev.)	697 (0.00)	15,179.67 (437.89)	43.56 (1.26)	53.01 (1.62)	0 (0.00)	372.22 (17.68)	61.39 (3.06)	23.87 (1.16)	12.69 (1.62)	608.16 (4.65)	87.25 (0.67)	9.42 (0.38)	70.57 (1.88)
P	—	—	—	—	—	—	24.00	8.30	3.90	8.30	8.30	—	—
6 (1778–1792) Observed	532	20,646	77.62	106.20	0	685	37	16.56	5	486	91.35	12.67	74.82
Course voyages removed	491	14,325	58.35	82.53	0	475	42	22.96	8	431	87.78	9.82	60.78
Simulation Means (Std. dev.)	491 (0.00)	17,584.55 (607.27)	71.63 (2.47)	97.97 (3.29)	0 (0.00)	622.79 (34.62)	35.84 (2.07)	17.18 (0.86)	4.75 (0.77)	446.87 (2.31)	91.01 (0.47)	12.13 (0.61)	70.04 (2.10)
P	—	—	—	—	—	—	0.10	0.00	0.00	0.00	0.00	—	—
All periods (1681–1792) Observed	3,250	120,347	74.06	109.24	0	1,260	222	16.83	29	2,964	91.20	12.95	187.01
Course voyages removed	2,890	80,974	56.04	87.45	0	873	229	20.30	36	2,580	89.27	10.91	158.42
Simulation Means (Std. dev.)	2,890 (0.00)	95,095.55 (1,765.82)	65.81 (1.22)	97.11 (2.45)	0 (0.00)	1,094.25 (74.97)	211.47 (6.01)	17.86 (0.46)	27.08 (2.60)	2,619.30 (7.35)	90.63 (0.25)	12.12 (0.30)	169.56 (2.52)
P	—	—	—	—	—	—	0.20	0.00	0.00	0.00	0.00	—	—

Note: The first row for each period shows indicators of cohesion in the observed voyage-by-voyage network. The second row for each period reports the degree of cohesion after the removal of all course voyages. For comparison, the simulation means (and standard deviations) document the degree of cohesion after removing as many randomly selected voyages as there are course voyages in each period (one thousand iterations). For each period, the *P*-value reports the percentage of the one thousand simulated networks (with randomly selected voyages removed) that yield the same or an even higher degree of fragmentation as the network where all course ventures are removed.

Source: Data for the observed network from *AD-IV* 9B165-9B176; 9B587; 4E5277-4E5278; 4E5343; 4E5364; 1F1914.

APPENDIX TABLE A.3 Cohesion Within the Merchant-by-Merchant Network (1681–1792): Observed Network, Removal of *Course* Partnership Ties, and Removal of Randomly Selected Partnership Ties Compared

			PARTNERSHIP TIES					NETWORK COHESION						
PERIOD	NETWORK	MERCHANTS	TOTAL	MEAN DEGREE	STD. DEV. DEGREE	MIN. DEGREE	MAX. DEGREE	ISOLATES	UNREACHABLE PAIRS [%]	NUMBER OF COMPONENTS	MAIN COMP. SIZE	MERCHANTS IN MAIN COMP. [%]	MEAN COMP. SIZE	STD. DEV. COMP. SIZE
1 (1681–1697)	Observed	723	5,124	14.17	19.83	0	234	4	12.82	14	675	93.36	40.17	158.44
	Course ties removed	723	3,496	9.67	17.29	0	209	185	53.32	14	494	68.33	3.63	34.94
	Simulation Means (Std. dev.)	723 (0.00)	3,496 (0.00)	9.67 (0.00)	13.64 (0.18)	0 (0.00)	160.37 (6.30)	16.23 (3.51)	15.30 (0.8)	12.84 (1.52)	665.32 (3.35)	92.02 (0.46)	25.13 (2.54)	123.53 (6.69)
	P		—	—	—	—	—	0.00	0.00	12.40	0.00	0.00	—	—
2 (1698–1720)	Observed	1,246	19,786	31.76	50.90	0	437	8	8.17	17	1,194	95.83	49.84	238.37
	Course ties removed	1,246	9,335	14.98	26.67	0	202	386	59.30	22	795	63.80	3.05	39.31
	Simulation Means (Std. dev.)	1,246 (0.00)	9,335 (0.00)	14.98 (0.00)	24.19 (0.17)	0 (0.00)	212.28 (8.51)	59.58 (6.62)	15.22 (1.02)	15.80 (2.61)	1,147.23 (6.91)	92.07 (0.56)	16.63 (1.32)	132.32 (5.91)
	P		—	—	—	—	—	0.00	0.00	1.00	0.00	0.00	—	—
3 (1721–1740)	Observed	1,343	7,544	11.23	25.11	0	248	47	37.68	86	1,060	78.93	10.10	91.74
	No *Course*	—	—	—	—	—	—	—	—	—	—	—	—	—
4 (1741–1755)	Observed	1,330	8,678	13.05	21.19	0	199	38	28.30	55	1,126	84.66	14.30	116.55
	Course ties removed	1,330	4,557	6.85	11.03	0	114	237	53.27	60	909	68.35	4.48	52.68

Simulation Means (Std. dev.)	1,330 (0.00)	4,557 (0.00)	6.85 (0.00)	11.27 (0.11)	0 (0.00)	104.75 (6.50)	160 (10.16)	43.11 (1.47)	54.53 (4.49)	1,002.85 (12.95)	75.40 (0.97)	6.21 (0.27)	68.44 (2.18)
P	0.00	0.00	—	—	—	—	0.00	0.00	10.10	0.00	0.00	—	—
5 (1756–1777) Observed	1,604	15,049	18.76	36.25	0	380	20	24.77	56	1,391	86.72	21.11	159.25
Course ties removed	1,604	10,260	12.79	25.23	0	380	187	41.94	58	1,222	76.18	6.55	77.99
Simulation Means (Std. dev.)	1,604 (0.00)	10,260 (0.00)	12.79 (0.00)	24.8 (0.14)	0 (0.00)	260.88 (7.80)	84.81 (7.75)	30.77 (0.87)	54.18 (3.36)	1,334.36 (8.39)	83.19 (0.52)	11.57 (0.58)	113.15 (3.40)
P	0.00	0.00	—	—	—	—	0.00	0.00	10.00	0.00	0.00	—	—
6 (1778–1792) Observed	1,471	34,099	46.36	87.82	0	1,140	14	11.48	28	1,384	94.09	35.02	213.23
Course ties removed	1,471	11,065	15.04	42.51	0	736	425	58.64	35	946	64.31	3.20	44.06
Simulation Means (Std. dev.)	1,471 (0.00)	11,065 (0.00)	15.04 (0.00)	28.67 (0.21)	0 (0.00)	369.90 (15.50)	191.81 (11.01)	32.24 (1.22)	27.97 (3.94)	1,210.83 (10.87)	82.31 (0.74)	6.71 (0.31)	81.68 (2.52)
P	0.00	0.00	—	—	—	—	0.00	0.00	3.00	0.00	0.00	—	—
All periods Observed	6,298	90,280	28.67	67.76	0	1,544	108	15.36	143	5,794	92.00	25.09	365.59
(1681–1792) Course ties removed	6,298	46,257	14.69	40.02	0	1,140	1,192	45.09	158	4,667	74.10	4.67	126.99
Simulation Means (Std. dev.)	6,298 (0.00)	46,257 (0.00)	14.69 (0.00)	34.82 (0.13)	0 (0.00)	790.78 (18.18)	567.52 (19.63)	27.51 (0.55)	136.72 (7.61)	5,362.00 (20.22)	85.14 (0.32)	8.95 (0.22)	202.06 (3.15)
P	0.00	0.00	0.00	0.00	0.00	0.00	0.00	0.00	0.30	0.00	0.00	—	—

Note: The first row and second row for each period reproduce the network descriptives and cohesion results in table 6.3 (see chapter 6). For comparison, the simulation means (and standard deviations) document the degree of cohesion after removing as many randomly selected partnership ties from the observed network as there are *course* partnership ties in each period (one thousand iterations). For each period, the *P*-value reports the percentage of the one thousand simulated networks (with randomly selected partnership ties removed) that yield the same or an even higher degree of fragmentation as the network where all *course* partnership ties are removed.

Source: Data for the observed network from *AD-IV* 9B165–9B176; 9B5B7; 4E5277–4E5278; 4E5343; 4E5364; 1F1914.

APPENDIX TABLE A.4 Cohesion Within the Merchant-by-Merchant Network (1681–1792): Removal of *Course* and *Pêche* (Newfoundland Fishing) Partnership Ties Compared

		PARTNERSHIP TIES						NETWORK COHESION					
PERIOD	NETWORK	MERCHANTS	TOTAL	MEAN DEGREE	STD. DEV. DEGREE	MIN. DEGREE	MAX. DEGREE	ISOLATES	UNREACH-ABLE PAIRS [%]	NUMBER OF COMPO-NENTS	MAIN COMP. SIZE	MER-CHANTS IN MAIN COMP. [%]	MEAN COMP. SIZE	STD. DEV. COMP. SIZE
2 (1698–1720)	Observed	1,246	19,786	31.76	50.90	0	437	8	8.17	17	1,194	95.83	49.84	238.37
	Course ties removed	1,246	9,335	14.98	26.67	0	202	386	59.30	22	795	63.80	3.05	39.31
	Pêche ties removed: Means (Std. dev.)	996.78 (3.39)	16,264.82 (70.11)	32.63 (0.12)	49.53 (0.15)	0 (0.00)	420.50 (2.54)	8.00 (0.00)	9.11 (0.29)	15.17 (0.58)	950.29 (3.79)	95.34 (0.15)	43.05 (1.10)	197.05 (2.92)
	P		—	—		—	—	0.00	0.00	0.00	0.00	0.00	—	—
4 (1741–1755)	Observed	1,330	8,678	13.05	21.19	0	199	38	28.30	55	1,126	84.66	14.30	116.55
	Course ties removed	1,330	4,557	6.85	11.03	0	114	237	53.27	60	909	68.35	4.48	52.68
	Pêche ties removed: Means (Std. dev.)	1,200.28 (10.70)	7,592.75 (125.28)	12.65 (0.16)	19.96 (0.32)	0 (0.00)	189.55 (5.33)	36.41 (1.11)	30.28 (1.45)	55.96 (2.26)	1,001.93 (8.98)	83.48 (0.87)	13.00 (0.33)	104.07 (2.07)
	P		—	—		—	—	0.00	0.00	2.40	0.00	0.00	—	—
5 (1756–1777)	Observed	1,604	15,049	18.76	36.25	0	380	20	24.77	56	1,391	86.72	21.11	159.25
	Course ties removed	1,604	10,260	12.79	25.23	0	380	187	41.94	58	1,222	76.18	6.55	77.99
	Pêche ties removed: Means (Std. dev.)	1,475.9 (17.17)	13,332.68 (333.66)	18.07 (0.31)	34.06 (0.67)	0 (0.00)	332.81 (10.68)	19.86 (1.25)	27.59 (1.10)	57.74 (2.20)	1,255.67 (19.77)	85.08 (0.65)	19.04 (0.68)	142.31 (3.87)

P	—	—	0.00	0.00	0.00	0.00	0.00	34.60	5.30	0.00	—	—	
6 (1778–1792) Observed	1,471	34,099	46.36	87.82	0	1,140	14	11.48	28	1,384	94.09	35.02	213.23
Course ties removed	1,471	11,065	15.04	42.51	0	736	425	58.64	35	946	64.31	3.20	44.06
Pêche ties removed: Means (Std. dev.)	1,409.22 (10.16)	32,800.23 (421.48)	46.55 (0.53)	85.92 (1.34)	0 (0.00)	1,062.99 (29.13)	12.96 (1.01)	11.37 (0.55)	26.38 (1.64)	1,326.66 (10.38)	94.14 (0.29)	35.90 (1.71)	211.37 (5.68)
P	—	—	0.00	0.00	0.00	0.00	0.00	0.00	0.00	0.00	0.00	—	—
All periods Observed	6,298	90,280	28.67	67.76	0	1,544	108	15.36	143	5,794	92	25.09	365.59
(1681–1792) *Course* ties removed	6,298	46,257	14.69	40.02	0	1,140	1,192	45.09	158	4,667	74.1	4.67	126.99
Pêche ties removed: Means (Std. dev.)	5,859.27 (25)	82,696.15 (652.49)	28.23 (0.18)	64.59 (0.73)	0 (0.00)	1,328.74 (40.89)	106.94 (2.15)	16.72 (0.36)	145.54 (3.57)	5,346.88 (26.62)	91.25 (0.19)	23.21 (0.40)	336.42 (3.70)
P	—	—	0.00	0.00	0.00	0.00	0.00	0.00	0.00	0.00	0.00	—	—

Note: The first row and second row for each period reproduce the network descriptives and cohesion results in table 6.3 (see chapter 6). The third row for each period reports network descriptives and cohesion results when as many *pêche* (fishing) voyages to Newfoundland are removed from the network as there are *course* voyages. First, voyages are removed from the two-mode network, then the one-mode merchant-by-merchant network is used to measure all cohesion indicators. Because there are more *pêche* than *course* ventures (see table 6.2 in chapter 6), repeated random selections of *pêche* ventures are used (one thousand iterations). For each period, the *P*-value reports the percentage of the one thousand networks where *pêche* ventures are removed that yield the same or an even higher degree of fragmentation as the network where all *course* partnership ties are removed. Results for period 3 are not reported because it was a period of peacetime that did not offer any opportunity for commerce raiding. Results for period 1 are not reported because, for the years 1681–1686, the specific type of trade cannot be identified unambiguously within the first set of archival documents (*AD-IV* 9B165). See note in chapter 6.

Source: Data for the observed network from *AD-IV* 9B165-9B176; 9B387; 4E5277-4E5278; 4E5343; 4E5364; 1F1914.

NOTES

1. INTRODUCTION

1. Collas (1949a, 47–67).
2. Note that privateering was not a French or English specialty, but rather was practiced by most maritime powers of the time. See Rodger (2014).
3. Martin-Deidier (1976, data appendix). See Collas (1949b) for details on the investments and returns of Chateaubriand's privateering ventures. The captain's report of the *Amaranthe*'s voyage can be found in *Archives départementales d'Ille-et-Vilaine à Rennes (AD-IV): AD-IV* 9B523.
4. Collas (1949a, 87–108); Roman (2001, 76).
5. Greif (2006).
6. Braudel (1992, vol. III, chaps. 1–4); Findlay and O'Rourke (2007, chaps. 4–5); Mancke (1999); Tracy (1990, 1991).
7. Given its prime role in international trade at the time, Marseille should be added to that list, even though it is a Mediterranean port.
8. Hancock (1995); Lespagnol (1991).
9. Butel (1999); Canny and Morgan (2011); Emmer, Pétré-Grenouilleau, and Roitman (2006); Greene and Morgan (2009); McCusker and Morgan (2000).
10. See, among many others, Caracausi and Jeggle (2014); Curto and Molho (2002); and Herrero Sánchez and Kaps (2017). Esteves and Mesevage (2019) survey recent empirical applications of social network analysis to economic history. Graham (2013) offers a review essay of recent monographs on early modern merchant networks in particular.
11. Alfani and Gourdon (2012); Erikson and Samila (2018); Zahedieh (2010, 106–13).
12. Van Doosselaere (2009); Hillmann (2008a); Padgett and McLean (2006); Padgett (2010).
13. For example, Hancock (2005).
14. McCusker and Morgan (2000); Morgan (1993); Zahedieh (2010).
15. Hancock (2009).
16. Graham (2013, 279).
17. For example, Baldassarri and Diani (2007); Crozier and Friedberg (1977); Gould (1995); Safford (2009); Traugott (1985).
18. Berg et al. (2015); Boulle (1981); Erikson (2014); Haudrère (2005); Haudrère, Le Bouëdec, and Mézin (2015).

19. *AD-IV* 1F1914.
20. For the most systematic statement of this concept, see Moody and White (2003).
21. Calhoun (1982); Homans (1941).
22. For the now-classic study of the concept of structural holes, see Burt (1992).
23. Gould and Fernandez (1989); Stovel and Shaw (2012).
24. Friedkin (1998, 127–28, 135–36).
25. Granovetter (1973).
26. Any reference to the idea of crosscutting social circles is indebted to the pioneering work of Georg Simmel, in particular the essays in his foundational *Soziologie* (1908).
27. Feld (1981).
28. Friedkin (1998, chap. 8). Elsewhere, I have likewise shown that *individual* brokers who are embedded in multiple networks at once are ideally positioned to mobilize otherwise-separate interest groups in joint political action (Hillmann 2008a). Also close in spirit is the recent work of Balazs Vedres and David Stark who argue that structural folding—membership overlap among cohesive groups—is conducive to the performance of business groups and their capacity for innovation (Vedres and Stark 2010; De Vaan, Vedres, and Stark 2015). Their focus, however, is primarily on team performance, whereas my concern is with community-wide cohesion.
29. Friedkin (1998, 128).
30. Johnsen (1985); Friedkin (1998, 137–46).
31. In the original French: "cette forteresse du Commerce est une pépiniére d'Armateurs, un séminaire de Héros." Coyer (1756, 75).
32. Again, in Coyer's own words: "la marine Marchande est la nourrisse de la Marine guerriére" (1756, 75).
33. Most important, Lespagnol (1991).
34. Lachmann (2000) is perhaps the most comprehensive statement on elite competition in early modern Europe.
35. *AD-IV* 9B167, ff 95v-96r.
36. For example, the partnership contract for the four-hundred-ton *Le Sage*, intended for a long-distance voyage to Spanish America in 1719, lists three *coarmateurs*: the Dame de Grandville, and the brothers André Lévesque sieur de la Souctière and François Lévesque sieur de Beaubriand (*AD-IV* 4E5278).
37. Bromley (1987, 374); Lespagnol (1991, 139); Morel (1957, 36).
38. *Ordonnance du commerce*, 1673, title 1, printed in Isambert, Decrussy, and Taillander (1829, 93–94); for a recent discussion, see Kessler (2004).
39. Carrière (1973, vol. I, 237–52); Jeannin (2002, 282–85); Kessler (2004); Martinetti (2013, 30–36); Nières (2004, 105); Takeda (2011, 57–60). For the quotes from *Le Parfait Négociant*, see Savary (1675, book II, chap. 42, 1–2).
40. Likewise, the *Ordonnance du commerce* of 1673, title 1, distinguishes between "négocians et marchands en gros et en détail" in article 6, whereas article 7 makes no such distinction and refers simply to "marchands en gros et en détail" (printed in Isambert et al., 1829, 94).
41. Nières (2004, 104–105).

2. SAINT-MALO IN THE FRENCH ATLANTIC ECONOMY

1. Sée (1928, 3).
2. Tuloup's (1976) narrative account offers a general history of Saint-Malo. For a collection of systematic essays on pivotal periods, see Lespagnol (1984).
3. Lespagnol (1991, 43), actually refers to the reign of Louis XIV, but the characterization applies just as well to these earlier times.

4. Tuloup (1976, 132–47).

5. The narrative of state centralization that confronts localism can be traced back at least to Alexis de Tocqueville ([1835–1840] 2004), and it is still present in comparative-historical sociology, including Downing (1992), Ertman (1997), Gorski (2003), Mann (1986), Sahlins (1989), and Tilly (1992).

6. Beik (2005) summarizes the work of revisionist historians who emphasize cooperation between the crown and provincial powers. The literature on the role of privilege under the absolutist monarchy is legion: see, among others, Beik (1985), Bien (1987), Bossenga (1991), Horn (2015), Kwass (2000), Root (1994), and Swann (2003).

7. Lespagnol (1991, 51–52).

8. Chateaubriand suggests the reference to Columbus in his *Mémoires* ([1849–1856] 1957, vol. I, book I, 28).

9. The notion of an Atlantic Economy is still a matter of debate and not without its critics. Some recent contributions to the vast literature include Butel (1999); Coclanis (2005); Emmer, Pétré-Grenouilleau, and Roitman (2006); Gervais (2011); Hancock (1995, 2009); and McCusker and Morgan (2000). For comparative-historical scholarship on the cultural and political exchanges that resulted from the European expansion across the Atlantic, see the recent collections by Bailyn and Denault (2009), Canny and Morgan (2011), and Greene and Morgan (2009). For the French Atlantic world, see the detailed treatment in Cabantous, Lespagnol, and Péron (2005) and the overviews by Dubois (2009) and Marzagalli (2011). I do not mean to imply that exploration and economic activities of European merchants were confined to the strict geographic boundaries of transatlantic exchanges. The emergence of an Atlantic trading system should rather be understood as the necessary gateway toward overseas expansion on a global scale. Le Bouëdec (1997) and Pétré-Grenouilleau (1997a) offer valuable general surveys of said overseas expansion, with an emphasis on the French experience. On long-distance fishery around Newfoundland, see Brière (1990). Pritchard's (2004) comprehensive study is indispensable for understanding the emergence of the French colonial empire and trade in the Americas. Haudrère (2005, vol. I, 11–29), considers the earliest ventures of the French into the East Indies. For the role of Saint-Malo in most of these early developments, see André Lespagnol's magisterial *Messieurs de Saint-Malo* (1991).

10. See in particular Fox (1971) on the theme of "the two Frances." Roche (1998, chaps. 4–5), likewise contrasts the social structures of "peasant France" and "merchant France." Braudel (1992b, vol. III, 335–47) discusses the various boundaries separating them from each other. Cheney (2010, 73–74) places the theme in the context of emerging ideas about commerce among eighteenth-century French *philosophes*. More recently, Acemoglu, Johnson, and Robinson (2005) have extended this idea and suggested a distinct commercial and political culture within those parts of Western Europe that were engaged in Atlantic trade and whose merchant elites benefited from favorable market-supporting political institutions.

11. Bromley (1987, 280); Cabantous et al. (2005, 322–35); Lespagnol (1984, 90–93); Lespagnol (1991, 52–53).

12. Cited in Braudel (1992b, vol. III, 347). Arbellot (1973) reports the duration of eighteenth-century itineraries based on the *Indicateur fidèle ou Guide des Voyageurs*, a contemporary travel guide, first published in 1764. For a discussion of the network of roads, rivers, and canals linking the towns and villages of eighteenth-century Brittany, see Nières (2004, 41–71).

13. The names of captains are included in the contracts of share partnerships (*actes de société*) in maritime trade (*AD-IV* 9B165–9B176). The 95.5 percent represent 599 individual names, excluding all multiple entries for which the same captain was hired for more than one voyage. Half of these Breton and Norman captains (299) resided in towns other than Saint-Malo.

14. Lespagnol (1991, 54–60).

15. Collins (1994, 46–47). See Bromley (1986, 1987) on the ambivalent relationship between Saint-Malo and the English Channel Islands—extensive trade during peace and mutual commerce raiding by privateers during war.

16. All statistics are based on trade data published in Delumeau (1966).

17. Collins (1994, 35) even notes the existence of "remarkably dense urban networks connecting Rennes and Saint-Malo," which supports the observation that Saint-Malo was not as disconnected from interior markets as the merchants of competing port cities would have the royal government to believe.

18. In comparison, although not entirely absent, merchants from Saint-Malo showed less of a presence in the northern trade with Scandinavia and the Baltic Sea. On French shipping in the northern trade in general, see, in particular, Pourchasse (2006). Earlier works include Bamford (1954), Cieslak (1977), and Pelus-Kaplan (1997).

19. On the increasing consumption of *bacalao* (dried codfish) as a staple food on the Iberian Peninsula, see Grafe (2012, 52–79).

20. Pritchard (2004, 139–50) recounts the difficulties the French royal government faced in their repeated attempts to establish a colonial fishery in New France and Newfoundland.

21. Bromley (1987, 283–85); Brière (1990); Cabantous et al. (2005, 136–50); Le Bouëdec (1997, 5–30); Lespagnol (1984; 1991, 235–306); Pritchard (2004, 139–50).

22. Statistics, combining departure and arrival tonnages, are based on trade data in Delumeau (1966).

23. Lespagnol (1984, 106).

24. The royal intendant at Brest reportedly claimed that "an element of Malouin seamen was essential to a good crew" (Bromley 1987, 284).

25. See again Delumeau (1966) as well as Labourdette (1988, 649–50) for the underlying data.

26. Lespagnol (1984, 107).

27. Cabantous et al. (2005, 205–6).

28. The trade statistics are taken from Delumeau (1966, 238–39); Cabantous et al. (2005, 211); and Lespagnol (1991, 408). For in-depth studies of Saint-Malo's commerce with Spain, see in particular Lespagnol (1991, 403–94) and Malamud Rikles (1986). Classic accounts of the involvement in the Spanish and colonial trade include Dahlgren (1909) and Sée (1928, [1925] 2001).

29. Sée (1926, 487–520) published and introduced a transcription of the "Mémoire Touchant Le Commerce Des Indes Occidentales Par Cadix." See also Sée (1928) and Le Bouëdec (1997, 31–34).

30. Grafe (2012, 83, 228) likewise emphasizes that the licensing of exclusive trade with the Spanish Americas was rather limited as a monopoly in a strict economic sense. For one, internal competition among Castilian traders was still maintained. Furthermore, as noted in the section on "Traditional Pillars of Commerce," even foreign traders were able to sidestep their nominal exclusion by hiring intermediaries among the licensed private traders.

31. On the role of local agents in the commerce with Cadiz, and *metedores* and *cargadores* in particular, see Braudel (1992a, vol. II, 145–53); and Sée (1926). Greif (2005) offers a thorough treatment of the commitment problem in economic exchange, with a particular emphasis on institutional solutions to the problem in various historical settings.

32. Lespagnol (1991, 114–17). The kinship relations among the various branches of the large Magon family as well as the birth, marriage, and burial dates of their individual members are meticulously documented in the Saint-Malo parish registers as edited by the abbé Paul Paris-Jallobert (2004).

33. *AD-IV* 9B167, f 113v, and 4E5277 document the two business partnership contracts (*actes de société*).

34. Lespagnol (1991, 442–54); Bromley (1987, 283–84); Cabantous et al. (2005, 316–18); Sée (1928). Sée ([1925] 2001) also dedicated an entire monograph to the exploits of the Magon merchant dynasty.

35. Lespagnol (1991, 444–45).

36. Chateaubriand ([1849–1856] 1957, vol. I, book I, 30–31) (my translation).

37. The gist of Tilly's argument can be found in his *Coercion, Capital, and European States* (1992). Classic accounts of the military revolution include Fritz Redlich's *The German Military Enterpriser and His Work Force* (1964–1965), Geoffrey Parker's *The Military Revolution: Military Innovation and the Rise of the West, 1500–1800* (1996), and Jan Glete's *Navies and Nations: Warships, Navies, and State Building in Europe and America* (1993). Just as influential have been the contributions

of Otto Hintze (1975) to the study of military organization and the rise of states. The literature on the early modern nexus between state-building, war, and political conflict keeps growing. Notable recent contributions include Black (1998); Downing (1992); Ertman (1997); Hoffman (2015); Mann (1986); and Parrott (2012). For innovations in fiscal administration and their links to warfare in the formation of the fiscal-military state, see Bonney (1999); Brewer (1988); Dincecco (2011); Glete (2002); Hoffman and Rosenthal (1997); Le Goff (1999); O'Brien (1988); O'Brien and Hunt (1993); Stone (1994); and Storrs (2009). Stasavage's work (2003, 2011) in particular has contributed to our understanding of the political link between public finance and the existence of representative assemblies in early modern state-building.

38.   For the quote, see Pares (1936, 179). The economic thought and policies of mercantilism, particularly with an eye on the French case, are treated in the classic studies of Cole (1939, 1943); Schaeper (1983); and, recently, Cheney (2010) and Horn (2015). The idea that mercantilism was a coherent system of economic thought in early modern Europe remains hotly disputed. So, too, is the view that commercial competition inevitably gave rise to military confrontations. See, among a plethora of contributions, Coleman (1980); Magnusson (1994); Pincus (2012); Stern and Wennerlind (2013); and, in particular, the chapters by Reinert (2013), who shows to what extent trade rivalry was intertwined with and nurtured political rivalry among European powers, and by Shovlin (2013), who casts a rather skeptical view on the causal link between rivalry in trade and the outbreak of war. See also Pagden's (1995) argument that Britain's and France's early empire-building in the Americas rested on the primacy of commerce, whereas Spain, at least initially, favored military conquest. On the notion of the Second One Hundred Years' War, see Bromley (1987, 495–503) and Crouzet (1996, 2008). On the British-French rivalry for the dominance of world trade during the long eighteenth century, see Black (1986); Crouzet (2008); and Findlay and O'Rourke (2007, 245–62).

39.   See Clark (1970) and Symcox (1976).

40.   Pincus (2009, 305–8).

41.   Findlay and O'Rourke (2007, 247–52); Le Roy Ladurie (1996, chap. 6); Lynn (1999, chaps. 6–7); Pritchard (2004, 391–401); Sonnino (1987).

42.   Tuloup (1976, 175–83); Clark (1970, 246, 249).

43.   Baugh (2011, 307–11); Dull (2005, 118); for a detailed study of the British coastal raids during the Seven Years' War and the battle of Saint-Cast, see Lagadec, Perréon, and Hopkin (2009).

44.   Saint-Malo was not alone in its vulnerability. Nearly all seabound towns in the province of Brittany found themselves exposed to the threat of Dutch and English naval attacks. Consequently, Vauban and his successors in the royal government undertook considerable efforts to reinforce urban defenses, including the installation of artillery batteries and the construction of citadels. See Nières (2004, 443–56).

45.   All statistics refer to figure 2.4, and are based on Delumeau (1966).

46.   On the economic consequences of war for French maritime commerce at large, see Horn (2015); Pétré-Grenouilleau (1997a, 50–54). Bromley (1987, 43–72) examines the impact of both the Nine Years' War and the War of the Spanish Succession on commercial relations across the North Sea. Brière (1983) and Pritchard (2004, 346–57, 393–401) consider the contest between Britain and France over the control of the Newfoundland fisheries. The studies by Bromley (1987, 279–95, 389–406) and Lespagnol (1991, 199–230) are particularly valuable for understanding the dampening effect of both wars on Saint-Malo's trade.

47.   For comparative studies of both naval strategies, see Symcox (1974) and Villiers (1991, vol. I, 75–92, 121–78). Dull (2009, 10–33); Harding (1999, 54–58, 149–85); Lynn (1999, 93–104); and Rodger (2005, 156–59) discuss the role of both naval strategies in the establishment of seapower during the Nine Years' War and the War of the Spanish Succession.

48.   See *AD-IV* 9B565: the Admiralty at Saint-Malo issued 2,178 notes of ransom (*billets de rançon*) between April 1706 and January 1710, in the midst of the War of the Spanish Succession. These

notes, however, are best interpreted as expectations to take foreign ships for ransom. For the number of ransoms that were actually taken, see chapter 5, table 5.2.

49. Bromley (1987, 187–212); Martin-Deidier (1976, 49–51).

50. Just how absolute and centralized the French absolutist state really was, and to what extent the king did cooperate with local and national elites, and thus accommodated their private interests, remains the subject of a lively debate among historians of the Ancien Régime. See Beik (2005) for a valuable review of traditionalist and revisionist accounts.

51. Privateering was not exclusive to the French. While a comparative discussion of other historical settings is beyond the scope of the present study, interested readers may consult Crowhurst (1977, 1989), Meyer (1981, 1983), Starkey (1990), and Hillmann and Gathmann (2011) on English privateering; Jamieson (1986) on Channel Island privateers; Lunsford (2005) on Dutch privateers; and Lydon (1970) and Swanson (1991) on colonial North America.

52. For the quote, see Bromley (1987, xi). On the historical origins, legal usage and often faux romanticism of the terms piracy, privateering, *corsaire*, and *course*, see Le Guellaff (1999, 40–53); Meyer (1971); and Rodger (2014). Additional misunderstandings arise because "corsair" and "privateer" may refer both to the ships employed in commerce raids and the captains who commanded them as well as to the private merchants who financed these ventures.

53. See *AD-IV* 9B583–585, 587; 9B591; 9B599–640; 9B679–9B680; Mollat (1975, 539–44) for regulations stipulated in the *Code des Prises*; and Le Guellaf (1999) for a comprehensive study of the legal foundations of the private war at sea.

54. Tuloup (1976, 161–65).

55. For instance, see Lespagnol (1984, 116).

56. All information on corsair commissions is taken from *AD-IV* 9B408; 9B435, (1)–(3). Data on declared prizes come from *AD-IV* 9B583–585, 587, and from surviving prize dossiers for the years 1688–1713 in *AD-IV* 9B599–622. These archival sources are coupled with evidence collected and printed in Morel (1958) and Martin-Deidier (1976). The numbers include only vessels that explicitly set out to sea to engage in commerce raiding (*armements en guerre*). Not included are armed merchantmen that carried commissions of *guerre et marchandise*. The latter primarily pursued trade, but they were legally entitled to seize prize ships as an act of self-defense. Somewhat confusing, these semi-corsairs are called "letter of marque" ships in English. For the distinction between these two types of commissions, see Aumont (2013, 107–26); Le Guellaf (1999, 203–5); Lespagnol (1991, 329–30); Rodger (2005, 156).

57. Studies of ports other than Saint-Malo that armed corsairs include Aumont (2013) on Granville; Bromley (1987) on Dunkirk (73–101, 103–19) and on Marseille (243–78); and Villiers (2000) on Dunkirk, Calais, and Boulogne.

58. Figure 2.7 draws on the list of privateering vessels compiled by Demerliac (1995, 294–322). Vessels on loan from the French royal navy are not included. Demerliac states that he restricted his list to ships that were larger than one hundred tons, although a few of his entries are of smaller tonnages. He further estimates that his list is likely to be complete for all corsairs larger than one hundred tons that sailed from Dunkirk, Cherbourg, Saint-Malo, Port-Louis, and Ciboure/Saint Jean de Luz. The entries for Calais, Boulogne, Dieppe, Le Havre, Honfleur, Granville, Brest, Nantes, Rochefort, Bordeaux, Bayonne, Marseille, La Ciotat, and Toulon are not as complete and thus report lower-bound estimates.

59. Bromley (1987, 227–29).

60. Bromley (1987, 311–20); Tuloup (1976, 199–205). Vergé-Franceschi (1996) recounts Duguay-Trouin's career as he rose from being a young, ambitious corsair captain to his ennoblement and promotion to *chef d'escadre de l'Amérique* in the royal navy during his later years.

61. Little agreement seems to exist among naval historians as to what extent privateering complemented or substituted for regular trades. Rodger (2005, 157) maintains that "ports whose trade prospered in

wartime seldom bothered with privateering." Bromley (1987, 301), in a more nuanced view, suggests that in some ports, such as Calais, "privateering was stimulated because peacetime income was cut off." But, referring to other ports such as Saint-Malo, he continues that "seeking substitutes for the loss of peacetime traffic was never enough to create a successful privateering port." On the role of privateering enterprise in Saint-Malo, see especially Bromley (1987), *passim*, and Lespagnol (1991, 307–402).

62. Butel (1974, 24–39); Cabantous et al. (2005, 212–13); Lespagnol (1991, 495–540); Malamud Rikles (1986), *passim*; Pritchard (2004, 43–70, 320–33).

63. Pritchard (2004, 386–87).

64. Lespagnol (2013a); Pritchard (2004, 350–51).

65. Alternatively, the same company was also referred to as the *Compagnie de la mer du Sud*. The surviving documents suggest that Danycan and Jourdan went through some disagreement concerning the original idea of a South Sea venture, its intended scope, and the role of other associates from Saint-Malo; see Dahlgren (1907, 425; 1909, 108, 115–22).

66. Bromley (1987, 290).

67. Lespagnol (1991, 577) even calls it "un style d'armement 'en guerre.'"

68. Lespagnol (1991, 400–1).

69. Dahlgren (1907, 449). In the same volume, Dahlgren details the—usually just as lengthy— itineraries of another 174 French vessels bound for the South Sea (1907, 447–554). For more details on the South Sea route and the rhythm of its shipping seasons, including the average durations, see Lespagnol (1991, 581–96).

70. Pritchard (2004, 358–61); Lespagnol (1991, 496–500).

71. *AD-IV* 4E5278. To the best of my knowledge, this is the only direct mention of the "mers du Sud" in any of the contracts.

72. See the partnership registrations of the *L'angelique* (1701; Athanaze Jolif, owner): *AD-IV* 9B167, f 133r; *Le Saint Jean Baptiste* (1706; François Baillon, sieur de Blanc-Pignon, owner): *AD-IV* 4E5277; *Le René Jullien* (1716; Jullien Godet, sieur des Grèves, owner): *AD-IV* 9B168, f 93v.

73. *AD-IV* 4E5278; see also Bromley (1987, 288).

74. Dahlgren (1909, 113).

75. Savary (1675). Lespagnol (1984, 131–32); Lespagnol (2013a, 197); Meyer (1985, vol. I, 225, 279; vol. II, 960). For Danycan's poll-tax, see *AM-SM* CC41, f 94v.

76. Dahlgren (1907, 446) reports a slightly larger number of vessels (n = 163) for the 1695–1724 period. I rely on the more conservative estimate suggested by Lespagnol (1991, 551–52, 818–19). Lespagnol also points out how close the number of French interloping ventures actually was to the 164 official Spanish ships (totaling 30,525 tons) that were sent to the American colonies between 1701 and 1715. The number of Spanish ships is based on Kamen (1969, 178).

77. *AD-IV* 9B165–9B168; 9B587; Lespagnol (1991, 555, 566–67, 820–21).

78. Lespagnol (1984, 126–27; 1991, 824–27). On the flow of silver from Potosí, see Malamud Rikles (1986, 215–31).

79. See Gottman (2013) for a valuable review of recent scholarship on the French East Indies connection.

80. Adams (2005, 50–51).

81. Boulle (1981, 105–8); Haudrère (2005, vol. I, 23–27); Manning (1996, 20–21).

82. Haudrère (2005, vol. I, 27–29); Lespagnol (1979; 1982; 1991, 647–70); Manning (1996, 21–23).

83. *AD-IV* 1F1914, ff 13r, 24r, and 27v include exemplary listings of the names of directors and main shareholders as well as the contributions they made to the company's capital. The accounts in the manuscript cover the years 1715 through 1727.

84. For the specific numbers of shares and capital amounts, see *AD-IV* 1F1914, ff 24v–26r. On the relationships among the associates and their social standing, see Lespagnol (1979, 432–43; 1991, 662–64, 672–80) and Paris-Jallobert (2004).

85. Lespagnol (1982; 1991, 681–710, 830–31).

86. Rivalries among French merchant communities were frequent, especially concerning trading privileges that had been granted to some ports at the exclusion of others. See, for example, Cheney (2010, 170–73); Haudrère (2005, vol. I, 73); Schaeper (1983, 93–95); Scoville (1962, 241–44).

87. Lespagnol (1979, 438–40; 1991, 665–66).

88. Lespagnol (1979, 431–32; 1991, 667–68, 677). On the use of privilege as an instrument of economic policy under the French Old Regime, see Horn (2015, 96–131) and Schaeper (1983).

89. See Pritchard (2004, 358–401) for an assessment of French colonial politics during the War of the Spanish Succession and their economic consequences.

90. AD-IV 9B435, (4), ff 1rv; Martin-Deidier (1976, appendix).

91. Lespagnol (1984, 133).

92. Haudrère (2005, vol. I, 46–68); Haudrère, Le Bouëdec, and Mézin (2015, 19–45); Manning (1996, 23, 27–29).

93. Lespagnol (1991, 787).

94. The underlying data, together with a contemporary *Mémoire* on the rationale behind the *Balance du commerce* and its administration, are printed in Romano (1957). Crouzet (1966, 260–62) has suggested that increases in current prices applied primarily to French import and export values of the 1780s, and hence to years beyond the period considered in figure 2.9. Consequently, the upward bias in import and export values may be less pronounced before 1780. Crouzet has further suggested that, even if we were to account for inflation in prices, the volume of French foreign trade still increased to levels close to Britain by the eve of the French Revolution. For assessments of the *Balance du commerce* as a source and France's expansion in foreign trade in this period, see Butel (1993, 77–120); Daudin (2005, 191–360); Horn (2015, 96–131); Pétré-Grenouilleau (2006, 225–50).

95. Lespagnol (1984, 134–35; 1991, 788); see also Butel (1990); Crouzet (2008, 103–33); Meyer (1985, vol. I, 346–47). On the role of Bordeaux in the West Indies, see Butel (1974, 24–39); for Marseille, see Carrière (1973, vol. I, 331–74); on the dominance of Nantes in the slave trade, see Pétré-Grenouilleau (1996); for La Rochelle, see Clark (1981); Martinetti (2013).

96. Brière (1983); Pritchard (2004, 400–1). The available partnership contracts (*actes de sociétés*) also reveal that the first Malouin fishing voyages to Cape Breton began in 1717, well after the Treaty of Utrecht (*AD-IV* 4E5278; 9B168).

97. Haudrère (2005, vol. I, 28–29, 47).

98. Cheney (2010, 170); Horn (2015, 110–11).

99. Roman (2001); Lespagnol (1984, 136).

3. SOCIAL SOURCES OF ECONOMIC GROWTH

1. The registers of venture partnership contracts are full of references to the "port de Sollidor" where *armateurs* intended to have their ships built, see *AD-IV* 9B165–176.

2. Chateaubriand ([1849–1856] 1957, vol. I, book I, 29).

3. Collins (1994, 32).

4. For the previous paragraphs, see Bromley (1987, 280); Lespagnol (1991, 22–33, 52–53).

5. Schaeper (1983, 57–58, 87–94); Takeda (2011, 31–35, 41–48).

6. In later years, traders from Saint-Malo and other Breton ports would resume their engagement in the commerce with Asia in a different form, this time based on free trade, as discussed in chapter 7.

7. Lespagnol (1991, 51–52, 62–68); see also chapter 2.

8. For the idea of poisedness, that is, an institutional environment that offers a particularly fertile ground for entrepreneurial opportunities and innovation, see Johnson and Powell (2015).

9. Lespagnol (1984, 1989a).

10. Lespagnol (1991, 107–8); Nassiet (2012, 326).

11. For a detailed study of provincial jurisdictional institutions in Brittany under the Ancien Régime, and the *sénéchaussées* in particular, see Debordes-Lissillour (2006).

12. On the salience of oligarchy in municipal politics under the Ancien Régime, see Beik (2009, 105–8) and Temple (1973); and on the case of Nantes, see Saupin (1996, especially chap. 12, 323–43). Other places besides Saint-Malo that come to mind include Marseille (Carriere 1973; Takeda 2011), Bordeaux (Butel 1974; Huetz de Lemps 1975), La Rochelle (Clark 1981; Martinetti 2013); Nantes again (Pétré-Grenouilleau 1996), and Le Havre (Delobette 2005).

13. Lespagnol (1991, 88–90).

14. Lespagnol (1991, 90). For the two *quartiers* in the 1701 poll tax rolls, see *AM-SM* CC41, ff 94v-103r, and ff 54v-59v.

15. Lespagnol (1991, 94–95).

16. Paris-Jallobert (2004, 3458, 3551, 3904). The Saint-Malo parish registers list 334 cases of abjuration between 1668 and 1790 (Paris-Jallobert 2004, 3904–3911).

17. *AD-IV* 4E5277; 9B168, f 40r; 9B171, f 1v. I am not the first to point out the significance of ship names: see Lespagnol (1991, 95), or Pétré-Grenouilleau (1996, 110–12), for the symbolism implied in the names of slave-trading ships armed at Nantes.

18. For example, in a letter dated May 17, 1754, and addressed to the *Parlement* of Brittany, the citizens of Saint-Malo wrote: "Exposant qu'il n'y a dans ladite ville qu'une seulle paroisse, desservie en l'eglise cathedralle par un curé ou vicaire perpetuel" (Paris-Jallobert 2004, 3454).

19. For an illustration, consider just one among many examples included in the registers of partnership contracts that refer to the *Bourse Commune* as the primary place for business affairs in town: "A Comparu le Sieur Pierre Fournier fils négociant en Cette ville, lequel a déclaré avoir achepté En vente publique et volontaire Sur le Ravelin ou Bourse Commune . . . un Batiment nommé le Marie Joseph du port de Trente deux Tonneaux ou Environ . . . [*sic*]" (*AD-IV* 9B174, f 71v, dated May 10, 1768).

20. Lespagnol (1991, 90–94).

21. The observed marriage practices were not unique to Saint-Malo. Collins (1994, 80–89), for example, finds comparable rates of endogamy (anywhere between 70 and 90 percent) and similar patterns of elite intermarriage in other parts—villages and cities alike—of early modern Brittany. Likewise, in the case of eighteenth-century La Rochelle, Martinetti (2013, 90), finds that about 65 percent of a sample of 178 sons of overseas traders married daughters from other trader families. Similarly, in his sample of 245 daughters of Rochelais trader elite families, 65 percent married a son from another trader family—and when they didn't, they wedded a son of the nobility, which underscores the selectivity in their marriage choices.

22. Lespagnol (1991, 103).

23. Their present ties also helped to translate their sense of community into municipal politics, in particular, the defense of local autonomy in governance and hard-won economic and political privileges; see Lespagnol (1991, 43–52).

24. Patterns of strong community bonds were of course not exclusive to Saint-Malo and may be found in other places as well. See, among others, Alfani and Gourdon (2012); Beik (2009, 224–52); Follain (2008); Mauro (1990).

25. "Enfermés le soir sous la même clef dans leur cité, les Malouins ne composaient qu'une famille" Chateaubriand ([1849–1856] 1957, vol. I, book I, 31).

26. Lespagnol (1991, 80–81); Paris-Jallobert (2004). Nières (2004, 149–54) considers both professional migration from nearby places and the arrival of foreign migrants in Brittany's port cities.

27. Lespagnol (1991, 81). Note that these noblemen were descendants of some of the oldest and most esteemed families in Brittany whose estates and titles can be traced back for centuries. Although their activities in maritime trade were similar, they are not to be confused with the heads of merchant

dynasties in Saint-Malo and elsewhere, who rose into the nobility through marriage alliances and the purchase of royal offices (see also the section "Status Attainment and Relative Decline" in this chapter). For obvious reasons, this group of ennobled merchants is sometimes referred to as a *noblesse commerçante* as well (Lespagnol 1991, 777). For the original idea and portrait of the *noblesse commerçante*, see Coyer (1756). Nassiet (2012) offers a recent comprehensive study, focusing on the lesser nobility in Brittany. See also Collas (1949a) who has traced the entire career of René-Auguste de Chateaubriand.

28. Lespagnol (1991, 82–83); Paris-Jallobert (2004).

29. One exception to this rule was the Italian Natale Stefanini, originally from Livorno, a somewhat quirky character who displayed a bottomless talent for making a fortune in no time and losing it all just as quickly.

30. Within the parish registers (Paris-Jallobert 2004), one finds fifteen entries—births, deaths, marriages—that refer to "Irlande" as the country of origin between 1600 and 1660; twelve such entries for the years 1670–1699; and another seventeen references for the years 1700–1760. One case even goes back to 1563. Three more cases, in the 1660s, in 1686, and in the 1690s, list "Hybernie" as the country of origin. Note that these numbers do not include all family members listed under an entry (e.g., when a marriage is mentioned, I count this as one case, leaving out all their children that follow in the register). The appropriate way to think of these numbers is probably as a lower-bound estimate of Irishmen whose births, baptisms, marriages, and deaths happened to be registered in Saint-Malo.

31. In places, the Saint-Malo parish registers hint at the refugee status of Irishmen and their families, such as the écuyer André Morrogh and Marie Sall "de Cork en Hybernie, réfugiés à cause des troubles." See Paris-Jallobert (2004, 3781).

32. For this estimate and this paragraph on Irish migration into Saint-Malo, see in particular Lyons (2001). For comparison, Meyer (1985, vol. I, 1017–41) considers the migrant nobility (*noblesse débarquée*) moving from Ireland to Nantes and Saint-Malo, and Martinetti (2013, 121–25) portrays the establishment of the *noblesse débarquée irlandaise* in La Rochelle by tracing the branches of the Butler merchant dynasty.

33. Bromley (1987, 144–47). Note Bromley's remark that "privateering was almost a badge of the true Jacobite in St. Malo" (145).

34. *AD-IV* 9B167–168, 4E5277–5278, 4E5343; Paris-Jallobert (2004, 3511, 3781, 3881–3882). Lespagnol (1991, 86, 100–101); Lyons (2001, 121–24).

35. It is also conceivable that success in commerce was an antecedent, and not an outcome, such that traders who had collaborated successfully in business partnerships subsequently arranged marriages among their offspring to solidify their bond, and decided to take up residence in the same neighborhood, which in turn led them to share a strong attachment to the same local place. My point is different, however: to understand how exactly one gets from shared religion, residential choice, marriage ties, and local identity to economic growth (or vice versa), one has to go beyond recognizing them as correlates and identify the linking mechanism between them.

36. Cabantous, Lespagnol, and Péron (2005, 316–18); Lespagnol (1991, 114–17, 442–54).

37. Cabantous et al. (2005, 314–15); Lespagnol (1991, 112–14).

38. For Saint-Malo, see Lespagnol (1991, 101–102, 107–108); for La Rochelle, see Martinetti (2013, 75); and for the mercantile classes in France at large, see Roche (1998, 140–73).

39. Roche (1998, 162).

40. Roche (1998, 161).

41. Roman (2001, 18); Pétré-Grenouilleau (1998, 113).

42. These observations seem to counter organizational theories that tell us too much cohesion may stifle entrepreneurship and innovation. In this view, excessive reliance on tightly knit community networks can lead to lock-in and complacency because they tend to privilege codified knowledge and

routines, whereas the exploration of new ideas and opportunities is discouraged (e.g., see March 1991). Saint-Malo's elite merchants were less susceptible to these pitfalls because they successfully complemented social cohesion by attracting outside shareholding partners in seaborne ventures whose very purpose was exploration; they welcomed migrants from as far as Ireland, Flanders, and the Netherlands; and they sent their young sons as apprentices out to sea or to foreign trading places. Consequently, little evidence suggests that, in the long run, social cohesion dampened the Malouins' entrepreneurial spirit. Nor did it narrow the diversity of their ventures to routine undertakings (see the findings on investment careers in chapter 7). In recent work with Brandy Aven, I show in greater detail how complementarity promotes entrepreneurship (Aven and Hillmann 2018).

43.   Lespagnol (1991, 733–89).

44.   *AM-SM* CC41; Lespagnol (1991, 719).

45.   Livorno, situated along the board of the Ligurian Sea, was a hotbed of Tuscan corsairs, authorized by the grand duke to raid Muslim shipping, especially by the end of the sixteenth century (Fontenay 2010, 227–228).

46.   *AD-IV* 9B167–9B168, 4E5277; Lespagnol (1991, 720). The partnership contract for Stefanini's ship to the coast of Guinea, the 160-ton *Le Saint François Xavier*, registered on January 18, 1701, can be found in *AD-IV* 9B167, ff 121v–122r.

47.   See Meyer (1985, vol. I, 331–49) for the illustrative cases of Duguay-Trouin, Luc Trouin de la Barbinais, René Moreau de Maupertius, and Nicolas Magon de la Chipaudière, all successful *négociants* and esteemed citizens of Saint-Malo. This interpretation is not without its critics. Pétré-Grenouilleau (1996, 126–48), drawing on the case of the Nantais merchanty, remains skeptical of a fusion between *négociants* and the nobility, despite all visible signs of cultural imitation. In contrast to Lespagnol's account, he suggests that the economic success of trader elites did not necessarily imply an upward social mobility, in particular because the ordered society of the Ancien Régime offered no recognizable position for them.

48.   Lespagnol (1984, 131–32; 1991, 733–86). On the venality of offices, see Beik (2009, 135–46) and Bien (1987).

49.   Lespagnol (1991, 734, 788); Meyer (1969, 60–63); Sée (1928, 7–9).

50.   Findlay and O'Rourke (2007, 227–310).

51.   A related puzzle concerns the rise of a new generation of *Messieurs de Saint-Malo*, to borrow Lespagnol's term, later in the 1750s and 1760s. If the members of the first generation around Danycan and Magon de la Lande were indeed so successful in turning away from trade and toward an aristocratic lifestyle based on landed property, and if they were also successful in steering the occupational training of their sons away from seaborne commerce and toward careers in the royal administration, then why do we observe the emergence of *new men* out of the leading Malouin families by the second half of the eighteenth century? I address this question in chapter 7 when I examine the development of trader careers and how they contributed to the observed venture partnership networks.

52.   I am not the first to note some of these limitations. See, for example, Pétré-Grenouilleau's (1997b) review essay on Lespagnol's monograph. One could read the causal relationship in reverse order such that the desire to achieve noble status prompted engagements in commercial ventures that were likely to be successful. Accordingly, their rise into the ranks of the nobility was what the Malouin traders had been aiming for all along; and consequently, they would have tried to leave commerce behind and enter the nobility as soon as they had accumulated the financial means to do so. However, little systematic evidence, if any, exists to support this view.

53.   Bearman (1993), Hillmann (2008a), Lachmann (2000), McLean (2004), and Padgett (2010), among others in historical sociology, address the consequences of elite stratification and competition for early modern politics and commerce.

54.   Collins (2009, 216–17); Kwass (2000, especially 21–61); Le Goff (1999). See also Bonney (1999); Brewer (1988); Hoffman (1994); Hoffman and Rosenthal (1997); Storrs (2009).

55. Duby ([1962] 1998, 242–52).
56. Root (1994).
57. Bluche and Solnon (1983, 99–114).
58. *AM-SM* CC41.
59. Bluche and Solnon (1983); Guery (1986).
60. Collins (1994, 7–9); Guery (1986, 1065).
61. *AM-SM* CC41, ff 94v-95r.
62. Servants and valets in the household were included in the tax rolls because the *capitation* required masters such as Danycan or Magon to pay their servants' dues (Collins 2009, 172).
63. In contrast to the neglect of *négociants* as a distinct category, the tax system even distinguished between different ranks of privateering captains, depending on the number of cannons their corsair ships would carry (Bluche and Solnon 1983, 24, 109–11).
64. Nières (2004, 104–5) similarly notes that rarely more than some twenty residents were explicitly documented as *négociants* for the purpose of taxation in most towns in Brittany, except for larger ports such as Nantes or Lorient.
65. Hence, Nicolas Magon de la Chipaudière is referred to as "Connestable de St. Malo [*sic*]" and Noël Danycan de l'Epine is listed with his positions as "Secrétaire du Roy" and "Seigneur du Comté de Rieux" (see figure 3.2). Apparently, these positions were more salient to denote their social rank and to determine their tax duties than their profession as ship-owning traders in long-distance commerce; see also Lespagnol (1991, 74–75).
66. Kessler (2007, 141–87); Le Bouëdec (1997, 316–20); Pétré-Grenouilleau (1997a, 63–67); Vignols (1931).
67. Lespagnol (1991, 159–64), arrives at a similar distribution, using the *capitation* values for the merchants who were explicitly labeled as *négociants* in the tax rolls.
68. Lespagnol (1991, 713–32, 834).
69. One may wonder if merchants near the bottom of the tax distribution should be counted among the trader elites, especially when they are compared with those at the very top. Still, even those I have called the traders of modest means were elite enough to sponsor their own ventures or acquire shares in the ventures organized by their peers. The defining characteristic for my purpose, then, is whether or not someone belonged to the "entrepreneurial milieu" of Saint-Malo (cf. Lespagnol 1991, 76).
70. The partnership records (*acte de société*) for both ventures are included in the notarial registers *AD-IV* 4E5277.
71. *AD-IV* 4E5277–5278; 4E5343; 9B165, 167, 168; 9B587; and Lespagnol (1991). Information on fitting costs is only sparingly available for the Spanish trade ($n = 6$) and *long cours* destinations ($n = 14$, including two voyages with no precise destinations beyond the *long cours* designation). The information is available for a greater number of interloping ventures, however ($n = 48$). Because they all concern long-distance trading, in contrast to fishing or privateering, I combine them into a single *long cours* category in table 3.3.
72. For exemplary cases with 1/256 shares, see the *actes de société* of the 250-ton corsair *L'Intrepide* in 1746 (*AD-IV* 9B172, ff 4rv), the 400-ton *Saint Luc*, bound for America in 1748 (*AD-IV* 9B172, f 30r), or the 300-ton *Le Merlin*, destined for Newfoundland in 1783 (*AD-IV* 9B175, f 87v).
73. The partnership records are full of cases in which shares were resold. For example, one Jullien Barbot entered the partnership of the *Jean Baptiste*, a ship destined for the "etroit de Gibraltar et ailleurs" in 1710–1711, for a sixty-fourth share. One Jean Lossieux bought another sixty-fourth share in that same enterprise. Both gentlemen purchased their shares from the portfolio of Nicolas Lemarchand, sieur de la Chapelle who himself invested in three-sixteenth shares in the same partnership. For similar cases, see the corsair *Bonne fortune* in 1702, the *guerre et marchandise* vessel *L'Union* in 1703, or the 150-ton *La Reyne Anne*, bound for Newfoundland in 1711–1712. All four cases are documented in *AD-IV* 4E5277.

74. Lespagnol (1991, 127–42).
75. With any such partition, one has to balance nuance and pattern. Because the number of cases is too limited for a fine-grained partition, I opt for the ability to reveal pattern rather than nuance in the activities of individual merchants. One particular alternative is to use the four groups I suggested to interpret figure 3.3: (1) less than 50 *livres tournois* (*lt.*), (2) between 50 and 100 *lt.*, (3) between 100 and 200 *lt.*, and (4) more than 200 *lt.* Using this alternative partition yields findings that are virtually indistinguishable from those presented in table 3.4.
76. Bluche and Solnon (1983, 104–109).
77. Lespagnol (1991, 142).
78. Lespagnol (1991, 365–67). Little, if any, evidence suggests that the democratic character of the *course* with its numerous small-scale investment opportunities emerged only once the richest merchants had left behind the world of trade; the idea being that smaller investments were encouraged to compensate for the capital influx that was lost. If this were indeed the case, it would defy the idea that the *course* served as a mediating organization among different merchant elite strata.
79. If the *course* and the partnership networks it spawned were indeed so central as an organizational platform for forging cohesive bonds, we may wonder how social cohesion within the merchant community was ever possible before the *course* became available as an opportunity. On one hand, it is an empirical question to what extent *course* partnerships contributed to cohesion before 1681, the first year in my observation window. Historically, we know that French privateering enterprise existed well before the 1680s (Bromley 1987). But precisely because my available data are left-censored, a conclusive empirical response is beyond the scope of this study. On the other hand, it is explicitly not my intention to suggest the singularity of the *course* in the creation of community, whether in Saint-Malo or elsewhere. The network ties that arose from *course* partnerships are a case in point to examine how organizational linchpins work. Hence, rather than searching for *course* networks whenever we encounter similar settings, my suggestion would be to focus on identifying functional equivalents to the linchpin role that *course* networks happen to have served in this particular place and time.

4. THE *COURSE*: ITS ORIGINS AND ORGANIZATION

1. *AD-IV* 9B408; 9B435, (1)–(5).
2. Martens (1801, 1).
3. Symcox (1974, 6).
4. Quoted in Pares (1938, 1). The wording in the current online edition of the *Oxford English Dictionary* varies ever so slightly from the edition that Pares referenced.
5. Fontenay (2010, 212–213, 341); Le Guellaff (1999, 40–53); Villiers (2000, 11–43). In addition to the absolute concept of piracy as raiders who supposedly defied any law, relative and locally bounded notions of piracy were probably much more common, including infringements of local law by authorized corsairs. For example, the revolutionary government of France punished as an act of piracy any campaign that a corsair pursued under several flags besides the French banner (Le Guellaff 1999, 42). Likewise, Rodger (2014, 7) criticizes the absolute definition of the pirate as the enemy of all mankind (*hostis humani generis*) as lacking an empirical basis.
6. Rodger (2014). Some earlier attempts to offer a more sober view of the differences between piracy and privateering under the French Ancien Régime include Meyer (1971, 1997) and Vignols (1927).
7. See Le Guellaff (1999, 54–55); Rodger (2014, 10–11). Among the earliest critics of designating the *Barbaresques* as corsairs, not without nationalist overtones, was the pioneer of Saint-Malo's maritime history, Léon Vignols (1899, 20).

8.   On the Barbary and Maltese corsairs and the *corso* in the Mediterranean, see in particular the excellent collected studies of Michel Fontenay (2010, especially chaps. 5–8). See also Malcolm (2015, 76–81), for situating the opponents in the *corso* on the broader canvas of historical developments in the sixteenth-century Mediterranean.

9.   The *Oxford English Dictionary* dates the first use in English of *corsales*, together with the word *pyrates*, to 1549, whereas the first mention of *privateer* apparently did not appear until 1641. Le Guellaff (1999, 40, 46–47) finds the word *pirate* in use as early as 1213. She dates the appearance in print of the term *course* in French to the late-fourteenth century, and the noun *cursaire* or *corsaire* to either 1443 or 1477, which in turn derived from the ancient provençal word *corsari*, known since the twelfth century. Tai (2003) goes back even further, to the practice and legal opinions of late-medieval piracy and corsairs in the Mediterranean.

10. See again Fontenay (2010, 278). Not included in this tripartite list are the *flibustiers*, a rather ambivalent class of raiders, sitting in between *course* and piracy, who roamed the Caribbean in search for booty in the seventeenth century. They may have carried government commissions to begin with, thus resembling the venturers engaged in the Atlantic *course*. But eventually they crossed the line into organized pillage, which drew them closer to the Mediterranean *corso*. Just as religious zeal pitted Christian and Muslim corsairs against each other in the *corso*, the mostly Protestant *flibustiers* often directed their attacks at Spanish Catholic opponents. See Fontenay (2010, 342–44); Le Guellaff (1999, 56–58); Villiers (1991, vol. I, 179–200).

11. For the identification of the three historical roots of the *course*, see Pares (1938, 1–4). Rodger (2014, 6) has criticized historical studies wherein " 'the state' makes an appearance when any sixteenth-century commentator would have written 'the prince', and the author implicitly assumes that this 'state' has a monopoly of the lawful use of force, even against an enemy in wartime." In what follows, I will keep referring to "the state" because, first, I am concerned with the late-seventeenth and eighteenth centuries, when, at least in France, the building of the absolutist state was in full swing, and, second, both the registrations of *corsaires* and the voyage partnerships (*sociétés de navire*) that sponsored them explicitly speak of the state whenever commissions were granted to pursue the "Course Sur les Ennemies de L'Etat" (see *AD-IV* 9B165–176; 9B408; 9B435, (1)–(5); 9B587).

12. Pares (1938, 1), referring to the English case. In France under Louis XIV, it was likewise common practice for the crown to lend navy ships to *armateurs* engaged in the *course*—what André Lespagnol (1995, 88–89, 114–117) has called *armements mixtes*. See also Bromley (1987, 187–212) and chapter 2.

13. Symcox (1974, 7). From a legal point of view, Le Guellaff (1999, 64–69) objects to the interpretation of corsairs as true auxiliaries to the regular navy because they retained their quintessential nature as privately armed ventures.

14. See Clark (1933) for an intriguing discussion of the thirteenth- and fourteenth-century English practice of reprisals.

15. The legal terms in French were spelled out under the "Titre des Lettres de Marques et de Représailles" in the *Ordonnance de la Marine* of August 1681, printed in Chardon (1784, vol. I, xxv). The quote refers to this document. On the wartime versus peacetime distinction between *lettres de marque* and *lettres de représailles*, see likewise Le Guellaff (1999, 301, fn. 402).

16. Chavarot (1991); Le Guellaff (1999, 301–302, fn. 402); de Mas-Latrie (1866, especially 530–31); Pares (1938, 2–3); and Rodger (2014).

17. The change in meaning and practice is illustrated in article XVI of the Treaty of Utrecht, March 31, 1713, as printed in Chardon (1784, vol. I, 330): "Toutes Lettres de représailles, de marque ou de contre-marque, ci-devant accordées, sont révoquées; & n'en pourra être ci-après donné par l'un desdits Rois, si ce n'est seulement en cas de déni de Justice." The clause first implies little distinction between letters of reprisal and letters of marque that had been issued during the war. Yet, within the second part of the same clause, it references the original meaning of such letters as an instrument for redress when justice had been denied to the injured party in peacetime.

18. Aumont (2013, 113–26); Pares (1938, 3–4).

19. Thus, the first article of the *Ordonnance de la Marine* of August 1681 stated: "Aucun ne pourra armer Vaisseau en guerre, sans Commission de l'Amiral" (Chardon 1784, vol. I, i). For example, in December 1760, the French *Conseil des prises* ordered the confiscation of four English prize ships because two French corsairs, the *Opale* and the *Brune*, had taken them without a lawful commission to do so. In their defense, the *armateurs*, the sieurs Gradis of Bordeaux, argued that both corsairs were frigates on loan from the royal navy and commanded by officers of his majesty. Hence, they assumed that there was no need to obtain a *commission en guerre* (Chardon 1784, vol. I, 535–36). For a similar case of confiscation of a prize ship by the Admiralty in 1706, see the corsair *la Susanne*, whose *armateur* likewise failed to obtain a proper commission (Chardon 1784, vol. I, 270–76).

20. For example, in the instructions of the *course et marchandise* registration of the three-hundred-ton *Le François* of Saint-Malo we read the following: "estant necessaire de pourvoir à la Seurete des vaissaux des nos Sujets qui entreprennent des voiages de long cours et de leur permettre de se mettre en estat de resister aux insultes qui leur pourvoir estre faites dans leur navigation par les ennemis des nostres estat ou par les pirates fourbans et gens sans adveu et mesmes de leur courrir Sus . . . [*sic*]" (*AD-IV* 9B381, ff 2rv).

21. As noted in chapter 2, the English equivalent to the *guerre et marchandise* commissions were known as letter-of-marque vessels. Their regulation, including the payment of wages and allotment of prize shares, closely resembled their French counterparts (Starkey 1990, 33–55; Rodger 1986, 128–30).

22. "Règlement Pour les Officiers, Matelots & Soldats des Vaisseaux armés en Course, concernant les avances qui leur seront faites," November 25, 1693, printed in Chardon (1784, vol. I, 144–52); Pares (1938, 8, 10–11). *AD-IV* 9B598 ("Etat des Prises qui ont été Conduites et Vendues au Port de St. Malo depuis la déclaration de la guerre avec L'angleterre") lists the full prize accounts of some nine corsairs that had their prizes adjudicated at Saint-Malo and other French ports in 1756 and 1757, at the beginning of the Seven Years' War. Depending on the value of the prize, the third to be paid to the crew varied greatly. It ranged from a moderate 2,198 *lt.* for a single ransom up to an impressive 234,946 *lt.* for a dozen prizes seized by the two-hundred-ton *Puisieulx*, fitted out by Grandclos Meslé, father and son. We learn more about the latter's career in detail in chapter 7.

23. Bromley (1987, 213–41); Lespagnol (1991, 312–21).

24. For the perennial Anglo-French rivalry, see Crouzet (2008). On the link between mercantilist policy, commercial rivalry and military conflict between early modern European powers, see the discussion and references in chapter 2.

25. Hillmann and Gathmann (2011).

26. Le Goff (1999).

27. See chapter 2, figures 2.6 and 2.7, and chapter 7, figure 7.1, for the number of *course* ventures fitted out in Saint-Malo and other French ports.

28. Pares (1938, 33–38); Bromley (1987, 286).

29. Chardon (1784, vol. I, 60–61, 86–87; vol. II, 965–66, 969–70).

30. Pritchard (1987, 80–81); Le Goff (1990, 216).

31. Braudel (1992b, vol. III, 116–36, 157–74); Cipolla (1993, 160–64); Goldberg (2012, chap. 5); Lopez (1976, 73–78); Pryor (1984); Udovitch (1970).

32. A considerable scholarly debate has surrounded the historical roots of the *commenda* partnership contract. Sociologists will recall Max Weber's ([1889] 2008) dissertation on medieval trade partnerships. For seminal modern-day contributions, see Pryor (1977) and Udovitch (1970, 170–248). Çizakça (1996, 10–22), offers a short summary of the debate.

33. Braudel (1992a, vol. II, 434); Gonzáles de Lara (2008, 253); Pryor (1977, 6–7; 1983, 134–35); Sayous (1929, 166–67); Udovitch (1970, 170–71). For a selection of original *commenda* contracts transcribed and translated from the Latin, see Lopez and Raymond (2001, 174–84).

34. Lopez (1987, 364).

35. Somewhat confusingly, contemporaries frequently applied the term *compagnia* also to bilateral *commenda* or *societas* contracts (Sayous 1929, 167). As Pryor (1977, 10–13) has noted, however, such inconsistencies in the use of nomenclature, even by notaries, were most likely not systematic but rather a result of variation in local custom and convenience.

36. Braudel (1992a, vol. II, 436–37); Lopez (1987, 364–65); Origo ([1957] 2017, 105–36); Sayous (1929, 168–69). For a selection of translated original *compagnia* partnership contracts, see again Lopez and Raymond (2001, 185–211).

37. Blomquist (1971); Sayous (1931).

38. Lopez and Raymond (2001, 186), suggest that it was this undivided and unlimited liability that kept merchants from using the *compagnia* contract in the much more risk-prone trade at sea. On Datini's merchant career and his multiple partnerships, see the classic account of Origo ([1957] 2017, especially 29–136), the recent studies collected in Nigro (2010), and Orlandi's (2014) analysis of his network of correspondents across the Western Mediterranean.

39. Greif (2006, chap. 3); Kessler (2007, 148); Pryor (1984, 413, 438–39).

40. Origo ([1957] 2017, 84–102). The quote is taken from pages 89–90.

41. See the discussion of polyvalence as an investment strategy in chapter 3 and chapter 7.

42. Ogilvie (2011, 315–43). For general treatments of the principal-agent model, see Laffont and Martimort (2002); Pratt and Zeckhauser (1991).

43. Greif (2005) offers a comprehensive discussion of the commitment problem in economic exchanges.

44. Gonzáles de Lara (2008).

45. Carlos (1992, 1994); Carlos and Nicholas (1990).

46. In some instances, however, opportunistic behavior of agents in a company's service played an essential part in weaving a global trading network. When companies tried to suppress this behavior through strict institutional enforcement, they risked detrimental consequences, as Emily Erikson has recently shown for the English East India Company (Erikson 2014; Erikson and Bearman 2006; Erikson and Samila 2018). In a similar case of organizational adaptation, Sgourev and van Lent (2015) demonstrate that the Dutch East India Company also came to permit private trade of its overseas agents as a response to declining company returns (see also Adams 1996).

47. Landa (1981).

48. Greif (2006, 58–88).

49. Later, in early modern times, even such a highly regulated organization as the Dutch East India Company seems to have relied on social bonds and community norms as an effective means to discourage overseas agents from opportunistic pursuits, such as misusing company-specific knowledge and resources for private gains (Wezel and Ruef 2017).

50. Goldberg (2012, 56–92).

51. Origo ([1957] 2017, 81–85).

52. Pryor (1983, 135–36). Nevertheless, the *tractator* in a *commenda* partnership usually had to post security (Pryor 1977, 12).

53. Pryor (1984, 431–33).

54. See Granovetter (1973) for a classic statement of transitivity and triadic closure in social relationships.

55. Moody and White (2003).

56. Silver (1990, 1477–78).

57. Van Doosselaere (2009, chaps. 4–5).

58. Padgett and McLean (2006).

59. Hillmann (2008b).

60. This paragraph summarizes the discussion of *société* and sociability in Kessler (2007, chap. 4), with the quotes taken from 141–42. On the natural-law foundation of commercial society in Ancien Régime France, see in particular Clark (2007, chaps. 3–4).

61. Beyond such ideals of virtuous merchants, it probably helped that all associates in a *société* had personal stakes in their venture and were fully liable for the debts or losses incurred by any of their partners.

62. Kessler (2007, 177–81).

63. Silver (1990, 1482–84).

64. It just so happened that one of the key advocates of liberal ideas in France, Vincent de Gournay (1712–1759), came from a wealthy trader dynasty of Saint-Malo. He thus embodied a bridging role as someone who straddled the practical world of commerce, the world of intellectual disputes about the ideals of economic exchange, and even the world of politics as an influential government official. See Clark (2007, 168); Roche (1998, 154–55).

65. Roman (2001, 58, 75, 209, 227, 278). The brothers Marion were relative newcomers to Saint-Malo and did not belong to the dynasty of the Marion, sieurs du Fresne. Their father was an architect, originally from the town of Quettou in Normandy. See Paris-Jallobert (2004, 3763).

66. Lespagnol (1991, 344–50); Martin-Deidier (1976, 47–48); Morel (1957, 40–41). Prize ships were repurposed as well, both for the *course* and trade: the *Vierge Sans Maculle* used to be a Dutch prize ship from Middelburg that was seized by a Malouin corsair, sold at auction, renamed, and eventually equipped for a trading voyage to Stockholm and the Baltic (*AD-IV* 9B168, f 40r). Similarly, the Dutch ship *Le St. Pierre Apostre de Roterdam* was taken as a prize and sold to a new Swedish owner in Carlshaven (*AD-IV* 9B167, ff 99rv).

67. Lespagnol (1991, 343); Martin-Deidier (1976, 53); Morel (1957, 44).

68. Martin-Deidier (1976) reports the tonnage of the *Duchesse de Polignac* in her data appendix.

69. For more detail on the build of privateering vessels and their weaponry, with an eye to the Norman port of Granville near Saint-Malo, see the recent monograph by Aumont (2013, especially 275–331).

70. Meyer (1971, 321).

71. Lespagnol (1991, 351).

72. Martin-Deidier (1976, 57–58).

73. *Règlement Pour les Officiers, Matelots & Soldats des Vaisseaux armés en Course*, November 25, 1693, article V (Chardon 1784, vol. I, 147). Fifteen additional days were granted for bringing in prize ships, or for replenishing victuals. Identical regulations were still in place in 1778: see *Déclaration Du Roi, Concernant la Course sur les Ennemis de l'État*, June 24, 1778, article 21 (Chardon 1784, vol. II, 641).

74. Martin-Deidier (1976, 59–62); Morel (1957, 46–50); Pritchard (1987, 75).

75. Lespagnol (1991, 351–54).

76. *AD-IV* 9B598, *Département de St. Malo. Remise Du Bureau des Repartitions des parts de prises.*

77. For selected corsairs from Granville in Normandy, Aumont (2013, 375–76) likewise finds that 94 percent of crew members came from Granville and its surrounding *quartier maritime* in 1745, with 81 percent in 1747, and still 52 percent in 1780. Bromley (1987, 172–73) finds smaller contingents for twenty-three armaments in 1702 (71.8 percent recruited from Brittany) and thirty-six armaments in 1711 (56.5 percent).

78. Morel (1957, 51–54). Sociologically inclined readers interested in recurrent patterns may be reminded of Bearman's (1991) analysis of a similar effect of localism on the rate of desertion among Confederate units in the U.S. Civil War. See also Hechter, Pfaff, and Underwood (2016) for a recent sociological study that considers mutinies on British Royal Navy vessels as cases of high-risk collective action caused by grievances on board.

79. Morel (1957, 44–46).

80. At the helm of *La Duchesse de Polignac*, Captain Guidelou went on to capture seven prizes on her commission, including trade ships on their way from Grenada to Amsterdam, another to Scotland, and apparently two English privateers sailing from Bristol, the *Heart of Oak* and the *Hope*. See Martin-Deidier (1976, data appendix). On Bristol's privateers, see Powell (1930).

81. Lespagnol (1991, 321–26).

82. Unfortunately, I have no systematic information on credit for sponsoring trade or *course* ventures—unless we are prepared to treat the purchase of shares as a form of extending credit to the *armateurs*. But see Gervais (2011) on the role of credit networks, especially book credit, for merchant success. Focusing on the Parisian credit market, Hoffman, Postel-Vinay, and Rosenthal (2000) show that notaries in particular acted as effective brokers in the matching of creditors and debtors. Again, I am not aware of systematic evidence that notaries in Saint-Malo played a similar brokerage role in their local networks—although the absence of evidence does not necessarily mean evidence for absence.

83. For a comparative view of voyage partnerships in other ports, see Meyer (1969, 95–117) on Nantes; Butel (1974, 172–79, 200–11) on Bordeaux; Martinetti (2013, 68–75) on family ties in *sociétés* formed in La Rochelle; and Hancock (1995, 104–14) on the experience of a group of global traders based in London.

84. Lespagnol (1991, 365).

85. Quotes from Kessler (2007, 142, 170, 177).

86. Meyer (1969, 101).

87. Kessler (2007, 178) suggests that *sociétés anonymes, sociétés en commandite par actions* and other such *sociétés de capitaux* were rarely, if ever, addressed in treatises of commercial law because they tended to be companies owned and directed by the crown itself, and thus were of public rather than private interest.

88. *AD-IV* 9B168, f 1r.

89. Meyer (1969, 101–05). See also Lespagnol (1991, 364).

90. All quotes from *Ordonnance du commerce*, March 1673, *Titre IV*, "Des Sociétés," printed in Isambert, Decrussy, and Taillander (1829, vol. 19, 96–97). For discussion and interpretation, see Kessler (2007, 162–66).

91. *Déclaration Du Roi, Concernant la Course sur les Ennemis de l'État*, June 1778, article 14, printed in Chardon (1784, vol. II, 639); Le Guellaff (1999, 269–71). As Kessler (2007, 166) notes, this applied particularly to nobles who preferred to remain anonymous, anxious as they were that their participation in a commercial undertaking would still be regarded as not becoming of their social station.

92. The reason may well have been, as Kessler (2007, 172) suggests, that "any business association that departed from the equal sharing of powers, profits, and losses that characterized the general partnership—namely, any *société en commandite*—was potentially suspect."

93. *AD-IV* 9B168, ff 51v-52r.

94. *AD-IV* 4E5278.

95. *AD-IV* 4E5278.

96. *AD-IV* 9B168, f 47v. See also the choice of *armateur* for the corsair *Le Natal* in 1703, *AD-IV* 9B168, f 22v.

97. Lespagnol (1991, 365–66) suggests a similar reading of the partnerships' composition.

98. *AD-IV* 9B175, ff 50v-51r, 54r, 58r.

99. *AD-IV* 4E5343. Martin-Deidier (1976, 41) describes similar instances of resales of shares.

100. *AD-IV* 4E5277.

101. *AD-IV* 4E5277.

102. *AD-IV* 4E5278. A similar choice of words can be found in other partnership agreements. See, for example, the corsairs *Le Cigne* in 1702, *AD-IV* 9B168, ff 12r-13v; *La galère de guinée* in 1696, *AD-IV* 9 B167, ff 83v-84v; and *Le Dauphin de Grandville* in 1693, *AD-IV* 9B167, ff 20v-21v; and likewise the *Saint-Pierre*, armed (presumably with a *guerre et marchandise* commission) for a voyage to the French islands in the Americas in 1738, *AD-IV* 4E5278.

103. *Ordonnance de la Marine*, August 1681, articles 1–3, printed in Chardon (1784, vol. I, i–ii). Le Guellaff (1999, 294–310) considers the detailed legal history of these regulations.

104. *AD-IV* 9B435, (1), f 3r; 9B435, (4), f 2r; 9B435, (5), f 13r; Robidou ([1919] 1998, 207).

105. For the total number of *course* raids launched from Saint-Malo and the number of prizes they seized, see chapter 2, figure 2.6, and chapter 7, figure 7.1. Likewise, see chapter 2, figure 2.7, for a comparative perspective on the scale of privateering enterprise in Saint-Malo and other eminent French ports in the years 1688–1713.

106. The tripartite typology has been proposed by Meyer (1971, 320–22) and refined by Lespagnol (1991, 334–43).

107. *Ordonnance de la Marine*, article 21, printed in Chardon (1784, vol. I, xii).

108. *AD-IV* 9B515–524, covering the years 1702–1783, which indicates that the requirement of captains to submit reports was still in force in the late-eighteenth century. Note that historian Léon Vignols transcribed the captains' reports for two selected campaigns of Malouin corsairs from 1695 (*AD-IV* 1F1930).

109. See also Morel (1957, 62–63).

110. *AD-IV* 9B517, ff 83rv.

111. *AD-IV* 9B521, ff 11v.

112. *AD-IV* 9B515, f 60r.

113. *AD-IV* 9B518, f 36r.

114. *AD-IV* 9B519, ff 136r–137r.

5. RETURNS TO PRIVATEERING

1. Le Guellaff (1999, 83–129).

2. For the paragraph that follows, see Symcox (1974, 221–33).

3. Bromley (1987, 311–20); Tuloup (1976, 199–205).

4. *AD-IV* F g67 ("Armement en Course à Saint-Malo, de la Frégate *La Duchesse de Polignac*," 1780).

5. Symcox (1974, 222–24).

6. Readers interested in the strategic-military role of the *guerre de course* in French naval policy may refer again to Symcox (1974), and especially Villiers's (1991) comprehensive two-volume work. Additional, more concise treatments may be found in Dull (2009, 10–33); Harding (1999, 54–58, 149–85); and Rodger (2005, 156–59).

7. The argument that the French *course* developed as a substitute for, or as a continuation of, normal trade by other means during bouts of armed conflict is addressed by Meyer (1971, 313); Rodger (2005, 157); and Lespagnol (1991, 308, 378–79), among others.

8. Symcox (1974, 231–33).

9. Fontenay (2010, 279–80).

10. On the Malouins' display of their "corsair mentality," see Bromley (1987, 289–90) and Lespagnol (1991, 577).

11. *AD-IV* 4E5278.

12. In the words of Emmanuel Le Roy Ladurie (1996, 292), France merely opposed "its Bourbon cousins in Madrid. . . . Inexpensive and relatively bloodless, the conflict was more of an argument amongst friends."

13. This handwritten "Liste d'Armements et Désarmements à St. Malo, de 1706 à 1739" is included in the Fonds Léon Vignols, *AD-IV* 1F1930. Vignols found the registers to be in very good condition, with most *course* ventures included, but it is apparently less complete for the coastal trade and excludes much of the Mediterranean trade. For my purpose, this means that the numbers for normal trade are conservative lower-bound estimates, and hence there may have been even more regular ventures during war than are documented in the registers, and consequently even less substitution by privateering enterprise.

14. Bromley (1987, 301).

15. For the three paragraphs that follow, see Morel (1957, 68–75) and Martin-Deidier (1976, 90–114). The work of Le Guellaff (1999) is probably the most comprehensive among recent treatments of the legal regulations of the *guerre de course*, even though her focus is on the revolutionary period.

16. Chardon (1784, vol. I, ix).

17. Chardon (1784, vol. I, xii). By 1691, a seat of the Admiralty had been established at Saint-Malo (Morel 1957, 33); Martin-Deidier (1976, 91–92).

18. Chardon (1784, vol. I, xiii–iv).

19. See, for example, "Procédure de Liquidation de prise. *L'Achille, La Gloire, L'Astrée, L'Amazone*, armés en course au commandement de Dugué-Trouin, 1709" (*AD-IV* 1F g124); "*Le plaisir des jeunes gens*, prise de *Joseph*," armateur Nicolas Lhostelier sieur des Naudières, June 22, 1689 (*AD-IV* 9B599); "*La Providence*, prise du corsair *Le Mahon* de Saint-Malo," armateur le sieur de Blessin, September 4, 1756 (*AD-IV* 9B 629). Series *AD-IV* 9B599–640 (*Dossiers de prises*) contains numerous prize dossiers spanning the entire 1688–1782 period.

20. "Lettres Patentes Du Roi, Portant établissement des Commissaires pour juger les Prises auprès de M. le Duc de Vendôme. Du 20 Décembre 1659" (Chardon 1784, vol. I, 41–43).

21. "Règlement Pour l'Assemblée du Conseil de Marine ou des Prises, & sur la manière dont il y sera procédé. Du 23 Septembre 1676" (Chardon 1784, vol. I, 69–73). "Extrait de l'Ordonnance de la Marine, du mois d'AoÛt 1681. Titre des Prises" (Chardon 1784, vol. I, i–xxv). "Règlement Que Le Roi veut être observé dans l'Instruction & le Jugement des Prises. Du 9 Mars 1695" (Chardon 1784, vol. I, 160–67).

22. "Lettres Patentes Du Roi, Portant nomination des Commissaires, pour tenir le Conseil des Prises, près M. l'Amiral de France. Du 9 Mars 1695" (Chardon 1784, vol. I, 168–69). See also "Règlement Pour l'Établissement du Conseil des Prises. Du 22 Avril 1744" (Chardon 1784, vol. I, 387–92).

23. Morel (1957, 31) notes that, in practice, it was often just the *Secrétaire d'État* who decided the case, as not to burden the *Conseil* with every single submission.

24. Series *AD-IV* 9B583–585, 587 includes the registers of the judgments of the *Conseil des prises* for the years 1695–1706 and 1709–1714. Series *AD-IV* 9B591 complements them for decisions on prizes made during the Seven Years' War (1756–1763).

25. Morel (1957, 30–32).

26. Morel (1957, 72–75).

27. *AD-IV* 4F g67.

28. In 1743, the crown sought to increase the incentives for the *course* by reducing the Admiralty's share of the prize money from a tenth of the gross proceeds obtained from the auction sale (i.e., before any fees and deductions) to a tenth of the net benefit (*bénéfice nu*) that accrued to the *armateurs* and shareholding partners after the *liquidation générale* of a *course* campaign had been concluded. See the "Édit du Roi Concernant le Dixième de M. l'Amiral de France, sur les Prises faites en mer," August 1743 (Chardon 1784, vol. I, 383–86). In September 1758, the Admiralty's tenth was abolished altogether. See "Édit du Roi, Portant Suppression à perpétuité du droit de Dixième sur les Prises & conquêtes faites en mer, attribué à la charge d'Amiral de France" (Chardon 1784, vol. I, 519–22).

29. One of the rare cases concerns the sale of prizes captured by the Malouin corsair *Le Loup*, dated September 13, 1748 (*AD-IV* 9B628, "Etât Et procès verbal d'apurement et Liquidation générale du produit de la course du navire corsaire *Le Loup* de Saint-Malo"). Results of the sales of some single prizes have survived in the prize dossiers (*AD-IV* 9B599–640). Yet, more than just the usual handful of complete balance sheets of costs and benefits exist primarily for the Revolutionary and Napoleonic wars, both of which are beyond my observation window. Some examples include the account of the privateer *le Passe-Partout*, manned with a one-hundred-men-strong crew, armed with fourteen cannons, launched by *armateurs* Dupuy, père et fils in 1793, and commanded by a certain Captain Michel (Mollat 1975, 545–48); the privateer *La Constance* of Saint-Malo, finalized in March

1806 (Mollat 1975, 549–54); and the corsair *Le Tigre* of Saint-Malo in 1793 (Robidou [1919] 1998, 189–93). See Martin-Deidier (1976, 326–342), for a systematic documentation.

30. Lespagnol (1991, 360–63, 817).

31. *AD-IV* 4E5277–5278; 4E5343.

32. Careful readers may also wonder if the estimated costs should be deflated, as they reflect investments made over a considerable span of time (1744–1783). Setting aside the difficulty of finding a suitable price index, my interest is primarily in the returns on investments for individual ventures. Hence, later, in the section "Profitability of the *Course*," I relate costs and benefits *within* the same ventures. As worthwhile as it may be for other research questions, I am less interested in the development of fitting costs over time. Consequently, the need for deflating the costs does not impose itself for my purposes.

33. The focus on these three major wars excludes the relatively minor conflict with Spain in 1718–1719. See note 12 in this chapter.

34. *AD-IV* 9B171–175. I am not the first to rely on the *actes de société* to assess the finances of French privateering ventures. Both Bromley (1972, 75) and Lespagnol (1991, 364) have suggested their use. For the case of Marseille in the years 1705–1712, Bromley had access to some eighty rare contracts that offer detailed insights into the financial structure of privateering campaigns. Although they may be preferable, similar contracts in comparable quantities do not seem to have survived for Saint-Malo.

35. Some caveats and their solutions should be mentioned. First, in three cases, information on the ship's tonnage was missing in the *actes de société*. I replaced these missing values with period-specific mean ship sizes. Second, when information on the share value was missing for an associate within a venture, I used the average share value (in *livres tournois*) within that particular venture. Obviously, disregarding these missing share values would underestimate the true cost of a venture, and thus overestimate the benefits. Third, in cases of privateers for which none of the associates have share values listed, I used the value of the ship (in *livres tournois*) instead, to the extent that this information was available. If neither share values nor the value of the ship were available, I imputed the fitting costs by using the period-specific average costs per ton.

36. Le Guellaff (1999, 312–19) discusses the shifting government policies and legal regulations concerning ransom-taking by French corsairs, sometimes encouraging and other times prohibiting it. Pares (1938, 19–25) considers the substantive pros and cons of ransoms, contrasting the points of view of the individual corsair and the royal government. A few examples of preprinted forms of ransom bills can be found among the prize dossiers, for example, *AD-IV* 9B620, for the *Ares*, Captain Michel Tanquerey, signed on June 25, 1711.

37. In his attempt of a comprehensive study of French privateering, Villiers arrives at slightly lower, yet close enough, estimates, with 422 commission granted in 1688–1697, amounting to a total of 79,485 tons (188 tons per vessel, on average) of armed privateers. At 234 ransoms taken by Malouin corsairs, his count is slightly higher than my estimates in table 5.2. For the 1702–1713 war, Villiers reports merely 236 privateering vessels involved in 425 ventures armed at Saint-Malo, yielding 528 prizes and ransoms taken (Villiers 1991, vol. I, 130–31, 142).

38. *AD-IV* 9B598 ("Etat des Prises qui ont été Conduites et Vendues au Port de St. Malo depuis la déclaration de la guerre avec L'angleterre"). The two auction sales pertain to prizes seized by the Malouin corsairs *Le Puisieulx* and *La Victoire*.

39. Lespagnol (1991, 385–92).

40. In 1702–1713, the Admiralty's tenth still applied to the gross sales value, after the deduction of a few smaller fees. See Bromley (1987, 227–28); Martin-Deidier (1976, 432–37).

41. See, among others, Clark ([1923] 1971, 120–29); Morel (1957, 92–97).

42. Thus, for the Spanish Succession war, Martin-Deidier (1976, 437) concluded that the *guerre de course* at Saint-Malo ran into an overall deficit of 4,286,952 *livres tournois* (*lt.*).

43. For the scale of privateering, see chapter 2, figures 2.6 and 2.7, and chapter 7, figure 7.1.

44. Lespagnol (1991, 388–90).

45. For instance, Martin-Deidier (1976, 437).

46. For two later examples, see "Etat de répartition & de compte général des Parts de Prises de L'équipage du corsaire *La Levrette*" (April 16, 1782), and "Etat des parts de prises payées a l'équipage du Corsaire *la jeune Olimpe*" (March 26, 1783), both in *AD-IV* 9B598. See also Lespagnol (1991, 390–92).

47. For the sources, see the notes to table 5.3.

48. Chardon (1784, vol. I, 383–86).

49. Martin-Deidier (1976, 441–42) has suggested that the Admiralty deemed merely four of the other fifty *course* campaigns launched during this period as even worthy of imposing the Admiralty's tenth. The implication is that forty-six (or 52 percent) of the total eighty-eight campaigns ran into a deficit.

50. More precisely, I use the cost per ton (in *livres tournois*) in each war period, multiplied by the tonnage of the corsair vessel. Cost per ton can be calculated directly whenever a vessel included in Martin-Deidier's (1976) list for the Admiralty's tenth can be matched to the same vessel in the partnership contracts (*actes de société*). When such matches could be made, I used the sum of shares contributed by the *armateurs* and their shareholding associates. When I could not make such a match, I multiplied a vessel's tonnage by the average costs per ton (e.g., 190.66 *lt.* in 1744–1748), as reported in table 5.1.

51. Under the first variant of calculating profits, six ventures led to a deficit. Under the alternative calculation, only three ventures made losses.

52. *AD-IV* 9B598 ("Etat des Prises qui ont été Conduites et Vendues au Port de St. Malo depuis la déclaration de la guerre avec L'angleterre"). I have supplemented this source with the results of three *course* campaigns of the 150-ton *L'Amaranthe* and the 70-ton *La Providence*, all three organized by René-Auguste de Chateaubriand in 1760–1761, and documented in Collas (1949b).

53. Setting aside particularly successful ventures, it is conceivable that *course* campaigns undertaken during later years of the war were less beneficial (see Martin-Deidier 1976, 443–48). Likewise, another document from 1758 reports that some dozen corsairs armed at Saint-Malo did not seize any prizes and were themselves captured by the English (*AD-IV* 9B598, "autres Corsaires armés à St. Malo pris par les anglais Sans avoir fait des prises").

54. For sources, see the notes to table 5.3.

55. The surviving balances for some seven ventures in the last column of table 5.3 also list gross values (in English guineas) for up to six ransoms that each of the privateers took during their campaigns (Martin-Deidier 1976, data appendix). Drawing on McCusker (1992, 6, 11, 312), I applied an exchange rate of 24.15 *lt.* for 1 guinea (gold coin). Even though these ransoms amounted to anything between 1,200 *lt.* and 100,800 *lt.*, including them in the profit estimates was not sufficient to offset the investment costs and to turn negative into positive balances. Adding the ransoms to those campaigns with a positive balance would render them even more profitable.

56. Table 5.3 does not present summary costs and profits, as Lespagnol (1991, 392) has done for the 1688–1697 and 1702–1713 wars. Because I relied on selected samples, I opted for a more restrained presentation.

57. The list of prize ships in *AD-IV* 9B598 ("Etat des Prises qui ont été Conduites et Vendues au Port de St. Malo depuis la déclaration de la guerre avec L'angleterre") documents at least twenty-one enemy vessels that were brought into other French ports in 1756–1757, in particular Brest, Cherbourg, Granville, Le Havre, and Morlaix.

In a similar vein, the particular profits presented for the American Revolutionary War are conservative estimates because they do not include at least another forty-eight prize ships that were captured by Malouin privateers, but whose sales values are unknown. Clearly, just about any solution to replace these missing observations (e.g., using median auction prices for prize ships in the same period) would increase the returns.

58. For the tonnage, ownership, number of prizes, and the amount of the Admiralty's tenth in the cases of the ships *L'Heureux* and *La Vestale*, see Martin-Deidier (1976, data appendix). For estimated costs and benefits, see the notes to table 5.3.

59. *AD-IV* 9B173, f 29r for the registration of the *société* on February 18, 1757, including the list of shareholding associates. For the prizes seized by the *Puisieulx*, see once more *AD-IV* 9B598 ("Etat des Prises qui ont été Conduites et Vendues au Port de St. Malo depuis la déclaration de la guerre avec L'angleterre").

60. See Collas (1949b) for investments, and Martin-Deidier (1976, data appendix) for the results of the venture. For the report of Claude Avice, captain of the *Amaranthe* during this campaign, see *AD-IV* 9B523 (folios not numbered). I treat the activities of Chateaubriand and Grandclos Meslé at length in chapter 7.

6. DYNAMICS OF PARTNERSHIP NETWORKS

1. *AD-IV* 4E5277.
2. Lespagnol (1991, 830).
3. *AD-IV* 9B165–9B176; 9B587; 4E5277–4E5278; 4E5343; 4E5364. Because of its significance for Saint-Malo's involvement in East Asian commerce, I also include the list of shareholding associates who formed the board of directors of the *Compagnie des Indes Orientales de Saint-Malo* (*AD-IV* 1F1914).
4. Multiple dates for the same partnership result primarily from the entrance of additional partners and shareholders into the contract at later dates. In most of the 223 cases (67 percent) when the documents list multiple dates per voyage contract, the earliest and the latest date fall into the same year. Only the months and days differ. Because I distinguish period-specific networks by year, these cases are unproblematic. The difference between the earliest and the latest date in the contract exceeds more than one year (maximum = six years, in three cases) in merely nineteen voyages. On average, the first and last recorded dates are about half a year apart from each other (standard deviation = 1.07).
5. Lespagnol (1991, 132) confirms this observation and suggests that the lack of a fixed ending date points to the long-term character of most undertakings. Partnerships that were explicitly established for a single venture, however, seemed to have been prevalent among long-distance voyages that often took years to complete.
6. To be precise, the local clustering tendency reveals itself once two-mode affiliation networks between ventures and merchants are transformed into one-mode networks wherein merchants are connected to other merchants if they participated as partners in the same ventures.
7. In practice, it is computationally more efficient to use edgelists instead of matrices to transform such large networks and calculate the statistics I report in tables 6.3 through 6.8. The substantive logic behind matrices and edgelists is the same, although matrices may be more intuitive. To visualize an edgelist for a given period, consider five columns. The first column lists individual merchants, and the second column lists individual voyages, thus creating pairs of merchants and the voyages they invested in (i.e., an edge between the two nodes). In column three, we find the type of trade for this voyage. Column four lists the share value the merchant invested in this voyage. Finally, column five lists the day, month, and year of the onset of the investment. The merchant-by-voyage pairs that correspond to empty cells in a matrix are not included in an edgelist. Just as in matrix transformations, merchant-by-voyage pairs are straightforward to transform into edgelists of merchant-by-merchant pairs or voyage-by-voyage pairs.
8. The *actes de société* appear to be less comprehensive as a source for two types of ventures (I thank André Lespagnol for pointing out this potential caveat; personal communication). One concerns

grand-scale privateering operations in the years 1692–1712 that relied on the loan of royal navy ships to private *armateurs*. The cohesion-supporting role of privateering enterprise in the merchant network, however, can be readily identified even without data on this specific subtype of the *course*. If anything, then, the findings of this chapter are conservative: adding information on these otherwise missing ventures would only strengthen the mediating function of the *course*. The other type concerns long-distance ventures directed by Malouin merchants and destined for the East Indies during the free trade period after 1769. Yet, as shown in chapter 3, these resource-intensive undertakings attracted primarily the wealthiest strata of the merchant community and hence were unlikely candidates for a mediating role similar to the *course*.

9. Lespagnol (1991, 140–42).

10. Magon de la Lande was not alone in his engagement in the cloth trade through Cadiz, either as a commissioner or on his own account. Others also speculated on valuable colonial imports such as piastres or cochineal (carmine dye) on the markets of Amsterdam and in particular Marseille (Lespagnol 2016). Such business activities beyond the formation of voyage partnerships are unfortunately not documented in the *actes de sociétés*.

11. Cabantous, Lespagnol, and Péron (2005, 317).

12. The case refers to the 130-ton *Le Don de Dieu* that left Saint-Malo in the summer of 1719 (*AD-IV* 9B168, f 113v).

13. The voyage to "Spanish America, both to the northern coast [i.e., the Caribbean] and to the seas and coasts of the South [i.e., Peru and Chile], and further beyond where the aforementioned associates have decided to send said letter-of-marque ship to sell, deal, stay, and trade its said cargo, while pursuing privateering war against the enemies of the State" (my translation) (*AD-IV* 4E5278, "Société du navire nommé *Le Sage*").

14. The number of ventures with unknown destinations or purposes in table 6.2 appears to be rather large. Although there are cases with missing descriptions across all periods, nearly a third ($n = 151$) belong to the first period alone. The reason is that, with few exceptions, the first set of partnership declarations that were registered by the Admiralty (*AD-IV* 9B165) does not list any destinations or purposes of the voyages. What we do know is that none of these missing cases were privateering ventures because the set is limited to peacetime years (1681–1686). Furthermore, a sizeable portion (41 percent) of merchants who held shares in unknown trades pursued investment careers that closely resembled the careers of merchants who invested in the coastal trade. The available evidence thus suggests that these investments in unknown trades were most likely investments in the coastal trade.

15. For the means comparison between *course* and all other trade ventures, $t = -18.6978$; $p = .0000$.

16. Adopting this cutoff value strategy assumes that the size of shares is equivalent across different trades. It is not immediately obvious, however, that, for example, a one-third share in a privateering venture is directly comparable to a one-third share in a long-distance voyage destined for the Indian port of Pondichéry.

17. The consequence of not considering investment ties with missing share values would be particularly severe for *course* partnerships, where 1,408 (41 percent) of all 3,450 investments lack this particular piece of information. For comparison, there are far fewer cases with missing share values in other major trades: 5 percent of investments in the *cabotage*, 11.5 percent in the Spanish trade, and 9 percent in the Newfoundland fisheries, but 27 percent in the West Indies trade.

18. These counts are lower-bound estimates because they include only those merchants who were manifestly active as business partners within a given period. For example, a merchant may have been listed as one of the partners in a voyage contract in period 1 (1681–1697), but he may not have joined any further partnerships in the subsequent period 2 (1698–1720). In the following period 3 (1721–1740), he was found once again among the investors of another overseas trading venture. In this scenario, our merchant would be included as a node in the networks for periods 1 and 3, but not in the network for period 2. For comparison with each discrete period-network, table 6.3. also considers the

entire duration from 1681 through 1792 as a single cross-section—that is, as a network in which people never die and ties never decay. The results show that the network pattern is robust across all periods—exempting again the visible fragmentation in period 3.

19. Considering the entire time span between 1681 and 1792, merely 108 *armateurs* (1.7 percent of the total) worked without any partners. Most of them were active in coastal shipping (15.7 percent), or their trade activities are unknown (26.9 percent), or the surviving records do in fact refer to the sale of a ship to a new owner (29.6 percent). None of the 108 loners was involved in more than one transaction.

20. The following two paragraphs draw on Hillmann and Aven (2011, 507–10); we used the same empirical strategy to examine social cohesion and fragmentation in similar partnership networks, although set in a very different historical context.

21. Moody and White (2003).

22. Technically, the conditional random set-up starts with the observed two-mode edgelist for each period, one column vector for merchant IDs and one column vector for voyage IDs. The merchant ID column remains unchanged. Voyage IDs are then drawn from their list, using simple random sampling without replacement, and stacked to form a new reordered column vector of voyage IDs. Effectively, merchant IDs and their degree centrality are held constant, and only the specific voyages they are connected with are rearranged. The number of merchant IDs assigned to each voyage ID also remains the same as in the observed network.

23. Because the randomly generated two-mode networks do not contain isolates by definition, the same number of isolates as in the observed network is appended to the one-mode projections of the randomly generated networks.

24. Appendix Table A.1 reports the full results for the comparison between the observed and simulated random networks.

25. See chapter 3.

26. The few exceptions to this observation are one isolated dyad of partners in periods 2, 5, and 6, and an additional clique of four partners in period 5. Otherwise, a single component is indeed the pattern that emerges.

27. This analogy and the panels shown in figure 6.2 may lead us to interpret the subgraphs of privateering merchants and their ties as a highly centralized core within their respective period networks, whereas most other trades were relegated to the periphery. One way to evaluate this idea is to examine how congruent the observed network matrix is with an ideal-typical core–periphery partition. Within such an ideal-typical partition, the density of affiliations in the core reaches its maximum, whereas it tends toward zero in the periphery and is minimal for the ties between core and periphery (for details, see Borgatti and Everett 1999). Because there were never as many *armateurs* and investors in privateering enterprise as in some other trades, they were unlikely to account for the entire network core. Plus, the *guerre de course* was not an option in period 3. These caveats notwithstanding, fitting the ideal core–periphery model to the observed network suggests that *course* ventures were indeed more likely than ventures in other trades to belong to the network core. In period 2, 42.2 percent among the *course* ventures belonged to the core, whereas only 11.9 percent among other trades did so. Likewise, in period 4, we find 30.5 percent versus 10.7 percent; in period 5, 26.9 percent versus 13.8 percent; and in period 6, 40 percent versus 15.2 percent. In period 1, the balance was reversed with only 4.2 percent of *course* ventures, yet 15.9 percent among other trades in the core. The magnitudes of these differences in proportions speak for themselves. For those interested, all differences are statistically significant ($p < .034$, at least). The tendency in these patterns thus seems to be consistent with the idea that the *course* occupied a central structural position. Just the exception in the first period prevents the evidence from being conclusive.

28. Recall that the merchant-by-merchant network we have examined derives from a two-mode affiliation network. Removing the *course* has a similar effect in the alternative voyage-by-voyage network,

and likewise reduces cohesion, albeit at a lower level (see appendix table A.2). Because the patterns are comparable, I focus on the person-level merchant network in this chapter. In addition, the network of person-level relations is the natural unit of analysis when I turn to the unfolding of individual merchant careers in chapter 7.

29. For the full results, see appendix table A.3.

30. Using the percentage of nodes within the main component as a statistic is often not meaningful for comparing observed and randomly generated networks. Large random networks in particular tend to converge into a single component, whereas observed networks often exhibit several disconnected clusters. There is no such concern here because the random selection applies only to ties that are to be removed from the observed network, and not to a wholesale random generation of new networks for comparison.

31. For the full results of this comparison, see appendix table A.4 in. The statistics are not calculated for period 1 because the first set of records (*AD-IV* 9B165), for the years 1681–1686, does not offer sufficient information to identify what particular trade a partnership engaged in. We know only that they were not privateering ventures because no armed conflict occurred during these years. Likewise, period 3 offered no privateering opportunities and hence no results for comparison are shown.

32. The recent studies collected in Padgett and Powell (2012) identify various mechanisms, whereby the overlap of multiple social networks favors innovation in markets and organizations. As I have shown elsewhere, the matter may differ in politics, where multiple network affiliations often separate interest groups to such an extent that they impede coalition-building (Hillmann 2008a).

33. See, among others, Adams (1996, 2005) on the Dutch case; Hancock (1995) on groups of London trader elites; Lespagnol (1991) on the *Messieurs de Saint-Malo*; Martinetti (2013) on merchant elites in La Rochelle; and Sabean, Teuscher, and Mathieu (2007) for a recent collection of studies across early modern Europe.

34. See chapter 2.

35. Particularly useful for this purpose has been the detailed compilation of parish records for Saint-Malo and what is now the Départment d'Ille-et-Vilaine, all painstakingly collected by the abbé Paris-Jallobert (2000–2004, 2004), and now available in digital format.

36. In my earlier work on economic elites in a different historical setting, the same method of identifying kinship networks has proven effective for an even larger set of individual observations; see Hillmann and Aven (2011).

37. For an exemplary study of the role of spiritual kinship in cementing business relationships among merchant entrepreneurs in late medieval and early modern Europe, see Alfani and Gourdon (2012).

38. Catholicism was so dominant in Saint-Malo that heterogeneity in religious affiliation was virtually absent and hence was unlikely to have influenced the selection into partnerships or shifts in network pattern over time. See chapter 3, and Lespagnol (1991, 94–100).

39. One should bear in mind, however, that these numbers reflect average levels of kin homophily. Some traders could and did have higher percentages of kin among their sharepartners, for instance, 50 percent and more in the ninety-fifth percentile, in line with the salience of kinship bonds among elite families, as discussed in chapter 3.

40. Note, however, that, for the first two measures, a value of one does not necessarily imply that all partners belonged to one single family—although empirically, this is the outcome we observe. Likewise, the measures are size dependent in the sense that the logically possible outcomes in between the minimum and maximum are limited for smaller partnerships. For example, with just three partners fitting out a voyage, there are just three possible results for the measure of homophily in dyads (0; 0.3; 1).

41. *AD-IV* 9B175, ff 7v, 25r, 28r, 40v–41r, 76r. Long-distance voyages were usually expedited from the port of Lorient on the southern coast of Brittany. As a note of caution, such capital-intensive enterprises probably attracted hidden outside investors who, by their very nature, may not always be revealed in the partnership contracts.

42. *AD-IV* 9B175, ff 16r, 23r-23v, 25r, 31r-31v, 36r, 43r.

43. *AD-IV* 9B176, f 61r.

44. Paris-Jallobert (2000–2004, 2004).

45. The dispersion of merchants with unknown places of residence is found within each of the six period-specific networks: the average number of ties per person ranged between 2.34 and 5.6 (standard deviation between 2.81 and 6.76); the number of separate components ranged from 36 to 108; and the percentage of unreachable pairs ranged from 59.9 percent to 97.8 percent.

46. Cheney (2010, 170–73); Horn (2015, 110–11).

47. For the Lyon connection, see, for example, *AD-IV* 9B175, f 38r.

48. The finding likewise confirms a fundamental tenet of classical structural sociology (Blau 1977), namely, that density and closeness in physical space heighten opportunities for social interactions and interdependencies between people.

49. The measure was originally proposed by Gould and Fernandez (1989) to study brokerage in networks of resource flows and hence focused on directed ties. Because affiliation networks such as the Malouin partnerships contain undirected ties only, the distinction between what they call gatekeeper and representative roles does not apply. Table 6.8 reflects the fact that the two roles are indistinguishable in the present case. The original measure also considers the role of coordinators who broker between members of their own group. My interest is much less in the potential of *course* ventures to broker among other *course* ventures, but rather in their ability to bridge between ventures operating in all kinds of trades. Because the relevance of the coordinator role is marginal for my argument, I do not consider it here.

50. The labels of *itinerant*, *liaison*, and *gatekeeper* roles do not carry any inherent meaning in the historical setting at hand. I merely retain the labels that Gould and Fernandez (1989) established in their original article for the sake of consistency.

51. Table 6.8 reports brokerage findings for the organizational network encompassing the full 1681–1792 period. The pattern of results for the period-specific networks is nearly identical: in all three roles, *course* ventures had significantly more brokerage opportunities than ventures in fishing or any other trades. The only exceptions are slightly stronger itinerant and liaison roles on the part of fishing partnerships in period 1, and on the part of other trade partnerships in period 2.

52. Comparing proportions of the *course* and other trades among the highest-scoring brokerage positions (ninetieth percentile) differs only marginally from the means comparison. *Course* ventures still represented the largest proportion of itinerant brokers (23.7 percent). For liaison brokers, *course* ventures (24.3 percent) held the largest proportion, along with the Newfoundland fishing trade. Finally, for gatekeeping brokers, the *course* represented the second-largest proportion (31.1 percent).

7. THE RISE OF *NEW MEN*

1. Roche (1998, 154–56).

2. Lespagnol (1991, 733–89).

3. Roche (1998, 412).

4. In all fairness, note that the emergence of this new generation in the second half of the eighteenth century is beyond the temporal scope of Lespagnol's study, which is primarily concerned with the fate of the Malouin elite under the reign of Louis XIV.

5. See Crouzet (2008) for a recent summary treatment of the "economic war" between France and Britain in the eighteenth century. Findlay and O'Rourke (2007, 247–62) offer a succinct overview of the so-called Second Hundred Years' War between Britain and France, and how it related to commercial expansion.

6. On the historical origins of the *Asiento* monopoly and its licensing system, see Daget (1990, 44–53).

7. This is the interpretation that Brière (1983) has suggested in his work on the Newfoundland fisheries in the early eighteenth century. For the following paragraph, see Pritchard's balanced discussion (2004, 400–401).

8. I borrow the term "Elusive Empire" from Pritchard (2004, chap. 9).

9. See Butel (1974, chap. 2) for a study of the plantation economy and sugar trade of the French Antilles through the lens of Bordeaux—one of the key ports in this trade. For systematic evidence on the prosperity of French foreign trade during the eighteenth century see in particular Daudin (2005, chaps. 4–5).

10. On war and sugar trade in the West Indies, see Richard Pares's (1936) classic study, and Crouzet (2008, chap. 3) for a recent assessment. On Anglo-French tensions in the Ohio River region, see Baugh (2011, 46–66).

11. On the North American conflict, see Anderson (2000).

12. Baugh (2011) portrays all the events of the Seven Years' War on a detailed and comprehensive canvas. Manning (1996, especially chap. 10) shows how French policy in India turned from pure trading interests toward warfare—not primarily because it was driven by an Anglo-French commercial rivalry, but rather as a consequence of becoming embedded in local Indian power politics.

13. Crouzet (2008, 341–66).

14. Rodger (2005) has set the gold standard for understanding Britain's naval eminence in the long eighteenth century. Brewer (1988) provides an influential account of the British fiscal-military state. The collection of studies in Bonney (1999) places it in a comparative setting of early modern European states.

15. For an overview of French privateering enterprise under Louis XV, see Villiers (1991, vol. I, 315–436).

16. Pritchard (1987, 80–81).

17. Magon de la Blinaye's correspondence is cited by Henri Sée in his classic study of *Le commerce maritime de la Bretagne* ([1925] 2001, 90–91). The translation of the quote is mine.

18. Villiers (1991, vol. II, 654–71) examines the *guerre de course* organized by French metropolitan ports during the American Revolutionary War.

19. See Lespagnol (1991, 400–401).

20. Boulle (1981, 106–107).

21. Lespagnol (1979, 431–32).

22. Lespagnol (1982, 336–44; 1991, 830–31).

23. That merchants from Saint-Malo, and not another port city, took over the affairs of the East Indies Company is also not surprising if one considers the important role the Malouins played in supplying personnel for the French commerce with Asia throughout much of the eighteenth century. Haudrère's estimates suggest that the largest share (41 percent) of naval officers on ships bound for the east came from Brittany, and Saint-Malo alone accounted for 38.9 percent of all 763 Breton officers. Likewise, between 1725 and 1768, some 3,247 (25 percent) of the 12,894 junior officers and sailors were based in Saint-Malo, a contingent second only to Port-Louis (Haudrère 2005, vol. II, 897, 903). Manning (1996, 65–67) echoes the dominance of the Bretons as mariners in East Indian shipping, yet also notes how company representatives resented the directorate of the Malouin merchants, with all their "greed, arrogance and unhelpfulness."

24. On the fate of the French Indies Company under Law's *Système* and after its dismantlement, see Haudrère (2005, vol. I, 33–114).

25. On the sieur de Maupertius, see Haudrère (2005, vol. II, 1060); Lespagnol (2013b).

26. For the preceding paragraph, see Haudrère (2005, vol. I, 115–53).

27. Schaeper (1983, 53–56); Tarade (1972, vol. I, 369–70). The irony is that many of the deputies held prominent positions in the very companies they criticized so vehemently, which only goes to show that their views were a far cry from our present-day understanding of laissez-faire economic policies.

Privilege, it seems, was welcomed when it served one's own interests, but condemned whenever it benefited one's competitors. For instance, La Motte-Gaillard's request that Saint-Malo should be granted the status of a free port as well as access to direct trade with the West Indies earned little support from its rival ports that held such exclusive trading rights. See Horn (2015, 111); Schaeper (1983, 58, 93–95).

28. Le Bouëdec (1997, 111–18).

29. Tarade (1972, vol. I, 56–59); Terjanian (2013, chap. 4).

30. Cabantous, Lespagnol, and Péron (2005, 242). On the Franco-British contest in India, from its beginnings in the 1740s to Governor Dupleix's expansionist politics and eventually French defeat in 1763, see Baugh (2011, 66–71, 282–97, 462–83).

31. Haudrère (2005, vol. II, chap. 10).

32. Pierre-Henri Boulle (1981) has even argued that private enterprise, especially of the Atlantic port cities, was the real engine of growth in French colonial commerce throughout the eighteenth century. But according to Boulle, it came at the price of "plunder from within," whereby the same merchant groups who benefited most from the workings of the company were gradually encroaching upon its privileges.

33. For the English case, see in particular Erikson (2014). On the French country trade in Asia, see Manning (1996, chap. 4). For a recent comparative discussion of the relation between chartered companies and private trade, see Berg et al. (2015).

34. The same rising pattern obtains if we consider the distribution of tonnages of merchantmen destined for the Indian Ocean. Indeed, something may be said in favor of the free trade advocates: the available evidence tells us that under its monopoly regime, it took the *Compagnie des Indes* as many as forty-two years (1730–1771) to arm 220 vessels to India and 70 vessels to China, whereas private traders needed just seventeen years (1769–1785) to dispatch 135 vessels to India and another 45 vessels to China. See Meyer (1982, 300).

35. I use the French term *la traite des Noirs* interchangeably with its commonly employed English equivalent, the slave trade. McWatters (2008, 179), points to an ongoing discussion in the French scholarly literature where *traite des Noirs* seems the preferred term because it refers to captured Africans, and not necessary to humans who were slaves all along.

36. For general histories of the transatlantic slave trade, see Daget (1990), Eltis (2000), and Klein (2010, especially chap. 4, on the European organization of the trade). The slave trade in the Indian Ocean has received far less attention—but see Allen (2015) for a recent assessment. Pétré-Grenouilleau (2004) examines the global scale of the market for enslaved Africans, beyond the usual focus on European merchants.

37. All estimates are based on the *Trans-Atlantic Slave Trade Database* (Eltis 2016). To put these numbers in context, I consider a historical period (1681–1790) as close as possible to the one used in chapter 6.

38. All estimates of slave-trading expeditions are drawn from the *Trans-Atlantic Slave Trade Database* (Eltis 2016) and refer to the number of vessels registered in British, French, Portuguese, and Dutch ports.

39. For overviews and general histories dedicated to the French slave trade, see Stein's (1979) earlier monograph, and more recently, Geggus (2001) and Régent (2007).

40. Pritchard (2004, 123–39, 162–86).

41. On the role of indentured servants in the French Caribbean, see Huetz de Lemps (1991).

42. On plantation economies and their consequences for labor demand, see Allen (2015, chap. 1); Pétré-Grénouilleau (2004, 44–67); and Régent (2007, chap. 2).

43. Pétré-Grénouilleau (2004, 119–143) portrays the acquisition and transport of enslaved Africans to the colonies. As the estimates in table 7.2 illustrate, the import of slaves into the French colonies was not provided exclusively by French traders. Beyond provision by other national carriers, an illicit

trade thrived as well. Banks (2005), for example, considers slave smuggling in the French West Indies, with a focus on Martinique.

44.   Allen (2008, 2015); Roman (2001, 221–26); Stein (1979, chap. 9). The estimated 63,700 slaves carried off from South-East Africa and Indian Ocean islands made up little more than 1 percent of all slave embarkations from Africa during the 1681–1790 period. Estimates are based on the *Trans-Atlantic Slave Trade Database* (Eltis 2016).

45.   On the centrality of the slave trade in Nantes, see Pétré-Grenouilleau (1996); on the activities of Le Havre's merchantry, see Delobette (2005); on the merchant *armateurs* of La Rochelle, see Martinetti (2013); and for the case of Bordeaux, see Butel (1974).

46.   Tuloup (1976, chap. 31); Zmuda (2004, 17).

47.   That the true purpose of these voyages was so rarely expressed is remarkable because the Malouin merchants were acutely aware of foreign competition in the slave trade. Permitting foreign traders to sell slaves in the French Antilles, they feared, would undermine national interest in this commerce. Hence, if such competition truly worried them, then being open about the business certainly would have helped their cause. See, for example, the correspondence of Meslé de Grandclos with his business partners in Nantes, April 22, 1786 (cited in Roman 2001, 55).

48.   *AD-IV* 4E5278, "société du navire *le Don de dieu* a Monsieur Des Vaux," May 1719.

49.   *AD-IV* 4E5278, "Société du Navire, 200 tx, *Sainte Famille*, armateur Mr. De La Villejosselin," 1721.

50.   *AD-IV* 4E5278, "acte De société du navire *L'hirondelle*," 1730.

51.   *AD-IV* 9B175, f 61v.

52.   *AD-IV* 9B176, ff 86v-87r. See also Roman (2001, 227).

53.   This is not the place to enter a detailed discussion of the profitability of the French slave trade. Much like the *course*, it apparently was a seafaring lottery, with high-risk investments and high returns for some, and significant losses for others. For recent studies based on systematic evidence, see Daudin (2004), McWatters (2008), and McWatters and Lemarchand (2012); and, for Saint-Malo slave traders, in particular, see Roman (2001, chap. 8); Zmuda (2004, chaps. 12–13).

54.   *AD-IV* 9B175, ff 55r, 61v.

55.   Lespagnol (1991, 817, 820–21, 830); *AD-IV* 4E5277.

56.   Daudin (2005, 305, 321).

57.   *AD-IV* 4E5277; 4E5278; 9B167–9B176; 9B2587.

58.   Lespagnol (1984, 136); Roman (2001, 41–43, 209–12); Zmuda (2004, chap. 3).

59.   I draw on the *armateurs* and slave traders listed by Roman (2001, 58–59) to identify the second generation of the *Messieurs de Saint-Malo*. Compared with Roman's list, my estimates of the number of their investments are more conservative because they consider only those ventures that are included in the partnership contracts (*actes de société*).

60.   Daudin (2004, 146).

61.   Anecdotal evidence suggests that just as much as *armateurs* and their partners switched from one trade to another, so were their ships repurposed: in 1765, the business partners Alain Le Breton, sieur de Blessin, and Guy Jean Sébire, sieur des Saudrais, bought the 120-ton *Le Sphinx* from the Comte de Bougainville, France's famous circumnavigator. Under Bougainville's command, the *Sphinx* was part of the expedition to establish a French colony on the Îles Malouines, known today as the Falklands or Islas Malvinas. The two Malouin *armateurs* Le Breton and Sébire, however, showed less interest in exploration, renamed the ship *Le Brocateur*, and turned it into a slaver for a voyage to the coast of Guinea (*AD-IV* 9B174, ff 23r-24v). Besides the reminder of the historical link between the remote South Atlantic islands and Saint-Malo, we may read this anecdote as an illustration of the tangible connections that existed between various trades, in this case, between expeditions to the South Sea and the African slave trade.

62.   Cabantous et al. (2005, 317); Lespagnol (1991, 140–42); Roman (2001, 110–12, 209–12).

63.   Roman (2001, 205) arrives at a similar conclusion, based on the 1790 *capitation*.

64. Recall that each tax quota in the *capitation* was based on a classification of taxpayers into twenty-two hierarchical classes according to their station in Old Regime society. See Bluche and Solnon (1983); Guery (1986).

65. The average tax quota in 1763 was 12.76 *livres tournois* (*lt.*) (median = 2 *lt.*; top ten percentile = 30 *lt.*; top five percentile = 60 *lt.*; *n* = 3,738 listed taxpayers). In 1789, the average tax quota was 23.17 *lt.* (median = 3 *lt.*; top ten percentile = 50 *lt.*; top five percentile = 107 *lt.*; *n* = 3,556 listed taxpayers).

66. Similar settings where merchant elites shaped the course of municipal politics include Bordeaux (Butel 1974, 328ff) and La Rochelle (Martinetti 2013, 153ff), among others. See Guignet (1996) for a short overview, and Saupin (1996) for one of the most comprehensive studies of municipal governance under the Ancien Régime, focusing on Nantes. Mousnier (1979, 563–605) compares the governance of *bourgeois* towns, such as Lyon, Marseilles, Toulouse, Bordeaux, and presumably Saint-Malo, to that of *seigneurial* towns and *communes*. Temple (1973) traces how oligarchy in town governance arose from local electoral systems that favored the interests of the wealth-holding bourgeoisie rather than from the creation of venal municipal offices. Follain's (2008) study likewise provides in-depth insights into communal governance under the Ancien Régime (especially 218–312 on the role of assemblies and officeholding in French municipalities). The recent volume edited by Saupin (2010) offers further details on the political institutions of town governance along the French Atlantic seaboard.

67. Register of the assembly of the city council of Saint-Malo on December 27, 1764; December 31, 1764; and January 9, 1765 (*AD-IV* C432); on May 6, 1766, and October 15, 1767 (*AD-IV* C438); list of the municipal officers of the community of Saint-Malo in 1764 (*AD-IV* 1F1948); Sée and Lesort (1911, 64). On the position of aldermen among the *notables* in municipal government and administration, see Mousnier (1979, 598–600). Beik (2009, 106, 294–300) notes that the role of *échevins* was indeed prestigious but that any influence was derived primarily from the officeholders' reputation among their peers in the community—an assessment that certainly befits the three named Malouin *échevins*.

68. For Sébire des Saudrais, see Sée and Lesort (1911, 9). For Marion (supposedly Louis Marie Marion de la Brillantais), see Sée and Lesort (1911, 73). For le Bonhomme de la Fontaine, see Sée and Lesort (1911, 13–14).

69. For Marion de la Brillantais and Fichet des Jardins, see Sée and Lesort (1911, 12); for Blaize de la Maisonneuve, see Sée and Lesort (1911, 9–10).

70. Paris-Jallobert (2004, 3837); Sée and Lesort (1911, 70, 87).

71. Sée and Lesort (1911, 9–10).

72. Beik (2009, 145–46); Sée and Lesort (1911, 9). For a recent discussion of the *secrétaires du roi*, see Schapira (2004).

73. I use both variants of his name—Grandclos Meslé or Meslé de Grandclos—interchangeably. He apparently preferred the first, as he used to sign documents as Grandclos Meslé (e.g., see *AD-IV* 9B173, f 46r, or 9B174, f 14r).

74. François-René de Chateaubriand recounts his ancestry in his autobiography ([1849–1856] 1957, vol. I, book I, 7–11; vol. II, 945).

75. Nassiet (2012, 333) shows the family tree of the Guérande lineage. For a detailed biography of René-Auguste de Chateaubriand, see Collas (1949a).

76. All quotes from Chateaubriand ([1849–1856] 1957, vol. I, book I, 12–15). See also Collas (1949a, 13–16); Nassiet (2012, 330). On inheritance rules, see also Giesey (1977). For a comprehensive study of relative impoverishment among the lesser nobility in early modern Brittany, see Nassiet (2012).

77. For both quotes, Coyer (1756, 150); see also Meyer (1985, vol. II, 1041–46). Coyer's ideas were of course not without critics. Among more recent assessments of the contemporary debate surrounding the *noblesse commerçante*, see Clark (2007, 135–44, 155–56); Kessler (2004); Shovlin (2000); Smith (2000).

78. Keber (2002, 17, 132–38); Roche (1998, 412–19).

79. Keber (2002, 2–3); Nassiet (2012, 190–98, 326–29, 441).

80. Collas (1949a, 19–45); Nassiet (2012, 341–47, 411); Roman (2001, 66–67, 277).

81. Roman (2001, 63–66).

82. Keber (2002, 133). Pineau-Defois (2010) observes a similar upward mobility of merchant traders into the nobility in Nantes at the eve of the French Revolution. Roche (1998, 412) notes that most of the three hundred Frenchmen ennobled during the eighteenth century were drawn from the merchantry or the navy.

83. Readers familiar with the structural analysis of labor markets in sociology will recognize that I am referring to the idea of vacancy chains of job mobility within organizations (White 1970).

84. Lespagnol (1991, 400–401).

85. *AD-IV* 9B173, f 46r.

86. Roman (2001, 65–66); *AD-IV* 9B173–176.

87. *AD-IV* 9B173 f 35r, f 42v, f 50r, ff 58v-59r, 9B174 f 9r, 9B175 ff 48v-49r; Collas (1949a, 47–67); Roman (2001, 277–78).

88. Chateaubriand had another priority as well. In 1761, he used the fortune he made in his early privateering enterprises to purchase, for 300,000 *lt.*, the Château de Combourg and its surrounding county to the southeast of Saint-Malo (Collas 1949a, 69–85; Roman 2001, 197). Given the portrait the son sketched of his father in the *Mémoires d'Outre-Tombe*, we may imagine just how much it must have meant for René-Auguste, now known as the chevalier comte de Combourg, to finally have redeemed his name and noble heritage: "Mon père y rêva son nom rétabli, la fortune de sa maison renouvelée" (Chateaubriand ([1849–1856] 1957, vol. I, book III, chap. 16). The purchase underlines the profound conservatism of the traders of noble descent, and hence how wedded they were to the importance of holding landed property. For merchants of lesser standing, profits from commerce may have paved the way to ennoblement; for nobles in trade, they were a means to reaffirm their aristocratic status in Old Regime society (Keber 2002, 137; Roche 1998, 412–13).

89. *AD-IV* 9B173–176; Collas (1949a, 87–108); Roman (2001, 76).

90. Bromley (1987, 289–90).

91. Although talent and skill imply intention, it is not strictly necessary for social cohesion to emerge in this manner among the merchant partners. For the idea of the *bricoleur*, see Lévi-Strauss (2008, 576–83).

92. Similar to my interest in the link between personal partnership networks and overall cohesion in the merchant community, a well-established research tradition in social network analysis has shown how different macrostructural patterns of communities and even entire cities may arise from variation in transitivity within local social relationships. See, for example, Baldassarri and Diani (2007); Friedkin (1998); Johnsen (1985); Martin (2009).

93. It just so happened that our two exemplary *armateurs* connected as well, when Chateaubriand became an investor of 40,000 *lt.* in the expedition to China that Grandclos Meslé undertook in 1783 (Roman 2001, 201).

94. Herein lies the difference to the vacancy chain models of mobility I alluded to earlier: in this historical setting, enchainment meant the union of past and present relationships, whereas vacancy chains usually are assumed to operate through a Markov process such that the history of one's ties is not salient for one's move to another position, nor is the history of that new position (Chase 1991, 138).

95. *AD-IV* 9B165–9B176; 9B587; 4E5277–4E5278; 4E5343; 4E5364; 1F1914.

96. Because all key measures in table 7.5 and table 7.6 directly capture the sequential ordering of activities and network ties among individual merchants over time, the robustness of the findings to potential period effects is of limited concern. I later consider potential differences across cohorts of traders.

97. Even someone who never stepped outside the world of privateering still could have held a broker position in the merchant network. From a purely structural point of view, ties to at least two ventures, no matter in what kind of commerce, were the only prerequisites for a role as a potential

mediator between one's partners. The rather low average number of partnerships they engaged in, however, suggests that they were not as well positioned as brokers as others who opted for a mixed investment strategy. Note also that comparisons of mean career lengths, both in terms of years and the number of ventures, reveal significant differences among all four patterns of career trajectories listed in table 7.5 ($p < .0000$; one-tailed t-tests).

98. Granted, just because a career pattern happened to be prevalent it does not necessarily mean that it was particularly uniform in its composition. That is exactly what we find in this setting, however: the most commonly observed sequence among those who never held an interest in the *course* consisted of two successive fishing voyages (*pêche*) to Newfoundland. The second-most-common pattern did not add much variety either, as it consisted of three, instead of two, successive fishing voyages.

99. One may suspect that variation in the career patterns of the three other groups, in columns (1), (3), and (4) in table 7.5, is similarly driven by differences in length alone. However, even the most active merchants—who combined *course* and regular trades—participated only in fourteen (seventy-fifth percentile) and, in rare cases, up to thirty-nine (ninety-fifth percentile) successive partnerships. Consequently, if variation across patterns would come entirely from variation in sequence length, then we would find less than forty different sequence patterns. This result also means that length alone cannot account for the 249 (column 3) and 313 (column 4) different patterns we observe in the case of merchants who joined both privateering and regular trade partnerships. The contrast is even more glaring in the group of those who invested solely in regular trades and never in the course (column 1): even their most active traders (in the ninety-fifth percentile) joined only nine successive partnerships. Here as well, length alone cannot possibly account for the 469 different sequence patterns.

100. This comparison does not apply to privateering partners who never contributed to a joint venture in any of the regular trades.

101. Recall that the available evidence from the Admiralty records allows me to distinguish fourteen different branches of maritime commerce, including privateering. Consequently, the numerator of the spread ratio is limited to a maximum value of fourteen as well. The implication is that, all else being equal, merchants with longer careers (more partnerships) will score lower than their peers with shorter careers (fewer partnerships). If anything, then, my finding that merchants who combined privateering and regular trades scored higher is in fact conservative because they also tended to have substantially longer careers than investors in regular trades alone (see table 7.5).

102. We may wonder to what extent results for this measure of diversity are determined by concurrent investments. It was certainly possible that two or more of one's partnership contracts were registered on the same date, which matters for an accurate sequential ordering of investments in the dataset. Hence, whenever they belonged to different branches of commerce, a separate category would be necessary to encode such concurrent partnerships. Many concurrencies would therefore inflate the diversity score for no substantive reason, and solely based on a coding decision. The issue, however, is far less severe than one might expect: just 13 percent ($n = 290$) of all 2,145 serial investors in my dataset had more than one partnership registered on the same date. Even more negligible are the thirty-four merchants—a mere 1.6 percent of all serial investors—who had more than two partnerships registered on the same date.

103. Here as well, means comparisons for the diversity measures between the groups of merchants in table 7.5 yield significant differences ($p < .0000$; one-tailed t-tests).

104. It is conceivable that much of the diversity that characterizes the 718 cases in the two bottom panels in figure 7.7 stems primarily from long careers with a uniform pattern where the same two activities took turns, such as {*course*} → {*pêche*} → {*course*} → {*pêche*} → {*course*}, and so forth (see also the last example in figure 7.6). Little empirical evidence, however, supports this scenario: none of the sequences that were shared by at least two merchants exhibited such a prolonged repetitive pattern. The only two sequence patterns that came even close were {*pêche*} → {*pêche*} → {*course*} → {*pêche*} and {coastal trade} → {*course*} → {coastal trade}, each shared by merely two merchants.

105.   Diversity in one's portfolio was certainly helpful, but not strictly necessary, for successful mediation and, hence, for an effective contribution to overall cohesion. Being well-positioned as a broker within the web of affiliations of a single trade might have worked just as well. Therefore, the coupling of substantive diversity in investments with favorable structural positioning is important.

106.   See chapter 6, table 6.2.

107.   Another way to put this is to say that power and influence accrue to those who are linked to powerful and influential others. For a classic statement of this idea, see Bonacich (1987). I use a related iterative algorithm of eigenvector centrality, based on Kleinberg (1999) and implemented in PAJEK 4.10 (Mrvar and Batagelji 2016), to assess hubness within the one-mode merchant-by-merchant projection of the two-mode merchant-by-venture affiliation network.

108.   Bromley (1987, 289).

109.   Note that such closure and enchainment mechanisms point to the inherently processual nature of mediation. When brokers succeed with building bridges to link otherwise separate parties, they eventually render their own roles obsolete.

110.   These findings are not limited to the generation of traders around Grandclos Meslé and Chateaubriand. They remain robust when comparing the average number and density of transitive ties across successive cohorts of merchant traders. Based on the date of the first partnership they participated in, I assign merchants to one of six cohorts that match the period networks in chapter 6 (1681–1697, 1698–1720, 1721–1740, 1741–1755, 1756–1777, and 1778–1792). One exception is the third cohort because it falls into a period of peacetime, and thus *course* ventures were not legally available as a first investment.

111.   For the means comparison between these trajectories, $t = -16.5172$ with $p < .0000$ (one-tailed).

8. THE COMING OF THE REVOLUTION

1.   See chapter 2.

2.   As evident in Danycan's tax returns for 1701 (see chapter 3).

3.   See, for example, *AD-IV* 9B167, ff 121v-125r. The list of partners in this venture reads like an honor roll of the Malouin merchant patriciate around 1700, including Pierre Grout, sieur de la Villejacquin; Luc Lefer, sieur du Val; Etienne Picot, sieur de Presmenil; Guillaume Moreau, sieur de la Primerais; Pierre de la Haye, sieur de Plouër; Macé Lefer, sieur de La Lande; Jeanne Martin, Dlle du Valéon; François Lefer, sieur de Beauvais; Nicolas Geraldin; Pierre Jolif, sieur du Clos; René Hérisson, sieur des Chesnais; Françoise Cheville, Dlle du Fougeray; Pierre François Nouail, sieur du Fougeray; François Lefer, sieur du Pin; Jean Gaubert; and Eon, sieur de la Baronnie.

4.   Both Noël Danycan's and Nicolas Magon's places of residence are documented in AM-SM CC41, f 94v. Their involvement in the South Sea project is examined at length by Dahlgren (1909).

5.   *AD-IV* 4E5277, partnership contracts for the corsair vessels *Le François Auguste* and *Le Comte de Toulouse*.

6.   *AD-IV* 1F1914, and chapter 2.

7.   See chapters 3 and 7.

8.   Bromley (1987, 290).

9.   Savary (1675).

10.   See Lespagnol (1991). Hence, here we find an early modern instance of the formation of a professional identity, a phenomenon that we, as social scientists, usually associate with distinctly modern occupations, such as career bankers (Stovel and Savage 2005; Stovel, Savage, and Bearman 1996) or psychiatrists (Abbott 1988).

11.   See chapter 7.

12. See figure 7.5.

13. See Lespagnol (1989b, 33–34).

14. How deeply ingrained this sense had become among the Malouins is apparent in Louis Blaize de Maisonneuve's refusal of the king's offer of ennoblement: he declared that one already should be considered noble by virtue of being a *bourgeois* of Saint-Malo (Sée and Lesort 2011, 9). One of the *new men*, Blaize de Maisonneuve's statement clearly carried political undertones and a distinct understanding of what "noble" meant. It is no surprise that he would later emerge as a leading figure of the patriotic cause during the revolutionary years (Lespagnol 1989b).

15. Brucker (1962, 20–29, 40–45).

16. Becker (1962); Brucker (1962, 87–90, 116–32, 159–72).

17. Brucker (1962, 40), and in particular Becker's entire 1962 article.

18. Padgett and Ansell (1993, 1284–85).

19. For a brilliant study of Henry VII's *new men*, see Gunn (2016).

20. This paragraph draws directly on my earlier work on elite mobilization before the English Civil War (Hillmann 2008a). The definitive study of the new merchants and their revolutionary role has been written by Brenner (1993).

21. Dupuy (1984, 215–25); Herpin (1931, 11–187). Herpin's book remains the classic narrative history of Saint-Malo under the French Revolution.

22. Collas (1949a, 259).

23. Roman (2001, 244–48).

24. Lespagnol (1989b, 29); Pineau-Defois (2010).

25. Herpin (1931, 272–73).

26. Roman (2001, 248–49); Herpin (1931, 184). Meslé de Grandclos was not sent to the guillotine in July 1794, as Herpin notes. On the émigrés of Saint-Malo, see Audran (2006), and the listing in Herpin (1931, 387–88).

27. See chapter 7.

28. *AD-IV* C 4098, f 104r.

29. Furet (1992, 55–60).

30. Sée and Lesort (1911, 13).

31. Sée and Lesort (1911, 14); Herpin (1931, 24).

32. Paris-Jallobert (2004, 3485).

33. Lespagnol (1989b, 32–33).

34. See chapter 2.

35. Lespagnol (1989b, 35–37).

36. As defined in Lespagnol (1989b, 1991). The four names are Alain Charles Marie Magon de Coëtizac, Alain Le Breton de Blessin, Jean-Baptiste Porée du Breil, and Pierre-Jacques Le Breton de la Vieuville.

37. These calculations are based on all *course* partnerships documented in *AD-IV* 4Fg67, 9B173, and 9B175.

38. Note, however, that three of the four *armateurs* held structurally central positions, and thus they contributed their fair share to maintaining the network. Their hubness scores are all well above the average (.007; standard deviation = .023) of all partners in the *course*: Magon de Coëtizac (.034), Le Breton de Blessin (.051), and Porée du Breil (.023).

39. See also Lespagnol (2018).

40. Le Guellaff (1999, 131–81).

41. As I have shown for the period between the War of the Spanish Succession and the War of the Austrian Succession, this role could not always be filled successfully, and its absence resulted in network fragmentation (see chapter 6).

42. Audran (2005); Bonnel (1961); Crowhurst (1989); Le Guellaff (1999).

43. Robidou ([1919] 1998, 189).

BIBLIOGRAPHY

MANUSCRIPT SOURCES

Archives départementales d'Ille-et-Vilaine à Rennes (AD-IV):

Sous-Série 9B—Fonds de l' Amirauté de Saint-Malo

9B165–176	Registre des contrats de vente et de société pour les navires, 1681–1792. [9B168 continues in 9B587].
9B380–389	Enregistrement des congés et commissions de navires, 1686–1693, 1721–1731.
9B408	Enregistrement des commissions de corsaires, 1709–1713.
9B435, (1)–(5)	Enregistrement des commissions de corsaires, 1702–1782.
9B515–524	Enregistrement des rapports des capitaines de corsaires, 1702–1783.
9B565	Enregistrement des billets de rançon, 1706–1710.
9B583–585, 587	Enregistrement des jugements du Conseil des prises, 1695–1706; 1709–1714.
9B591	Déclarations de bonnes prises, 1756–1762.
9B597	Registres des parts de prises, 1786-An III.
9B598	Etats des parts de prises de divers bâtiments, 1746–1783. Etats des prises amenées et vendues à Saint-Malo, 1756–1758.
9B599–640	Dossiers de prises, 1688–1782.
9B679–680	Code des prises.

Série C—Fonds de l'Intendance et des Etats de Bretagne

C432, 436, 438, 439, 804	Villes et communautés: Saint-Malo.
C1583	Députés de Saint-Malo au Bureau de Commerce.
C4070	Capitation—Rôles—Diocèse de Saint-Malo, 1740.

C4086   Capitation—Rôles—Diocèse de Saint-Malo, 1763.

C4098   Capitation—Rôles—Diocèse de Saint-Malo, 1789.

C4259   Capitation de la noblesse—Rôles—Diocèse de Saint-Malo, 1734,
                         1735, 1739, and 1740.

C4262   Capitation de la noblesse—Rôles—Diocèse de Saint-Malo, 1766,
                         1767, and 1788, 1789.

                         Sous-Série 2E—Fonds de familles
2Ed11   Fond Danycan: Livre de bord du *Phelypeaux*, 1706–1709.

                         Sous-Série 4E—Fonds notariaux
4E5277–5278   Première Etude de notaires royaux à Saint-Malo: Notaire Charles
                         Pitot: actes de société, 1702–1734.

4E5343   Deuxième Etude de notaires royaux à Saint-Malo: Notaire Michel
                         Le Roy: actes de société, 1709–1712.

4E5364   Deuxième Etude de notaires royaux à Saint-Malo: Notaire Pierre
                         François Morel: actes de société, 1721; 1723.

                         Sous-Série 1F—Collections et grands fonds
1F1914   Fonds Magon de La Balue: Journal comptable de la Compagnie
                         des Indes Orientales de Saint-Malo.

1F1930, 1948   Fonds Léon Vignols.

                         Sous-Série 4F—Marine et Colonies
4F g62–63, 67   Corsaires malouins: pièces diverses.

4F g124   Liquidation des prises faites par Duguay-Trouin, 1709.

Archives municipales de Saint-Malo (AM-SM):

Série CC41   Rôle de répartition de la capitation de 1701.

PUBLISHED SOURCES

Abbott, Andrew. 1988. *The System of Professions: An Essay on the Division of Expert Labor.* Chicago: University of Chicago Press.

Acemoglu, Daron, Simon Johnson, and James Robinson. 2005. "The Rise of Europe: Atlantic Trade, Institutional Change, and Economic Growth." *American Economic Review* 95(3): 546–79.

Adams, Julia. 1996. "Principals and Agents, Colonialists and Company Men: The Decay of Colonial Control in the Dutch East Indies." *American Sociological Review* 61(February): 12–28.

——. 2005. *The Familial State. Ruling Families and Merchant Capitalism in Early Modern Europe.* Ithace, NY: Cornell University Press.

Alfani, Guido, and Vincent Gourdon. 2012. "Entrepreneurs, Formalization of Social Ties, and Trustbuilding in Europe (Fourteenth to Twentieth Centuries)." *Economic History Review* 65(3): 1005–28.

Allen, Richard B. 2008. "The Constant Demand of the French: The Mascarene Slave Trade and the Worlds of the Indian Ocean and Atlantic during the Eighteenth and Nineteenth Centuries." *Journal of African History* 49(1): 43–72.

——. 2015. *European Slave Trading in the Indian Ocean, 1500–1850*. Athens: Ohio University Press.

Anderson, Fred. 2000. *Crucible of War: The Seven Years' War and the Fate of Empire in British North America, 1754–1766*. New York: Alfred A. Knopf.

Arbellot, Guy. 1973. "La grande mutation des routes de France au XVIIIe siècle." *Annales: Économies, Sociétés, Civilisations* 28(3): 765–91.

Audran, Karine. 2005. "La course à Saint-Malo sous la révolution et l'Empire." *Neptunia* 240(December): 34–41.

——. 2006. "L'accusation d'émigration des négociants malouins: une justification abusive de la politique terroriste à Saint-Malo." *Annales historiques de la Révolution française* 345: 31–53.

Aumont, Michel. 2013. *Les Corsaires de Granville. Une culture du risque maritime (1688–1815)*. Rennes, France: Presses Universitaires de Rennes.

Aven, Brandy, and Henning Hillmann. 2018. "Structural Role Complementarity in Entrepreneurial Teams." *Management Science* 64(12): 5688–5704.

Bailyn, Bernard, and Patricia L. Denault, eds. 2009. *Soundings in Atlantic History: Latent Structures and Intellectual Currents, 1500–1830*. Cambridge, MA: Harvard University Press.

Baldassarri, Delia, and Mario Diani. 2007. "The Integrative Power of Social Networks." *American Journal of Sociology* 113: 735–80.

Bamford, Paul Walden. 1954. "French Shipping in the Northern European Trade, 1660–1789." *Journal of Modern History* 26(3): 207–19.

Banks, Kenneth J. 2005. "Official Duplicity: The Illicit Slave Trade of Martinique, 1713–1763." In *The Atlantic Economy during the Seventeenth and Eighteenth Centuries. Organization, Operation, Practice, and Personnel*, ed. Peter A. Coclanis, 229–51. Columbia: University of South Carolina Press.

Baugh, Daniel. 2011. *The Global Seven Years War, 1754–1763*. London: Routledge.

Bearman, Peter S. 1991. "Desertion as Localism: Army Unit Solidarity and Group Norms in the U.S. Civil War." *Social Forces* 70(December): 321–42.

——. 1993. *Relations into Rhetorics: Local Elite Social Structure in Norfolk, England, 1540–1640*. New Brunswick, NJ: Rutgers University Press.

Becker, Marvin B. 1962. "An Essay on the "Novi Cives" and Florentine Politics, 1343–1382." *Mediaeval Studies* 24: 35–82.

Beik, William. 1985. *Absolutism and Society in Seventeenth-Century France: State Power and Provincial Aristocracy in Languedoc*. Cambridge: Cambridge University Press.

——. 2005. "The Absolutism of Louis XIV as Social Collaboration." *Past and Present* 188(August): 195–224.

——. 2009. *A Social and Cultural History of Early Modern France*. Cambridge: Cambridge University Press.

Benedict, Philip. 1989. "French Cities from the Sixteenth Century to the Revolution: An Overview." In *Cities and Social Change in Early Modern France*, ed. Philip Benedict, 6–66. London: Routledge.

Berg, Maxine, Timothy Davies, Meike Fellinger, Felicia Gottmann, Hanna Hodacs, and Chris Nierstrasz. 2015. "Private Trade and Monopoly Structures: The East India Companies and the Commodity Trade to Europe in the Eighteenth Century." *Political Power and Social Theory* 29: 123–45.

Bien, David D. 1987. "Offices, Corps, and a System of State Credit: The Uses of Privilege Under the Ancien Régime." In *The Political Culture of the Old Regime*, ed. Keith Michael Baker, 89–114. Oxford: Pergamon Press.

Black, Jeremy. 1986. *Natural and Necessary Enemies: Anglo-French Relations in the Eighteenth Century*. London: Duckworth.

——. 1998. *War and the World: Military Power and the Fate of Continents, 1450–2000.* New Haven, CT: Yale University Press.

Blau, Peter M. 1977. *Inequality and Heterogeneity: A Primitive Theory of Social Structure.* New York: Free Press.

Blomquist, Thomas W. 1971. "Commercial Association in Thirteenth-Century Lucca." *The Business History Review* 45(Summer): 157–78.

Bluche, François, and Jean-François Solnon. 1983. *La véritable hiérarchie sociale de l'ancienne France. Le tarif de la première capitation (1695).* Geneva, Switzerland: Droz.

Bonacich, Phillip. 1987. "Power and Centrality: A Family of Measures." *American Journal of Sociology* 92(5): 1170–82.

Bonnel, Ulane. 1961. *La France, les États-Unis et la guerre de course (1797–1815).* Paris: Nouvelles Editions Latines.

Bonney, Richard, ed. 1999. *The Rise of the Fiscal State in Europe, c. 1200–1815.* Oxford: Oxford University Press.

Borgatti, Stephen P., and Martin G. Everett. 1999. "Models of Core/Periphery Structures." *Social Networks* 21: 375–95.

Bossenga, Gail. 1991. *The Politics of Privilege: Old Regime and Revolution in Lille.* Cambridge: Cambridge University Press.

Boulle, Pierre-Henri. 1981. "French Mercantilism, Commercial Companies and Colonial Profitability." In *Companies and Trade*, ed. Leonard Blussé and Femme Gaastra, 97–117. Leiden, Netherlands: Leiden University Press.

Braudel, Fernand. 1992a. *Civilization and Capitalism, 15th–18th Century.* Vol. II, *The Wheels of Commerce.* Trans. Siân Reynolds. Berkeley: University of California Press.

——. 1992b. *Civilization and Capitalism, 15th–18th Century.* Vol. III, *The Perspective of the World.* Trans. Siân Reynolds. Berkeley: University of California Press.

Brenner, Robert. 1993. *Merchants and Revolutionaries: Commercial Change, Political Conflict and London's Overseas Traders, 1550–1653.* Princeton, NJ: Princeton University Press.

Brewer, John. 1988. *The Sinews of Power: War, Money, and the English State, 1688–1783.* Cambridge, MA: Harvard University Press.

Brière, Jean-François. 1983. "Pêche et politique à Terre-Neuve au XVIIIe siècle: la France véritable gagnante du traité d'Utrecht?" *Canadian Historical Review* 64(June): 168–87.

——. 1990. *La pêche française en Amérique du Nord au XVIIIe siècle.* Montréal, QC: Éditions Fides.

Bromley, John S. 1972. "Projets et contrats d'armement en course marseillais, 1705–1712." *Revue d'histoire économique et sociale* 50(1): 74–109.

——. 1986. "A New Vocation: Privateering in the Wars of 1689–97 and 1702–13." In *A People of the Sea: The Maritime History of the Channel Islands*, ed. A. G. Jamieson, 109–47. London and New York: Methuen.

——. 1987. *Corsairs and Navies, 1660–1760.* London: Hambledon Press.

Brucker, Gene A. 1962. *Florentine Politics and Society, 1343–1378.* Princeton, NJ: Princeton University Press.

Burt, Ronald S. 1992. *Structural Holes: the Social Structure of Competition.* Cambridge, MA: Harvard University Press.

Butel, Paul. 1974. *Les négociants bordelais, l'Europe et les Îles au XVIIIe siècle.* Paris: Aubier.

——. 1990. "France, the Antilles, and Europe in the Seventeenth and Eighteenth Centuries: Renewals of Foreign Trade." In *The Rise of Merchant Empires. Long-Distance Trade in the Early Modern World, 1350–1750*, ed. James D. Tracy, 153–73. Cambridge: Cambridge University Press.

——. 1993. *L'Économie française au XVIIIe siècle.* Paris: SEDES.

——. 1999. *The Atlantic.* London: Routledge.

Cabantous, Alain, André Lespagnol, and Françoise Péron. 2005. *Les Français, la terre et la mer. XIIIe–XXe siècle.* Paris: Fayard.

Calhoun, Craig J. 1982. *The Question of Class Struggle.* Chicago: University of Chicago Press.

Canny, Nicholas, and Philip Morgan, eds. 2011. *The Oxford Handbook of the Atlantic World: 1450–1850.* Oxford: Oxford University Press.

Caracausi, Andrea, and Christof Jeggle, eds. 2014. *Commercial Networks and European Cities, 1400–1800.* London: Pickering & Chatto.

Carlos, Ann M. 1992. "Principal-Agent Problems in Early Trading Companies: A Tale of Two Firms." *American Economic Review, Papers and Proceedings* 82(2): 140–45.

——. 1994. "Bonding and the Agency Problem: Evidence from the Royal African Company, 1672–1691." *Explorations in Economic History* 31: 313–35.

Carlos, Ann M., and Stephen Nicholas. 1990. Agency Problems in Early Chartered Companies: The Case of the Hudson's Bay Company." *Journal of Economic History* 50(4): 853–75.

Carrière, Charles. 1973. *Négociants marseillais au XVIIIe siècle. Contribution à l'étude des économies maritimes.* 2 vols. Marseille, France: Institut Historique de Provence.

Chardon, Daniel Marc Antoine. 1784. *Code des prise ou Recueil des édits, déclarations, lettres patentes, arrêts, ordonnances, règlements et décisions sur la course et l'administration des prises, depuis 1400 jusqu'à présent.* 2 vols. Paris: L'imprimerie royale.

Chase, Ivan D. 1980. "Social Process and Hierarchy Formation in Small Groups." *American Sociological Review* 45: 905–924.

——. 1991. "Vacancy Chains." *Annual Review of Sociology* 17: 133–54.

Chateaubriand, François-René, vicomte de. [1849–1856] 1957. *Mémoires d'Outre-Tombe.* 3rd corr. ed. 2 vols. Edited by Maurice Levaillant and Georges Moulinier. Bibliothèque de la Pléiade. Paris: Gallimard.

Chavarot, Marie-Claire. 1991. "La pratique des lettres de marque d'après les arrêts du parlement (XIIIe–début XVe siècle)." *Bibliothèque de l'école des chartes* 149: 51–89.

Cheney, Paul. 2010. *Revolutionary Commerce. Globalization and the French Monarchy.* Cambridge, MA: Harvard University Press.

Cieslak, Edmund. 1977. "Sea-borne Trade Between France and Poland in the XVIIIth Century." *Economic History* 6(1): 49–62.

Cipolla, Carlo M. 1993. *Before the Industrial Revolution: European Society and Economy 1000–1700.* 3rd ed. London: Routledge.

Çizakça, Murat. 1996. *A Comparative Evolution of Business Partnerships. The Islamic World and Europe, With Specific Reference to the Ottoman Archives.* Leiden, Netherlands: Brill.

Clark, George. 1970. "The Nine Years War, 1688–1697." In *The New Cambridge Modern History*, Vol. VI, *The Rise of Great Britain and Russia, 1688–1715/25*, ed. John S. Bromley, 223–53. Cambridge: Cambridge University Press.

Clark, G. N. [1923] 1971. *The Dutch Alliance and the War Against French Trade, 1688–1697.* New York: Russell & Russell.

Clark, Grover. 1933. "The English Practice with Regard to Reprisals by Private Persons." *American Journal of International Law* 27(October): 694–723.

Clark, Henry C. 2007. *Compass of Society: Commerce and Absolutism in Old-Regime France.* Lanham, MD: Rowman & Littlefield.

Clark, John G. 1981. *La Rochelle and the Atlantic Economy During the Eighteenth Century.* Baltimore, MD: Johns Hopkins University Press.

Coclanis, Peter A., ed. 2005. *The Atlantic Economy During the Seventeenth and Eighteenth Centuries: Organization, Operation, Practice, and Personnel.* Columbia: University of South Carolina Press.

Cole, Charles Woolsey. 1939. *Colbert and a Century of French Mercantilism.* New York: Columbia University Press.

——. 1943. *French Mercantilism, 1683–1700.* New York: Columbia University Press.

Coleman, D. C. 1980. "Mercantilism Revisited." *The Historical Journal* 23(4): 773–91.

Collas, Georges. 1949a. *Un cadet de Bretagne au XVIIIe siècle: René-Auguste de Chateaubriand, Comte de Combourg, 1718–1786. D'après des documents inédits sur la vie maritime, féodale et familiale en Bretagne au XVIIIe siècle.* Paris: Librairie A. G. Nizet.

———. 1949b. "Les procès de corsaires de M. de Chateaubriand." *Mémoires de la Société d'Histoire et d'Archéologie de Bretagne* 29: 101–19.

Collins, James B. 1994. *Classes, Estates, and Order in Early Modern Brittany.* Cambridge: Cambridge University Press.

———. 2009. *The State in Early Modern France.* 2nd ed. Cambridge: Cambridge University Press.

Coyer, abbé Gabriel François. 1756. *La noblesse commerçante.* London: Duchesne.

Crouzet, François. 1966. "Angleterre et France au XVIIIe siècle: essai d'analyse comparée de deux croissances économiques." *Annales. Économies, Sociétés, Civilisations* 21(2): 254–91.

———. 1996. "The Second Hundred Years War: Some Reflections." *French History* 10(4): 432–50.

———. 2008. *La guerre économique franco-anglaise au XVIIIe siècle.* Paris: Fayard.

Crowhurst, Patrick. 1977. *The Defense of British Trade, 1689–1815.* Folkestone, UK: Dawson.

———. 1989. *The French War on Trade: Privateering, 1793–1815.* Aldershot, UK: Scolar Press.

Crozier, Michel, and Erhard Friedberg. 1977. *L'Acteur et le système. Les Contraintes de l'action collective.* Paris: Seuil.

Curto, Diogo Ramada, and Anthony Molho, eds. 2002. "Commercial Networks in the Early Modern World." EUI Working Paper HEC No. 2002/2. Florence, Italy: European University Institute.

Daget, Serge. 1990. *La traite des Noirs.* Rennes, France: Éditions Ouest-France.

Dahlgren, M. E. W. 1907. "Voyages Français à Destination de la Mer du Sud avant Bougainville (1695–1749)." *Nouvelles Archives des Missions scientifiques* XIV: 423–568.

———. 1909. *Les Relations Commerciales et Maritimes Entre la France et les Côtes de l'Océan Pacifique.* Vol. I, *Le Commerce de la Mer du Sud jusqu'à la Paix d'Utrecht.* Paris: Librairie Ancienne Honoré Champion.

Daudin, Guillaume. 2004. "Profitability of Slave and Long-Distance Trading in Context: The Case of Eighteenth-Century France." *Journal of Economic History* 64(March): 144–71.

———. 2005. *Commerce et prosperité. La France au XVIIIe siècle.* Paris: Presses de l'Université Paris-Sorbonne.

Debordes-Lissillour, Séverine. 2006. *Les Sénéchaussées royales de Bretagne. La monarchie d'Ancien Régime et ses juridictions ordinaires (1532–1790).* Rennes, France: Presses Universitaires de Rennes.

Delobette, Edouard. 2005. "Ces Messieurs du Havre. Négociants, commissionnaires et armateurs de 1680 à 1830." PhD diss., Université de Caen.

Delumeau, Jean. 1966. *Le Mouvement du port de Saint-Malo, 1681–1720. Bilan statistique.* Paris: Klincksieck.

Demerliac, Alain, Cdt. 1995. *La Marine de Louis XIV. Nomenclature des vaisseaux du Roi-Soleil de 1661 à 1715.* Nice: Editions Omega.

De Vaan, Mathijs, Balazs Vedres, and David Stark. 2015. "Game Changer: The Topology of Creativity." *American Journal of Sociology* 120(4): 1144–94.

Dincecco, Mark. 2011. *Political Transformations and Public Finances: Europe, 1650–1913.* Cambridge: Cambridge University Press.

Downing, Brian M. 1992. *The Military Revolution and Political Change: Origins of Democracy and Autocracy in Early Modern Europe.* Princeton, NJ: Princeton University Press.

Dubois, Laurent. 2009. "The French Atlantic." In *Atlantic History: A Critical Appraisal*, ed. Jack P. Greene, 137–62. Oxford: Oxford University Press.

Duby, Georges. [1962] 1998. *Rural Economy and Country Life in the Medieval West.* Trans. Cynthia Postan. Philadelphia: University of Pennsylvania Press.

Dull, Jonathan R. 2005. *The French Navy and the Seven Years' War.* Lincoln: University of Nebraska Press.

———. 2009. *The Age of the Ship of the Line. The British and French Navies, 1650–1815.* Lincoln: University of Nebraska Press.

Dupuy, Roger. 1984. "Un monde qui s'estompe (1789–1848)." In *Histoire de Saint-Malo et du pays malouin*, ed. André Lespagnol, 215–34. Toulouse, France: Éditions Privat.

Eltis, David. 2000. *The Rise of African Slavery in the Americas.* Cambridge: Cambridge University Press.

———. 2016. Trans-Atlantic Slave Trade Database. Expanded data set. Atlanta, GA: Emory University. http://www.slavevoyages.org/ (accessed September 2016).

Emmer, Pieter C., Olivier Pétré-Grenouilleau, and Jessica V. Roitman, eds. 2006. *A Deus Ex Machina Revisited: Atlantic Colonial Trade and European Economic Development*. Leiden, Netherlands: Brill.

Erikson, Emily. 2014. *Between Monopoly and Free Trade: The English East India Company, 1600–1757*. Princeton, NJ: Princeton University Press.

Erikson, Emily, and Peter Bearman. 2006. "Malfeasance and the Foundations for Global Trade: The Structure of English Trade in the East Indies, 1601–1833." *American Journal of Sociology* 112(July): 195–230.

Erikson, Emily, and Sampsa Samila. 2018. "Networks, Institutions, and Uncertainty: Information Exchange in Early-Modern Markets." *Journal of Economic History* 78(4): 1034–67.

Ertman, Thomas. 1997. *The Birth of the Leviathan: Building States and Regimes in Medieval and Early Modern Europe*. Cambridge: Cambridge University Press.

Esteves, Rui, and Gabriel Geisler Mesevage. 2019. "Social Networks in Economic History: Opportunities and Challenges." *Explorations in Economic History* 74(October): 101299.

Feld, Scott L. 1981. "The Focused Organization of Social Ties." *American Journal of Sociology* 86(5): 1015–35.

Findlay, Ronald, and Kevin H. O'Rourke. 2007. *Power and Plenty: Trade, War, and the World Economy in the Second Millennium*. Princeton, NJ: Princeton University Press.

Follain, Antoine. 2008. *Le village sous l'Ancien Régime*. Paris: Fayard.

Fontenay, Michel. 2010. *La Méditerranée entre la Croix et le Croissant. Navigation, commerce, course et piraterie (XVIᵉ–XIXᵉ siècle)*. Paris: Classiques Garnier.

Fox, Edward Whiting. 1971. *History in Geographic Perspective: The Other France*. New York: Norton.

Friedkin, Noah E. 1998. *A Structural Theory of Social Influence*. Cambridge: Cambridge University Press.

Furet, François. 1992. *Revolutionary France, 1770–1880*. Trans. Antonia Nevill. Oxford: Blackwell.

Geggus, David. 2001. "The French Slave Trade: An Overview." *William and Mary Quarterly* 58(1): 119–38.

Gervais, Pierre. 2011. "A Merchant of a French Atlantic? Eighteenth-Century Account Books as Narratives of a Transnational Merchant Political Economy." *French History* 25(1): 28–47.

Giesey, Ralph E. 1977. "Rules of Inheritance and Strategies of Mobility in Prerevolutionary France." *American Historical Review* 82(2): 271–89.

Glete, Jan. 1993. *Navies and Nations: Warships, Navies, and State Building in Europe and America, 1500–1860*. Stockholm, Sweden: Almqvist and Wiksell International.

——. 2002. *War and the State in Early Modern Europe: Spain, the Dutch Republic, and Sweden as Fiscal-Military States, 1500–1660*. London: Routledge.

Goldberg, Jessica L. 2012. *Trade and Institutions in the Medieval Mediterranean: The Geniza Merchants and their Business World*. Cambridge: Cambridge University Press.

Gonzáles de Lara, Yadira. 2008. "The Secret of Venetian Success: A Public-Order, Reputation-Based Institution." *European Review of Economic History* 12: 247–85.

Gorski, Philip S. 2003. *The Disciplinary Revolution: Calvinism and the Rise of the State in Early Modern Europe*. Chicago: University of Chicago Press.

Gottmann, Felicia. 2013. "French-Asian Connections: The Compagnies des Indes, France's Eastern Trade, and New Directions in Historical Scholarship." *Historical Journal* 56(2): 537–52.

Gould, Roger V. 1995. *Insurgent Identities: Class, Community, and Protest in Paris from 1848 to the Commune*. Chicago: University of Chicago Press.

Gould, Roger V., and Roberto M. Fernandez. 1989. "Structures of Mediation: A Formal Approach to Brokerage in Transaction Networks." *Sociological Methodology* 19: 89–126.

Grafe, Regina. 2012. *Distant Tyranny: Markets, Power, and Backwardness in Spain, 1650–1800*. Princeton, NJ: Princeton University Press.

Graham, Aaron. 2013. "Mercantile Networks in the Early Modern World." *Historical Journal* 56(1): 279–95.

Granovetter, Mark S. 1973. "The Strength of Weak Ties." *American Journal of Sociology* 78(May): 1360–80.

Greene, Jack P., and Philip D. Morgan, eds. 2009. *Atlantic History: A Critical Reappraisal*. New York: Oxford University Press.

Greif, Avner. 2005. "Commitment, Coercion, and Markets: The Nature and Dynamics of Institutions Supporting Exchange." In *Handbook of New Institutional Economics*, ed. C. Ménard and M. M. Shirley,
727–86. Dordrecht, Netherlands: Springer.

———. 2006. *Institutions and the Path to the Modern Economy. Lessons from Medieval Trade*. Cambridge:
Cambridge University Press.

Guery, Alain. 1986. "État, classification sociale et compromis sous Louis XIV: la capitation de 1695." *Annales.
Économies, Sociétés, Civilisations* 41(5): 1041–60.

Guignet, Philippe. 1996. "Municipalités: organisation et pouvoirs." In *Dictionnaire de l'Ancien Régime*, ed.
Lucien Bély, 861–67. Paris: Presses Universitaires de France.

Gunn, Steven. 2016. *Henry VII's New Men and the Making of Tudor England*. Oxford: Oxford University
Press.

Hancock, D. 1995. *Citizens of the World: London Merchants and the Integration of the British Atlantic Community, 1735–1785*. Cambridge: Cambridge University Press.

———. 2005. "The Trouble with Networks: Managing the Scots' Early-Modern Madeira Trade." *Business History Review* 79(Autumn): 467–91.

———. 2009. *Oceans of Wine: Madeira and the Emergence of American Trade and Taste*. New Haven, CT: Yale
University Press.

Harding, Richard. 1999. *Seapower and Naval Warfare from 1650–1830*. London: UCL Press.

Haudrère, Philippe. 1999. "The French India Company and Its Trade in the Eighteenth Century." In *Merchants, Companies and Trade: Europe and Asia in the Early Modern Era*, ed. Sushil Chaudhury and
Michel Marineau, 202–11. Cambridge: Cambridge University Press.

———. 2005. *La Compagnie française des Indes au XVIIIe siècle*. 2nd rev. and corr. ed. 2 vols. Paris: Les Indes
Savantes.

Haudrère, Philippe, Gérard Le Bouëdec, and Louis Mézin. 2015. *Les Compagnies des Indes*. 4th ed. Rennes,
France: Editions Quest-France.

Hechter, Michael, Steven Pfaff, and Patrick Underwood. 2016. "Grievances and the Genesis of Rebellion:
Mutiny in the Royal Navy, 1740 to 1820." *American Sociological Review* 81(1): 165–89.

Herpin, Eugène. 1931. *Saint-Malo sous la Révolution, 1789–1800*. Rennes, France: Riou-Reuzé.

Herrero Sánchez, Manuel, and Klemens Kaps, eds. 2017. *Merchants and Trade Networks in the Atlantic and
the Mediterranean, 1550–1800*. London: Routledge.

Hillmann, Henning. 2008a. "Mediation in Multiple Networks: Elite Mobilization Before the English Civil
War." *American Sociological Review* 73: 426–54.

———. 2008b. "Localism and the Limits of Political Brokerage: Evidence from Revolutionary Vermont."
American Journal of Sociology 114(September): 287–331.

Hillmann, Henning, and Brandy L. Aven. 2011. "Fragmented Networks and Entrepreneurship in Late Imperial Russia." *American Journal of Sociology* 117(September): 484–538.

Hillmann, Henning, and Christina Gathmann. 2011. "Overseas Trade and the Decline of Privateering." *Journal of Economic History* 71(3): 730–61.

Hintze, Otto. 1975. *The Historical Essays of Otto Hintze*, ed. Felix Gilbert. Oxford: Oxford University Press.

Hoffman, Philip T. 1994. "Early Modern France: 1450–1700." In *Fiscal Crises, Liberty, and Representative
Government 1450–1789*, ed. Philip T. Hoffman and Kathryn Norberg, 226–52. Stanford, CA: Stanford
University Press.

———. 2015. *Why Did Europe Conquer the World?* Princeton, NJ: Princeton University Press.

Hoffman, Philip T., and Jean-Laurent Rosenthal. 1997. "The Political Economy of Warfare and Taxation
in Early Modern Europe: Historical Lessons for Economic Development." In *The Frontiers of the New
Institutional Economics*, ed. John N. Drobak and John V. C. Nye, 31–55. San Diego, CA: Academic
Press.

Hoffman, Philip T., Gilles Postel-Vinay, and Jean-Laurent Rosenthal. 2000. *Priceless Markets: The Political
Economy of Credit in Paris, 1660–1870*. Chicago: University of Chicago Press.

Homans, George C. 1941. *English Villagers of the Thirteenth Century*. Cambridge, MA: Harvard University Press.

Horn, Jeff. 2015. *Economic Development in Early Modern France. The Privilege of Liberty, 1650–1820*. Cambridge: Cambridge University Press.

Huetz de Lemps, Christian. 1975. *Géographie du commerce de Bordeaux à la fin du règne de Louis XIV*. Paris-La Haye: Mouton.

——. 1991. "Indentured Servants Bound for the French Antilles in the Seventeenth and Eighteenth Centuries." In *"To Make America": European Emigration in the Early Modern Period*, ed. Ida Altman and James Horn, 172–203. Berkeley: University of California Press.

Isambert, Decrussy, and Taillander. 1829. *Recueil Général des Anciennes Lois Françaises*. Vol. XIX, *Janvier 1672–Mai 1686*. Paris: Belin-Leprieur & Verdière.

Jamieson, A. G., ed. 1986. *A People of the Sea: The Maritime History of the Channel Islands*. New York: Methuen.

Jeannin, Pierre. 2002. *Marchands d'Europe. Pratiques et savoirs à l'époque moderne*. Paris: Éditions Rue d'Ulm/Presses de l'École normale supérieure.

Johnsen, Eugene. 1985. "Network Macrostructure Models for the Davis-Leinhardt Set of Empirical Sociomatrices." *Social Networks* 7: 203–224.

Johnson, Victoria, and Walter W. Powell. 2015. "Poisedness and Propagation: Organizational Emergence and the Transformation of Civic Order in 19th-Century New York City." NBER Working Paper No. 21011. Cambridge, MA: National Bureau of Economic Research.

Kamen, Henry. 1969. *The War of Succession in Spain, 1700–1715*. London: Weidenfeld & Nicolson.

Keber, Martha L. 2002. *Seas of Gold, Seas of Cotton. Christophe Poulain DuBignon of Jekyll Island*. Athens: University of Georgia Press.

Kessler, Amalia D. 2004. "A 'Question of Name': Merchant-Court Jurisdiction and the Origins of the Noblesse Commercante." In *A Vast and Useful Art: the Gustave Gimon Collection on French Political Economy*, ed. Mary Jane Parrine, 49–65. Stanford, CA: Stanford University Libraries.

——. 2007. *A Revolution of Commerce. The Parisian Merchant Court and the Rise of Commercial Society in Eighteenth-Century France*. New Haven, CT: Yale University Press.

Klein, Herbert S. 2010. *The Atlantic Slave Trade*. 2nd ed. Cambridge: Cambridge University Press.

Kleinberg, Jon M. 1999. "Authoritative Sources in a Hyperlinked Environment." *Journal of the Association for Computing Machinery* 46(5): 604–32.

Kwass, Michael. 2000. *Privilege and the Politics of Taxation in Eighteenth-Century France*. Cambridge: Cambridge University Press.

Labourdette, Jean-François. 1988. *La nation française à Lisbonne de 1669 à 1790. Entre Colbertisme et Liberalisme*. Paris: E.H.E.S.S. & Fondation Calouste Gulbankian.

Lachmann, Richard. 2000. *Capitalists in Spite of Themselves: Elite Conflict and Economic Transitions in Early Modern Europe*. Oxford: Oxford University Press.

Laffont, Jean-Jacques, and David Martimort. 2002. *The Theory of Incentives: The Principal-Agent Model*. Princeton, NJ: Princeton University Press.

Lagadec, Yann, Stéphane Perréon, and David Hopkin. 2009. *La bataille de Saint-Cast (Bretagne, 11 Septembre 1758): Entre histoire et mémoire*. Rennes, France: Presses Universitaires de Rennes.

Landa, Janet T. 1981. "A Theory of the Ethnically Homogeneous Middleman Group: An Institutional Alternative to Contract Law." *Journal of Legal Studies* 10(June): 349–62.

Laurent, Catherine. 1986. "Saint-Malo, Ille-et-Vilaine." *Atlas Historique des Villes de France*, ed. Ch. Higounet, J.-B. Marquette, and Ph. Wolff. Paris: Editions du C.N.R.S.

Le Bouëdec, Gérard. 1997. *Activités maritimes et sociétés littorales de l'Europe atlantique, 1690–1790*. Paris: Armand Colin.

Le Goff, T. J. A. 1990. "Problèmes de recrutement de la marine française pendant la Guerre de Sept Ans." *Revue Historique* 574(April–June): 205–33.

——. 1999. "How to Finance an Eighteenth-Century War." In *Crises, Revolutions And Self-Sustained Growth. Essays in European Fiscal History, 1130–1830*, ed. W. M. Ormrod, Margaret Bonney, and Richard Bonney, 377–413. Stamford, UK: Shaun Tyas.

Le Guellaff, Florence. 1999. *Armements en course et Droit des prises maritimes (1792–1856)*. Nancy, France: Presses Universitaires de Nancy.

Le Roy Ladurie, Emmanuel. 1996. *The Ancien Régime. A History of France, 1610–1774*. Trans. Mark Greengrass. Oxford: Blackwell.

Lespagnol, André. 1979. "Négociants et commerce indien au début du XVIIIe siècle: l'épisode des 'Compagnies malouines', 1707–1719." *Annales de Bretagne et des pays de l'Ouest* 86(3): 427–57.

——. 1982. "Cargaisons et profits du commerce indien au début du XVIIIe siècle—Les opérations commerciales des Compagnies Malouines 1707–1720." *Annales de Bretagne et des pays de l'Ouest* 89(3): 313–50.

——. 1984. "Saint-Malo port mondial (16ᵉ–18ᵉ siècles)." In *Histoire de Saint-Malo et du pays malouin*, ed. André Lespagnol, 89–137. Toulouse, France: Éditions Privat.

——. 1989a. "Entreprise individuelles et associations commerciales dans le capitalisme malouin au XVIIe siècle." In *Le négoce international: XIIIe–XXe siècle*, ed. François Crouzet, 115–25. Paris: Economica.

——. 1989b. "Négociants et Ancien Régime en Bretagne à la fin du XVIIIe siècle: le cas malouin." In *La Bretagne, une province à l'aube de la Révolution*, 29–39. Brest, France: C.R.B.C./Société Archéologique du Finistère.

——. 1991. *Messieurs de Saint-Malo. Une élite négociante au temps de Louis XIV.* Saint-Malo, France: Éditions L'Ancre de Marine.

——. 1995. *Entre l'argent et la gloire. La course Malouine au temps de Louis XIV.* Rennes, France: Éditions Apogée.

——. 2013a. "Danycan Noël, sieur de l'Épine." In *Dictionnaire des corsaires et pirates*, ed. Gilbert Buti and Philippe Hrodej, 196–98. Paris: Éditions CNRS.

——. 2013b. "Moreau, René, sieur de Maupertuis." In *Dictionnaire des corsaires et pirates*, ed. Gilbert Buti and Philippe Hrodej, 547. Paris: Éditions CNRS.

——. 2016. "Saint-Malo, les Malouins et Marseille. Une relation particulière." Reprinted in André Lespagnol. 2019. *Saint-Malo et la Bretagne dans la première mondialisation*. Brest, France: Centre de Recherche Bretonne et Celtique, Université de Bretagne Occidentale Brest, 239–55.

——. 2018. "Saint-Malo, pôle marchand de la 'première Modernité.' " *Annales de Bretagne et des Pays de l'Ouest* 125(3): 285–300.

Lévi-Strauss, Claude. 2008. *La Pensée sauvage*. In *Œuvres*, ed. Vincent Debaene, Frédéric Keck, Marie Mauzé, and Martin Rueff, 555–872. Bibliothèque de la Pléiade. Paris: Gallimard.

Lopez, Robert S. 1976. *The Commercial Revolution of the Middle Ages, 950–1350*. Cambridge: Cambridge University Press.

——. 1987. "The Trade of Medieval Europe: the South." In *The Cambridge Economic History of Europe*, Vol. II, *Trade and Industry in the Middle Ages*, ed. M. M. Postan and Edward Miller, 306–401. 2nd ed. Cambridge: Cambridge University Press.

Lopez, Robert S., and Irving W. Raymond, eds. 2001. *Medieval Trade in the Mediterranean World: Illustrative Documents*. 3rd imprint. New York: Columbia University Press.

Lunsford, Virginia West. 2005. *Piracy and Privateering in the Golden Age Netherlands*. New York: Palgrave MacMillan.

Lynn, John A. 1999. *The Wars of Louis XIV*. London: Longman.

Lydon, James G. 1970. *Pirates, Privateers, and Profits*. Upper Saddle River, NJ: Gregg Press.

Lyons, Mary Anne. 2001. "The Emerge of an Irish Community in Saint-Malo, 1550–1710." In *The Irish in Europe 1580–1815*, ed. Thomas O'Connor, 107–26. Dublin, Ireland: Four Courts Press.

Magnusson, Lars. 1994. *Mercantilism: The Shaping of an Economic Language*. London: Routledge.

Malamud Rikles, Carlos Daniel. 1986. *Cádiz y Saint Malo en el comercio colonial peruano (1698–1725)*. Cadiz, Spain: Diputación Provincial de Cádiz.

Malcolm, Noel. 2015. *Agents of Empire. Knights, Corsairs, Jesuits and Spies in the Sixteenth-Century Mediterranean World*. London: Allen Lane.

Mancke, Elizabeth. 1999. "Early Modern Expansion and the Politicization of Oceanic Space." *Geographical Review* 89(2): 225–36.

Mann, Michael. 1986. *The Sources of Social Power*, vol. 1. Cambridge: Cambridge University Press.

Manning, Catherine. 1996. *Fortunes à faire: The French in Asian Trade, 1719–48*. Aldershot, Hampshire, UK: Variorum Ashgate.

March, James G. 1991. "Exploration and Exploitation in Organizational Learning." *Organization Science* 2: 71–87.

Martens, Georg Friedrich de. 1801. *An Essay on Privateers, Captures, and Particularly on Recaptures According to the Laws, Treaties, and Usages of the Maritime Powers of Europe*. Trans. Thomas Hartwell Horne. London: E. and R. Brooke.

Martin, John Levi. 2009. *Social Structures*. Princeton, NJ: Princeton University Press.

Martin-Deidier, Annick. 1976. "La guerre de course à Saint-Malo de 1688 à 1814." PhD diss., Paris I, Sorbonne.

Martinetti, Brice. 2013. *Les Négociants de La Rochelle au XVIIIᵉ siècle*. Rennes, France: Presses universitaires de Rennes.

Marzagalli, Silvia. 2011. "The French Atlantic World in the Seventeenth and Eighteenth Centuries." In *The Oxford Handbook of the Atlantic World: 1450–1850*, ed. Nicholas Canny and Philip Morgan, 235–51. Oxford: Oxford University Press.

de Mas-Latrie, René. 1866. "Du droit de marque ou droit de représailles au Moyen Âge." *Bibliothèque de l'école des chartes* 27: 529–77.

Mauro, Frédéric. 1990. "Merchant Communities, 1350–1750." In *The Rise of Merchant Empires: Long Distance Trade in the Early Modern World 1350–1750*, ed. James D. Tracy, 255–86. Cambridge: Cambridge University Press.

McCusker, John J. 1992. *Money and Exchange in Europe and America, 1600–1775*. Chapel Hill: University of North Carolina Press.

McCusker, John J., and Kenneth Morgan, eds. 2000. *The Early Modern Atlantic Economy*. Cambridge: Cambridge University Press.

McLean, Paul D. 2004. "Widening Access While Tightening Control: Office-Holding, Marriages, and Elite Consolidation in Early Modern Poland." *Theory and Society* 33: 167–212.

McWatters, Cheryl S. 2008. "Investment returns and la traite négrière: evidence from eighteenth-century France." *Accounting, Business and Financial History* 18(2): 161–85.

McWatters, Cheryl S., and Yannick Lemarchand. 2012. "Accounting for Triangular Trade." In *French Accounting History: New Contributions*, ed. Yves Levant, 115–38. London: Routledge.

Meyer, Jean. 1969. *L'armement nantais dans la deuxième moitié du XVIIIe siècle*. Paris: S.E.V.P.E.N.

——. 1971. "La Course: Romantisme, Exutoire Social, Réalité Économique. Essai de Méthodologie." *Annales de Bretagne* 78(June): 307–44.

——. 1982. "La France et l'Asie: essai de statistiques, 1730–1785: état de la question." *Histoire, économie et société* 1(2): 297–312.

——. 1985. *La noblesse bretonne au XVIIIe siècle*. 2nd ed. 2 vols. Paris: Éditions de l'École des Hautes Études en Sciences Sociales.

——. 1997. "La guerre de course de l'Ancien Régime au XXᵉ siècle: essai sur la guerre industrielle." *Histoire, économie et société* 16(1): 7–43.

Meyer, William R. 1981. "English Privateering in the War of 1688–1697." *Mariner's Mirror* 67(3): 259–72.

——. 1983. "English Privateering in the War of Spanish Succession, 1703–1713." *Mariner's Mirror* 69(4): 435–46.

Mollat, Michel, ed. 1975. *Course et Piraterie. Etudes présentées à la Commission Internationale d'Histoire Maritime à l'occasion de son XVᵉ colloque international pendant le XIVe colloque international pendant le XIVᵉ Congrès International des Sciences historique, San Francisco, August 1975*. Paris: Editions du C.N.R.S.

Moody, James, and Douglas R. White. 2003. "Structural Cohesion and Embeddedness: A Hierarchical Concept of Social Groups." *American Sociological Review* 6: 103–27.

Morel, Anne. 1957. "La guerre de course à Saint-Malo de 1681 à 1715, 1ère partie." *Mémoires de la Société d'histoire et d'archéologie de Bretagne* 37: 5–103.

———. 1958. "La guerre de course à Saint-Malo de 1681 à 1715. 2ème partie, tableaux des armements malouins." *Mémoires de la Société d'histoire et d'archéologie de Bretagne* 38: 29–169.

Morgan, Kenneth. 1993. *Bristol and the Atlantic Trade in the Eighteenth Century*. Cambridge: Cambridge University Press.

Mousnier, Roland E. 1979. *The Institutions of France Under the Absolute Monarchy, 1598–1789*. Vol. I, *Society and State*. Chicago: University of Chicago Press.

———. 1984. *The Institutions of France under the Absolute Monarchy, 1598–1789*. Vol. II, *The Organs of State and Society*. Chicago: University of Chicago Press.

Mrvar, Andrej, and Vladimir Batagelji. 2016. PAJEK 4.10. University of Ljubljana, Slovenia.

Nassiet, Michel. 2012. *Noblesse et pauvreté. La petite noblesse en Bretagne, XVe–XVIIIe siècle*. Rennes, France: Presses Universitaires de Rennes.

Nières, Claude. 2004. *Les Villes de Bretagne au XVIIIe siècle*. Rennes, France: Presses Universitaires de Rennes.

Nigro, Giampiero, ed. 2010. *Francesco di Marco Datini. The Man, the Merchant*. Fondazione Istituto Internazionale di Storia Economica "F. Datini." Florence, Italy: Firenze University Press.

O'Brien, Patrick K. 1988. "The Political Economy of British Taxation, 1660–1815." *Economic History Review* 41(February): 1–32.

O'Brien, Patrick K., and Philip A. Hunt. 1993. "The Rise of a Fiscal State in England, 1485–1815." *Historical Research* 66: 129–76.

Ogilvie, Sheilagh. 2011. *Institutions and European Trade. Merchant Guilds, 1000–1800*. Cambridge: Cambridge University Press.

Origo, Iris. [1957] 2017. *The Merchant of Prato. Daily Life in a Medieval Italian City*. London: Penguin.

Orlandi, Angela. 2014. "Networks and Commercial Penetration Models in the Late Medieval Mediterranean: Revisiting the Datini." In *Commercial Networks and European Cities, 1400–1800*, ed. Andrea Caracausi and Christof Jeggle, 81–106. London: Pickering & Chatto.

Padgett, John F. 2010. "Open Elite? Social Mobility, Marriage, and Family in Florence, 1282–1494." *Renaissance Quarterly* 63(2): 357–411.

Padgett, John F., and Christopher K. Ansell. 1993. "Robust Action and the Rise of the Medici, 1400–1434." *American Journal of Sociology* 98: 1259–319.

Padgett, John F., and Paul D. McLean. 2006. "Organizational Invention and Elite Transformation: The Birth of Partnership Systems in Renaissance Florence." *American Journal of Sociology* 111(5): 1463–568.

Padgett, John F., and Walter W. Powell, eds. 2012. *The Emergence of Organizations and Markets*. Princeton, NJ: Princeton University Press.

Pagden, Anthony. 1995. *Lords of All the World: Ideologies of Empire in Spain, Britain and France, c. 1500–c.1800*. New Haven, CT: Yale University Press.

Pares, Richard. 1936. *War and Trade in the West Indies, 1739–1763*. Oxford: Oxford University Press.

———. 1938. *Colonial Blockade and Neutral Rights, 1739–1763*. Oxford: Oxford University Press.

Parker, Geoffrey. 1996. *The Military Revolution: Military Innovation and the Rise of the West 1500–1800*. 2nd ed. Cambridge: Cambridge University Press.

Paris-Jallobert, Paul. 2000–2004. *Anciens registres paroissiaux de Bretagne, d'après les travaux de l'abbé Paris-Jallobert. Ille-et-Vilaine, tomes I–VI*. CD-ROM. Rennes, France: Sajef.

———. 2004. *Anciens registres paroissiaux de Bretagne, d'après les travaux de l'abbé Paris-Jallobert. Ille-et-Vilaine, tome VII: Saint-Malo*. CD-ROM. Rennes, France: Sajef.

Parrott, David. 2012. *The Business of War: Military Enterprise and Military Revolution in Early Modern Europe*. Cambridge: Cambridge University Press.

Pelus-Kaplan, Marie-Louise. 1997. "Les Européens et la Baltique (1690–1790)." *Bulletin de la Société d'Histo-rie Moderne et Contemporaine* 1–2: 99–129.

Pétré-Grenouilleau, Olivier. 1996. *L'argent de la traite. Milieu négrier, capitalisme et développement: un modèle.* Paris: Aubier.

——. 1997a. *Les négoces maritimes français, XVIIe–Xxe siècle.* Paris: Belin.

——. 1997b. "Dynamique sociale et croissance. À propos du prétendu retard du capitalisme maritime français (note critique)." *Annales. Histoire, Sciences Sociales* 52(6): 1263–74.

——. 1998. *Nantes au temps de la traite des Noirs.* Paris: Hachette.

——. 2004. *Les traites négrières. Essai d'histoire globale.* Paris: Gallimard.

——. 2006. "Colonial Trade and Economic Development in France, Seventeenth to Twentieth Centuries." In *A Deus Ex Machina Revisited. Atlantic Colonial Trade and European Economic Development*, ed. Pieter C. Emmer, Olivier Pétré-Grenouilleau, and Jessica V. Roitman, 225–61. Leiden, Netherlands: Brill.

Pineau-Defois, Laure. 2010. "Une élite d'ancien régime : les grands négociants nantais dans la tourmente révo-lutionnaire (1780–1793)." *Annales historiques de la Révolution française* 359(January–March): 97–118.

Pincus, Steve. 2009. *1688: The First Modern Revolution.* New Haven, CT: Yale University Press.

——. 2012. "Rethinking Mercantilism: Political Economy, the British Empire, and the Atlantic World in the Seventeenth and Eighteenth Centuries." *William and Mary Quarterly* 69(1): 3–34.

Pineau-Defois, Laure. 2010. "Une élite d'ancien régime: les grands négociants nantais dans la tourmente révolutionnaire (1780–1793)." *Annales historiques de la Révolution française* 359(1): 97–118.

Pourchasse, Pierrick. 2006. *Le Commerce du Nord: Les échanges commerciaux entre la France et l'Europe septentrionale au XVIIIe siècle.* Rennes, France: Presses Universitaires de Rennes.

Powell, J. W. Damer. 1930. *Bristol Privateers and Ships of War.* Bristol, UK: J. W. Arrowsmith.

Pratt, John W., and Richard Zeckhauser, eds. 1991. *Principals and Agents: The Structure of Business.* Cambridge, MA: Harvard Business School Press.

Pritchard, James. 1987. *Louis XV's Navy, 1748–1762. A Study of Organization and Administration.* Kingston, ON: McGill-Queen's University Press.

——. 2004. *In Search of Empire. The French in the Americas, 1670–1730.* Cambridge: Cambridge University Press.

Pryor, John H. 1977. "The Origins of the Commenda Contract." *Speculum* 52(January): 5–37.

——. 1983. "Mediterranean Commerce in the Middle Ages: a Voyage under Contract of Commenda." *Viator: Medieval and Renaissance Studies* 14(January): 133–94.

——. 1984. "Commenda: the Operation of the Contract in Long Distance Commerce at Marseilles During the Thirteenth Century." *Journal of European Economic History* 13(Fall): 397–440.

Redlich, Fritz. 1964–1965. *The German Military Enterpriser and His Work Force: A Study in European Eco-nomic and Social History.* 2 vols. Wiesbaden, Germany: Steiner.

Régent, Frédéric. 2007. *La France et ses esclaves. De la colonisation aux abolitions (1620–1848).* Paris: Grasset.

Reinert, Sophus A. 2013. "Rivalry: Greatness in Early Modern Political Economy." In *Mercantilism Reimag-ined: Political Economy in Early Modern Britain and Its Empire*, ed. Philip J. Stern and Carl Wennerlind, 348–70. Oxford: Oxford University Press.

Robidou, François, l'Abbé. [1919] 1998. *Les derniers corsaires malouins. La course sous la Révolution et l'Empire, 1793–1814.* Rennes, France: La Decouvrance.

Roche, Daniel. 1998. *France in the Enlightenment.* Cambridge, MA: Harvard University Press.

Rodger, Nicholas A. M. 1986. *The Wooden World: An Anatomy of the Georgian Navy.* New York: W. W. Norton.

——. 2005. *Command of the Ocean. A Naval History of Britain, 1649–1815.* New York: W. W. Norton.

——. 2014. "The Law and Language of Private Naval Warfare." *The Mariner's Mirror* 100(February): 5–16.

Roman, Alain. 2001. *Saint-Malo au temps des négriers.* Paris: Karthala.

Romano, Ruggiero. 1957. "Documenti e prime considerazioni alla 'Balance du commerce' della Francia dal 1716 al 1780." In *Studi in onore di Armando Sapori*, 1267–300. Milan, Italy: Istituto Editoriale Cisalpino.

Root, Hilton L. 1994. *The Fountain of Privilege: Political Foundations of Markets in Old Regime France and England*. Berkeley: University of California Press.

Safford, Sean. 2009. *Why the Garden Club Couldn't Save Youngstown: The Transformation of the Rust Belt*. Cambridge, MA: Harvard University Press.

Sahlins, Peter. 1989. *Boundaries: The Making of France and Spain in the Pyrenees*. Berkeley: University of California Press.

Sabean, D. W., Teuscher, S., and Mathieu, J., eds. 2007. *Kinship in Europe. Approaches to Long-term Developments (1300–1900)*. Oxford: Oxford University Press.

Saupin, Guy. 1996. *Nantes au XVIIe siècle: vie politique et société urbaine*. Rennes, France: Presses Universitaires de Rennes.

——. ed. 2010. *Histoire sociale du politique. Les villes de l'Ouest atlantique français à l'époque moderne (XVIe–XVIIIe siècle)*. Rennes, France: Presses Universitaires de Rennes.

Savary, Jacques. 1675. *Le Parfait Négociant, ou Instruction générale pour ce qui regarde le commerce de toute sorte de marchandises tant de France que des pays étrangers*. Paris: Louis Billaine.

Sayous André-Émile. 1929. "Les transformations des méthodes commerciales dans l'Italie médiévale." *Annales d'histoire économique et sociale* 1(2): 161–76.

——. 1931. "Dans l'Italie à l'intérieur des terres: Sienne de 1221 à 1229." *Annales d'histoire économique et sociale* 3(10): 189–206.

Schaeper, Thomas J. 1983. *The French Council of Commerce, 1700–1715. A Study of Mercantilism After Colbert*. Columbus: Ohio State University Press.

Schapira, Nicolas. 2004. "Occuper l'office. Les secrétaires du roi comme secrétaires au XVIIe siècle." *Revue d'histoire moderne et contemporaine* 51(1): 36–61.

Scoville, Warren C. 1962. "The French Economy in 1700–1701: An Appraisal by the Deputies of Trade." *Journal of Economic History* 22(June): 231–52.

Sée, Henri. [1925] 2001. *Le commerce maritime de la Bretagne au XVIIIè siècle*. Rennes, France: La Découvrance.

——. 1926. "Documents sur le commerce de Cadix (1691–1752)." *Revue de l'Histoire des Colonies Françaises* 14: 465–520.

——. 1928. "The Ship-Owners of Saint Malo in the Eighteenth Century." *Bulletin of the Business Historical Society* 2(June): 3–9.

Sée, Henri, and André Lesort, eds. 1911. *Cahiers de doléances de la sénéchaussée de Rennes pour les états généraux de 1789*. Vol. III, *Évêchés de Saint-Malo et de Saint-Brieuc*. Rennes, France: Oberthur.

Sgourev, Stoyan V., and Wim van Lent. 2015. "Balancing Permission and Prohibition: Private Trade and Adaptation at the VOC." *Social Forces* 93(3): 933–55.

Shovlin, John. 2000. "Toward a Reinterpretation of Revolutionary Antinobilism: The Political Economy of Honor in the Old Regime." *Journal of Modern History* 72(March): 35–66.

——. 2013. "War and Peace: Trade, International Competition, and Political Economy." In *Mercantilism Reimagined: Political Economy in Early Modern Britain and Its Empire*, ed. Philip J. Stern and Carl Wennerlind, 305–27. Oxford: Oxford University Press.

Silver, Allen. 1990. "Friendship in Commercial Society: Eighteenth-Century Social Theory and Modern Sociology." *American Journal of Sociology* 95(May): 1474–1504.

Simmel, Georg. 1908. *Soziologie: Untersuchungen über die Formen der Vergesellschaftung*. Berlin, Germany: Duncker & Humblot.

Smith, Jay M. 2000. "Social Categories, the Language of Patriotism, and the Origins of the French Revolution: The Debate Over Noblesse Commerçante." *Journal of Modern History* 72(June): 339–74.

Sonnino, Paul. 1987. "The Origins of Louis XIV's Wars." In *The Origins of War in Early Modern Europe*, ed. Jeremy Black, 112–31. Edinburgh, Scotland: Donald.

Starkey, David J. 1990. *British Privateering Enterprise in the Eighteenth Century*. Exeter, UK: University of Exeter Press.

Stasavage, David. 2003. *Public Debt and the Birth of the Democratic State: France and Great Britain, 1688–1789*. Cambridge: Cambridge University Press.

——. 2011. *States of Credit: Size, Power, and the Development of Modern European Polities*. Princeton, NJ: Princeton University Press.

Stein, Robert Louis. 1979. *The French Slave Trade in the Eighteenth Century. An Old Regime Business*. Madison: University of Wisconsin Press.

Stern, Philip J., and Carl Wennerlind, eds. 2013. *Mercantilism Reimagined: Political Economy in Early Modern Britain and Its Empire*. Oxford: Oxford University Press.

Stone, Lawrence, ed. 1994. *An Imperial State at War: Britain from 1689 to 1815*. London: Routledge.

Storrs, Christopher, ed. 2009. *The Fiscal-Military State in Eighteenth-Century Europe*. Burlington, VT: Ashgate.

Stovel, Katherine, and Michael Savage. 2005. "Mergers and Mobility: Organizational Growth and the Origins of Career Migration at Lloyds Bank." *American Journal of Sociology* 111(4): 1080–1121.

Stovel, Katherine, Michael Savage, and Peter Bearman. 1996. "Ascription into Achievement: Models of Career Systems at Lloyds Bank, 1890–1970." *American Journal of Sociology* 102(2): 358–99.

Stovel, Katherine, and Lynette Shaw. 2012. "Brokerage." *Annual Review of Sociology* 38: 139–58.

Symcox, Geoffrey. 1974. *The Crisis of French Sea Power, 1688–1697. From the Guerre d'Escadre to the Guerre de Course*. The Hague: Martinus Nijhoff.

——. 1976. "Louis XIV and the Outbreak of the Nine Years War." Pp. 179–212 in *Louis XIV and Europe*, ed. Ragnhild Hatton. Columbus: Ohio State University Press.

Swann, Julian. 2003. *Provincial Power and Absolute Monarchy. The Estates General of Burgundy, 1661–1790*. Cambridge: Cambridge University Press.

Swanson, Carl E. 1991. *Predators and Prizes: American Privateering and Imperial Warfare, 1739–1748*. Columbia: University of South Carolina Press.

Tai, Emily S. 2003. "Piracy and Law in Medieval Genoa: The *Consilia* of Bartolomeo Bosco." *Medieval Encounters* 9(2–3): 256–282.

Takeda, Junko Thérèse. 2011. *Between Crown and Commerce. Marseille and the Early Modern Mediterranean*. Baltimore, MD: Johns Hopkins University Press.

Tarade, Jean. 1972. *Le commerce colonial de la France à la fin de l'Ancien Régime: L'évolution du régime de 'l'Exclusif' de 1763 à 1789*. 2 vols. Paris: Presses Universitaires de France.

Temple, Nora. 1973. "Municipal Elections and Municipal Oligarchies in Eighteenth-Century France." In *French Government and Society, 1500–1800. Essays in Memory of Alfred Cobban*, ed. J. F. Bosher, 70–91. London: Athlone Press.

Terjanian, Anoush Fraser. 2013. *Commerce and Its Discontents in Eighteenth-Century French Political Thought*. Cambridge: Cambridge University Press.

Tilly, Charles. 1992. *Coercion, Capital, and European States, AD 990–1990*. Rev. ed. Oxford: Basil Blackwell.

de Tocqueville, Alexis. [1835–1840] 2004. *Democracy in America*. Trans. Arthur Goldhammer. New York: Library of America.

Tracy, James D., ed. 1990. *The Rise of Merchant Empires. Long-Distance Trade in the Early Modern World, 1350–1750*. Cambridge: Cambridge University Press.

——, ed. 1991. *The Political Economy of Merchant Empires. State Power and World Trade, 1350–1750*. Cambridge: Cambridge University Press.

Trans-Atlantic Slave Trade Database. Expanded data set, accessed September 2016. http://www.slavevoyages .org.

Traugott, Mark. 1985. *Armies of the Poor: Determinants of Working-Class Participation in the Parisian Insurrection of June 1848*. Princeton, NJ: Princeton University Press.

Tuloup, François. 1976. *Saint-Malo. Histoire Générale*. 2nd rev. ed. Paris: Klincksieck.

Udovitch, Abraham L. 1970. *Partnership and Profit in Medieval Islam*. Princeton, NJ: Princeton University Press.

Van Doosselaere, Quentin. 2009. *Commercial Agreements and Social Dynamics in Medieval Genoa*. New York: Cambridge University Press.

Vedres, Balazs, and David Stark. 2010. "Structural Folds: Generative Disruption in Overlapping Groups." *American Journal of Sociology* 115(4): 1150–90.

Vergé-Franceschi, Michel. 1996. "Duguay-Trouin (1673–1736): un corsaire, un officier général, un mythe." *Revue Historique* 598(April–June): 333–52.

Vignols, Léon. 1899. "La course et les corsaires: la légende et l'histoire." *Bulletin de la Société d'Études Historiques et Geographiques de Bretagne* 3(1): 20–25.

——. 1927. "La course maritime: ses conséquences économiques, sociales, et internationales." *Revue d'histoire économique et sociale* 15(2): 196–230.

——. 1931. "Le commerce maritime et les aspects du capitalisme commercial à Saint-Malo, de 1680 à 1792." *Revue d'histoire économique et sociale* 19: 9–26.

Villiers, Patrick. 1991. *Marine Royale, Corsaires et Trafic dans l'Atlantique de Louis XIV à Louis XVI*. 2 vols. Reprint ed. Lille: Atelier national de reproduction des thèses.

——. 2000. *Les Corsaires du Littoral: Dunkerque, Calais, Boulogne, de Philippe II à Louis XIV (1568–1713)*. Villeneuve d'Ascq: Presses Universitaires du Septentrion.

Weber, Max. [1889] 2008. *Zur Geschichte der Handelsgesellschaften im Mittelalter. Schriften 1889–1894*. Max Weber-Gesamtausgabe, vol. I/1, ed. Gerhard Dilcher and Susanne Lepsius. Tübingen, Germany: J. C. B. Mohr (Paul Siebeck).

Wezel, Filippo Carlo, and Martin Ruef. 2017. "Agents with Principles: The Control of Labor in the Dutch East India Company, 1700 to 1796." *American Sociological Review* 82(5): 1009–36.

White, Harrison C. 1970. *Chains of Opportunity: System Models of Mobility in Organizations*. Cambridge, MA: Harvard University Press.

Zahedieh, Nuala. 2010. *The Capital and the Colonies: London and the Atlantic Economy, 1660–1700*. Cambridge: Cambridge University Press.

Zmuda, Mehdi. 2004. *Saint-Malo, port négrier? XVIIème–XIXème siècles*. Villiers-sur-Marne: Phénix Éditions.

INDEX

Page numbers in *italics* indicate figures or tables.

voyages: (*continued*)
    long-distance, 284n41; participants in, 146;
    partnerships of, tied to kinship, *175*, 176;
    of privateering enterprise as organizational
    platform for repeated partnerships and
    transitive closure, *232*; of Saint-Malo to Spanish
    America and East Asia, *49*; sponsors for, 74

Wailsh, Philippe, 72
Walsh, Jacques, 72
Walsh, Pierre, 121
wandering fishery (*pêche errante*), 29
war, 12, 27; commissions for commerce
    raiding during declared, 94–95; economic
    opportunities from, 40, 55; naval warfare,
    40–41, 91, 93–94; rise of new opportunities
    and, 36–54; as rule rather than exception, 37
War of the Austrian Succession, 13, 139, 141, *195*,
    216; as dynastic, 193; outbreak of, 55, 166
War of the League of Augsburg. *See* Nine Years'
    War

War of the Spanish Succession, 27, 37–39, 41;
    end of, 42, 58; French defeat during, 192;
    height of, 117; impact of, 263n46; political
    allegiances shifting before, 46; privateering
    enterprise during, 41, *42*, 43, 117, 123, 126, 133,
    238; shipping during, 39–40; vulnerability of
    French trading posts revealed during, 51
war of trade: Anglo-French confrontations in West
    Indies as, 37
wartime strategy: undermining commerce of
    competing states as, 94
wealth: accumulation of, 77, 151; distribution of,
    79–83; fitting costs and variation in, 86, *87*;
    growth of, in Saint-Malo, 22; information
    on taxable, 80; as inherited, 70; of merchant
    elites, 13–14; self-interest and, 103; social status
    and, 79; socioeconomic stratification and, 112,
    144–45; as taxable, 76, 208; variation of, within
    merchant elites, *82*, 89, 191
William III, King, 37
Wyatt, Henry, 242